THE GROWTH OF
THE BRITISH PARTY SYSTEM
VOLUME I
1640–1923

IVOR BULMER-THOMAS

The Growth of
the
British Party System

VOLUME I
1640–1923

JOHN BAKER
5 ROYAL OPERA ARCADE
PALL MALL, LONDON, SW1

Printed in Great Britain by Richard Clay (The Chaucer Press), Ltd.,
Bungay, Suffolk.

PREFACE TO THE FIRST EDITION

SINCE *The Party System in Great Britain* was published in
1953 there have been several major books on what G. M.
Trevelyan in his Romanes lecture called "the vast, unwritten
theme of party history". Mr. R. T. McKenzie in his *British
Political Parties* has dealt in detail with one aspect of the
struggle between the two chief contenders for supremacy
("the distribution of power within the Conservative and
Labour parties"), and Sir Ivor Jennings has covered the whole
field more discursively in the three volumes of his *Party
Politics*. Before the close of next year, Mr. Peter Goldman's
history of the Conservative party from 1832 to 1951 may have
made its appearance. There have been many valuable books
and articles throwing light on particular aspects of, or episodes
in, the party conflict.

The Party System in Great Britain has been out of print for
a number of years, and I have been urged to bring out a new
edition. This I hope eventually to do, but with Trevelyan's
words in my ears I have thought it well first to attempt a
sketch of the growth of the party system from its origins in the
Civil War to its all-pervading influence today. There are many
features of the British party system that cannot be properly
understood except in terms of their historical evolution. The
different approaches of Conservatives and Labour to the leadership and the party conference—and there is a real difference in
approach however similar the terminal action may be—cannot be explained except by the different histories of the two
parties.

It needs to be emphasized that this is a sketch of the growth
of the party system, not a political history, and many political
events of great magnitude find no mention in these pages
because they have no bearing on the evolution of party. For
the same reason what I have called the "pre-history" of the
party system is treated fairly lightly, and the narrative increases in detail as the parties become more highly organized
and their grip on the national life tightens.

I have not sought in these pages to plead any cause or point
any moral—only to give a plain account of the rise of parties

to their present dominance in British political life. If there is one thing that emerges at the end, it is the unpredictable character of the evolution of party. The course that parties have taken has been governed, not by the pursuit of abstract principles, but by men who are of like passions with ourselves; and the only lesson that can be safely drawn is an old one—Politics is about People. It will not escape notice how frequently men have done their greatest work in parties different from those in which they began; and it is good to see how often the leaders have been prepared to shatter their parties and ruin their political fortunes rather than compromise what they believe to be the public interest. This is healthy; yet the readiness of men to work with their political associates in all normal matters, and to subordinate their personal inclinations and ambitions to the general wish of their party, is one of the greatest gifts that can be bestowed upon a nation. It is not lightly to be cast aside.

This book is mainly about the party system at the national level. The development of party in local government is a large theme for which, except in such special cases as London, the materials have hardly been gathered together. To have attempted to include it in this book would have swelled its dimensions unacceptably.

I am deeply grateful to Mr. Roger Fulford, President of the Liberal Party, to Mr. Carol Johnson, M.P., secretary of the Parliamentary Labour party for sixteen years, and to Mr. Geoffrey D. M. Block, Assistant Director (Information) of the Conservative Research Department, for reading the typescript and making many valuable suggestions out of their great knowledge of their own parties. While I have done my best to profit by their advice, they are in no way responsible for any errors that may be found in this book or for any expressions of judgement. Wherever I have erred in any question of fact or shown any bias in judgement I shall be glad to be corrected.

Ivor Bulmer-Thomas

London, June 1965

PREFACE TO THE SECOND EDITION

IN this second edition I have added a new chapter bringing the narrative to the year 1966. The opportunity has been taken to correct a few errors and possibilities of misunderstanding that have come to light, and I have added a new series of notes, distinguished from the notes to the first edition by the use of index letters instead of index numbers. These are mainly for the purpose of taking account of the many new books on particular aspects of the theme that have appeared since the first edition was written; but I have occasionally enlarged my thoughts on various matters where recent developments, such as the new material about the Zinoviev letter, or friendly criticism, such as that about my treatment of the rise of the modern Cabinet, has made this course desirable. As a result I hope that the usefulness of the book to students will be increased.

I have done my best to profit by the notices of reviewers, and I readily acknowledge my debt to the helpful comments of such writers as Dr. H. J. Hanham, Professor Bernard Crick and Mr. Robert Rhodes James. It has not, however, always been easy to do what I have been enjoined to do. One reviewer who took me severely to task for not expatiating, in a work clearly announced as ending in 1964, on the courage of Mr. Desmond Donnelly and Mr. Woodrow Wyatt in opposing the nationalization of steel in 1965 may feel satisfied—honour has been done to them in the new chapter; but I must still decline, in what professes to be a work of history, to speculate about the future of the parties (and especially the possibility of a Lib-Lab pact, as Mr. Wyatt himself wanted me to do, *Sunday Times*, 16th January 1966).

One group of reviewers I have found it particularly hard to please, as it appeared to be their main object to indicate how much better a book they could have written if they had been able to give their attention to it. No doubt this is so, but the fact remains that, apart from the second volume in the late Sir Ivor Jennings's trilogy—which, as the untypical product of a great scholar's declining years it is kinder to leave to posterity—it is the only book in existence known to

me which covers the history of the party system from its
origins to the present day. Perhaps the subject is too vast
for one man, or at any rate for this one man, but it is worth
attempting.

Though complete histories of the subject do not abound,
there has been no lack of literature on particular aspects.
Since the first edition was prepared there have been published
three important studies of episodes in the history of the
Liberal party, one on the early days of the Irish Home Rule
party, one on the Independent Labour party, one on the
Fascists and some minor books on the Labour party. Only
the Tories maintain their traditional silence about themselves, and even Mr. Peter Goldman's history of the modern
Conservative party is still awaited. (For Tories politics remains
to some extent a mystery with *arcana* to which the uninitiated
may not penetrate.) There have been at least two widely
read series of academic reflections on the British party system.
The fascination that the British party system has had for
people in other lands since Ostrogorski first theorized about
it continues, and long may it do so, for is not the British
parliamentary system one of our best exports? Nevertheless,
the word of caution that Bryce sounded in introducing Ostrogorski to the English-reading world is still needed, and I doubt
whether anyone who has not been immersed in the British
party system can fully understand all its nuances. It is only
when we come to biography and autobiography—"history
teaching by examples"—that the Englishman feels really at
home. It is in the flood of biographical works that we must
chiefly seek the English contribution to the history of the
party system, bearing in mind, of course, that the memoirs
of statesmen, and sometimes their official lives, are meant
to conceal as well as to reveal, or at any rate to strike a
pose at the bar of history. Since the first edition was prepared there have been notable biographical studies of Prime
Ministers Addington, Canning, Peel, Palmerston, Disraeli,
Gladstone, Balfour, Asquith, Churchill, Eden and Macmillan,
of Foreign Secretary Castlereagh, of Chancellor Snowden, and
of the party breakers Parnell and Joseph Chamberlain, all of
whom left a deep impression upon the party system. Important studies of Carteret and Newcastle, Chatham and Liverpool that had gone out of print have again been made available. A new life of Baldwin is in preparation, and there is
hope that the one great gap—a satisfactory biography of Mac-
Donald—will eventually be filled.

Since the first edition was prepared there have also been
two further Nuffield election studies, and like many others I

have benefited from them. I have been taken to task in some quarters for my "unsophisticated" approach to the party system, but, as I said in the earlier preface, Politics is about People, and until recently the people who shaped the party system were also unsophisticated. "Baldwin knifed me, and I shall knife Baldwin"—that is the way the British party system has been shaped. Since the public opinion polls became a feature of British party life I trust I have given due weight to them; but happily it is still not possible to learn all there is to know about the British party system by feeding the facts into a computer and waiting for the results to come out at the other end. Having started my life as a mathematician I could feel a certain self-interest in the quantification of history; but mercifully this nightmare is still in the future.

Ivor Bulmer-Thomas

London, April 1967

ACKNOWLEDGEMENTS

I N the first place among my acknowledgements I desire to express my gratitude to Her Majesty The Queen for her gracious permission to quote from papers in the Royal Archives at Windsor. At the same time I should like to record my indebtedness to Mr. R. Mackworth-Young, the Librarian at Windsor, for his unfailing courtesy and helpful advice.

I have made some use also of the photostat copies of the reports of Cabinet meetings sent to Sovereigns by Prime Ministers and now deposited by the gracious permission of Her Majesty at the Public Record Office.

I wish further to express my gratitude to the following for permission to quote from the documents mentioned: Sir Max Aitken—the Bonar Law papers; Mr. Mark Bonham Carter—the Asquith manuscripts at Oxford; Mrs. Stephen Lloyd—the diary of her father, Mr. Neville Chamberlain; the Passfield Trustees—Beatrice Webb's diaries; Lord Rosebery—a memorandum written by his father for Queen Victoria; Lord Samuel—his father's papers written during the political crisis in 1931 and now deposited in the House of Lords; Mr. R. J. Topping—a memorandum written by Sir Robert Topping for Mr. Neville Chamberlain; Lord Younger—a letter written by his grandfather to Mr. Bonar Law.

Quotations from manuscript sources that have already appeared in print have been checked wherever possible against the originals. This accounts for slight variations that may be noticed.

A list of the printed works from which I have quoted, and in which copyright still subsists, will be found at the end of the second volume, and I there record my thanks to the authors, publishers and owners of the copyright for the permissions given.

Ivor Bulmer-Thomas

CONTENTS OF VOLUME I

PART ONE
THE PRE-HISTORY OF PARTY

To place its origin still farther back, as some distinguished writers have done,[2] in the great national cleavage wrought by Henry VIII's decision to break with Rome is too ambitious. There were parties, certainly, at that time as there always have been when men are divided on great issues, but they were religious rather than political, they have no continuity with the parties of later history, and they did not constitute a system.

It is more plausible to argue, as one great historian has done,[3] that the party system was born on that fateful day in February 1641 when the abolition of episcopacy was proposed to Parliament, and "two parties stood opposed to one another in the House of Commons, not merely on some incidental question, but on a great principle of action which constituted a permanent bond between those who took one side or the other". If they had continued their debate in the chamber, and not transferred it to the field, this day, when episcopalians became royalists, would have an undeniable claim; but because the issue was taken to arms, we have to look to the resumption of parliamentary government in the days of Charles I's easygoing son for the fusion of parties into a system.

There were certainly parties in Parliament by 1679, and the names Whig and Tory, which were to remain in currency for the next two hundred years, and one of which is still in use today, were then borrowed from current slang to denote supporters and opponents of the Exclusion Bill, designed to prevent James, Duke of York, from succeeding his brother on the Throne. The names were not complimentary. "Whig" is probably a shorter form of whiggamore, and the whiggamores were a body of insurgents from the west of Scotland who in 1648 marched on Edinburgh. The name Whig was properly given to adherents of the Presbyterian cause in Scotland in the latter half of the seventeenth century and was applied to the exclusioners in derision. The term Tory, an anglicized form of an Irish word meaning a pursuer, was even less polite. In its original sense it was used in the seventeenth century to denote one of the dispossessed Irish who became outlaws and lived by killing and plundering the English settlers and soldiers. It was equivalent to "bog trotter", and was applied by the exclusioners to their opponents because they noticed that the Duke of York tended to favour Irishmen for his friends. Narcissus Luttrell in 1681 wrote of the duke's supporters and the exclusioners: "The latter party have been called by the former whigs, fanaticks, covenanteers, bromigham protestants, &c.; and the former are called by the latter tories, tantivies, Yorkists, high flown church men, &c." These nicknames, given in mockery, were accepted with pride, and came to be used to denote the two great parties in the state during the next two centuries. Mr. Nigel Birch has aptly compared the way in which the survivors of the British Expeditionary Force, derided by the German

Kaiser in 1914 as a "contemptible little army", gloried in the name "Old Contemptibles".[4]

Though the names Whig and Tory came into use about 1679, the parties they denoted were already in existence and to understand how they arose it is necessary to go back to the beginning of the reign. The Cavalier Parliament elected in 1660 was strongly royalist, but so long as Clarendon was the King's chief minister he sought to pursue a moderate policy that would heal the wounds of the Civil War. To this end he arranged for discussions every day of the session with members of the House of Commons regarded by reason of personal prestige or family connexions as having influence with other members. The object was to let it be known what was the King's policy and to win support for it in advance, and the members favoured with the Lord Chancellor's confidence were known as "undertakers".[5] This implied and to some extent created a "Court party", with the "undertakers" as the precursors of the later whips; and there was inevitably a tendency for those royalist members who did not like Clarendon's moderation to concert together and form a "Country party". Partly as a result of their opposition Clarendon fell in 1667, and the five ministers who then gained the King's ear, called the Cabal from their initial letters (Clifford, Ashley, Buckingham, Arlington and Lauderdale), not only continued his method of using "undertakers" to ensure support in Parliament for the King's new policies but made increased use of patronage with the same objective. Clarendon's followers then took over the rôle of the "Country party".

This use of "undertaking" is the first example of the mechanics of a party system, but it is still too early to say that a party system had come into being. The Court and Country parties were not identical with the Cavaliers and Parliamentarians of an earlier generation, nor yet with the Tories and Whigs of a later. They were a by-product of the real power that the Sovereign continued to enjoy, and until the Sovereign's power was finally eliminated they appeared from time to time in the parliamentary scene, under William and Mary, Anne and the first three Georges, alongside Whigs and Tories, to confuse the true evolution of party.

There were some things that the most efficient "undertaking" could not win from the Cavalier Parliament, and in order to get money for the war in 1673 Charles had to agree to the repudiation of the Declaration of Indulgence and the passing of the Test Act, which had as early consequences the fall of Clifford (a Roman Catholic) and the dismissal of Anthony Ashley Cooper, Earl of Shaftesbury, as Ashley had by then become. Before long the Cabal had been destroyed and Thomas Osborne, soon to be created Earl of Danby (and later Duke of Leeds) became the King's chief adviser, with Shaftesbury as his chief opponent. It was in the struggles of Danby and Shaftesbury during the next few years that the British party system was moulded, and these men may justly be regarded as the founders of the Tory and Whig parties.

It was Danby's achievement to rally a parliamentary majority on the association of Church and King, which had inspired the Cavaliers in the Civil War and was to be a rallying cry of the Tories for many years to come. The weakness of the policy was the fact that the King was only too ready to desert the Church in favour of a faith which the great majority of Englishmen at the time distrusted deeply. Danby's strength lay almost entirely in Parliament, where he showed great skill in manipulating support for his policies. Shaftesbury, who had deserted Charles I for the parliamentary cause in 1644 because he saw danger to the Protestant religion in the King's service, had since that date been a consistent supporter of toleration for Protestant dissenters, but he excepted Roman Catholics from his indulgence. He forged the link between the Whigs and the Non-conformists which was to remain strong even after the Whigs had yielded place to the Liberals. Shaftesbury was a powerful figure in Parliament, when it was allowed to meet, and has some claims to be considered the founder of parliamentary oratory, but much of his strength lay outside and especially in the municipal corporations.

The public terror roused by Titus Oates's pretended revelation of a Popish Plot in 1678 led to the impeachment of Danby and the dissolution of the Cavalier Parliament. Three elections followed in quick succession and three predominantly Whig Parliaments. In the first of these Parliaments the Court had no more than twenty-five or thirty supporters. The Exclusion Bill was read a second time in the Commons and Charles II frustrated its further passage by dissolving. The new legislature proved similar in composition to the old, and was prorogued before it could meet. Shaftesbury, dropped from office, and his friends organized petitions for the meeting of Parliament while their opponents expressed abhorrence of this attempt to encroach on the royal prerogative. The two parties became known as petitioners and abhorrers, but these were inconvenient and transient names. Someone started calling the petitioners Whigs and the abhorrers Tories. The country liked the names, and they stuck. When Parliament did eventually meet, the attempt of the Whigs to secure the succession for Charles's illegitimate son, the Duke of Monmouth, was more than the Tories could stomach, and they caused the Exclusion Bill to be thrown out in the Lords, notably helped by the oratory of George Savile, then Earl and later Marquess of Halifax, who gladly accepted the title of "Trimmer", and on this occasion greatly helped to keep the ship of state on an even keel.[6] Parliament was once more dissolved and a new one summoned to meet in Tory Oxford, but that also was quickly dissolved, and thereafter Charles ruled without a Parliament.

In these dramatic years the British party system, which had been in gestation since 1640, experienced the trauma of birth and emerged into the light of day. Though elections were very different then from what they are now, we shall not err greatly in saying that the elections of 1679–81 were fought on party lines, and were the first to be so fought. As G. M. Trevelyan has said:

"From the Exclusion Bill struggle date not only the names of Whig and Tory, but a new perfection of party organization and propaganda, and the peculiarly English art of 'electioneering'. A country that had once exerted itself so profoundly in electoral and parliamentary strife was not likely to be long quiet under a despotism. Shaftesbury and his enemies had introduced the astonishing customs of the Eatanswill election, with all its noise, expense, anger and fun—a peculiar and valuable national heritage, because it fostered that interest in the conduct and result of elections for want of which the parliamentary system has withered and wilted in more than one continental country in our own day."[7]

Sir Keith Feiling fills in some of the details of those original elections. "Printed manifestoes, choice of candidates from headquarters, red rosettes for Tories and the true blue for Whigs, Shaftesbury's 'Green Ribbon' club in the City answered by 'loyal' societies, rival newspapers, all the paraphernalia of party were in formation." And as another historian, Mr. David Ogg, observes: "It was not in the tepid amenities of academic debate, but in the vituperation of the street, the coffee-house, and the scaffold that the distinction of Whig and Tory took hold on the minds of Englishmen. The distinction, as it emerged, pervaded almost the whole field of national life, and was as potent an inspiration for the frivolous as for the serious."[8]

G. M. Trevelyan has passed severe judgement on the height to which party passions ran at this time,[9] and again in the reign of Queen Anne, but a kindlier view is possible. The questions that divided Englishmen in 1679–81 were not dissimilar from those that made their fathers take to arms in 1642. That " '41 was come again" was, indeed, a common saying at the time. The prerogatives of the Crown, the rights of the legislature, the claims of the Church, toleration for dissent, the supremacy of the law—these were the same issues that led Charles to raise his standard at Nottingham and Hampden to fall at Chalgrove. If they scratched a Tory, the men of 1679 saw the lineaments of a Cavalier; if a Whig, the round head of a Parliamentarian. But there was one big difference. Whatever wild ideas they entertained, and whatever crimes they committed, they stopped short of the supreme evil of civil war. The passions that might have been spent on the field were released on the hustings; and when the real crisis came in 1688 Tories and Whigs showed that they could put the nation before party and united in a glorious because bloodless revolution. This, surely, is no mean achievement for the first years of the new and untried party system.

The steps that led up to that crisis can soon be told.[a] The Whig triumph of 1679–81 was followed by a period of Tory supremacy, sharpened when some old Roundhead soldiers failed in their plot in 1683 to murder the royal brothers at Rye House. The Tories took advantage of the public indignation to strike at the Whig leadership by sending Russell and Algernon Sidney to the scaffold, thereby providing the Whigs with a martyrology for many years to come. Shaftesbury had fled abroad and had died earlier the same year. Having got rid of the leaders, the Tories struck at the roots of Whig power by depriving over sixty towns, including London, of the freedom from royal control they had hitherto enjoyed under their charters. In these circumstances it was safe for James II, when he ascended the Throne, to summon a Parliament. It was packed with Tories strongly royalist in sentiment and holding the doctrine of non-resistance to the Lord's anointed taught in every Anglican pulpit; but it was not prepared to see England subjected to Rome, and as this was the lynch-pin of James's policy a rupture was bound to come. Monmouth's rebellion at first strengthened his position; but the savage revenge taken in his name by Kirke and Jeffreys sickened the nation; and with the decapitated body of Monmouth in a traitor's grave the way was open for Whigs and Tories to unite in the choice of Mary and her husband the Prince of Orange for the succession. When the invitation to William was sent, it was signed by three Tories as well as four Whigs.[10]

We must be careful not to think of the parties in the seventeenth century in modern terms. They were no more than loose groupings of men who found it convenient to work together in Parliament. They had little in the way of organization. Each member felt free to pursue his own ideas, or, if he was bound, it was not to his party but to the territorial magnate or municipal corporation who had provided him with his seat. There were almost as many Tory opinions as there were Tories, and Whig opinions as there were Whigs. Though there were many gradations within the ranks of the two parties, the difference between Tories and Whigs was not itself meaningless or trivial. Fundamentally the difference between Tory and Whig was a difference of outlook, and in particular it is permissible to detect a difference of temper which inclined men to be Whigs or Tories according to their readiness or reluctance to accept change. Those who thought, as Falkland[b] told the Commons, "When it is not necessary to change, it is necessary not to change" were more likely to be found in the Tory ranks; and those who were ready to overturn existing institutions were more likely to range themselves with the Whigs. It is tempting, but not altogether convincing, to seek the division along a line of social cleavage, and we are justified

in seeing a tendency among the rising merchant classes to ally themselves with the Whigs and a tendency among the Tories to identify
themselves with the landed interest. This found expression in many
Tory efforts to insist on a landed qualification for members of
Parliament and in Whig measures to encourage trade and banking.
It accords with the fundamental difference of outlook already
noted, for the land is permanent but other forms of property come
and go. Yet too much must not be made of this difference, for there
were merchants among the Tories and no lack of great landlords
among the Whigs. This distaste for change and attachment to the
land on the one side, the appetite for experiment and zest for trade on
the other, agree also with what was the earliest and deepest and most
lasting of the policy differences between Tories and Whigs, support
of the Church by the Tories and toleration of dissent by the Whigs;
for the Church was a conservative force relying upon tithe for the
stipends of its clergy, whereas Nonconformity was an explosive
force and by its teaching encouraged trade and industry. These are
real contrasts, but like the others they must not be pushed too hard.

Brought together by the practical necessity of standing together
on great issues, and constantly evolving to meet changing situations,
the British parties have been empirical but not devoid of guiding
principles. From earliest days they have not lacked theoreticians to
justify their policies. Among the many writers who taught Tory
households to respect the divine right of Kings, the best remembered
is Sir Robert Filmer, whose *Patriarchia* was published in the fateful
year 1680, though written earlier. In his view the rule of a family by
a father is the true model of all government. Filmer is best remembered, not for any intrinsic merits, but because he was attacked by
John Locke, who provided the Whigs with a more carefully
reasoned philosophy for many years to come. Locke was the physi-
cian and friend of Shaftesbury, and in those stormy days was
already working out his contractual theory of the state which he
set down in writing in his *Two Treatises of Government* published
in 1689. According to Locke, civil society was created by a compact
in which individuals agreed with each other (not with a sovereign)
to surrender to the community as a whole the right of enforcing the
law of reason; but the compact was limited to this right of enforcing
the law of reason and the individual retained his natural rights. The
main reason why men chose to enter into such a compact, in
Locke's view, was to preserve their private property, and the chief
object of legislation was to provide "guards and fences" to that
property. This was a philosophy wholly agreeable to the Whig magnates and merchants among whom Locke moved. It can be argued
endlessly whether political parties have embarked on courses of
action in obedience to their philosophies or political philosophies
have been framed to justify their courses of action.[11]

2

PARTY MINISTRIES
1689–1714

Parties regarded as factions—Burke's defence of party—Tory abandonment of the principle of divine right—acceptance of Harley as leader—Tories split by the Hanoverian succession— George I turns to the Whigs—William I's "Junto", the first party ministry—Whigs and Tories as "ins" and "outs"—Queen Anne's dislike of party ministries

THOUGH parties had been brought into existence by practical necessity, many years were to pass before they were accepted as respectable institutions. They were usually called factions in a highly pejorative sense. Halifax thought them a conspiracy against the rest of the nation,[1] but this was perhaps an exercise in trimming, when he did not know on which side he was going to cast his weight. Bolingbroke wrote *A Dissertation upon Parties* and several other treatises on the same theme, but he was then in the wilderness trying to recover his position, and it was the only line for a Tory Jacobite to take.[2] Pope put the feeling into one of his couplets:

> *The names of party I detest,*
> *Badges of slavery at best—*

just as Macaulay was to do in the next century:

> *Then none was for a party;*
> *Then all were for the state.*

This distaste helps to account for the fact that even today the name of party is unknown in the written constitution.

No one seems to have had a good word for party until Edmund Burke wrote *Thoughts on the Cause of the Present Discontents* in 1770. He set out to demolish the doctrine enunciated by Bute a few years earlier: "That all political connexions are in their nature factious, and as such ought to be dissipated and destroyed; and that the rule for forming administrations is mere personal ability."[3] He began by distinguishing between connexion and faction.

"Where men are not acquainted with each other's principles, nor experienced in each other's talents, nor at all practised in their mutual habitudes and dispositions by joint efforts in business; no personal confidence, no friendship, no common interest, subsisting among them; it is evidently impossible that they can act a public part with uniformity, perseverance, or efficiency. In a connexion, the most inconsiderable man, by adding to the weight of the whole, has his value, and his use; out of it, the greatest talents are wholly unserviceable to the public. No man, who is not inflamed by vain-glory into enthusiasm, can flatter himself that his single, unsupported, desultory, unsystematic endeavours, are of power to defeat the subtle designs and united cabals of ambitious citizens. When bad men combine, the good must associate; else they will fall, one by one, an unpitied sacrifice in a contemptible struggle."[4]

It is a powerful defence, and Burke rams the argument home by challenging the notion "that patriotism was a bloody idol, which required the sacrifice of children and parents, or dearest connexions in private life, and of all the virtues that rise from those relations", and ridiculing "the cant of *Not men but measures*" as a "a sort of charm, by which many people get loose from every honourable engagement".

We can still share Burke's scorn "that a man's connexions should degenerate into faction, precisely at the critical moment when they lose their power, or he accepts a place". What will trouble the conscience of the modern student of politics is his refutation of the charge "that you are blindly to follow the opinions of your party, when in direct opposition to your own clear ideas". This charge had been devised, said Burke, "to throw an odium on political connexion", and it implied "a degree of servitude that no worthy man could bear the thought of submitting to; and such as, I believe, no connexions (except some Court Factions) ever could be so senselessly tyrannical as to impose". It cannot be so confidently asserted today that this is an invention of the enemies of party, and we shall need to give more careful consideration to it than Burke thought necessary; but we may readily agree with the continuation of his argument:

"Men thinking freely will, in particular instances, think differently. But still as the greater part of the measures which arise in the course of public business are related to, or dependent on, some great *leading general principles in government*, a man must be peculiarly unfortunate in the choice of his political company if he does not agree with them at least nine times in ten. If he does not concur in these general principles upon which the party is founded, and which necessarily draw on a concurrence in their application, he ought from the beginning to have chosen some other, more conformable to his opinions."[5]

These words were doubtless thrown at Burke, some twenty or more years later when he broke with the Whigs and began to associate with the Tories, or, as some prefer to say, helped to found a new Tory party. Before he wrote his apology, the parties had gone through many vicissitudes and the party system itself had significantly evolved. The Tories had been compelled to make a painful adjustment when one-half of their chosen platform of Church and King fell from beneath them, and that not once but twice. We have already seen how the teachers of the divine right of kings and non-resistance to the Lord's anointed had swallowed their words in 1688 and joined in calling a Dutch Calvinist to be (along with his English wife) Supreme Governor of the Church of England. That James must go few Tories doubted; but many would have liked to salve their consciences by a regency, or the settling of the Crown on Mary alone with William as consort. These expedients were unacceptable to the man most concerned, and many Tory clergymen, led by Archbishop Sancroft, though they knew William had to be King chose to become a sect of Non-Jurors rather than forswear themselves.

To save faces, especially Tory faces, James's flight was treated as abdication rather than expulsion; but the fact that the Convention Parliament could offer the Throne to a prince of its choice, and accompany it with a Bill of Rights settling the succession on Anne in default of issue to William and Mary and excluding Roman Catholics, involved the abandonment of the Tory principle of divine right and acceptance of the Whig principle of a contract. The Tories not only made this adjustment in their fundamental principles, but in 1701, when they had again attained the seats of power, they underlined it by introducing the Bill that became the Act of Settlement, which vested the succession in the Protestant House of Hanover. It is hardly less significant that their leader on this occasion was Robert Harley, the future Earl of Oxford, whose very churchmanship was doubtful. Born in a Presbyterian atmosphere in Herefordshire, and educated at a dissenting academy, Harley had established himself in Parliament as a leader of the "new Country party" and was closely associated with the Whigs. Towards the close of the seventeenth century, as the Whigs attained power he moved into the Tory orbit, but he retained not a few of his Whiggish beliefs and no small degree of his early sympathy with dissent. In this latter respect Harley must be regarded as a freak or sport of nature, for the connexion between the Church of England and the Tory party remained close until the present century, and we have to wait until Bonar Law to find an open Nonconformist at the head of its counsels—though the religious views of his predecessor, Arthur Balfour, which are not easily discovered or defined, may have had more affinity with the ecclesiastical establishment north of the border than south of it.

The adjustment in beliefs had been made, and so successfully that in the closing years of Anne the Tories were as powerful as ever they had been. Then came the dreaded moment that Anne, like Elizabeth before her, had refused to contemplate. In 1714 the word ran round, "Queen Anne is dead." Though the Act of Settlement was on the statute book, when it came to the point many Tories found it hard to accept a German Protestant on the Throne of England. Their rival leaders, Oxford and Bolingbroke, had spared no effort to get James II's son, the Old Pretender, to abandon or dissemble his Roman Catholic religion, but he gave them no help. The Whigs were already ingratiating themselves at the Hanoverian Court, which the Tory ministers dared not do for fear of displeasing their royal mistress. The Tories were split between those who were willing to accept a Hanoverian prince, however grudgingly, and those who gave their loyalty and their toasts to the King across the water. This time the Tory party found it harder to adjust itself to the imperious demands of the hour. Its leaders were discredited, the rank and file dismayed. The rising in favour of the Old Pretender in 1715 made it possible for the Whigs to label all Tories as Jacobites, and they did not scruple to do so. For themselves they were content to bask in the favours of the lawful successor and to enjoy the discomfiture of their rivals. As a disappointed ally in the late war, George disliked the Tory Peace of Utrecht; he knew that half the Tories would always be sighing for a Stuart king; the security of his title rested upon a Whig philosophy of government; and he had made up his stubborn Teutonic mind that, unlike William III, he would have no Tories for ministers but rely exclusively on Whigs.

This reliance on a ministry drawn from one party is now accepted as a fundamental of the constitution, but when George I called Townshend and Stanhope, Cowper and Walpole to office it was still novel. It had arisen without premeditation, not out of any theoretical considerations but out of the needs of the hour, in the reign of William and Mary. William was conscious that he owed his Throne to Tories as well as Whigs, and saw danger to himself in allowing the revolution to be claimed as an exclusively Whig triumph. Partly for reasons of national unity, and partly for his personal comfort, in the first years of his reign he distributed offices among the two parties with the Tory Danby in the leading place. In his reign, as in that of all his predecessors, the choice of his servants and advisers lay within his unfettered discretion. There was no reason in law or precedent for expecting him to limit his choice to men of one party. Though one minister might stand out from the others by reason of his talents or the favours bestowed on him, there was no Prime Minister in the modern sense of the word; and no minister would have dreamed of making it a condition of office that he should have the choice of his colleagues, still less that his resignation should bring the whole ministry down. Such notions lay in the distant future.

In appointing a mixed ministry William was following the constitutional norm, but in 1693–4 one by one the Tories were dropped, and from 1694 to 1698 he had exclusively Whig ministers—Somers as Lord Keeper, Montagu at the Treasury, Russell at the Admiralty and Shrewsbury as Secretary of State, with Wharton as the party organizer[6] in the office of Comptroller of the Household. The King had no deep constitutional aim in view. It was simply that he found it easier to work with these Whig ministers, especially as they were more compliant than Tories in raising money for the expensive war with France. In founding the Bank of England and making a new issue of coinage in place of the debased currency this Whig ministry illustrated the close connexion of the party with trade and commerce. Its five leading members, constituting a "steering committee" in Mr. Carswell's happy phrase, are known to history as the Junto.[7] Derived from the Spanish, like some other uncomplimentary terms in British party history, the word is defined by the dictionary as meaning a clique, faction, cabal, club or coterie, which implies no more than that it was an innovation. The expedient showed the advantage of drawing the executive servants of the Crown from a body of men with like views;[8] and by excluding from office the men who did not belong to the government party it provided them with a powerful motive for wishing to overthrow the administration and so gave a stimulus to the party struggle. Unconsciously William had stumbled upon a major constitutional discovery.

In the remaining years of his reign and in that of Anne there was an alternation of predominantly Whig and Tory governments. It began to seem in the nature of things that Whigs and Tories should take it in turn to be "ins" and "outs". A pattern was virtually established by which the Whigs waged the wars and the Tories made the peace; the Whigs were better at waging war because they were prepared to spend more money, but high taxation made them unpopular as the years passed. After negotiating the Treaty of Ryswick that terminated the eight-year war with Louis XIV, William turned to Tory ministers, and Tory ministers were in office in the first years of Anne. "The maxim laid down at Court," Burnet has told us,[9] "was to put the direction of affairs in the hands of the Tories." The Queen, a devout churchwoman who attended service daily, did not conceal her own Tory sympathies, but for the conduct of the War of the Spanish Succession she found it politic to call in the Whigs. Marlborough waged the battles, his wife Sarah dominated the Queen and Godolphin (not at first a Whig but by necessity made a bedfellow with them) led the ministry.

It was an expensive war, and when Henry Sacheverell was brought to trial for sermons reviving the high Tory doctrines of divine right and non-resistance the light penalty showed that a Tory reaction had set in. Sarah Marlborough *née* Jennings found to her horror that she was being supplanted at Court by her low-born cousin Abigail Masham, in 1710 Godolphin and the Whigs were dismissed, and Tory ministers, among whom the moderate Oxford and the extremist Bolingbroke strove for the pre-eminence, were called to office. It was the great achievement of this ministry, and of Bolingbroke especially, to make in the Peace of Utrecht a just and enduring settlement after a bitter and protracted war. For the rest, they spent their great talents and energies in securing the passage of measures to strengthen the position of their own party and permanently disable their opponents—in 1711 an act requiring every member of Parliament to draw an income of at least £300 a year from land, and an act punishing the occasional conformity by which Nonconformists held office in defiance of the Test, in 1714 an act intended to destroy dissenting schools. This last was too much for Oxford, mindful of his own schooldays, but his course was almost run. When he and Bolingbroke quarrelled in a painful scene in the Queen's presence, Anne had to choose, and she chose Bolingbroke. He was afflicted by none of Oxford's hesitations, and had made it his confessed object "to fill the employments of the kingdom down to the meanest with Tories" so as to put those "who may outlive the Queen beyond the reach of Whig resentment".[10] Alas for the vanity of human wishes! Within five days of his rival's dismissal Queen Anne was dead, and when the box with the names of lords justices was opened they were found to be almost entirely Whigs.

Throughout her reign Queen Anne had party governments, or predominantly party governments, but she knew it was a constitutional innovation, and dreaded it, perceiving truly that it would weaken the position of the Crown. In a letter written in 1706 to Godolphin when the Whigs were trying to get Sunderland made Secretary of State in place of Sir Charles Hedges she protested:[11]

"May be some think I would be willing to be in the hands of the Tories; but whatever people may say of me, I do assure you I am not inclined, nor never will be, to employ any of those violent persons, that have behaved themselves so ill towards me. Besides, I must freely own to you, I am of the opinion, that making a party man Secretary of State, when there are so many of their friends in employment of all kinds already, is throwing myself into the hands of a party, which is a thing I have been desirous to avoid ... All I desire is, my liberty in encouraging and employing all those that concur faithfully in my service, whether they are called Whigs or Tories, not to be tied to one, nor the other; for if I should be so unfortunate as to fall into the hands of either, I shall not imagine myself, though I have the name of Queen, to be in reality but their slave, which as it will be my personal ruin, so it will be the destroying all government; for instead of putting an end to faction, it will lay a lasting foundation for it. You press the bringing Lord Sunderland into business, that there may be one of that party in a place of trust, to help carry on the business this winter; and you think if this is not complied with, they will not be hearty in pursuing my service in the Parliament. But is it not very hard that men of sense and honour, will not promote the good of their country, because everything in the world is not done that they desire! when they may be assured Lord Sunderland shall come into employment as soon as it is possible. Why, for God's sake, must I, who have no interest, no end, no thought, but for the good of my country, be made so miserable, as to be brought into the power of one set of men?"

The answer of history to her last despairing question is that it was for the good of the country that the Sovereign should be brought into the power of one set of men drawn from the predominant party; and apart from brief periods of coalition, the exceptions that have tested the rule, the country has had party ministries in the whole of the period since her death. It began with nearly half a century of unbroken Whig ministries.[a]

3

THE WHIG OLIGARCHY
1714–1761

Tory office-holders eliminated and Tory acts repealed—Tory strength in the Church of England—and in the country gentlemen—factions among the Whigs—developments in party system under George I and II—principle of Cabinet solidarity—emergence of Prime Minister—rise in importance of the House of Commons—ministry drawn from the party having the confidence of the Commons—use of patronage and bribery to support the government—growth of the Prime Minister's power to seek a dissolution—Bolingbroke's attempt to unite Tories and dissident Whigs—the Lancaster House opposition—rule of the Pelham Whigs—William Pitt the Elder's attitude to parties—his alliance with Henry Fox—accession of George III and end of the Whig ascendancy

AT the accession of George I it seemed as though the Whigs might crush their rivals for ever. They took a leaf from Bolingbroke's book, and almost every Tory office-holder throughout the country down to the local exciseman was eliminated in favour of a Whig. Oxford was imprisoned and impeached, and though the impeachment collapsed he played no further part in politics. Ormonde was impeached and fled the country for the rest of his days. An act of attainder was obtained against Bolingbroke, who had fled to the Pretender's court, and though he obtained his pardon in 1723 he never recovered his former ascendancy or even his seat in the Lords. The acts punishing occasional conformity and banning dissenters' academies were repealed in 1719.

Though the supremacy of the Whigs was consolidated by these measures, there were limits to what they could do. At heart England remained Tory, and the Whig oligarchy who dominated at Court and in Parliament never represented more than a minority in the country. The Church of England almost to a man and the country gentry in large part were powerful Tory forces which the Whigs were prudent enough to leave undisturbed. There was no part of England that was not in a parish, and the parish priest was almost certainly a man of Tory convictions whose prayers for the King were uttered with reservations. The Industrial Revolution and the Methodist movement were still in the future, and in this rural England almost everyone attended church, and Sunday by Sunday heard long sermons impregnated with Tory doctrine. As vacancies arose on the episcopal bench the Whigs were able to put a string of Whig bishops into sees, but they soon realized that they could not remove the tests excluding from office those who did not conform to the Church of England, and from 1727 were content with an annual act indemnifying those who omitted to take the Anglican sacrament. The national Church retained its privileged legal position well into the next century, and so long as it retained that position the Tory party could not wholly die. Bound up with the Church were the squires. Partly by virtue of their own position as landlords and partly by virtue of their commissions as justices of the peace, they had been the unpaid agents of local administration in England throughout Tudor and Stuart times. It was part of James II's folly to try to make the country gentlemen his instruments in effecting the conversion of England, and their stubborn refusal was not the least element in his defeat. Their success was so complete that they were effectively free from control by the central government throughout the whole of the next century, more free indeed than they had been under Elizabeth and James I. As far as the mass of the people in the countryside were concerned, they and not some unknown lords in remote Whitehall were the real government in social and economic as well as in political and religious matters; and most of them were Tories. The Whigs did not dare, or at any rate did not seek, to disturb this arrangement, which in their own capacity as country gentlemen suited them well enough. As Trevelyan has said:[1]

"The justices of the peace held their commissions from the Crown, through the selection of the Lord Chancellor, but they were not paid by the Crown, and their wealth and local influence came to them from their landed estates, which the government could not touch. Thus the political power of the Whig oligarchy at the centre was effectually limited in the localities by the oligarchy of the squires, who were mainly Tory. But there was nothing to limit the social power of the landed gentry, Whig and Tory together. It was the rural landlords who formed the true oligarchy, no longer controlled by the central power, which rather they themselves controlled."

The Church of England and the Tory gentry provided a solid base on which the Tory party could raise itself again, though shattered at its apex; and there was yet another factor founded in human nature that prevented Whig ascendancy from becoming Whig tyranny. When the Tory menace to the Whigs dissolved, the Whigs began to dispute among themselves. Though Whig ministries held office continuously from 1714 to 1761, there was no lack of party struggles, but they were struggles between different groups of Whigs. These struggles had the same characteristics as the old contests of Tories and Whigs, and are proof that if party did not exist it would be necessary to invent it.

The Whigs were seldom left unmindful of what the dissenters expected from them. Though Mr. John Brooke in his introductory survey to *The House of Commons 1754–1790* can identify only nineteen members known to have been dissenters in that period, he finds plenty of evidence that they formed a considerable portion of the voters in the English boroughs and counties, and in certain constituencies their help was almost essential. They needed no lessons in bringing pressure to bear on political leaders, and they have some claim to have formed the earliest pressure group in British politics. Shortly before the general election of 1734, a body called the "Dissenting Deputies" was formed with a view to political action in defence of Nonconformity. It consisted of delegates from the Presbyterian, Congregational and Baptist churches within easy reach of London. The deputies extracted from Walpole a pledge of support, and in return they gave him their backing at the election. It was a factor in securing his majority, but when they asked him to redeem his promises by giving them relief from the Test and Corporation Acts he played for time on the ground that it would revive the cry of "The Church in danger", and finally he told them that he could do nothing. When the proposal came before the house he said the proposal was ill-timed, and it was defeated by 251 votes to 123. Though baulked in their main object, the "Dissenting Deputies" were successful in stopping many local acts of unlawful persecution. They remained in being throughout the eighteenth and nineteenth centuries, and were ever vigilant in bringing their grievances to those in authority until complete toleration was secured.

The reigns of the first two Hanoverians saw several developments of major importance in the party system. Like most developments in British constitutional history, they came about without fore-thought. The way for them had been prepared by Queen Anne, who, being a woman, and not a woman having the heart of a King as Elizabeth I, leant upon the advice of ministers more than her male predecessors had done. What Anne had done by reason of the frailty of her sex, George I was obliged to do by his lack of fluency in the English language and the rise of an "efficient" or inner Cabinet which he never attended. Though the "nominal Cabinet" remained in existence, the "efficient" Cabinet became the reality and is the prototype of the modern Cabinet.[a] This not only increased the importance of the Cabinet as an organ of government but enabled the doctrine of Cabinet solidarity to grow up. When their

C

Sovereign was no longer at the table, men could speak their mind freely, and so long as they held together it was impossible for the Monarch to blame any one of them for the advice tendered. By a further natural development, when the King withdrew from Cabinet the office of Prime Minister came into being. Hitherto all English sovereigns had been in a real sense their own Prime Minister. When they no longer sat in Cabinet, someone had to preside, and his pre-eminence among his fellows was soon recognized. At first it was a primacy among equals, and the term "Whig oligarchs", which slips so easily from the pen, is properly applied to this period of the first two Georges; but as the years passed the duties discharged by the Prime Minister made it inevitable that he should become more than a first among equals. It was he who made known the wishes of the King to the Cabinet, and conveyed the advice of the Cabinet to the King. By a natural process his advice on men was sought as well as on measures. Almost inevitably the choice of the King's servants slipped from the Sovereign to the Prime Minister. It was as much as George I could be expected to do, with his limited know-ledge of England, to choose one suitable man to be his chief adviser; and fortunately in 1721, when Stanhope died of apoplexy (or perhaps of the South Sea Bubble), he did not make a mistake. For the next twenty-one years Sir Robert Walpole presided in Cabinet, and his long tenure of office allowed these new constitutional principles to take firm root.

We must not suppose that Cabinet government in its panoply as we know it today descended upon Hanoverian England like some Athena. George II, who had quarrelled violently with his father and had led an opposition to him from Leicester House,[2] could not be expected to take George I's ministers to his heart immediately. He knew English, and had come to England young enough to learn his way around. At his accession he made a half-hearted attempt to have Sir Spencer Compton as his Prime Minister, but Compton's inability and Queen Caroline's good sense kept Walpole in the seat of power. In later years George II did make a number of direct ministerial appointments, and in 1744 and 1757 he even tried to make whole Cabinets. It is nevertheless true that in the reigns of George I and George II the principle of Cabinet government became so firmly established as to resist the efforts of George III to break it.

The inability of George I to exercise the powers of his pre-decessors led to a corresponding rise in the importance of Parliament relative to the Crown; and as the House of Commons was the money-raising part of the legislature, and that at a time when money was sorely needed after the drain of great wars, this meant a rise in the constitutional position of the House of Commons. It is a sign of the times that Walpole chose to remain in the House of Commons throughout the whole period of his political life, and

accepted the earldom of Orford only when his downfall was immi-
nent. The relative strength of the House of Commons in relation to
the Crown had been further enhanced by two acts regulating its life.
The Triennial Act of 1694, which fixed the life of Parliament at
three years, took away the Sovereign's power to keep a subservient
legislature in being indefinitely, long after it had ceased to be representative; but the short period then fixed meant that members
always had an election just behind or ahead of them. The Septennial
Act, prolonging the normal duration of Parliament to seven years,
was passed for the empirical purpose of avoiding an election in the
troubled state of the country in 1716 soon after the Jacobite rising;
but as it applied also to future Parliaments it gave members a
greater sense of security on election, and therefore greater independence in relation to the Crown. The rise in the importance of
the lower house for these several reasons led to the tacit acceptance
of the principle that the ministry must be drawn from a party
having the confidence of the House of Commons, and ideally that
implied the command of a majority in that chamber.

There was an unpleasant consequence of this increased importance of the House of Commons. Elections to the House, and control
of it when elected, became matters of greater significance. Governments did not feel disposed to leave matters to chance, and both
patronage and bribery were used to influence the choice of electors
and the votes of members.

The significance of "Old Corruption", as Cobbett called it,[3] for
the story of the party system is three-fold. In the first place, governments did not lose elections. It was the duty of the Secretary of the
Treasury to see that they did not; and no election was lost by a
government until that of 1830 ushered in the Reform Bill. Since the
Reform Bill elections have made governments, but before the
Reform Bill governments made elections. For this purpose the secret
service funds were used to supplement those government supporters
who were not able to pay in full their own heavy expenses. It follows that the opposition, having to rely solely on their own purses,
were heavily handicapped in relation to the government. In the
second place, the expense of election was so great that compacts
were frequently made to avoid contests; and in a two-member constituency representation might be shared between a Whig and a
Tory. Contested elections were indeed rarer than uncontested,
though this has to be qualified by the thought that many more elections would have gone to the poll if the preliminary canvass had not
shown one of the candidates that he had no hope of success. In the
third place, as elections were so expensive, both to governments
and to candidates, Parliament normally ran out the full term of
seven sessions fixed by the Septennial Act in 1716. No instance of
Parliament being dissolved before its time occurs until 1780, when

George III dissolved on the advice of the Cabinet in order to strengthen Lord North's position in the House of Commons; and although
this Parliament would have expired in any case the following year
the principle was important. A new constitutional device had been
discovered, and it was employed again in 1784 and 1807 with the
same object, to strengthen the government of the day. A Prime
Minister's threat to dissolve, thereby subjecting both his followers
and his opponents to the inconvenience of a general election, has
long since been one of the recognized weapons in the British party
struggle, and is often the only way of resolving a difference of
policy on a major issue.

Walpole's long tenure of office was not unchallenged. Helped by
the pens of Swift and Pope, Bolingbroke made it his aim to unite the
Tories led in the House of Commons by Sir William Wyndham with
the dissident Whigs led by William Pulteney, later Earl of Bath. He
founded the *Craftsman* as a political magazine in which to express
his views, and in it there appeared in 1733–4 the instalments of *A
Dissertation upon Parties*. The argument was that the Revolution
settlement had been universally accepted; that the old strife of Whig
and Tory had ceased to have any meaning; that the only true parties
left were those of Court and Country; and that it was time for all
good men to come to the aid of the nation. These were lofty sentiments, but they failed in the object of unseating Walpole and
rehabilitating Bolingbroke. Later, in 1738, when he had joined the
Leicester House opposition—for George II had the mortification of
seeing his son Frederick assume the same rôle that he had played
against his father—Bolingbroke tried again, and in *The Patriot King*
he painted the portrait of a sovereign who should govern by
choosing the best men from all parties. It was to have a baneful
influence on the future George III, but none at the time.

When Walpole's arts eventually failed there was a brief period in
which his colleagues the two brothers Henry Pelham and the Duke
of Newcastle were joined by the opposition Whigs, William Pulteney and John Carteret, later made Lord Granville[b]; but the Pelhams
soon ousted the intruders, and between them held the office of Prime
Minister for thirteen years, Henry from 1743 to his death in 1754,
and thereafter the duke to 1756. In these years the duke proved
himself not inferior to Walpole in the sordid arts of manipulating
electors and elected, and his secret service accounts as brilliantly
annotated by Namier still make fascinating reading.[4] It was in an
early stage of the Pelham administration that the Young Pretender
made his bid for the Throne; immediately it doomed the Tories to
further frustration, but by finally demonstrating the futility of the
Jacobite cause it paved the way for an ultimate revival on a new
basis.

Newcastle resigned in 1756 only because popular clamour demanded that William Pitt should be entrusted with the conduct of the war, to be known to history as the Seven Years' War, that had just broken out. This soaring eagle of eighteenth-century politics defies classification in terms of party. He was not a Tory, and no Tory at that time could have hoped for the power that Pitt was avid to wield; but he has equally little title to be called a Whig, except that he associated with the Whigs who then had a monopoly of office. Men counted as nothing with him compared with the measures on which he had set his fiery heart. So unlike Walpole in his disinterested patriotism, he shared Walpole's love of the House of Commons; and the Great Commoner was a dearer title to him than the earldom of Chatham ever could become. He had hoped to become leader of the house when Pelham died in 1754, but Newcastle passed him over in favour of the nondescript Sir Thomas Robinson. For the purpose of baiting Robinson Pitt then joined forces with Henry Fox. It is the first time the names of Pitt and Fox, which were to mean so much in the history of party and in the greater history of England, were brought into conjunction. Fox had been a Tory, but had become a disciple of Walpole and had been given office in 1743. When Robinson was driven to resign—with a secret service pension of £2,000 a year—it was Fox who took his place as Secretary of State; and it was then that Pitt likened the union of Fox and Newcastle to the conflux at Lyons of "the Rhône and Saône : this a gentle, feeble, languid stream, and, though languid, of no depth—the other a boisterous and impetuous current—but they meet at last".[5]

The jest was no more to Newcastle's taste than Pitt's saying, when the war began disastrously, as English wars are apt to do : "I am sure I can save this country and nobody else can."[6] He was allowed to form a ministry with the Duke of Devonshire as its titular head, but in 1757 a better arrangement was made. Newcastle again became Prime Minister on the understanding that he should take charge of the patronage while Pitt should wage war. Fox was kept quiet with the office of Paymaster-General, which Pitt had left as a poor man, and proceeded to amass a vast fortune.

The new spirit that Pitt infused into the nation brought an accumulation of victories that made him the idol of all classes; but before he could bring the war to a glorious conclusion, George II had died (1760) and his grandson George III sat on the Throne.

We have come to the Years of Confusion in British party politics. "George, be a king" had been the constantly repeated injunction of his foolish German mother, and The Patriot King had been the staple of his education. Born in England, and wholly English except in lineage, he had made it his resolve to recover the kingly powers that his German grandfather and great-grandfather had thrown away.

His determination to end the war as speedily as possible led Pitt to resign in 1761. Newcastle was dismissed in the following year, and the young and headstrong King summoned his favourite, the Earl of Bute, to take the place that he vacated. It may or may not be just to call Bute a Tory,[7] but the long period of Whig ascendancy had come to an end.[6]

4

YEARS OF CONFUSION
1761–1782

Namier's analysis of the eighteenth-century House of Commons—
members dependent on patrons—or in the employment of the
Crown—office of Secretary of the Treasury—rise of an impartial
Civil Service—continuity of the Whigs and Tories—personal rule
of George III—fall of Bute—and of Grenville—Rockingham called
to office—the Rockingham Whigs—Grafton's ministry—destroyed
by Chatham—the King turns to Lord North—fall of North and end
of personal rule

NAMIER'S epoch-making study *The Structure of Politics at the Accession of George III* is acknowledged as a masterpiece of analytical history. In it he throws a cold light on the reasons why men went into Parliament and the methods by which they arrived there, and one of the chief conclusions to which he comes is:[1] "There were no proper party organizations about 1760, though party names and cant were current; the names and the cant have since supplied the materials for an imaginary superstructure."

In his later Romanes lecture *Monarchy and the Party System* Namier goes even farther, and bluntly says:[2] "In 1761 not one parliamentary election was determined by party." He contrasts it with the election of 1951, when "not one constituency returned a non-party member". According to his researches:

"Three broad divisions, based on type and not on party, can be distinguished in the eighteenth-century House of Commons: on the one side were the followers of Court and Administration, the 'placemen', *par excellence* a group of permanent 'ins'; on the opposite side, the independent country gentlemen, of their own choice permanent 'outs'; and in between, occupying as it were the centre of the arena, and focusing upon themselves the attention of the public and of history, stood the political factions contending for power, the forerunners of parliamentary government based on a party-system."

Namier draws the conclusion that "no consistent defence of parties was possible under the 'mixed form of government'", by which he means a form of government in which power was shared between the Crown and the legislature. There were two main ways in which the full development of the party system was impeded in the eighteenth century.

In the first place, a high proportion of the members of the House of Commons owed their seats to influence. The use of secret service funds by the government to buy the votes of electors and members has often been exaggerated—Namier shows it to have been "but a small rivulet, not a river, and not nearly as dirty as generally supposed"[3]—but the patronage of boroughs was a major element. Namier finds that 111 borough patrons determined or influenced the election of 205 seats, and as 30 seats were more or less under the immediate management of the government some 235 borough seats, almost half the representation of England, were under patronage; and there were others which were not free, but merely disputed between patrons.[4] A redeeming feature is that the members thus nominated voted in the House of Commons more freely than might have been expected.

The second factor impeding the proper functioning of the party system was the large number of members of Parliament in the employment of the Crown. Of thirty admirals on the flag list in 1761, no fewer than twenty sat in Parliament at one time or another; and in the general election of that year sixty-four serving Army officers were elected.[5] Even stranger by modern British standards is the number of permanent officials of government departments who sat in the House of Commons. In the Act of Settlement it had been laid down that "no person who has an office or a place of profit under the king shall be capable of serving as a member of the House of Commons"—which would have excluded ministers as well as civil servants—but the section was repealed before it could take effect; and a new statute disqualified the holders of new offices created after 1705, disqualified the holders of certain offices and pensioners at pleasure, obliged members of the House of Commons who accepted an old office to seek re-election and excepted commissions in the Army and Navy from the disqualification. In consequence, throughout the eighteenth century many civil servants sat in Parliament. As Namier observes, "the seat in the house added to the importance and standing of civil servants, and their presence in Parliament was useful to their chiefs".[6]

The most interesting of all these offices from the point of view of party history is that of Secretary of the Treasury. From 1714 there were two of them, of whom the senior managed elections in the government interest and mobilized members for divisions in the House of Commons. He was, as we should say today, the government chief whip, and in the eighteenth century, owing to the rise in importance of the Commons, whipping began to become both a science and an art. In any history of party the Secretaries of the

Treasury must play a part scarcely inferior to that of the political chiefs whom they served. Normally they sat in the House of Commons and retired with their political chiefs, but the cases of two of the more eminent among them show the first glimmerings of modern thought on the subject.

When Walpole fell in 1742 the Duke of Bedford assumed that dismissal would follow for Walpole's Secretary of the Treasury, John Scrope, "through whose hands such sums of money have passed, and who refused to give any answer to the Secret Committee about those dark transactions". Pulteney replied: "What your grace mentions is absolutely impracticable. Mr. Scrope is the only man I know, that thoroughly understands the business of the Treasury, and is versed in drawing money bills. On this foundation he stands secure, and is as immovable as a rock."[7]

In 1782 Lord North retired from the Treasury and of the two Secretaries Sir Grey Cooper followed him into opposition, but John Robinson, "conceiving himself absolved from any obligation to accompany his ancient principal through all the consequences of his new political alliances, quitted altogether that party".[8] Robinson had managed the elections of 1774 and 1780, and showed his impartiality by giving the benefit of his advice to Pitt in the election of 1784.

We can now see that it was desirable to separate the control of State finance from the management of the House of Commons. The two Secretaries of the Treasury continued to be political officers with seats in the House of Commons, and were named the Parliamentary Secretary and the Financial Secretary, but in 1805 there was created the office of Permanent Secretary, incompatible with a seat in Parliament. The Parliamentary Secretary continued to have the task of securing a majority for the government in and out of Parliament, and the Permanent Secretary, with charge of the daily work of the Treasury, had no responsibility for the management of elections or the House of Commons and no obligation to retire with his ministerial chief. Scrope and Robinson in the eighteenth century were groping towards the nineteenth-century conception of a Civil Service which should stand aloof from the party struggle and be at the disposal of the government of the day irrespective of political complexion. An impartial and politically neutral Civil Service is now recognized as an essential element in the successful working of the party system. We must not be surprised if the eighteenth century took some time to discover it.

To say that "there was no proper party organization about 1760" or that "in 1761 not one parliamentary election was determined by party" is not to say that parties did not then exist, though Namier's words have often been taken in that sense. This is going farther than the facts warrant. There were certainly in the middle of the eighteenth century innumerable men who called themselves Whigs and would not have denied belonging to the Whig party. There were many men who called themselves Tories and would have been surprised to be told that the Tory party did not exist. We can imagine what Dr. Johnson would have said if told there was no Tory party— he who always said the first Whig was the Devil, and who in his reporting of Parliament took care that the Whig dogs should not have the best of it. What is true is that there was no party organization outside Parliament, nor ever had been, nor could be until after 1832; and that in Parliament the alignment of parties had become confused. Though we may not go the whole way with Dr. Southgate[9] in saying that "when Whiggism had become the creed of the age, under the second George, it lost its significance as a term which could meaningfully be used to differentiate one set of politicians from another", we may readily agree that "by the accession of George III in 1760 nobody knew what Whiggery was because almost everybody who was anybody in the political world claimed to be a Whig".

The real problem is not whether parties existed but whether there was any continuity linking the Whig and Tory parties of the seventeenth century with the Whig and Tory parties of the nineteenth. It is as though two streams that had run in parallel courses for a hundred years merged their waters for the next twenty, and then divided once more into two parallel streams for another hundred years until one of them was finally lost in the sands. Despite much inter-mingling during the period of confusion it seems fair to say that the right-hand waters remained the right-hand waters and the left-hand waters remained the left-hand waters. Whatever the politicians might do in Parliament for the sake of office—and even a Chatham could turn completely round on the question of Hanover to gain his ends—there were ample groups of people in the country who remained loyal to the old ideals without question and perhaps without much thought. When we see two parties at the beginning of the eighteenth century, one of them allied to the Church and the landed interest, the other linked with dissent and the mercantile classes, and when we see at the end of the century two parties, one of them allied to the Church and the landed interest, and the other linked with dissent and the mercantile classes, and when we find the former party in each pair called Tory and the latter party in each pair called Whig, there is a presumption in favour of some degree of continuity that would need much evidence to overthrow it. It is not a continuity of structure and organization but a continuity of ideas and of men. Though Sir Keith Feiling is the historian of the Tory "parties", as the historian of the Whigs, Dr. Southgate, has pointed out,[10] and though he holds that in the eighteenth century "no Tory party existed, in the modern sense of party, perhaps till the death of the younger Pitt", we may applaud him for having kept in *The Second Tory Party 1714–1832* "a title which may serve as a reminder that there was none the less a continuous tradition and some elementary framework of party, and a descent of political ideas".[11]

The realization among Tories that after 1745 Jacobitism was a lost cause, and the weariness of the nation with an indefinite continuance of Whig rule, made people ready for a change in 1760, even if George III, fed with the precepts of the latter-day Bolingbroke, had not come to the Throne determined to rule without parties. For a score of years he maintained his personal rule by seeking what ministers he would where he would; and the results were so disastrous for the country that by a paradox "the reign of George III, who dedicated himself to the extirpation of party, created the parties of our modern history".

The means by which George III re-assumed the old powers of the Crown was to take into his own hands the patronage and corruption that Walpole and Newcastle had exercised. His supporters in Parliament, who would once have been the Court party, became appropriately known as "the King's friends". He claimed not only control over policy but the right of nominating individual ministers. For a Prime Minister to present the Sovereign with a list of ministers or a set of policies on which he would accept office was denounced as "storming the closet". The government being the King's, to oppose it was dangerously near treason in the eyes of the King and his friends, and a "formed opposition" was frowned upon. It was inevitable that the new men on whom the King called should be denounced by the Whigs as Tories, but the historian of the Tory party will not accept them, and retorts that Bute and his Treasury Secretary Jenkinson, chief organizer of the King's friends, Grenville and North were Whigs, for "till 1770 everyone in office was a 'Whig' ".[12] It is proof alike of the confusion in the party system and of the unpopularity of the policies of which they were the tools.

Bute was made so much the butt of the nation's wit and anger that he did not survive as Prime Minister beyond 1763. The King thereupon called on George Grenville, who had been Bute's Secretary of State but had previously served in the Whig administrations of Pelham and Newcastle. He and his elder brother Richard, Earl Temple, William Pitt (who married Hester Grenville) and George, Lord Lyttelton were some of "Cobham's boys", also known as "the cousinhood" and "the patriots", who had formed a distinct group among the Whigs in the time of Walpole and had opposed the Hanoverian connexion. Whether he is to be reckoned a Whig or a Tory at this time, Grenville fared no better than Bute, and, having incurred the displeasure of the King, he was dismissed in 1765. At the suggestion of his uncle the Duke of Cumberland (the "Butcher of Culloden"), the King in desperation then had recourse to a man whose title to the name of Whig was undeniable, Charles Watson Wentworth, Marquess of Rockingham. He is the harbinger of a new era in British party politics, for the Rockingham Whigs[a] were to be the basis of a new school of Whig thought and the foundation of a new Whig ascendancy; but in 1765 no one would have dared make such a prophecy, for Pitt would not join the ministry—it might have made a world of difference to British and American history if his vanity and inability to work with others had not forbidden him— and this kept Shelburne out and led Grafton to resign. The ministry had to be completed with two of the King's friends, Northington and Egmont. After barely a year of office Rockingham was dismissed, thought not without substantial achievements to his credit, and Pitt then agreed to come in, with Grafton as the titular head of the ministry, but the great commoner strangely prejudiced his chances of success by going at the same time to the House of Lords. The King made no secret of his wishes: "As I know," he wrote,[13] "the Earl of Chatham will zealously give his aid towards destroying all party distinctions", and he announced his intention to "withstand that evil called connexion", to "root out the present method of parties banding together" and "to distribute the functions of state by rotation". Whether Chatham could have achieved much with his royal master in such a mood is doubtful, but in any case it was too late. In the same year mind and body became unhinged, and henceforth only flashes of inspiration and activity illumined the darkness of the Earl of Chatham. Grafton's ministry survived the election of 1768, as eighteenth-century governments always did, and with much reshuffling dragged on till 1770. The old lion who had put Grafton in office then rose from his lair to destroy him. The result was to put Lord North, the eldest son of the Earl of Guilford, into office for twelve years. In this amiable House of Commons man the King found exactly the pliant tool he had been seeking as the instrument of his personal rule; and North did not strengthen his position by allowing George III to pay his personal debts to the tune of £20,000. In 1780, when the House of Commons carried Dunning's famous resolution, "that the power of the Crown has increased, is increasing, and ought to be diminished", there was good reason; but in the same year, as we have noticed, the King took advantage of a favourable turn to dissolve Parliament for the first time in advance of its normal end in order to keep North in office. That unfortunate man was helped in his unenviable task by divisions among the opposition, but as the American war proceeded on its disastrous course he would often have resigned but for the King's plea that he be not left to the mercy of the Whigs. After Cornwallis's surrender at Yorktown in 1782 he would no longer be kept and delivered the King to the Whig ministers whom he dreaded. The era of personal rule was over and that of party government had again begun.[14]

5

RE-FORMATION OF PARTIES
1761–1807

Burke joins the Whigs—and Fox—the Yorkshire petition—birth of Radicalism—the Rockingham ministry of 1782—a government responsible to the House of Commons—coalition of Fox and North —William Pitt founder of a new Tory party—Parliament dissolved in advance of its term—Whigs thrown into disarray by French revolution—Fox's New Whigs—stimulus to Radicalism—factions among the Tories—Grenville's "Ministry of All the Talents"— Portland forms a Tory ministry

WHILE George III was recovering his prerogatives and losing an empire, there were developments among the parties which were to change the character of the party system when the period of personal rule was over.

The Rockingham Whigs in 1765, when their leader first took office, were only one group among several in the amorphous body of Whiggery. It is common to regard them as in the political succession of the Pelham Whigs, but they belonged to different generations, Rockingham had not personally served under Pelham or Newcastle, and there have not been lacking historians to challenge the link.[1] In 1765 they had no monopoly of the name Whig, and theirs was only a caretaker administration. They might have cut no further figure upon the stage of history if Rockingham had not been persuaded to adopt as his "man of business" or secretary an Irishman of parts trying to establish himself in the political life of the capital. The Duke of Newcastle, still intriguing at the age of seventy-two, whispered that Edmund Burke was an Irish papist who had been a Jesuit and was an emissary from St. Omer. Rockingham asked Burke for his comments on these allegations. Burke denied them indignantly, and Rockingham expressed himself satisfied; but Burke, fearing that his patron's confidence had been impaired, asked leave to give up the post. Rockingham, recognizing integrity as well as ability, persuaded him to stay, and they lived in close mutual confidence till within a few months of Rockingham's death seventeen years later. Rockingham gave Burke a status that he could not have obtained, great as were his talents, by his independent exertions; and Burke gave to the Rockingham Whigs not only the powerful allies of his tongue and pen but a fervent inspiration and reasoned principles which lifted them above the ordinary factions of the time. He was returned to Parliament in 1766 and his maiden speech justifying Rockingham's policy towards the colonies was recognized at once as putting politics on a higher level. After Rockingham's administration fell, Burke in *Observations on a Late Publication on the Present State of the Nation* made a reply to Grenville that showed him to be a master of the details of finance as well as of broad principle, and in 1770 there came his great justification of party in *Thoughts on the Cause of the Present Discontents*.

It was above all a justification of the Rockingham Whigs, who were beginning to attract more and more of the able young men of the party. Pre-eminent among them was Charles James Fox, third son of Henry, now Lord Holland, the indulgent father whom he had cost for years a thousand guineas a week. Fox had started his parliamentary career in 1769 as a supporter of the Court and in the following year, when still only just of age, he was made a junior Lord of the Admiralty in North's administration. His character in the next few years, as delineated in the scintillating pages of Trevelyan's biography, gave no indication of his future steadiness of purpose: "During the earliest, and much the longest, portion of his first Parliament, Fox, as the spoilt child of the worst House of Commons that ever met, seemed bent upon ascertaining how much unsound argument and pert dogmatism would be tolerated from a ready and an agreeable speaker, and how often it was permissible to go in and out of place without any adequate reason for leaving office, or justification for resuming it."[2] The frivolity concealed a fundamentally serious nature, as he showed in 1772 when he resigned to be free to oppose the Royal Marriages Act on which the King was bent to spite his brothers for marrying commoners; and though he returned to office, his support of the attempt to relieve Nonconformist ministers and schoolmasters from the necessity of subscribing to the Thirty-nine Articles and his sympathy with the American colonists made him a marked man at Court and led to his final departure from North's administration in 1774. "Sick of a prison house whose secrets had so early been familiar to him," his biographer finely writes, "he dissolved his parnership with Sandwich and Wedderburn, and united himself to Burke, and Chatham, and Savile in their crusade against the tyranny which was trampling out English liberty in the colonies, and the corruption which was undermining it at home."[3] Between him and Burke there was already the respect that two men of abounding genius are bound to feel for each other, and Burke brought him into the circle of the Rockingham Whigs. They steered his wayward nature into the paths which his fundamental integrity had already selected, and he used his genius to give greater precision to those principles of public life that they were beginning to formulate.

Those principles needed re-formulation because conditions had greatly changed in the course of the century, and it was no longer sufficient merely to stand by the Revolution Settlement. It was still necessary to insist that the power of a King of England was not absolute, and in 1778 Fox bluntly reminded George III of the fates of Charles I and James II; but the Church of George III did not provoke passion and devotion as the Church of Charles the Martyr had done. Latitudinarianism and Whig bishops kept enthusiasm at a low ebb. This discouragement of zeal was to drive the followers of John and Charles Wesley into dissent, but not into the arms of the Whig party. Nothing was to be feared from the Church of England so long as its establishments and endowments were not tampered with, or the tests abolished, and it was even safe to offer some relaxation to those outside its calm fold. The Whigs remained faithful to the cause of toleration for Protestant dissenters, and at the other end of the scale they began to identify themselves with the relief of Roman Catholic recusants from their disabilities. In 1778 Sir George Savile was successful in obtaining an act permitting Roman Catholics to own land and open schools. The disgraceful Lord George Gordon riots two years later showed how delicately it was necessary to walk in this direction, but Fox never deviated from the policy of Roman Catholic emancipation.

As religious questions moved from the centre of the stage, others took their place. It is a coincidence that the year of George III's accession is the conventional date for the beginning of the Industrial Revolution, but that momentous change could hardly fail to transform the outlook of parties. By swelling the population of such towns as Birmingham and Manchester, it drew attention to the unreformed character of the constituent bodies that returned members to Parliament. What Chatham had called "the rotten part of our constitution" grew rottener every year. It is symptomatic of the change in outlook that Chatham, Burke and Fox first sat in Parliament for rotten boroughs—Old Sarum, Wendover and Midhurst—but the Rockingham Whigs before 1780 had begun to embrace the cause of reform, which was to lead to the greatest of all Whig triumphs, and to presage the elimination of corruption and the misuse of patronage, of which their Whig predecessors had been more guilty than anyone. They took up the cause of "public economy", notably in the years 1779–80 when the growing cost of the American war and the prospective loss of the colonies made men more receptive to criticism of the North administration. They were impelled to do so largely by the success of a Yorkshire clergyman, Christopher Wyvill, in organizing extra-parliamentary agitation in favour of "economical reform", not merely as an end desirable in itself but as a means of freeing Parliament from corruption. He presented to a meeting of Yorkshire freeholders a draft petition in favour of public economy, which was eventually presented to Parliament by Sir George Savile with 8,000 signatures; and after this "Yorkshire Petition" had been approved he carried a further resolution for the appointment of a committee "to carry on the necessary correspondence for effectually promoting the object of the petition and to support that laudable reform and such other measures as may conduce to restore the freedom of Parliament". As Mr. Ian R. Christie says in his narrative of these events:[4] "A committee simply to manage the petition would have been nothing new; but the resolution, stating the terms of reference of the committee in such vague form, indicated Wyvill's desire to keep on foot a machinery in Yorkshire for promoting his political programme." In his Yorkshire Association we see a foreshadowing of constituency organization; and although it had no permanence—it was allowed to die away in 1786 when Wyvill could no longer see his way clearly between the rival contenders for power—the example had a wide influence at the time. Twenty-five other counties—and a number of boroughs—presented petitions in 1780, and most of them set up committees of correspondence similar to the Yorkshire Association. Yorkshire in those days was a politically alert area and gave a lead to the rest of the country.

The Rockingham Whigs had wholeheartedly identified themselves with the cause of self-determination in the colonies, and although this was on grounds of justice and expediency rather than on abstract economic principle, it pointed to a break with the doctrines of the mercantile school, according to which colonies were milch cows for the mother country. It foreshadowed the later Whig championship of small nationalities everywhere and also the adoption of free trade as a principle; but this was still in the future, even though Adam Smith had published his *Wealth of Nations* in 1776. Linked with the freeing of the colonies was a growing distaste for the slave trade. The abolition of that grim trade in 1807 was destined to be Fox's bequest to the nation, for although this measure is correctly linked with the name of Wilberforce, it owed its passage through the House of Commons to the help of the government, of which Fox was the active mind.

The Rockingham Whigs had put their hibernation to good use, and when North was released from his misery in 1782 they constituted an able body of statesmen with a consistent set of principles. On this foundation the Whig party was eventually re-united and revivified, or, as some would prefer to say, a new Whig party was founded. The outlook was complicated, however, by a new phenomenon in British politics, the birth of Radicalism.

According to the historian of Radicalism,[5] this took place between 1762 and 1782; and in that period, so admirably illuminated by Dr. Maccoby, no date is more significant than 28th March 1768, when John Wilkes was elected member of Parliament for Middlesex, which was as near to being a popular election as any election could be in the eighteenth century. The second son of a London malt distiller and privately taught by a dissenting minister, he had lived a profligate life before and after he was elected member for Aylesbury in 1757, which by a complicated arrangement cost him £7,000. In answer to the *Briton* started by Bute to justify ministerial policy, he founded the *North Briton* in 1762, and the cleverly vicious attacks that he made on the favourite were as much as anything responsible for that nobleman's fall. When Grenville succeeded, Wilkes made a devastating attack upon the King's Speech in No. 45 of the *North Briton*. The King took it as a personal insult, a "general warrant" (one not naming the person to be arrested) was issued, and Wilkes was thrown into the Tower, from which he was released by the Lord Chief Justice on the ground of a breach of privilege. By a protracted series of legal proceedings he established the illegality of general warrants, which were abolished under Rockingham's first administration.

The government's next stroke was to attempt to prosecute Wilkes for printing on his private press his friend Thomas Potter's obscene parody of Pope, the *Essay on Woman*, of which only twelve copies had been run off, and those for private circulation. Wilkes thought it judicious to move himself to Paris—after fighting a duel with Samuel Martin, Secretary to the Treasury and the chief agent of official corruption. He was expelled from the House of Commons, but came back to fight the general election of 1768, and though defeated in London was successful in Middlesex. Answering the legal charges against him, he was sentenced to a fine of £500 and a year's imprisonment for No. 45 and the same for the *Essay on Woman*. The crowds that assembled outside his prison, dispersed on one occasion with loss of life, and the nation-wide cry, "Wilkes and Liberty", bore witness to his immense popularity, and testified to the rise of a new phenomenon in public life. Wilkes's imprisonment, it was instinctively felt throughout the nation, was not just one more move in the strife of Whig and Tory factions. He had stirred numbers of people who had hitherto been politically inarticulate, and did not feel that either the Whig or the Tory aristocracy had anything to do with them. His support lay most evidently in the lower middle and artisan classes who had benefited from the Industrial Revolution and were becoming conscious of their political disfranchisement. They were acquiring money, as their gifts to Wilkes showed, but they did not have the vote, and they were beginning to resent their deprivation. Though these were Wilkes's main supporters, con-

D

sciously or unconsciously he stirred depths far below them in what it was usual to call the mob, among men and women who did not yet aspire to the vote but wanted bread. With the Industrial Revolution there had begun the succession of trade cycles, and this was a time when the ministry found it prudent to relax the restrictions on the import of corn. The connexion between the rise and fall of trade and the rise and fall of governments is now a platitude, though still imperfectly investigated, but in those early days of the Industrial Revolution the hungry coal-heavers knew nothing about trade cycles, and in a vague way felt that Wilkes was the champion of their empty bellies. Perhaps those who cried "Wilkes and Liberty", whether in the middle or lower classes, did not know his private life or in that far from squeamish age did not care; they may even have liked his boast that he had "no small vices". If they had any hesitations, they were answered by the powerful pen of "Junius", who began at this time his campaign to unite the "patriot" forces against the King: "You will not suspect me of setting up Wilkes for a perfect character. The question to the public is, where shall we find a man, who, with purer principles, will go the lengths, and run the hazards that he has done? The season calls for such a man, and he ought to be supported."

That was, indeed, the question, and the wealthy Alderman Beckford answered it in the same way as "Junius", and induced the city of London, of which he had become Lord Mayor in 1762 and 1769, to present at court petitions couched in language that George III and his ministers had not previously heard. The words of the most famous, that of 1770, may still be seen on his monument at Guildhall. It may seem strange in the light of later history that the city of London should be allied with the Radical cause, but so it was in those unrepresentative days, and Beckford gave its freemen a *Political Creed* containing phrases that were to become battle-cries for generations:

"That the number of little paltry rotten boroughs, the number of placemen and pensioners, and the corruption of the electors as well as the elected, were the instruments that would in time prove the ruin of the state. To prevent these evils it was necessary that there should be a more equal representation of the people, that the number of placemen should be limited by law, and that the servants of the crown should be obliged to exhibit fuller accounts of the manner in which the public money was disposed of."[6]

We need not follow Wilkes through all his expulsions and re-elections until he was finally allowed to take his seat in 1774 and consolidated his hold on the city by himself becoming Lord Mayor of London. What does call for notice before we leave him is the formation in 1769 of the Society of Supporters of the Bill of Rights to help him in his campaign. The original members included three members of Parliament who had acquired notoriety by their opposition to the Court, several clergymen and lawyers, an apothecary, a wine-merchant and a wealthy owner of plantations who was promptly voted treasurer. The leading spirit was John Horne, who later called himself Horne Tooke after a benefactor, but is often called "Parson" Horne because of the deacon's orders that he had received. The Society of Supporters of the Bill of Rights has strong claims to be regarded as the first political association, and therefore holds an honourable place in the story of party. It is true that Wilkes regarded it as no more than an instrument for paying the debts incurred by his extravagant mode of life, and this led to a breach with Horne. He and others who had helped to found the Bill of Rights Society withdrew in 1771 and founded the Constitutional Society.

A few days before the Bill of Rights Society was founded the freeholders of Middlesex had met at the Mile End Assembly Rooms to pledge their support for Wilkes in the forthcoming election. Dr Maccoby accounts it to be the "first remarkable forerunner of the modern indoor election meeting",[7] and eight days later they held another meeting in the same place for the purpose of repledging themselves to Wilkes, who had in the meantime been expelled from the house. All these Wilkes proceedings have a curiously modern ring about them. One of Wilkes's admirers, Sir Joseph Mawbey, and his co-member Henry Thrale, even went to the length in 1769 of seeking from the electors of Southwark formal instructions as to their conduct in Parliament.[8] The Bill of Rights Society, as Mr. Rudé notes,[9] developed this "novel device of 'instructing' M.P.s on their conduct in Parliament, and, after that, of eliciting pledges from parliamentary candidates to support a listed number of popular causes at Westminster". In 1771 the society drew up a declaration under eleven heads which amounted in effect to a party programme It included "a full and equal representation of the people in Parliament", the requirement of an oath against bribery from all candidates, a Pension and Place Bill, the remedy of Irish and American grievances, and annual Parliaments.[10] We feel already to smell the breath of Chartism. Candidates were asked whether they would support this or a similar list of reforms. The first member of Parliament to be elected after giving such pledges to his constituents was one of Wilkes's associates, Frederick Bull, who took his seat for the city of London in 1773.[11] Before the election of 1774 Wilkes pledged himself to the meeting of Middlesex freeholders to support shorter Parliaments, more equal representation of electors, the exclusion of placemen and the repeal of the Quebec Act.[12] It was this novel tendency that led Burke to assert to the electors of Bristol the right of a member of Parliament to speak and vote according to his own judgement.[13]

The name Radical was not yet in use—the first example of the political use of the word appears to be in 1786 when "the necessity of a substantial and radical reform in the representation" was demanded—and Wilkes and his dozen followers in the Parliament elected in 1774 did not think of themselves as a party.[14] They nevertheless formed a recognizably distinct group in Parliament, campaigning vociferously for the enfranchisement of the lower classes, the suppression of rotten boroughs and freedom for the American colonies; and they mobilized support for their programme in meetings throughout the country. We are justified in seeing the origin of the Radical group of members of Parliament, who, without ever forming a separate party, formed a distinct group with clear ideas of their own, and by their determination and their strength of support in the country stirred the Whigs to bolder courses than they would themselves have adopted.

When North could no longer continue the King reluctantly sent for Rockingham, but insisted on having one of his friends, the Earl of Shelburne as Secretary for the Colonies to act as a brake on such Whigs as Fox at the Foreign Office and Burke in the Paymaster's department. Though he had been the main inspiration in the Whig revival, Burke was not offered a seat in the Cabinet, and the injury to his feelings was deep. The Cabinet belonged, as Fox put it, partly to the King and partly to the country, but though neither the King nor Fox realized it at the time, the era of personal rule was over. "From the day of Lord North's resignation in March 1782," as Trevelyan observes,[15] "Britain has never been governed save by a Prime Minister and Cabinet responsible not to the King alone but first and foremost to the independent judgement of the House of Commons." Though the Sovereign retained many real powers for a long time to come, the way to full party government was open.

Rockingham's second ministry was terminated after a few months by his death, but not before it had carried two measures of major importance. One freed Ireland from the jurisdiction of the British Privy Council and the sovereignty of the British Parliament, and repealed some of the anti-Catholic measures there. The other, Burke's Economic Reform Bill, fulfilled in large measure the hopes of the Yorkshire petitioners twelve years earlier by striking at the power of the government to corrupt the House of Commons. Government contractors were not allowed to sit in Parliament, large numbers of revenue officers were disfranchised, forty offices in the King's gift were abolished, and the secret service and pension funds were reduced.

On Rockingham's death the King gave his place to Shelburne, but Fox would not serve under him. The claim was then put forward specifically by Fox that the Prime Minister should be the choice of a majority of the Cabinet, not of the King, and he refused to serve except under the Duke of Portland. The King would not yield, and Fox resigned along with Burke, Portland, Cavendish and Sheridan, the dramatist, who had entered Parliament in 1780 and had been made Under-Secretary for Foreign Affairs.

Fox then committed one of those acts of folly to which his impulsive nature made him liable from time to time. Forgetting all the invective he had hurled at North's administration, he allied himself with that statesman for the ostensible purpose of opposing the unfavourable terms of the peace settlement, but for the real purpose of bringing down Shelburne. In this they were successful, but the country was shocked by what appeared to be the abandonment of principle in favour of opportunism; and still more shocked when Fox and North forced themselves on the King as Secretaries of State with Portland as the nominal Prime Minister. Words that he had used in the previous year were still ringing in men's ears : "From the moment I shall make any terms with one of them I will rest satisfied to be called the most infamous of mankind." For long afterwards the conjunction of Fox and North was known as *"The* Coalition", and it helped to give a bad name to coalitions for which there were better reasons.

One measure pushed through Parliament by Fox, increasing the opprobrium in which he stood, has a special interest in the story of party. The Prince of Wales, the future George IV, came of age in 1783, and it was necessary to vote an income to him for his separate establishment at Carlton House. Like George I and George II, it was the misfortune of George III to have an heir who thwarted him in everything and regarded it as his rôle to become the leader of the opposition. The King had not failed to observe his son's partiality for the Whigs, especially Fox and Sheridan, and this was a prime reason for his refusal to countenance Fox as the successor to Rockingham. Fox pressed for a substantial allowance, the King demurred. In the end a compromise was reached, and the Prince was given £50,000 a year from the Civil List (Fox had asked for £100,000) and £60,000 to pay his debts and set up Carlton House, which henceforth became as much as anything could the opposition headquarters.

Another measure that Fox sponsored—the India Bill—had more to commend it, for it would have transferred patronage in those vast territories from the East India Company to a commission appointed by the government and removable only by Parliament. The impeachment of Clive in 1773 and the presence in the house of "nabobs" who had bought themselves seats and immunity with wealth acquired in India had drawn attention to the power that Indian patronage offered. The King made it known that no peer who voted for the bill could be his friend. It was rejected by the Lords, and the coalition was dismissed at the end of 1783.

Thus William Pitt the Younger was called at the tender age of twenty-four, after Temple had failed, to the highest counsels of the state. It was an inspired choice, if indeed George III had any choice; but no one at that date could possibly have seen that Pitt would be Prime Minister, save for a brief interval, until his death in 1806; that he who never called himself a Tory would so rally the Tory forces as to cause himself to be venerated as the founder of a new Tory party; and that the Whigs would be out of office all that century and for practical purposes till 1830.

The second son of the Earl of Chatham whose name he bore and whose genius he inherited, William Pitt described himself as an independent Whig when he entered Parliament in 1781 for the pocket borough of Appleby, having been rejected by Cambridge University; and he made an orthodox Whig beginning in a maiden speech supporting economic reform which drew from Burke the praise: "He is not a chip of the old block, he is the old block itself."[16] He could have had a minor post in Rockingham's second administration, but with sublime assurance would accept nothing less than a place in the Cabinet, which Rockingham was not disposed to give to such a stripling. His chance came within a few months when Shelburne invited him to be Chancellor of the Exchequer; and as Shelburne was commonly regarded as Chatham's political heir it would have been surprising if he had declined. When the unfavourable turn of the negotiations at Versailles made it necessary for Shelburne to widen his support, Pitt was sent as an emissary to Fox. After Pitt's maiden speech Fox had joyously put up his name for Brooks's, and he had given way to him in the House of Commons when they rose simultaneously a little later. But Fox's detestation of Shelburne was so great that he would return to office only if Shelburne resigned as Prime Minister. Pitt retorted: "I did not come here to betray Lord Shelburne."[17] It was a critical moment. The course of party history has not infrequently been dictated by the likes and dislikes of party leaders; and from this moment we may date the beginning of the evolution that made Pitt the leader of a revived and united Tory party against which the brilliant declamations of Fox beat in vain.

The coalition with North increased the breach between Fox and Pitt, who in memorable phrases said to the House of Commons: "If, however, the baneful alliance is not already formed, if this ill-omened marriage is not already solemnized, I know a just and lawful inpediment, and in the name of the public safety I here forbid the banns."[18] The alliance was indeed consummated, but it proved barren. Out of office, Pitt announced his intentions: "I desire to declare," he said, "that I am unconnected with any party whatever. I shall keep myself reserved, and act with whichever side I think is acting right."[19] When he came back to office as Prime

Minister it was in a sense his own party that he created, but there were first great difficulties to overcome. His supporters were in a minority in the House of Commons, and ranged against him were orators of the calibre of Fox, Burke and Sheridan. The opposition were prepared to allow him to carry essential financial business, for they knew that at a general election they would pay for the unpopularity of the coalition; but he could not hope in that house to secure the passage of any constructive legislation and his thoughts turned to dissolution as the only remedy. The King agreed, and Parliament was dissolved in 1784 after only four of the seven years for which it could run. It is an even clearer case than the 1780 general election of a dissolution to suit the convenience of the Prime Minister; another convention of the constitution was being established. Though Fox was personally successful at Westminster, Georgiana Duchess of Devonshire gaining at least one vote for him by kissing a butcher, his followers were massacred throughout the country, and won the name of "Fox's martyrs". Some 160, as commonly reckoned,[20] lost their seats, and Pitt had a clear majority in the new house. With George Rose now Secretary of the Treasury, drawing on the knowledge and advice of Robinson about patrons and candidates, the King threw all his weight on the side of Pitt during the elections and allowed him a lavish number of new creations of peers afterwards, but this was as fair an election as had taken place in Great Britain for a long time. It was a sign of the growing political awareness in British public life that the freeholders of Yorkshire, who had hitherto had their members effectively chosen for them in the drawing-rooms of Wentworth Park, Bolton Abbey and Castle Howard, insisted on electing a banker's son, William Wilberforce, who happened also to be the close friend of Pitt. Among others successfully returned was Henry Dundas, who had been Lord Advocate in all the ministries from 1775 to 1783. Though Pitt and he had crossed swords, a mutual respect had deepened. Pitt took him into his administration as Treasurer of the Navy, which post he held for sixteen years; but though there was no lack of naval business in that period, he was even more helpful to Pitt in the indispensable rôle of party manager.

Pitt's administration is sharply divided between the early years of peace and the war with France following the outbreak of the French Revolution. In peace he addressed himself mainly to the restoration of the nation's financial credit, to Ireland and to India. His hard work, his tact with all men and especially his success in handling the King without concession of principle, and his manifest integrity made a favourable comparison with the flamboyant excursions of Fox and yearly brought him fresh respect and support. There was an awkward moment in the life of the parties in 1788 when the King's insanity became unmistakable and undeniable; for while it was agreed that the Prince of Wales must be Regent, Pitt said this position must be conferred by act of Parliament, and drafted an act that would limit the Regent's powers, while Fox asserted the Prince's right to the position by prerogative and without limitation. Happily for Pitt the King recovered, and his hold on the country generally, but especially on the merchants of the city of London, continued to grow.

The forces of the Whig opposition, which were thus being well contained, were thrown into complete disarray by the French Revolution. When the Bastille fell, the immediate reaction of most Whigs was that of Wordsworth

> Bliss was it in that dawn to be alive,
> But to be young was very heaven.

Fox was beside himself with delight. "How much the greatest event it is that ever happened in the world," he exclaimed, "and how much the best." Sheridan, Grey, Windham and Francis were equally enthusiastic, but there was one ominous note of dissent in the Whig ranks. Burke had visited France in 1773, and his Irish heart had been captured by the vision of Marie Antoinette, "glittering like the morning star, full of life, and splendour, and joy".[21] He had also met the encyclopaedists, and their cold atheism had disturbed him. On his return he warned his countrymen that the principles of civil society were being undermined across the channel, and if he felt forebodings in 1789 he could claim to be consistent. The march of the mob to Versailles and the forced transport of the King and Queen to Paris increased his dread, and he saw with anxiety the approval that these proceedings had received from "two clubs of gentlemen in London, called the Constitutional Society, and the Revolution Society".[22] He took his pen in hand, and in 1790 not only London but the whole of Europe was reading *Reflections on the Revolution in France*. From Catherine the Great in Russia to George III in his own capital he received the delighted thanks of sovereigns; but among his Whig friends there was surprise, disdain and coolness. A break was inevitable. Sheridan and he had already bickered in the house before publication, and in 1791 there was an open breach with Fox in the chamber. "There is no loss of friends," whispered the warm-hearted Fox. "I am sorry," replied Burke, in a voice audible to all, "but there is . . . Our friendship is at an end."[23] Fox and Burke never met again except for formal interviews in connexion with the trial of Warren Hastings, and the Whig party lost the man who, more than any other, had given it a soul.

The tragic sequence of events in France and the tales brought to England by the aristocratic *émigrés* made many others follow where Burke had led. The Duke of Portland and his followers, apprehensive about the course of events abroad, thought it was no time to proceed with further reforms of the Constitution at home; Fox and his followers, shrugging their shoulders at the terror in France, pressed on with schemes of reform in Britain; and a distinction was soon made between "Old Whigs" and "New Whigs". Pitt did not share Burke's emotional reaction to the Revolution, but the threat from the revolutionary armies to the Rhine delta would have compelled him to take to arms even if the republic in 1793 had not first declared war. The fight for national existence deepened the cleavage between those who supported and those who were alarmed by events in France. In 1794 Portland, Fitzwilliam, Windham and Grenville took office under Pitt. Fox and his followers in the House of Commons were reduced to a tiny minority, not enough it was said, to fill a hackney carriage. "That is a calumny," said one of the New Whigs, "we should have filled two." In fact, there was a faithful remnant of sixty.[24]

If Fox had not continued even in the threat of invasion to press for parliamentary reform, there were others who would have done so; and the New Whigs knew it. Wilkes had broken with his earlier self when, as City Chamberlain, he used troops to crush the Gordon rioters, and he lived to become a strong supporter of Pitt; but his accents were heard on other and in many ways more effective lips. There was Richard Price, the dissenting moral philosopher, who had caught the flame of freedom from America; John Cartwright, brother of the inventor of the power-loom and the author of *The Legislative Rights of the Commonalty Vindicated*, who had founded the Society for Constitutional Information to campaign for universal suffrage and annual parliaments; there was Joseph Priestley, famous chemist and Unitarian minister, who had been Shelburne's librarian, and whose sympathies with the stirrings among the masses was notorious; there was Thomas Hardy the eloquent shoemaker and secretary of the Corresponding Society, newly founded in admiration of the French Revolution; above all, there was Tom Paine, probably a deist, but near enough to an atheist for all but theological students not to see the difference, who held kings and hereditary chambers to be so much useless lumber. In brief, Radicalism was strong, though that name was still not in use. Richard Price's dying gloom was cheered by the success of the French Revolution; Burke's *Reflections* was provoked by the welcome given to it by Cartwright's society; and Paine set out to answer Burke in *The Rights of Man*. It was a good answer from his point of view, charging Burke with forgetting the wrongs of great masses of men in his indignation over a few nobles, and the prodigious sale when the first part appeared in 1791 alarmed the government, an alarm not diminished when he was elected by the department of Calais to the French Convention. According to Lady Hester Stanhope, Pitt "used to say that Tom Paine was quite in the right", but then he would add, "What am I to do? . . . As things are, if I were to encourage Tom Paine's opinions we should have a bloody revolution."[25]

The fear of bloody revolution oppressed Pitt's mind more and more as the war sharpened in intensity and the labouring masses began to feel want. As early as 1794 his Attorney-General, John Scott, later Lord Eldon, had demanded the condemnation of Hardy for advocating "representative government, the direct opposite of the government which is established here"; fortunately, the government was saved from itself by a jury of twelve sensible men.[26] All discussion of reform was silenced everywhere except within the walls of Parliament itself. The Corresponding Society and other political associations were suppressed by act of Parliament. The great right of *Habeas corpus* was suspended. Combinations of workmen, that is to say trade unions, were forbidden by statute. To enforce these measures, far severer than were really required by the war, Pitt's spies were everywhere, and the total effect was to create an image of Pitt and his supporters that took many years to dissolve. Meanwhile, by their nightly battles in the House of Commons, the little band of New Whigs were creating an image of themselves as the champions of liberty, even of license. No attempt was made to silence opposition within the privileged walls, or even to create a coalition as in later world wars; but from 1797 to 1799 the Whigs themselves, at last wearying of the futile fight, absented themselves from Parliament in an "Aventine secession" and left Pitt to wage the war.

By an odd turn of history he was obliged soon afterwards to hand over the task for a while. Irish rebellion and French attempts at invasion led to a proposal to merge Ireland in the United Kingdom, and the Irish Parliament was persuaded to vote itself out of exis-tence. The union came into existence with the new century. Pitt thought that it should be followed by a measure of Roman Catholic emancipation in Ireland, but the King was so upset by the thought that his mind became unbalanced, and on his recovery he extracted a promise from Pitt never again to make such a proposal in his life-time. Little thinking that the King would outlive him by fourteen years Pitt agreed, but resigned in favour of Addington, Speaker of the Commons. He had been in power from 1783 to 1801 and in that long period had established Cabinet government on firm founda-tions, and in the Cabinet and in dealings with the Sovereign the supremacy of the Prime Minister over all other servants of the Crown.

As Trevelyan so aptly points out,[27] the weakness of the Whig party between 1793 and 1830 had the same effect as the weakness of the Tory party from 1714 in reviving a group system on the floor of the House of Commons in place of a two-party system. "Just as the long weakness of the Tories caused the Whigs to divide into Walpole and anti-Walpole factions, so the Tories in the first year of the nineteenth century broke up into Pittites, Addingtonians and Whig–Tory followers of the Grenville family. These groups, personal rather than political in their differences, combined each in turn with the Foxite remnant to form the governments and oppositions of the remaining years of war."

Addington himself had a personal following of about fifty in the house. He was not a big enough man to command respect even in his own Cabinet, and when after the truce marked by the Peace of Amiens war broke out again there was a demand for Pitt's return. Rejecting any idea of serving under Addington, Pitt made a forceful declaration of the need for one minister to be pre-eminent among his colleagues—the clearest statement of the case for a Prime Minister ever heard before or since.[28] He had while in office gently substituted the personal rule of the Prime Minister for the personal rule of the King, but in such a tactful manner as to make it entirely acceptable to George III that King Pitt should rule and not he.

Pitt was back in Downing Street in 1804, and Prime Minister for the second time long enough to share the glory of Trafalgar and bear the blows of Ulm and Austerlitz, but he died within two years, worn out with the task of weathering the storm. His leadership had been so personal that there was no obvious successor, but his colleagues advised the King to send for Grenville, and when that statesman thought it expedient to form a broad-bottomed "Ministry of all the Talents" drawn from all the chief groups, including the Fox Whigs, the King made no demur. By this time the old issue of Jacobinism in France was dead. Napoleon's aim at world dominance was manifest, and the Foxites had long agreed with heavy hearts that he must be resisted.[29] Fox himself became Secretary of State, and although the presence of Addington, now known as Viscount Sidmouth, and the Earl of Moira, the Prince's favourite, justified the description of broad-bottomed all the talents came from Fox's followers—Grey, Henry Petty (Shelburne's son), Erskine and his nephew Holland—reinforced by a group of Whigs—Spencer, Windham and Fitzwilliam—who had joined Pitt in 1794 but broken with him when he gave way over Roman Catholic emancipation. It was virtually a Whig government, but it did not last long. Fox died in 1807, though not before he had carried the abolition of the slave trade, which Wilberforce had never been able to obtain from Pitt. Grenville carried on with Grey as Fox's successor both as Secretary of State and as Leader of the House of Commons. It was a further instalment of Roman Catholic emancipation that broke them. The King agreed to Grey's proposal that Roman Catholics should be allowed to hold commissioned rank anywhere, but when Grey asked that the highest commands should be open to them he talked of broken faith, and ministers resigned.

The aged Portland was brought in for the second time in his life to be a figurehead Prime Minister. As the head of a Revolution family, he would still regard himself as a Whig, but his Cabinet was unmistakably Tory, and contained three men who were to head indubitably Tory administrations. After the years of confusion a new Tory party had come into existence, and, as we now know, it was to govern the country for the next twenty or more years.[a] The first step in that process was to appeal to the country, though a general election had been held the previous year.

6

THE TORIES ENTRENCHED
1807–1830

*Grey as leader of the Whigs—"Peace, Economy and Reform"—the
Regent disappoints the Whigs—growing popularity of the Radicals
—Tory policy after 1815—Canning splits both parties—rising
influence of Peel in the Tory party—O'Connell's election—significance of the Catholic Association—rise of the Irish party—changes
in the Whig and Tory parties between Charles II and George IV—
little organization of parties inside Parliament—and none outside*

THE party that formed the government in 1807 was essentially
the party that Pitt had left on his death. At the Exchequer there
was Spencer Perceval, second son of the Earl of Egmont, a successful
lawyer who had entered Parliament in 1796 and won acclaim by his
speeches in support of Pitt's administration. Though he had served
Addington as Solicitor-General and Attorney-General, this implied
no disloyalty to Pitt, but whereas Pitt was obliged to stand firm
against Roman Catholic emancipation through necessity, Perceval
adopted that course by choice, and his speech against concession
had helped to bring down the Grenville ministry. The Home Secretary was Robert Banks Jenkinson—Lord Hawkesbury since 1804
and in due course to be Earl of Liverpool—who had been made
Master of the Mint by Pitt in 1799, and after serving Addington as
Foreign Secretary had been given the Home Office when Pitt returned to Downing Street. The most obvious of the Pittites was
George Canning, who had deliberately attached himself to Pitt on
coming down from Oxford, though his debating there had led
Sheridan to point him out to the House of Commons as a rising hope
of the Whigs. Canning's choice of Pitt as patron is not without its
significance in the understanding of parties at that time, for as the
son of a destitute mother forced to take to the stage, and a furious
hater of the aristocracy, he could not ally himself with the Whigs,
who then represented privilege and exclusiveness far more than the
Tories, however much at election times Charles James Fox might
be hailed "Man of the People". Entering Parliament in 1793, and

serving as Under-Secretary for Foreign Affairs, he was schooled by Pitt for higher office and was made Treasurer of the Navy in 1804. To him fell the task of delivering the eulogy on Pitt at his mentor's death. Refusing to take office with Fox in the "Ministry of All the Talents", he obtained the Foreign Office from the Duke of Portland. In that office he was brought into conflict with a man of very different upbringing, Robert Stewart, Viscount Castlereagh, but Castlereagh also had felt the magic of Pitt's spell as acting Chief Secretary for Ireland, and had worked closely with Pitt over the negotiations for union and the attempt to secure relief from Roman Catholic disabilities. Not in the government by choice, because he wished to clear himself of certain charges against him, but influencing it from outside, was Pitt's ally in his Indian policy, the Marquess Wellesley; and his brother, later to be Duke of Wellington, was Irish Secretary for a few months before being sent on the military tasks with which his name is imperishably connected. Another Pittite was William Huskisson, who first held office as Under-Secretary for War in 1795, was Secretary to the Treasury in Pitt's second administration, and held the same office under the Duke of Portland. Eldon—the John Scott whom Pitt had made his Attorney-General—was brought back to the Woolsack, which he occupied for twenty years, and from which he opposed all reform, but especially legal reform, all concessions to Roman Catholics, all change. Here already are all the great names in the history of the Tory party until the Reform Bill with the exception of Goderich and of Peel, who was then too young to enter Parliament; and Peel's father, sitting on the back benches of the House of Commons, was as strong a Pittite as anyone, rewarded by Pitt with a baronetcy. As it happened, the young Palmerston held junior office in this government, and if he called himself anything it would be a Tory, but he shunned high office for many years—he could have been Chancellor of the Exchequer in 1809—and when he overcame this reluctance it was with the Whigs.

The government of 1807 was thus a Tory government whose members nearly all owed their inspiration and training to Pitt. Of policy there could be little in those years except a policy of winning the war; only the negative policy of no parliamentary reform and no concessions to the labouring masses, because of the fear of revolution, and no Roman Catholic emancipation because of the King's conscience.

Just as clearly as the Tories were the heirs of Pitt, the Whigs were the successors of Fox's New Whigs. Their undisputed chief, though not technically their leader, was Charles Grey, son of the general created Earl Grey, who had sat for Northumberland since 1786, had delighted Whig ears by his assault on Pitt, had followed Fox with simple loyalty, and in those days was determined to be not a whit behind his leader in his sympathy with revolutionaries abroad or reformers at home. He even went beyond Fox in presenting the petition for parliamentary reform of the Society of the Friends of the People, founded in 1792 by Lauderdale; later he regretted his association with that body, though not to the extent of Lauderdale, who voted against the Reform Bill. He had moved the impeachment of Pitt and was the leading spirit in the secession of 1797. Addington offered him office, but he would not enter the ministry without Fox. Towards the end of Fox's life he began to take a less militant line, and could with difficulty be dragged from Howick; but it was his stand over Roman Catholic commissions that brought down Grenville. In the same year his father's death took him from the Commons, and leadership of the Whigs in that house fell on George Ponsonby, who held it till his death ten years later. There could be no doubt about his spirit of opposition, for he had opposed even the grant of funeral honours to Pitt. Sheridan had been disappointed of the leadership on the death of Fox, and it was now George Tierney's turn to be disappointed—he who had called Pitt out for not withdrawing a charge of obstructing public business, even when it was declared unparliamentary, and had exchanged pistol shots with him on Putney Heath. Spencer's son, Viscount Althorp, had been converted from Toryism by Fox and given a minor post by Grenville, and he was soon to ride hard with the more advanced members of the party such as Romilly and Whitbread, but for the present he was holding his horses. A rising Scottish barrister who had taken the high road to England, Henry Peter Brougham, was disappointed that his Whig friends had not yet found him a seat in the house, but he was rendering them valiant service by his articles in the *Edinburgh Review*, and it could be only a matter of time. Among the younger members a significant name was that of William Lamb, who had entered Parliament in 1806, but his fame was in the future, and mainly after he succeeded his father as Viscount Melbourne.

Such were the Whigs who went into opposition in 1807, and they naturally carried with them Fox's banner of "Peace, Economy and Reform". They could not then have peace, and because they could not have peace they could not have economy, but they continued to press, as opportunity offered, for reform and Roman Catholic emancipation. It was safe now to seek relief for Roman Catholics without fear of losing their traditional hold on dissent.

The Portland administration proved that it is not possible to have two kings in Brentford, and broke up in 1809 after Canning and Castlereagh fought their celebrated duel. Perceval became Prime Minister, at first without the services of either, and with Wellesley in place of Canning. In 1811 the incurable nature of the King's malady became evident, and the Prince of Wales was given the Regency, made permanent a year later. This was the great moment for which the Whigs had so long waited, but it was not to be, though their own obstinacy was as much to blame as the Regent's tergiversation. The Regent did invite Grenville to form a ministry but they could not agree on the address, and he became nervous about charges that the advent of the Whigs would ruin any chance of his father's recovery. He asked Perceval to continue. Wellesley's resignation in 1812 made a reconstruction necessary, and by that time there was no possibility of the King's recovery, but the Regent still shrank from a wholly Whig ministry. He offered his old friends a few places in the existing administration, but they declined on the ground that Roman Catholic emancipation could no longer be postponed, and that on this subject, as on the conduct of the war, there was no possibility of agreement between Perceval and themselves. Not long afterwards Perceval was shot dead in the lobby of the House of Commons by a half-mad bankrupt with a grievance,[1] and the question had to be raised once more. The Regent again offered the Whigs a certain number of places and again they declined. He thereupon turned to Lord Liverpool, as Jenkinson had now become, and Liverpool formed a purely party administration of men who called themselves Tories and thought of themselves as Tories. The position of the government was markedly strengthened by the general election in 1812. Liverpool remained in office until obliged by paralysis to resign in 1827, and was Prime Minister for longer than anyone has ever been save Walpole and Pitt.

The Whigs were put out of countenance by the Regent's defection. It became more and more difficult to get Grey to make the four-day journey to London. They were embarrassed, too, by the rise of eloquent new Radical leaders, who sometimes really were men of the people and in other cases caught the ear of the people as the proud Whigs could never do. A powerful stimulus was given to the Radical movement in 1809 when the discarded mistress of the Duke of York, commander-in-chief of the British armies during the greatest war they had fought, accused him of selling commissions to persons who had her ear. Sir Francis Burdett, elected with another Radical, Admiral Lord Cochrane, for the very constituency of Westminster in which the Parliament buildings stood, was then at the zenith of his Radical career and frequently in collision with authority; while William Cobbett's *Political Register* was thrilling the masses by its virile English and love of the countryside, and teaching them to detest equally the names of Whig and Tory.

The end of the war in 1815 brought Liverpool's government problems of a new but equal order, though it cannot be maintained that they were approached with any measure of intelligence or understanding. The suspension of *Habeas corpus* and the press prosecutions in 1817, the "Peterloo massacre" of 1819 and the repressive Six Acts that followed bit deeply into the minds of the manual workers and left an impression of the Tory party as unsympathetic to their interests. In some measure the problems were created by the government's financial and economic policy. In order to protect the farmers at a time when prices were dropping, Parliament passed in 1815 a Corn Law banning the import of foreign wheat until the home price stood at 80s. a quarter, and colonial wheat until the price reached 67s. a quarter; and this at a time when the population was so rising that oversea supplies were becoming essential. The income-tax, introduced by Pitt as a war measure, was abandoned, so that the national revenue—over half of which went to pay interest on the national debt—had to be mainly raised by indirect taxation, largely on the necessities of life. At a time when demand had dropped severely, the government pursued a deflationary policy, culminating in the restoration of cash payments by the Bank of England. There was a relaxation in these harsh measures after 1821, helped by an improvement in trade. Between 1821 and 1825 on the advice of Huskisson duties were greatly reduced on many raw materials, in 1824 and 1825 the Combination Laws were modified so as to legalize trade unions within limits, and in 1828 a sliding scale of duty on imported corn varying with the price was substituted for the fixed duty; but the unfortunate image of the Tory party created by the repressive legislation was not easily eradicated.

The resignation of Liverpool in 1827 threw the party system into the melting-pot once more. When it is considered that he enjoyed nothing like the power of influencing Parliament and the electors that Walpole or even Pitt possessed, and that for years his government was held in the deepest odium by the labouring classes, his achievement in keeping his ministry intact for fifteen years is remarkable, and shows that he must have possessed qualities greater than a superficial examination of his life would suggest.[a]

After spending seven years in the wilderness, Canning was reconciled to Castlereagh and again given office in 1816. When Castlereagh took his life in 1822, Canning succeeded to his "whole inheritance"[2] as Foreign Secretary and Leader of the House of Commons, and on Liverpool's resignation he was the natural successor as Prime Minister, and George IV accepted him as such, though with some reluctance on account of his sympathy with Roman Catholic emancipation and his trouncing of foreign despots. For the same reason Wellington, Peel and five others of his late colleagues refused to serve under him. What made him obnoxious to so many of his fellow-Tories, endeared him to most Whigs, though not, it must be admitted, to the patrician Grey, who could not forget the actress mother and thought him false. Most Whigs not only welcomed his open mind on the Roman Catholic question, but relished the support he had, unlike Castlereagh, given to nationalism abroad. When Canning's ministry was announced it was found to contain the

E

Duke of Devonshire, Melbourne and two other Whig members of Parliament; and although Grey held aloof, Lansdowne and Holland gave it support. Canning's accession to the highest post under the Crown is thus remarkable in party history in that it cleft both the Tories and the Whigs.[3] Most party leaders who have changed party lines have been content with splitting their own side. In consenting to the admission of Whigs, the King gave a "decided negative" to the "destructive project" of parliamentary reform—so far had the friend of Fox and Sheridan moved—and told Canning that while he would not be required to abjure his strong and settled opinions upon the subject of Catholic emancipation, if at any time this question was forced upon him from that moment the Cabinet was to be considered as dissolved.[4]

What further disintegration of the party system Canning might have wrought if he had lived we can only guess, for he died within a few months. Goderich would no doubt have continued on the same lines, for he gave Holland the Home Office, but he resigned without waiting to meet Parliament. So the strategic reserve, in the person of the Duke of Wellington, was summoned. The Duke, who was expected to entrench himself against all advocates of reform, at first belied his reputation, largely under the influence of Peel who now came to the front as Home Secretary and Leader of the House of Commons. The reactionary Eldon was dropped, and a group of Canning's followers brought in—Huskisson, Palmerston, Melbourne and Dudley. He soon lost them, ostensibly over the disfranchisement of East Retford and Penrhyn, but really over the dropping of Canning's foreign policy and Huskisson's desire for freer trade. The duke's government became a purely Tory government, but when the question of Nonconformist disabilities was raised, to the general surprise he made no attempt to stand his ground. Lord John Russell, scion of the great Revolution family, who had been elected to Parliament in 1813, was now playing a leading part on the Whig side, and persuaded the House of Commons to accept the repeal of the Test and Corporation Acts in so far as they restricted the holding of office by Protestant dissenters. Wellington advised the House of Lords to agree with the Commons, and repeal was carried.

In itself this was not a matter of great consequence, for various devices enabled Nonconformists to get round the acts; but it added to the arguments for the more controversial question of Roman Catholic emancipation. This had come to the fore again as a result of East Retford, for the filling of the Canningite places necessitated a by-election in County Clare, and it was won by Daniel O'Connell, to be known as the Liberator. At that time no Roman Catholic was able to sit in the House of Commons because he was required to make a declaration against transubstantiation, the invocation of saints and the sacrifice of the mass. Whatever might be said in the

light of history for enacting such a requirement in England, where
Roman Catholics were a small minority, it was an indefensible
hardship in Ireland, where the population was overwhelmingly
Roman Catholic; yet from the beginning of the union in 1801 Ireland had not been permitted to send a single Roman Catholic representative to the imperial Parliament. To remedy this and related
injustices, in 1823 O'Connell had formed the Catholic Association,
which is noteworthy in party history as the earliest mass organization for the return of political candidates, and one of the most
impressive of such bodies. The base of the organization was the
parish, and every Roman Catholic parish priest in Ireland was in
effect an agent for the Catholic Association. All efforts of the government to kill the Catholic Association were frustrated by O'Connell's
skill in keeping it within the law, while subtly conveying to authority the impression of a force superior to its own which was prepared
to shake society to its foundations. Faced by the demand of O'Connell to take his seat and by the knowledge of the forces behind him,
Wellington and Peel were placed in a dilemma. Peel was deeply
pledged by many public commitments to oppose Roman Catholic
emancipation, and in particular he had been preferred by the electors of Oxford University to Canning precisely because of his attitude on that question; yet as a former Irish Secretary, who had been
obliged to carry out a policy of coercion he knew that it was
necessary to give way. He offered to resign so that the measure
could be carried, but Wellington judged that the King and Parliament could be persuaded only if Peel himself urged that course. Peel
did not shrink from the necessary but to him distasteful task. The
King consented, withdrew and again consented. In the House of
Commons 173 Tories voted against Peel, and emancipation was
carried only with the help of Whig and Canningite votes. Wellington obtained the grudging assent of the Lords, but not without a
challenge to a duel from the Earl of Winchilsea. Peel thought it
proper to give the electors of Oxford University a chance to express
their opinion, and they turned him out; after a little wandering he
became member for Tamworth. O'Connell, the immediate cause of
all the trouble, took the new oath and his seat.

These memorable proceedings are noteworthy in the history of
party for many reasons. By relegating to the past the story of
Roman Catholic disabilities, they cleared the way for a reconciliation between the Tories and the Roman Catholic Church in England.
They foreshadowed Peel's break with his party, though that was to
come on another issue. They showed in the Catholic Association a
model for mass party organizations. They brought into the House of
Commons a compact body of Irish members, having interests and
allegiancies of their own and little in common with the Whig and
Tory parties, which they judged entirely by their attitude to Irish

questions. O'Connell's single vote in 1829 foreshadowed a substantial Irish party capable of holding the balance between the British parties, making and unmaking governments, and shaping policies. This was to be a major factor in British politics until 1914.

The religious concessions stimulated rather than satisfied the demand for reform. As we stand on the eve of the agitation that culminated in the Reform Bill, let us look back and see the ground we have traversed. At the beginning we started with a Tory party linked with the Church of England and believing in the divine right of kings. Faced by Charles II and James II with the necessity of choosing between Church and King, it adhered to the Church, and joined in bringing about the Revolution settlement on the basis of a compact between Sovereign and people. Henceforth the Tory still believed in Church and King, but his loyalty was to the Crown as an institution rather than to the King as a person. When Queen Anne failed to leave any direct heir, the conflict of loyalties between the King on the Throne and the King over the water destroyed the Tory party in Parliament, but the great mass of clergy and gentry preserved Tory feeling and the Tory name in the countryside. The advent of George III, glorying "in the name of Briton", and educated in the principles of their old chief Bolingbroke, reconciled Tories once more to the person of the Monarch, and Tories again began to appear at Court and in Parliament. When the King's attempt at personal rule failed, Tories to an ever-increasing extent found their ideals realized in the policies pursued during peace and war by William Pitt; and after his death the statesmen he inspired ruled Great Britain as Tories at the head of a Tory party.

In this long period the Tory policy evolved greatly by adaptation to changing circumstances, but there was an unbroken attachment to the Church of England, which found expression at the end in reluctance to remove the legal disabilities on Protestant and Roman Catholic dissenters. There was also continuous attachment to the landed interest, which found expression in bills requiring a property qualification for members and at the end in a corn law to protect home farmers from competition. Throughout all this long period it could be said that a Tory was a man who was averse to change until the need for it was completely proved. This habit of mind made many Tories ill at ease in the Revolution settlement, though their leaders had helped to bring it about; but as the years passed and the Revolution settlement became the established order of things, they came to regard themselves as its special guardians. This dedication to the established order, accentuated by war abroad and unrest at home, created an image of the Tory party in the years following the Napoleonic wars as hostile to the labouring masses and a brake on economic and political progress.

We started also with a Whig party championing the rights of

Protestant dissenters and holding that a King held his powers as part of a compact with his people, who could take away those powers if he broke the compact. This theory was given practical expression in the Glorious Revolution and the settlement of the Crown on the Hanoverians, and for nearly half a century after the accession of George I the government of the country fell entirely into the hands of the great Whig families—the Revolution families, the circle of the "great-grandmotherhood"—who had played the major part in bringing about these events. The Tory opposition in Parliament having collapsed, the Whigs divided into factions, and when the years of George III's personal rule ceased one of these factions under the leadership of Rockingham and the inspiration of Burke became the core of a revived Whig party. Many of its members, including Burke himself, joined Pitt's side during the struggle with revolutionary France, but the New Whigs who remained under the leadership of Charles James Fox preserved the name and the party, and dedicated themselves increasingly to parliamentary reform and the extension of liberty at home and abroad. One form which the extension of liberty took was the removal of religious disabilities. The Whigs remained faithful throughout to the cause of Protestant dissent, and at the end they extended their toleration to the removal of Roman Catholic disabilities. Though the Revolution families were the greatest landowners in the country, the Whig party was specially linked with the rising merchant classes, many of whom had been nurtured in dissent. This attachment to dissent and to the mercantile interest is a mark of continuity in the evolution of the Whig party. Throughout the whole period it can be said that a Whig was by temperament not averse to making changes in the political and economic order if it seemed desirable, and even to take risks in experimenting.

Though the names Whig and Tory are the only names of parties that occur in the period—except in so far as men talked of "Mr. Pitt's party" and so on for the personal followings of ministers—it would be a mistake to imagine that all the while a solid group of Whigs was ranged against a solid group of Tories either in Parliament or outside. Bolingbroke may have had his own reasons for protesting, "The bulk of both parties are really united", and Henry Fox for arguing "that Whig and Tory no longer subsisted", while Dr. Johnson would not have endorsed Gibbon in denouncing, "Those foolish, obsolete words Whig and Tory";[5] but there were long periods when the opposition of Whig and Tory practically ceased and the words were hardly used. We are nevertheless justified for the reasons already given in seeing a continuity between the Whigs and Tories of the Exclusion Bill in 1679 and the Whigs and Tories of the Reform Bill in 1832. To deny this continuity is possible only by an excessive concentration on parliamentary proceedings and forgetfulness of the great world outside. Sir Keith Feiling is right in seeing in Whigs and Tories "two twin schools of thought . . . decisively opposed to each other on the causes which most divide mankind—on religious truth and political power".[6]

The party system from 1679 to 1832 was a two-party system in that Whigs and Tories contested for the centre of the stage, and there was no other political party; but in the reign of George III the rise of men later called Radicals drew attention to the fact that outside the charmed circles holding or aspiring to political power there were great unenfranchised masses to whom Whig and Tory were equally anathema. The Radicals did not in this period, or ever, constitute a separate party, although, after 1807, such spokesmen of the Radicals in the House of Commons as Whitbread, Creevey and Brougham were increasingly out of sympathy with the official Whig leadership. Before 1832 there were not more than a dozen members of the House of Commons at any one time who could justly be called Radicals, but they stood for a large body of opinion in the country, and their influence on parties was far from negligible, especially in driving the Whigs faster along the road of reform than otherwise they would have gone.

The continuity of the Whig and Tory parties has been questioned because they stood for different policies at the end from what they stood for at the beginning. It would be a sorry state of affairs if parties were never allowed to admit that they had made a mistake; and in any case in a changing world it is necessary to change in order to remain consistent. Yet there is an impressive continuity of policy in one major respect "linking the party of Shaftesbury and Somers to that of Fox and Grey, the party of Danby and Bolingbroke to that of the younger Pitt and Canning". Trevelyan has found this continuity "mainly in the unbroken connexion of the Tories with the Church interest, and of the Whig aristocrats with the Protestant Nonconformist voters".[7] Many instances could be given to illustrate the continuity in Tory and Whig policy arising from their attitude to change and their link with the landed or mercantile interests.

In other respects the policy followed at any given moment by Whig or Tory administrations depended very much on the personality of the ministers filling the chief posts in those governments. There was no pre-determined pattern that Whig or Tory policy was bound to follow. What actually happened was determined, not only by the innate dispositions of the two parties, but by the likes and dislikes, the rivalries and ambitions, the unrewarded services and unforgiven snubs, the generous loyalties or unforgiving hatreds, the memory of some act of kindness or some fancied slight up school at Westminster or on the playing fields of Eton, the persuasion of some pretty face or the recollection of some good dinner. In this way, no less than by reasoned argument round a green baize table, policy has always been made. If Pitt had been less stiff with Fox when he bore Shelburne's message, if Burke had not chanced to be at Versailles when Marie Antoinette appeared in her glory, if Grey had not borne such dog-like loyalty to Fox, if Bellingham had vented his spleen on Liverpool instead of Perceval—these are the stuff out of which politics are made. The Tory party at the end of the Napoleonic wars acquired an odious reputation, for which it paid heavily later, of supporting tyranny abroad and repression at home. Yet how easily it might have been otherwise! If Canning had succeeded in getting rid of Castlereagh in 1809, if Peel had been Home Secretary in place of Sidmouth on the morrow of Waterloo, how different an image the Tory party would have borne in the first half of the nineteenth century! It is such thoughts that prompt men to say we learn nothing from history except that we learn nothing from history.[b]

Some may argue that Castlereagh rather than Canning, Sidmouth rather than Peel, represented the true soul of the Tory party; that Peel eventually left the party (or rather was left by it), and that Canning would have done so, after first splitting it, if he had lived. This cannot be proved. It can equally be argued that in the long reign of the Tories two sets of principles were struggling for possession of the soul of the party, and one set rather than the other could easily have prevailed.

In the field of foreign relationships Tories were divided between the principle of supporting the established order abroad, of which Castlereagh was the symbol, and the principle of championing nationalist movements, of which Canning was the exponent. The former principle eventually prevailed, and the Tory Palmerston, always the champion of small nations, took his place at the side of Russell among the Whigs, but it would not have needed many turns of the wheel for Palmerston to have carried out Canning's policy as a Tory Foreign Secretary in a Tory government. In any case, the differences must not be exaggerated. Castlereagh and Canning and all Tories were at one in a dislike of "abstract and speculative principles" and in making the maintenance and enhancement of British interests the object of their policy. The question at issue was the practical one whether British interests would better be served by non-intervention abroad or by intervention, and the answer could be different at different times according to circumstances; before his death Castlereagh had already moved towards Canning's position, as his famous paper of 5th May 1820[8] reveals, and the instructions he drew up guided Wellington's attitude at the Congress of Verona of "neutrality but not indifference".

In the realms of commerce and finance it was touch and go whether the Tories would become the party of protection or of *laisser faire*, of deflation or of inflation. The founder of the revived

Tory party, William Pitt, had studied Adam Smith's *Wealth of Nations* as a young man at Cambridge soon after its publication, was immediately converted, and made it his endeavour to put into practice the principles of "an author", as he told the House of Commons in 1792, "now unhappily no more, whose extensive knowledge of detail and depth of philosophical research will, I believe, furnish the best solution to every question connected with the history of commerce or with the systems of political economy". In spite of much pressure during the bread shortage of 1800, he pursued the policy, his biographer tells us, "of abstaining, as a government, from all interference in the purchase of corn in foreign markets, conceiving that the speculations of private individuals gave the most likely prospect of producing a sufficient supply".[9] In 1799 he introduced the revolutionary instrument of an income-tax, rising to ten per cent of incomes of £200 a year or more. To finance the war he relied on paper money, and accepted the resulting depreciation in the value of money with its diminution in the burden on debtors. If he had been leading the Tory party when peace returned, we may doubt whether he would have asked for the Corn Law or abolished the income-tax. We can only guess whether he would have restored cash payments, at any rate at so early a date. The economists whom he had studied would have approved it as a painful but necessary measure; and it was in obedience to the Bullion Committee, and against his first judgement, and in a sorrowful departure from his Pittite father's views that Peel adopted a deflationary policy. Tory economic policy after Waterloo was not consistent except in this, that the points in which they followed the "sophisters, economists and calculators" and the points in which they departed from them helped to create a picture of a Tory party sympathetic to landowners and bondholders and unsympathetic to the struggles of the labouring masses.

This image of the Tory party after Waterloo was heightened by its hostile attitude to proposals for a softening of the savage laws then in force for the protection of property. There was a genuine fear of the breakdown of society if the laws were relaxed; yet Romilly and Mackintosh would surely have had greater success if some more humane Tory than old Eldon had been sitting on the Woolsack. This was shown when Peel became Home Secretary in 1821, and abolished the death penalty for over a hundred offences; and the change is not entirely due to an end of the fear that statesmen were sitting on top of a revolution.

There were great families with a hereditary attachment to both parties, but on the eve of the Reform Bill the Whigs were more markedly aristocrats than the Tories. For the divine right of kings the Whigs had virtually substituted the divine right of the Revolution families. They regarded themselves as the equals, if not the superiors, of the Hanoverian princes they had put on the Throne. The principles of liberty that they advocated in public affairs they extended to their private lives, and some at any rate openly made free with each other's wives and daughters. There were great Tory landowners also, but not so many or so conspicuous, and a sense of solidarity and rectitude was given to the Tory pyramid by the large number of parsons and country gentry at its base. As nurseries of future statesmen, Eton tended to be more Tory than Westminster, Oxford than Cambridge. The links between the Whigs and the mercantile classes remained strong—though some rich merchants, in closer touch with the labouring masses, sympathized with the Radicals, and William Beckford had even been a strong supporter of Wilkes. It was another of the great gifts of Pitt to the Tory party that he began to win for the Tories the attachment of a considerable section of the merchants and industrialists. Like his father before him, he was for many years the idol of the city of London. Robert Peel, father of the statesman and a Lancashire cotton spinner, was typical of the new men brought into touch with the Tory party through Pitt's influence; and although the Tory party has remained to this day attached to the soil, the basis of its support was widening.

In the period we have traversed there have been developments not only in the parties but in the party system. At the outset the claim of the King to absolute rule had only just been defeated, and throughout the period the government of the country has been mixed, but with power tending to pass from the King to the Cabinet and Parliament. The facts that William was put on his Throne by Parliament, that Anne was a woman, that the Hanoverians owed their Throne more to Parliament than to their blood, that George I could speak no English, and that George II still felt an alien led to a strengthening of the rôle of the Cabinet and Parliament that George III's attempt at personal rule could not undo. As the power of the Crown diminished and that of Parliament increased, the party system developed as the most satisfactory form of parliamentary government. The successive stages are marked by the growth of several conventions of the constitution—that the Cabinet should be drawn from a single party (1694), that there should be a Prime Minister (1721), that this Prime Minister should select his colleagues from his own party rather than having them selected for him by the King, that the King's power to dissolve Parliament and hold a general election should be used to strengthen the party in power (1780, 1784, 1807). At the end of the period these conventions are not fully accepted, and one formidable power still remains in the hands of the Sovereign, the power to dismiss his ministers; but we have advanced far in the working of the party system as we know it today.

This party system was, however, virtually confined to Parliament. Even among members of Parliament there was little in the way of organization. A leader might invite like-minded persons to dinner or a meeting in his town or country house, or he might send letters to his friends indicating his views, or he might discuss policy and tactics with them in their favourite clubs. The Secretary of the Treasury would compile for the First Lord lists of the ways members might be expected to vote, and with the help of the patronage and secret funds at his disposal he might try to ensure they voted the right way; but these methods of influence had been severely curtailed since 1782. The Prime Minister still had the valuable power of recommending to peerages—for an attempt in 1719 to limit this power had failed—and thanks to the good relations he had with his Sovereign Pitt had considerably diluted the House of Lords. This was practically all that there was in the way of organizing parties in Parliament, and outside Parliament there was no permanent party organization either on the national scale or in the constituencies. The electorate was very small, elections took place infrequently, and the necessary arrangements for seeing that the electors voted the right way were made *ad hoc* as the need arose. There might be a lawyer who was acknowledged as my lord's man of business and looked after his political interests, but that was all. The Reform Bill was soon to change this state of affairs.

PART TWO
ORGANIZED PARTIES IN THE
NINETEENTH CENTURY

7

REFORM, CONSERVATIVES AND LIBERALS 1830–1841

The Tory government loses the election of 1830—Reform Bill—it gives a share of the government to the middle classes—but does not enfranchise the labouring masses—and is regarded by the Radicals as only an instalment—the Tories begin to be called Conservatives—and the more advanced supporters of the Whigs begin to be called Liberals—transformation of the Whigs into the Liberal party—divisions among the Whigs—Stanley moves towards the Conservatives—Lichfield House compact between Whigs and Irish—the House of Lords becomes a Tory stronghold—"His Majesty's Opposition"—rise of the Chartist movement—Disraeli's vision of a new Toryism—Gladstone "the rising hope of those stern and unbending Tories"

F OR many years Grey had despaired of seeing parliamentary reform carried. The King, so it seemed, would never agree, nor was public opinion strongly in its favour. As late as February 1830 he advised his son, Lord Howick, not to hamper his career with such a question. In June of the same year the death of George IV necessitated a general election, at which reform proved to be a burning issue. Wellington's government was left in a minority in the House of Commons. It was the first occasion since the history of such things that a government had lost an election. One of those great movements of opinion that periodically sweep the country had taken place. The concessions made in turn to Nonconformists and to Roman Catholics had left an impression on Radical minds that the government was in retreat, the Tory forces were in disarray, economic grievances swelled the chorus of discontent, it was a year of revolutions abroad. At some time or other reform was bound to come, and the longer it was delayed the more were the waters heaped up, but it still remains puzzling why a question that was academic at the beginning of 1830 dominated the scene at the end of the same year.

Whatever the etymology of the name, the House of Commons was originally a house of representatives of communities. There were two knights from each shire—from Rutland no less than from Yorkshire—and two burgesses from each borough. As the years passed, the belief grew that representation should bear some relation to the number of inhabitants in an area, and on this basis the constitution of the House of Commons had long been indefensible. By the autumn of 1830 there had spread an irresistible demand for the disfranchisement of rotten boroughs left with only a negligible population, the enfranchisement of the large towns created by the Industrial Revolution, and an enlargement of the electorate. The Duke of Wellington and more surprisingly Peel, who had given way twice already, nevertheless determined to resist the irresistible.

Their ministry survived the general election by only a fortnight. Defeated on a motion to reform the civil list, ministers resigned, and King William IV gave Grey the summons for which he had so long waited in the wings. The Revolution families were, of course, well represented, headed by Lord John Russell and Edward Stanley, later to be recognized (though he had by then ceased to be a Whig) as the "Rupert of debate" and fourteenth Earl of Derby. It was a thoroughly aristocratic Cabinet, as a Whig Cabinet should be; but it was not wholly Whig. Grey was able to include the Duke of Richmond, an ultra-Tory and extreme Protestant, disgusted with Wellington for his capitulation to Rome. Of greater consequence, he was able to recruit the Canningites, Melbourne and Palmerston among them, who were henceforth absorbed into the general body of the Whigs. What would have happened if the Canningite leader, Huskisson, had not been killed by one of the new steam locomotives it is hard to say. He was on the verge of a reconciliation with the Duke of Wellington and might have converted him to reform, but his own election address had given no promise on that subject. As it was, the Canningites gave the ministry valuable experience of office which in the nature of things the pure Whigs could not have possessed—Grey himself had not been in office except for a few months in 1806—and the Whig party the benefit of the cross-fertilization of minds. There was one member of this Cabinet whose inclusion gave special pleasure to the Radicals—John George Lambton, known to the Court as Lord Durham since his elevation to the peerage by Goderich but to the masses as "Radical Jack". Made wealthy beyond the dreams of avarice by royalties from rising coal production, he had married as his second wife a daughter of Grey—the Whigs were given to inter-marriage—but had moved far from the cautious opinions of Grey's later years. It was he who was asked to preside over a committee of four to prepare a Reform Bill, the others being Lord John Russell, Viscount Duncannon and Sir James Graham. Radicals nodded their heads in approval.

The Whig magnates did not really like reform any more than the Tories, but they wanted finality and they wanted a measure that would give them as strong a hold on the government of the country as their forefathers possessed under the first kings from Hanover. Therefore they were content that such men as Durham and Russell should produce it. On 1st March 1831 Russell introduced the Bill in the House of Commons, which learnt that no fewer than 160 seats were to be redistributed, that is, taken out of the hands of borough patrons. The Bill received a second reading by one vote—302 to 301—and was emasculated in committee. The King would not accept the resignation of the ministry. With the recollection of the 1807 election following on that of 1806 in his mind, Grey then asked for a dissolution and after some hesitation on the part of the King obtained it. The system being still unreformed, Grey's minions were able to use all the resources still open to ministers to secure a favourable result, and they, unlike Wellington in 1830, had the tide of opinion flowing strongly with them. They did not merely ask for the return of the King's ministers, which had been the issue in all previous elections. They asked the electors to endorse the principle of "The bill, the whole bill, and nothing but the bill". This election is the first in which a party asked for approval for a specific issue of policy, and they obtained it in no uncertain manner. In the new House of Commons 367 voted for the second reading of the bill against 231, and 345 voted for the third reading against 236. The bill on second reading in the House of Lords was thrown out by 199 votes to 158. The twenty-one bishops who voted against the bill were specially blamed by the masses as they could just have turned the scale if all had voted the other way. There were riots in Derby, Nottingham and Bristol, where the bishop's palace was burnt, and wild talk in political unions that had sprung up, after the example of Thomas Attwood[1] in Birmingham, to agitate for the bill. The prospect was that if reform was not obtained by parliamentary action, the unions themselves would organize the rioting. Great Britain was nearer to revolution than it had been for many a long year. There was still one constitutional weapon that could be used, the creation of peers. It was not new, for it had been used to secure approval of the Treaty of Utrecht in 1713, and the failure of the attempt to limit this act of the prerogative in 1719 was an acknowledgement that the power remained. Another bill was prepared, and was passed in the Commons and sent back to the Lords. This time they gave it a second reading by nine votes, but began obstructing in committee. Grey told the King that he must either ensure the passage of the bill by creating at least fifty new peers or find new ministers. King William, a simple sailor not meant by nature to deal with such problems, hesitated. Grey handed in his resignation, and the country ran with rumours that the victor of Waterloo was going to rule with the sword. Francis Place, the Radical tailor of Charing Cross, saw that London was plastered with placards, "Go for gold and stop the duke". Birmingham talked about refusing to pay taxes. Peel persuaded Wellington that it was time to yield, and also that a party pledged against reform could lend itself to bringing in a reform bill only by lowering the tone of public life. The King promised Grey that he would create enough peers, and Grey's ministers resumed the seals of office. In the end, the House of Lords shrank from the addition of fifty or more new peers even more than it shrank from the abolition of rotten boroughs. At the word from Wellington "About turn", sufficient peers absented themselves from their places, the Reform Bill passed the Lords, and it became law on 7th June 1832.

When the act is examined in the cool light 130 years later, it may sometimes be wondered why it stirred so much passion. Fifty-five boroughs returning two members and one returning a single member were disfranchised, and thirty boroughs returning two members were deprived of one. Such great cities as Manchester, Birmingham and Leeds and populous metropolitan districts were given the right of sending two members to Westminster. But the extension of the franchise (now to be given in the counties to certain copyholders, leaseholders and tenants-at-will as well as to the 40s. freeholders, and in the boroughs to all occupiers of premises having a yearly rental value of £10 or more) added fewer than a quarter of a million voters to the electorate. The act gave a share in the government of the country to the middle classes. Inevitably it could only be, as the Radicals warned, an instalment of reform, not, as most of the Whigs fondly hoped, a final settlement. Yet, limited as it was, it transformed the party system, and that in two ways. One was to bring about a profound change in the attitude of the two great parties to questions of the day. This was witnessed by the adoption of new names.

The *Quarterly Review*, founded to counter the *Edinburgh Review*, was then the leading Tory organ, and in January 1830 an article by J. Wilson Croker referred to "what is called the Tory, and which might with more propriety be called the Conservative, party". At a time when the name of Tory was held in as deep odium as ever it has been, the term pleased. It furnished a description of the aims of the party which supporters could accept and at which opponents could not cavil, and it had none of the controversial associations of Tory. The name was immediately adopted by others, and in 1831 even Peel was using it. "If the Tory party is gone to pieces," he wrote to Croker, "I doubt whether the new Parliament is to blame for the 'labefaction', as Dr. Johnson has it. I apprehend there are two parties among those who call themselves Conservatives"; and he proceeded to describe the faith of moderate and "ultra-Tories". In the following year O'Connell was saying to the House of Commons, "The learned Solicitor-General for Ireland ... admits that the details of the bill are Conservative—that is the fashionable term, the new-fangled phrase now used in polite society to designate the Tory ascendancy." Earlier that same fateful year of reform, *Blackwood's Magazine* had said *tout court* without thinking any explanation necessary, "The fortresses of the Conservative party in the nomination boroughs are to be entirely destroyed!"[2]

There was no document conferring the name Tory on the party of Danby, Bolingbroke, Liverpool and Wellington, and no change of name deed was necessary to call it Conservative. It was simply a matter of usage. Very quickly the name came into general use, and when later in the century party organizations came into existence and necessitated a formal designation, it was the term Conservative that was used rather than Tory. The name Tory has nevertheless never dropped out of use. It is probably the term generally used by opponents, perhaps because it is possible to hiss more hate into two syllables than into four, and to conjure up more opprobrium from the caverns of history, but there have always been members of the party who prefer to call themselves Tories, with all the associations of three centuries that the name evokes, and from time to time, notably in the eighteen-forties, the eighteen-eighties and the nineteen-forties, there have been powerful attempts to revive the use of this evocative term.

On the lips of Croker, a die-hard Tory who crossed swords frequently with Macaulay during the debates on the Reform Bill and refused to sit in the reformed house, the term Conservative could not have implied any reduction in the doctrines of Toryism; but in practice it came to have a softer *nuance* than Tory. This is doubtless why Peel so promptly encouraged the use of the new name, for he realized that the enlargement of the electorate must bring a considerable adaptation of the Tory party to new circumstances if it was to survive. This did not escape the notice of so acute an observer as Charles Greville, who wrote in his memoirs for 14th June 1835: "Peel clearly does not intend that there shall be (as far as he is concerned as their leader) a *Tory* party, though of course there must be a *Conservative* party, the great force of which is the old Tory interest."[3]

In their hour of victory the Whigs had no motive for changing their name, but a new name had come into existence to denote those members of the party who favoured more radical reforms than the general body. As early as 1816 Southey had written, "These are the personages for whose sake the continuance of the Alien bill has been opposed by the British *Liberales*", and in 1826 Scott's *Journal* referred to "Canning, Huskisson and a mitigated party of Liberaux".[4] The Spanish *Liberales* were a group of reformers at the

F

beginning of the nineteenth century who were in power from 1820 to 1823 and roused general abhorrence by the violence of their opinions and actions. There was a group of French *Libéraux* with similar aims held in like detestation by men of traditional views. In the second decade of the century the term Liberal came to be applied by opponents to the advanced section of the Whigs, often in the Spanish or French form, and no doubt with the implication that their views and conduct were un-English; but as the name was already used in a good sense, those advanced Whigs were not averse from accepting the designation. Like Whig and Tory, the word Liberal was a term of abuse derived from outside England and intended to be offensive, and like Whig and Tory it was accepted with pride; but unlike Whig and Tory, it had the advantage for those designated by it of bearing a good natural meaning in that it suggested a friend of liberty everywhere and in all its forms. It was never just an alternative for Whig as Conservative was for Tory. There was more than a difference of *nuance* between Whig and Liberal. No one would have mistaken a true Whig for a Liberal, however much Liberals may have supported, or even served in, Whig ministries. Within the fold of the same political grouping there were both Whigs and Liberals. At first the Whigs were in a great preponderance and the Liberals in a small minority. In those early days there might be some confusion between Liberals and Radicals. As the years passed, the balance within the fold began to alter, the Whigs began to decline in numbers and influence and the Liberals took possession of the party. There is no precise moment at which we can say it ceased to be Whig and became Liberal. It was a gradual process of evolution in which the change in the use of names matched a change in ideas. About the middle of the century it is fair to say that what used to be known as the Whig party had become the Liberal party; and as the balance had shifted towards the Liberals by the time national organizations were created, it was the term Liberal that was then adopted as the formal designation of the party. We can be more precise about individuals than about the party as a whole. The last Whig Prime Minister resigned in 1866, the first Liberal Prime Minister took office in 1868; but each had Whigs and Liberals in his Cabinet. In 1886 the remaining Whigs left the Liberal party, and thereafter ceased to play a recognizably distinct part in British politics, though even to this day there have been individuals who pride themselves on being "the last of the Whigs".

A new election based on the Reform Act was held in December 1832 and resulted on paper in a huge Whig majority. In a House of Commons of 658 members there were fewer than 150 avowed Tories or Conservatives. But the Whigs could not be sure of their Radical and Irish allies, nor indeed were the Whigs themselves a homogeneous body. In those days when governments had lost the power to influence members by corruption and party machines had not yet come into existence, no one could be sure how a member would vote on a particular issue except that he would please himself. With these qualifications we may reckon that there were about 360 Whigs with 70 Radicals and 70 Irish members nominally and normally supporting them. The Radical element had been greatly strengthened by the voices of Cobbett, Grote, Molesworth and Buller. Among the motley band of reformers Dr. Southgate detects the names "conservative", "Whig", "moderate", "constitutional", "liberal", "convinced", "Radical", "thoroughgoing" and "advanced" —an amalgam out of which the Liberal party was eventually to emerge.[5]

Despite its huge paper majority in the Commons, the Cabinet almost immediately ran into trouble over the related problems of Ireland and the Church. Ministers were being pressed to more drastic reform, but were obsessed by the thought of opening the floodgates of revolution. On the Radical wing Durham impatiently resigned in 1833, and on the other wing Stanley gave up office in 1834 rather than consent to the appropriation of revenues of the Irish Church to secular purposes. A bill for the suppressing of ten out of the twenty-two Irish bishoprics had been the immediate occasion in 1833 of the Oxford Movement, which gave new life to the Church of England, and by its resistance to liberalism in all forms helped to restore the fortunes of the Tory party and to avert the wilder schemes of the Radicals for disestablishment and disendowment. A proposal that some of the revenues obtained by the suppression of the bishoprics should be secularized had been dropped before the bill became law, but a similar proposal was made in connexion with the Irish tithe every year, and defeated in the Lords, until 1838. Stanley's resignation was provoked by Lord John Russell, then sulking after his great labours for reform in the reduced office of Paymaster-General. It was a momentous occasion for the leadership of both the major parties. Stanley, who had been Irish Secretary and was then Colonial Secretary, had no objection to the state regulation of the Irish Church, but he thought it wrong to confiscate Church revenues for secular purposes, and in particular for the education of Roman Catholics. Russell thought that justice to Ireland demanded appropriation of Church revenues for lay purposes, even for the benefit of Roman Catholics. In view of the disagreement, the matter was left an open one in the Cabinet—as Roman Catholic emancipation had been for so long. But in 1834, when Stanley made a mild speech in the Commons reiterating his views, Russell's mind heard more than his ears, and he rose to contradict, among the cheers of the Irish members. Stanley passed a note to Graham, "John Russell has upset the coach", and so he had.

Stanley resigned, and took with him Graham, Goderich and Richmond. He never worked with the Whigs again, and lived to be three times Prime Minister in a Conservative government. For the leadership of the Whigs Russell's action was equally momentous. In the spring of 1834 the two men marked out as future leaders of the Whigs were Stanley and Althorp; but the approaching death of Althorp's father would soon take him to the Lords as Earl Spencer, as happened in the autumn, and Russell's *coup* removed his main rival for the succession and opened the way to two periods of residence at 10 Downing Street.

Worse troubles were to follow for the Whigs before the year was out. The need to renew the Irish Coercion Act brought out the fact that Althorp and other members of the Cabinet were working with O'Connell to secure a milder measure. Grey threw up his office in despair and Althorp resigned his in honour. He came back when Melbourne succeeded Grey as Prime Minister, but on Earl Spencer's death King William IV dismissed the ministry. It was the last exercise of this royal power, but in the prevailing divisions among the Whigs it was little resented. Melbourne was reluctant to see Russell succeed Althorp as leader of the Commons, and perhaps it would be nearer the truth to say that the King took the opportunity of dismissal that Melbourne readily gave him. Peel became Prime Minister, but the ensuing general election, while greatly reducing the Whig majority, did not give him enough Tory support to last more than six months. It was the old question of lay appropriation of Irish Church revenues that led to his defeat, and it was engineered by a compact between the Irish members and the Whigs, which was the beginning of an alliance having fateful consequences throughout the century. After some inconclusive talk among the leaders, one of the Whigs sent to O'Connell for distribution among his followers some of the circulars sent by the Whig leaders to their followers. O'Connell replied assuring Russell of sixty-two votes and a steady alliance until the Tories were turned out. Because his letter was made known at a meeting of Whig members in a house in St. James's Square, it has come to be known as the Lichfield House compact. It survived the fall of Peel, and enabled Melbourne on his return to office to bear with composure the absence from his ministry of Althorp, Stanley, Brougham, Graham and Durham.

Without fully realizing what was happening, the Whig party was in process of losing its character and identity. From the Glorious Revolution to the French wars the Whigs had played at least as great a part in the House of Lords as the Tories. From the time of the Reform Act the House of Lords became a Tory stronghold, as it has remained to this day, a state of affairs made palatable to other parties only by the clipping of its powers. Pitt's numerous creations had helped to secure the Tory ascendancy, and the defection of

Jersey and Tankerville just before the Reform Bill had deprived them of two of their leading hostesses, a social fact in those days of major political importance; but the main reason was a feeling that in playing with reform and associating with Radicals and wild Irishmen the Whigs were being "traitors to their class". The loss of influence in the House of Lords was matched by a still further loosening of the connexion between the Whigs and the landed interest as they found the exploitation of the minerals under their soil more profitable than the rents decreed for surface farming. But in leaving the Lords and the land to the Tories, the Whigs planted the seeds of their own decay. They could not without incongruity become popular leaders. A "Tory working man" there could be, as was proved later in the century, but a "Whig working man" was a contradiction in terms, and even a Whig manufacturer was an oddity. For half a century after the Reform Bill the Whigs continued to exercise through their abilities and the traditional deference accorded to them a political influence out of all proportion to their numbers, but the future lay with the middle-class leaders whom they had called into existence.

The fact that the Tory party had now become the party of the Lords and the land as well as of the Church did not obtrude itself at first owing to the circumspect character of its new leader.[a] Peel, who might have given way on reform if he had not given way on so many things already, knew that the Reform Act could never be undone and strove to make it work in a manner acceptable to himself. He discovered one of the great secrets of party government that even an opposition can have much influence upon the government of the country. It was not many years earlier, in 1826, that John Cam Hobhouse had coined the phrase "his Majesty's opposition". At the time it was meant as a jest. "It was said to be very hard on his Majesty's ministers to raise objections to this proposition," he observed. "For his own part, he thought it was more hard on his Majesty's opposition [*a laugh*, records *Hansard*] to compel them to take this course."[6] What was only a jest on the lips of Hobhouse became a reality with Peel as leader of the opposition, though even Peel might have smiled at the thought that one day the leader of the opposition would be paid for opposing.

Peel was greatly helped, of course, by the knowledge that though Melbourne might carry the Commons he could get the last word in the Lords. The accommodating spirit of Peel was matched by the temperament of Melbourne, who was none too happy about the more fiery spirits in his following. In consequence the legislation of the decade—and there have been no more fruitful ten years in the legislative history of Great Britain—bears the stamp of Peel as much as of Grey and Melbourne.

Melbourne was Prime Minister for the whole period from 1835 to

1841, but for the last two years in a peculiar and to some extent humiliating manner. His majority in the Commons was precarious, and in 1838 he gladly seized the opportunity to tender his resignation to the young Queen Victoria when Tories and Radicals combined to block suspension of the constitution of Jamaica. The Queen sent for Peel, but would not grant his request for a dissolution; and when he asked for the substitution of Tory ladies for at any rate some of the Whigs in her household she declined. It became manifest that the old-world grace of Melbourne, who had set out to train the eighteen-year-old girl in the art of ruling, had captivated her completely. She had filled her household with Whigs, read only Whig newspapers, trusted only Whigs, was a Whig. She found Peel cold and forbidding, as O'Connell had done in describing his smile as like the silver plate on a coffin. The Queen kept the wife of Normanby, the sisters of Morpeth, the daughter of Duncannon and the sisters of Russell at her side, and Melbourne returned to office through the bedchamber. It was not constitutionally proper even in those days, but apart from receiving the honours and emoluments of office for two more years the Whigs could make little use of the extension; and in the course of it the Queen, in marrying Prince Albert, found a new and even more trusted adviser than Melbourne.

The close working together of Melbourne and Peel was not to the taste of the Radical members of Parliament nor to the unenfranchised industrial masses outside. The Radicals, though numerous and influential, never formed an organic party, not because they would not have welcomed it but because they were too individualistic and unpractical.

What looked like a more serious challenge to the old order[b] came from outside Parliament in the form of the Chartist movement, and though all its demands had been made in the previous century and all but one have since been granted, it seemed to Whigs and Tories alike to justify their forebodings of revolution. Disappointment with the Reform Bill had led William Lovett to found the London Workingmen's Association, and in 1838 he drafted a bill known as the Charter which embodied demands for equal electoral areas, manhood suffrage, payments of members, the abolition of property qualifications, vote by ballot and annual Parliaments. Missionaries were sent by the London Workingmen's Association to other parts of Great Britain, and among the factory workers of the Midlands and the North and the miners of South Wales they found ready ears. The economic depression was accentuated by the harshness of the new Poor Law, 1834, against which Richard Oastler and J. R. Stephens were campaigning in Yorkshire. Torchlight meetings were held on the moors and armed insurrection was advocated. Thomas Attwood conceived the election by the disfranchised of a Convention which should sit in London as a rival to Parliament. At the same time a petition for the enactment of the Charter received over a million and a quarter signatures. When it was rejected by Parliament, the Convention issued orders for a general strike, but cancelled them on realizing that it had no organization for seeing a strike through to success. Tempers became inflamed, and plans for a march on Newport from the mining valleys of Monmouthshire led to a bloody clash with the armed forces. The leaders were sentenced to death, later modified to transportation, and most of the Chartist leaders in other parts of the country were imprisoned. For the time being Chartism was suppressed, but Whigs and Tories had been given a sharp reminder that their gilded life was lived only on the surface of society.

There was a young man just elected to Parliament who took the warning to heart. A glance at the Whig and Tory parties had convinced Benjamin Disraeli that he could best start his political life as a Radical, but two defeats under that label cured him of independence. He began to draw near to Toryism, but Toryism with a difference, not the calculating conservatism of Peel but a rich, gorgeous Toryism in which devotion to Throne, reverence for the Church and deference to the nobility was balanced by a genuine zeal for the common people. Though this amalgam struck the House of Commons as an oriental extravagance when he first secured election in 1837, his speeches on the Chartist movement showed that his sympathy with the working classes was no affectation; and in a few years his novel *Sybil* revealed to thousands of readers the miseries of factory workers in the Industrial Revolution and the gap between the two nations that co-existed in England. By superb political artistry that took him to the top of the "greasy pole", he was able to convert the Tory party to his views, but this still seemed as far off in 1841 as it had a few years earlier, when Melbourne told him to put out of his head the notion that he might be Prime Minister.[7]

At that time it seemed more likely that the future leader of the Tory party might be the son of a Liverpool merchant who shared Peel's background and general outlook—even though Peel had thrown down his first book *The State in its relations with the Church* in disgust, with the words, "That young man will ruin a fine career if he writes such books as these." Thanks to the patronage of the Duke of Newcastle, he had been provided at Newark with what was still an easy way into Parliament in 1832. He had defended slavery in his maiden speech, and from the opposite benches Macaulay had discerned him to be "the rising hope of those stern and unbending Tories, who follow, reluctantly and mutinously, a leader, whose experience and eloquence are indispensable to them, but whose cautious temper and moderate opinions they abhor".[8]

Such are the vagaries of political life that he was to live to be three times Prime Minister in a Liberal administration. It is certain that he and Disraeli could not have worked together in the same party; it is not so evident that he could not have been a Conservative Prime Minister.

8

BEGINNINGS OF PARTY ORGANIZATION
1832–1841

*Need for local party organizations to ensure registration of sup-
porters—Peel perceives a "new element of political power"—
political clubs—relation of a member of Parliament to his constituents—printed election addresses—the first national party
manifesto—survival of proprietory boroughs and influence of landlords—most candidates still unopposed—slow development of
party organizations—shape of the House of Commons*

THE Reform Act of 1832 was not only responsible for a change
in the character and policies of the Whig and Tory parties but
led to the growth of extra-parliamentary party organizations previously unknown.

In the restricted electorates before reform there was no need for
such organizations. When Disraeli first stood at Wycombe in a by-
election in 1832 there were only thirty-two electors. The elder Pitt
sat for Old Sarum, where there was not a single inhabited house and
sheep grazed peacefully on the mound that marked the site of the
ancient city. Only in a few boroughs such as Westminster and Pres-
ton was the electorate large enough to call for serious attention on
the part of candidates; in these the standard £10 franchise of the
Reform Act had the effect of reducing the electorate, but these were
rarities. The county electorates were more numerous, but amenable
to the influence of the great territorial magnates. In the boroughs
the electors as often as not sold their votes to the highest bidders. In
the counties they generally followed the lead of the great lords. The
only organization required to win an election was to find the money
needed to feast or bribe the electors or to win the favour of the
magnate with the "prevailing interest". The manner in which Fox
became member of Midhurst in 1768 is exceptional, but will serve
as an illustration.[1] It was a burgage-borough consisting of a number
of small holdings, each marked by a stone set on end in the middle,

without any human resident. Viscount Montagu had bought all the holdings, and as the election drew near he made them over to his servants with instructions to nominate Charles James Fox and his cousin Lord Stavordale as members and then to return the holdings to him. Montagu's steward acted as returning officer, and in this manner Fox was elected to Parliament while enjoying himself in Italy without making a single speech or even canvassing one of the nominal electors. As Parliaments could normally be expected to run their full course, the member once elected had no need to meet his constituents again for six or seven years, and seldom did.

It is common now to think that such a system stands self-condemned, and by the standard of "one man, one vote" it does; this standard was not accepted anywhere in the eighteenth or most of the nineteenth century, and the old system was not without its merits in comparison with the new. The arts of persuading a selection committee to allow a man to stand, and a vast electorate to prefer him over some other, have frequently not proved less laborious, expensive or degrading than the methods by which the Pitts entered Parliament for Old Sarum and Appleby, Fox for Mid-hurst, Burke and Canning for Wendover, Gladstone for Newark; nor were they obliged, as soon as they were elected to be thinking how to win the next election. The old system for all its faults allowed men of ability relatively easy access to Parliament at a sufficiently early age for the full development of their faculties; and in Parlia-ment gave them leisure to think out the best policy for the country regardless of the electoral consequences for themselves.

By the standard of adult suffrage the Reform Act did not greatly increase the number of voters, but it enlarged the electorate suffici-ently to terminate these easygoing days. From 1832 onwards the need began to be felt for an organization in each constituency to secure the return of a member of the desired party complexion, and this involved an organization not only during the actual period of the election campaign to persuade electors to vote the desired way, but to ensure that they would continue to vote the right way in future, and that new electors would vote the right way, that is to nurse the constituency.

The need for local party organizations was accentuated by the provision made in the Reform Act for the registration of electors. Previously there had been no lists of electors, and the guarantee against a person voting without the right to do so had been the scrutiny of his claim by the returning officer at the election itself. The Reform Act provided that the overseers of the poor were to require all persons entitled to vote to send in claims by a certain date in each year, and before a further date the overseers were charged with the duty of publishing a list containing the names of all persons already on the register or claiming to be added to it;

except that in boroughs freemen were to appear on a Town Clerk's list and in the City of London a list of liverymen was to be made by the returning office. Provision was made for objections to names on the lists, and for the revisions of the lists in special courts held by "revising barristers" appointed by the judges of assize or the Lord Chief Justice. When the lists had been so revised, the entry of a name on the register was conclusive evidence that the person bearing it was entitled to vote.

These provisions made it essential for candidates to ensure that all their known supporters were duly entered on the register in force, and also that objection was made to the names of opponents appearing on the register if there was any evidence that they were not legally entitled to vote. For this some local party organization was desirable. From their main purpose they were often called registration societies or registration associations, and the actual work of scrutinizing the lists and making objection to opponents was usually done by a local solicitor. Lancashire gave a lead in this as in so many other matters, and the Rochdale Reform Association and the Liverpool Conservative Association were both founded in 1832. The former still exists as the local Liberal organization, and the latter as the local Conservative organization.

No one perceived the changes entailed by the Reform Act more clearly than Sir Robert Peel. In a letter to Charles Arbuthnot, who had been Secretary of the Treasury, Peel wrote on 8th November 1838:[2]

"The Reform Bill has made a change in the position of parties, and in the practical working of public affairs, which the author of it did not anticipate.

"There is a perfectly new element of political power—namely, the registration of voters, a more powerful one than either the Sovereign or the House of Commons.

"That party is the strongest in point of fact which has the existing registration in its favour. It is a dormant instrument, but a most powerful one, in its tacit and preventive operation.

"What a check it is at this moment upon the efficiency and influence of the existing government, backed as it is by all the favour and private goodwill of the Crown, and by a small majority of the House of Commons. It meets them every day, and at every hour. Of what use is the prerogative of dissolution to the Crown, with an unfavourable registry, and the fact of its being unfavourable known to all the world? The menace of dissolution is only laughed at.

"Then it is almost impossible to make any promotion, or vacate any office, for fear of sustaining a defeat.

"The registration will govern the disposal of offices, and determine the policy of party attacks; and the power of this new element will go on increasing, as its secret strength becomes better known, and is more fully developed. We shall soon have, I have no doubt, a regular systematic organization of it. Where this is to end I know not, but substantial power will be in the registry courts, and there the contest will be determined."

Peel was right. It was to take a long time before the example of Rochdale and Liverpool was universally followed, but this was the modest beginning of the vast party organizations covering the whole country that we know today. He himself urged upon his followers continuously the need to "register, register, register" "Where this is to end I know not"—nor perhaps do we. Every successive enlargement of the electorate—in 1867, in 1884, in 1918 and in 1929—increased the necessity for the nation-wide organization of parties. The vote was gradually extended to all adult men, and then in two stages to all adult women; and the problem of ensuring that no supporter's name gets omitted from the register of voters, and that he or she records a vote when the opportunity arises, remain two of the main duties of local party organizations. (Now that every adult with a few statutory exceptions is entitled to a vote the possibilities of objection to opponents have become more limited.) Peel's "regular systematic organization" has become far more regular and far more systematic than ever he foresaw. As for the watch that he realized governments would keep on opinion among the electorate, this has become far more developed than he could have foretold. The rough tests of personal observation and the results of by-elections have now given place to scientifically conducted polls of public opinion which enable the experts to say with a high degree of accuracy not only how the electorate would vote after an immediate dissolution but how many seats the main parties would obtain. The "secret strength" of parties has become regular front-page news, and politicians are always nervously looking over their shoulders at graphs of their and their party's popularity. Peel might not have liked the new world that in rough outline he saw; but beyond doubt he would have adjusted himself to it as to the changing circumstances of his own day.

The development of constituency organizations involved as a corollary the creation of national party organizations to guide, co-ordinate and foster their activities. The need was at first supplied in a typically British manner by two clubs, the one founded just before and the other a few years after the Reform Act. Brooks's Club had long been a Whig meeting-place and White's a Tory, but something different from these aristocratic and convivial clubs was needed to meet the needs of the new age. In 1831 fifteen Tory parliamentarians (including the Duke of Wellington and William Holmes, the whip, but not Peel) met at a house owned by Joseph Planta, in Charles Street, and agreed to rent it as a party headquarters. The experiment did not work, and it was decided instead to set up a club on a subscription basis which would give members social amenities. Opened in 1832 in Carlton Terrace, and named the Carlton Club, it moved in 1835 to Pall Mall. As it was supported by the great figures of the party, and engaged a French *chef*, it became a matter of prestige among Tories to belong to the Carlton, and provincial leaders welcomed it as a place in which they could hob-nob with the national leaders and learn the London gossip. As candidates who were not wanted need not be elected, the club had a unifying influence on the party. Here politicians who wanted seats could be put in touch with constituencies needing candidates. Here also was the office for the dispatch of the whips' circulars. Here also the task of fostering the formation of registration societies and giving advice to them when formed was undertaken. A non-practising barrister, Francis Robert Bonham, who had made himself an expert in election law, set himself up in the Carlton and built up what Sir Ivor Jennings calls "a central advisory system".[3] He was, in effect, the first national agent of the party. As early as 1836 the Marquess of Londonderry writing to the Duke of Buckingham could call it "the headquarters of the party organization". Bonham's was the hand that pulled a thousand strings.

The Whigs, having a seemingly impregnable position in the House of Commons, were slower off the mark and were nearly beaten by their Radical wing. Francis Place had set up a Parliamentary Candidates' Society in 1831, but it proved abortive. In 1834 Durham and Parkes set up a Reform Association to give central advice on registration, and a registration office with a solicitor, James Coppock, as secretary, was set up in Cleveland Row. Coppock fulfilled the same function for the Radicals as Bonham for the Conservatives, and was in effect a national agent. The example of the Carlton showed the advantage of combining social life with politics, and in 1834 a group of Radicals formed the Westminster Club, later known as the Westminster Reform Club, in Great George Street. It could not, however, compete in attractions or usefulness with the Carlton, and in 1836 Molesworth and a few others sent out an appeal to found a new reforming club. Without authority they sent out their letter in the name of fifty members of Parliament, and the whips were at last provoked to action. Talks took place between Molesworth, Joseph Parkes, Edward ("Bear") Ellice, who had been chief whip, and his successor, John Edward ("Ben Backbite") Stanley. The result was the Reform Club in Pall Mall. Helped by an even more famous *chef* than the Carlton's, none other than Alexis Soyer, the Reform quickly established itself as a social centre patronized by all the leading Whigs. This was not at all what was wanted by Molesworth, whose club would have consisted of "the best of the Radicals and no Whigs",[4] but the Radicals were always unpractical. The Westminster Club and the Reform Association were wound up, and the Reform

Club discharged the functions of a national headquarters for the Whigs as the Carlton for the Tories, and in the same ways.

The extension of the franchise was responsible for a change in the relation between a member and his constituents of major importance in the development of the party system. Before the Reform Act a member of Parliament did not normally regard himself as bound by pledges to his constituents as to how he should vote in the House of Commons. He regarded himself as sent to Parliament to use his best judgement about the country's affairs and to vote accordingly. In general he would be a supporter or opponent of the ministry, but with no obligation how he should speak or vote on a particular occasion, and though his patron might hold him accountable the electors could not. Burke put the doctrine in classic form in his speech at the conclusion of the poll at Bristol on 3rd November 1774:[5]

"Certainly, gentlemen, it ought to be the happiness and glory of a representative to live in the strictest union, the closest correspondence and the most unreserved communication with his constituents. Their wishes ought to have great weight with him; their opinion high respect; their business unremitted attention. It is his duty to sacrifice his repose, his pleasures, his satisfactions to theirs; and above all, ever and in all cases, to prefer their interest to his own. But his unbiased opinion, his mature judgement, his enlightened conscience, he ought not to sacrifice to you; to any man, or to any set of men living. These he does not derive from your pleasure; no, nor from the law and the constitution. They are a trust from providence, for the abuse of which he is deeply answerable. Your representative owes to you, not his industry only, but his judgement; and he betrays, instead of serving you, if he sacrifices it to your opinion."

Burke's conception of the duty of electors was to choose a good man and let him get on with the job; it would be open to them not to choose him again if he disappointed their expectations—as he found to his cost in 1780 when the electors of Bristol took their revenge for his advocacy of a measure of Roman Catholic emancipation and for denouncing commercial policy towards Ireland.

There was a notable exception to this doctrine in 1829 when Peel, having come out in favour of Roman Catholic emancipation, felt obliged to resign his seat at Oxford and, on presenting himself anew to the electors, was defeated. The circumstances in which he had become one of the University burgesses were so exceptional as to alter the case. It was his opposition to Roman Catholic emancipation that had led the University to prefer him to Canning, and he had expressed himself so definitely on the subject that he was morally bound to submit himself to re-election.

Post-reform electorates differed in two ways from pre-reform electorates. They were usually larger, and they were more interested in serious political argument. For both reasons it was no longer possible for a candidate merely to offer them his services in Parliament. Electors began to wish to know what a candidate stood for. The custom became general of setting out in a printed election address the policies which the candidate proposed to support in Parliament.

This process was carried a stage farther in 1834 when Peel, on the eve of the general election made necessary by the dismissal of the Whig ministers and the dissolution of Parliament, issued an address to his own electors at Tamworth which was in effect a Conservative party manifesto. In form it was a statement of government policy, for Peel had already kissed hands as Prime Minister, but in practice it was a party leader's manifesto for which the endorsement of the electorate was sought. In a memoir[6] he thus recorded the origin of the Tamworth manifesto:

"Immediately after the completion of the Cabinet I proposed to my colleagues that I should take advantage of the opportunity which the approaching election would afford, and in an address to the constituent body of Tamworth declare the general principles upon which the government proposed to act. My colleagues entirely approved of this course and of the address which I submitted to their consideration."

In the address itself, before turning to specific questions of policy, he said:[7]

"My acceptance of the first office in the government terminates, for the present, my political connection with you. In seeking the renewal of it, whenever you shall be called upon to perform the duty of electing a representative in Parliament, I feel it incumbent upon me to enter into a declaration of my views of public policy, as full and unreserved as I can make it, consistently with my duty as a minister of the Crown.

"You are entitled to this, from the nature of the trust which I again solicit, from the long habits of friendly intercourse in which we have lived, and from your tried adherence to me in times of difficulty, when the demonstration of unabated confidence was of peculiar value. I gladly avail myself also of this, a legitimate opportunity, of making a more public appeal—of addressing, through you, to that great and intelligent class of society of which you are a portion, and a fair and unexceptional representative—to that class which is much less interested in the contentions of party, than in the maintenance of order and the cause of good government, that frank exposition of general principles and views which appears to be anxiously expected, and which it ought not to be the inclination, and cannot be the interest, of a minister of this country to withhold."

Peel never had occasion again to fight a general election as Prime Minister, and as leader of the opposition in 1841 he did not follow the example he had set in 1834 as head of the government. His example was not, in fact, followed until his disciple Gladstone in 1874, at the close of five years of office, drafted an address to his constituents at Greenwich; and in justifying himself to the Queen for a procedure that must have struck her as novel he appealed to the precedent forty years earlier: [8]

"Large portions, and the most important portions, of Mr. Gladstone's address were read to and considered by the Cabinet, and it was in some respects amended at the suggestion of his esteemed colleagues. It is however so framed as not to commit them collectively equally with himself, except only as to the remissions of taxes, and aid to local rates, contemplated in the finance of the year. This method of stating generally the case of the government in substance corresponds with the proceedings of Sir R. Peel in 1834–5 when he addressed the electors of Tamworth."

Disraeli had not expected this move, but retorted with a similar address to the electors of Buckinghamshire. In his case there was no time to consult his colleagues. Having chanced to come to London from friends in Staffordshire, he learnt that there was to be a dissolution only when he read Gladstone's address in *The Times* of Saturday, 24th January. He promptly set himself to counteract any benefit that the Liberals might get from the "snap" election. He shut himself up in the hotel where he was then living as a widower and wrote what came into his head, but he wrote on behalf of the whole Conservative party. His address was published in *The Times* of Monday, 26th January.

The modern practice of issuing a manifesto on behalf of the whole party had been suggested by Disraeli as far back as 1838, when he wrote to Peel offering to draft anonymously "a species of manifesto of the views and principles of the Conservative party". His offer was not accepted, and it was not until 1892 that a Conservative leader issued a message to the electors at large. The term "manifesto" was commonly used in the press of the seventies and eighties to describe the election address of a party leader to his constituents or some other pronouncement by him in connexion with a forthcoming election, but from 1876 until the end of the century the Conservative party was led by peers, first Beaconsfield, then Salisbury, and peers suffered from the disability that they had no constituent body to address and by convention were expected not to intervene in elections to the lower house. In 1880 Beaconsfield, as we shall see, overcame the difficulty by writing what was in effect an election manifesto to the Lord Lieutenant of Ireland (the Irish question being a main issue). In 1885 Salisbury's manifesto took the form of a speech to the National Union, and a year later his speech to a fête at Hatfield, reinforced by other speeches, met the need. When in 1892 he conceived the idea of issuing a manifesto addressed not to any particular body of constituents but to the electors generally he hit on a device that has since been generally followed in the Conservative party; but this is to anticipate events, and it is time to return to Peel's original incursion into this field.[9]

The substance of the Tamworth manifesto was notable for its explicit acceptance of the Reform Act as "a final and irrevocable settlement of a great constitutional question—a settlement which no friend of the peace and welfare of this country would attempt to disturb, either by direct or by insidious means". Peel promised not to interrupt the progress of the inquiry into municipal corporations started by the late government. While refusing to alienate ecclesiastical property in any part of the United Kingdom (*i.e.* Ireland) from strictly ecclesiastical purposes, he favoured "an improved distribution of the revenues of the Church" if its influence could thereby be extended, and accepted the principle of commuting tithe for a cash payment.

The manifesto was successful in influencing votes, not enough to keep Peel in office for long but enough to ensure that the policies described in it were carried out.

It must not be supposed that all the developments in organization encouraged by the Reform Bill came about at once. There was not even a clean sweep of the nomination boroughs. Professor Gash reckons that after 1832 there were certainly forty-two proprietory boroughs in England and Wales, and perhaps as many as fifty-two; the number of members returned by the proprietors was certainly fifty-nine, and perhaps as high as seventy-three.[10] In the counties the influence of the landlords was to some extent strengthened. Voting was not to be by secret ballot until 1872, and so long as men could not vote without their landlords, employers or customers knowing how they had voted the development of a free party system was impeded. Despite the statutory provisions, bribery, whether in the direct form or in the form of treating was not to be eradicated for many years. Though the Reform Act gave the vote to a section of the middle classes, it still excluded the great mass of the country from any share of political power. The percentage of the adult population entitled to vote was increased only from 5·0 to 7·1 per cent. The most astonishing fact by modern standards is that in most constituencies candidates were still unopposed. A contest was still the exception until 1885. This does not mean that most constituencies were agreed on the member they wanted, for a candidate frequently withdrew in order to save expense if the preliminary canvas showed that he had no chance of winning; but it helps to explain why party organizations were slow to develop. It was not until the end of the century that the major parties had anything like

G

a complete network of constituency associations. The Carlton and Reform Clubs were amateurish forms of national organization, and half a century was to pass before they were put on a more professional and business-like basis. Peel's initiative in the matter of a national election manifesto was not generally followed, as we have seen, until the end of the century. Yet by 1841 all the essentials of modern party organization had been adumbrated, with a single important exception: no one had yet thought of a national party conference; and this brings out the fact that no one had yet thought of the rank and file of party members giving directions to their leaders. Such an idea would, indeed, have been unthinkable in the conditions of 1832–41. The purpose of such incipient party organizations as had sprung up in the country was to help the parliamentary leaders, and either directly or through the whips the parliamentary leaders kept a firm control over them.

There is one incident in the period which may not have an obvious connexion with the party system, yet all who have sat in Parliament know how potent it is. From the dissolution of the chantries in 1537 to 1834 the Commons had sat in St. Stephen's Chapel in the Palace of Westminster. In 1834 St. Stephen's Chapel was destroyed by fire, thanks to a decision to burn the wooden tallies with which the accounts of the medieval Treasury had been kept. The new chamber of the House of Commons, like the chapel, was built on a rectangular plan, with benches running down the two long sides. The physical fact that members had to sit on one side or the other, not in an infinity of gradations from Mr. Speaker's right to his left, has had no small part in encouraging the formation of two strong parties and in preventing the degeneration of parties into numerous groups based on personalities rather than on principles.[11]

9

CONSERVATIVE REVIVAL AND SPLIT 1841–1846

The Conservative triumph of 1841 helped by good registration— Peel's policies test the loyalty of his followers—demand for free trade in corn—Stanley leads protectionist Tories in the Lords—and Bentinck in the Commons—Peel harried by the Tory protectionists —but with Whig help carries the repeal of the Corn Laws—then defeated by a combination of Whigs and protectionist Tories— Peel "not a good party man"

IT is not possible to say exactly to what extent the careful attention given to the party's organization was responsible for the great Conservative victory at the general election of 1841. Immediately after the triumph of the Whigs in 1832 dissensions within their ranks and the swing of the pendulum of public opinion had begun to prepare the way for a return of the Conservatives to power. The summons to Peel in 1834 was premature, but the electoral results of 1835 and 1837 showed that the pendulum had passed the middle point, and at any time from 1839 onwards a Conservative victory at the polls would have been certain. Yet there can be no doubt that superior organization did play a big part in the triumph of 1841. In the preceding period Bonham had engaged in a "rather extensive correspondence as to the registrations, and the ensuing municipal elections", which gave him a quiet confidence. When Peel asked him to present the result of a dissolution by a Whig or alternatively a Tory ministry, he said it did not matter. "So entirely too are we prepared (some elections will always *regulate themselves* at the last moment) that I should *relatively to their preparation* be glad Parliament was dissolved next week."[1]

It is still not possible to classify members precisely by party, but in the first division in the new Parliament the Whigs were beaten by ninety-one votes and resigned, and Peel was called upon to form a government. The Queen, under Prince Albert's tutelage, had overcome her repugnance to Peel, and henceforth no cloud marred their relationship. The Crown ceased to be part of the Whig machinery. Stanley had declined to join Peel's ministry in 1834, but he had in practice worked with him from that date, and his acceptance of the office of Colonial Secretary in 1841 marked a further stage in his passage from the Whig to the Conservative ranks. Graham, who had left the Whigs with him, now became Home Secretary. Gladstone was made Vice-President of the Board of Trade and was to enter the Cabinet two years later as President. Such were the chief personages in what was by common consent one of the most brilliant administrations of the century. Before it fell five years later it was to reintroduce the income-tax, establish the gold standard, place trade upon sound foundations for growth and remove disabilities from Roman Catholics, Nonconformists and Jews. Its significance lies not only in major enactments, but in the fact that it marks the transition of the country from an agricultural to a manufacturing basis; and herein lies its importance in the history of party.

The romantic and imaginative mind of Disraeli had become increasingly restive as he saw the cold and calculating financier from Lancashire transforming the Tory party rooted in the Church and the land to a Conservative party based on the industrial and commercial middle classes. His own ideals were at once more aristocratic and more popular than those of Peel. His political philosophy gave a leading rôle to the Sovereign as the protector of the whole nation; to the Church, then being revitalized by the Oxford Movement; and to the landed aristocracy. But he also had deep sympathy with the labouring masses created by the Industrial Revolution, as he had already shown by his "most capital speech on Chartism"[2] in the previous Parliament. He was not content to believe with the economists that what was good for the masters must necessarily be good for the hands, or alternatively that nothing could ever be done to improve the lot of the industrial masses as they would only breed to the level of subsistence. Disraeli's natural antipathy to the policies of Peel had been sharpened by the Prime Minister's haughty rebuffal of his solicitations for office—though Peel was not free as Stanley had let it be known that "if that scoundrel were taken in, he would not remain himself".[3] He attached himself to a small band of young Tories who shared his romantic vision—George Smythe (later 7th Viscount Strangford), Lord John Manners (later 7th Duke of Rutland) and Alexander Baillie Cochrane. They were given the name Young England.[a] He put his ideals into two novels which took England by storm—*Coningsby, or the New Generation* in 1844, and *Sybil, or the Two Nations* in 1845. In *Sybil* Disraeli expressed his conviction that the rich and the poor formed "two nations; between whom there is no intercourse and no sympathy; who are ignorant of each other's habits, thoughts, and feelings, as if they were dwellers in different zones, or inhabitants of different planets; who are formed by a different breeding, are fed by a different food, are ordered by different manners, and are not governed by the same laws".[4] In *Coningsby* he made clear his view that the transformation of Toryism into Conservatism was more than a change of name.

"The Tamworth manifesto of 1834 was an attempt to construct a party without principles; its basis therefore was necessarily latitudinarianism; and its inevitable consequence has been political infidelity."

"There was indeed a considerable shouting about what they called Conservative principles; but the awkward question naturally arose, what will you conserve?"

"Conservatism assumes in theory that everything established should be maintained; but adopts in practice that everything that is established is indefensible."

"Conservatism discards prescription, shrinks from principle, disavows progress; having rejected all respect for antiquity, it offers no redress for the present and makes no preparation for the future."[5]

" 'Hush!' said Mr. Tadpole, 'the time has gone by for Tory Governments; what the country requires is a sound Conservative government.'

" 'A sound Conservative government,' said Taper, musingly. 'I understand: Tory men and Whig measures.' "[6]

Disraeli's biting sarcasm was not confined to the pages of novels. Even before *Coningsby* was written, he had been using the lash of his tongue upon the writhing back of Peel from his place behind him in the House of Commons. He called the Irish Arms Bill a measure which it was disgraceful to introduce and degrading to oppose.[7] When Peel showed his annoyance, Disraeli complimented him on "all that courtesy which he reserves only for his supporters". Graham advised "a crack or two of the whip". In 1844 Disraeli did not receive the usual circular requesting his attendance at the meeting of Parliament, or, as a later generation would say, the whip was withdrawn from him. When he found that the omission was not accidental Disraeli wrote a letter to Peel in which he acknowledged that his remarks might "have been deficient in that hearty good will which should be our spontaneous sentiment to our political chief", but excused himself by "the want of courtesy in debate" that he had experienced from his leader. In reply, Peel icily explained that he had not sent the circular because Disraeli's expressed opinions had led him to doubt whether he was entitled to send it.[8]

The great mass of Tory members had neither the ability nor the disposition to fling such taunts as Disraeli hurled at their leader, but from the beginning of his ministry Peel, regarding himself as the guide of the nation rather than the servant of a party, had tried their patience sorely. The re-introduction of the income-tax hit all men of property, and the reduction in agricultural protection offended the farmers, but not to the point of letting in the Whigs and Radicals. The Maynooth grant shook many more. In 1840 O'Connell, seeing that he could not rely much longer on a Whig government in London, had founded the Association for the Repeal of the Union, and though he had only twelve supporters in the House of Commons after the election of 1841 he gathered the great mass of Irishmen behind him and gave open countenance to the rule of violence. Peel retaliated by having him arrested, and he was sentenced to imprisonment but released on appeal. A fatal illness took hold of him soon afterwards, and Peel thought the moment had come to conciliate the Irish priesthood by increasing the grant for the seminary at Maynooth. It cost him the resignation of Gladstone, and infuriated half the Tory party, who recalled how he had turned round in 1829 on the question of Roman Catholic emancipation.

The final break came over the great change in the fiscal system which Peel was destined to inaugurate. From being an exporter of wheat on balance until the accession of George III, Great Britain had become, owing to the growth of population and the development of manufacturing industries, dependent on foreign sources of supply. A bad harvest in 1838 led seven Manchester merchants to form an association which next year became a national body under the title the Anti-Corn Law League. Under the leadership of Richard Cobden and John Bright it conducted a brilliant campaign for the removal of the duties on foreign corn, and as the first political mass-organization machine in Great Britain it holds an important place in the history of party, both for the results it achieved and for the example it set. As may be read in Norman McCord's record, *The Anti-Corn Law League*, it sent out speakers, distributed pamphlets, organized electioneering, created freehold franchises and did much work in connexion with registration. After 1846 many of its most capable officers took up political work with the parties. Under pressure from the Anti-Corn Law League the Whigs, as the last act of a dying ministry, proposed a fixed duty on imported wheat instead of the sliding scale drawn up in 1828. Peel's motion of lack of confidence was carried in the House of Commons by one vote—although the Whigs wheeled through the lobby a noble member well known to be in a state of total idiocy. Before he took office in 1841 Peel had been accustomed to justify the protection given to British farmers by saying that it was on a par with the protection given to British manufacturers; but between 1842 and 1845 he removed much of the protection given to manufacturers and so destroyed his own argument. In 1842 he lowered the sliding-scale duties on imported corn, and there are many signs that his mind was moving in the direction of eventual total repeal even before the failure of the Irish potato crop in 1845 galvanized him into action. It was not quite true, as Wellington said, "Rotten potatoes have done it all",[9] but the potato blight provided him with an occasion and a good reason for taking action of whose necessity he had already become convinced.

When he unfolded his thoughts to his Cabinet, there was apprehension. At this time he and Stanley performed a scissors-like motion, their paths finally crossing. Stanley became the mouthpiece of the protectionists in the Cabinet, and was at first supported by the Duke of Buccleuch. Failing to achieve unanimity Peel placed the Cabinet's resignation in the hands of the Queen, but as neither Russell nor Stanley was able to form a government he was asked to resume office with a commission to terminate the duty on foreign corn. He summoned his colleagues to meet him at 9.30 p.m. on 20th December, and most of them waited to hear that they were now out of office. Instead they heard Peel tell them that he was Prime Minister, commissioned to terminate the duties on foreign corn, and invite their support in that task. Stanley was the first to break the silence and refused. Wellington, true to his dogma that the Queen's government must be carried on, said he was delighted and would have done as Peel had done. He clearly believed in Peel more than in protection, and under his lead all the others present acquiesced in the about turn.[10]

Peel had carried his Cabinet, but he still had to face his party, and at this point the party split. They had followed Peel in many things, but only 112 Conservative members of the House of Commons were prepared to follow him in this rejection of a sacred Tory dogma. Stanley, having thoroughly outgrown his Whig past, was the natural leader of the protectionist Tories, but he could no longer lead in the House of Commons, for in 1844 he had sought refuge in the Lords from the late sittings of the lower house. In debating force and organizing ability Disraeli stood out above all Tory protectionists in the Commons, but he knew that he was still disliked by large numbers of them for his eccentricities and foreign origin. He showed great wisdom, unexpected self-restraint and an uncanny judgement of men in urging Lord George Bentinck to assume the leadership of the Tories in the Commons. Though Bentinck had sat in eight Parliaments, he had never spoken in any great debate, and when he did appear his hunting pink was often visible beneath his greatcoat. Peel's defection, as he judged it, completely changed his character, or at any rate his manner of life. He sold his horses, gave himself up to daily attendance at the house, and did not break his fast until he had left it for fear of succumbing to the family weakness of falling asleep after meals.[11]

Peel was harried mercilessly by Bentinck and Disraeli in the

Commons, but with the support of the Whigs he carried the abolition of the tax on imported corn. Gladstone was now back in his
government, as Colonial Secretary in place of Stanley, and lending
all help in that direction, but not yet back in the House of Commons, for his acceptance of office vacated Newark and he did not
stand there again as the Duke of Newcastle regarded him as a be-
trayer of the territorial interest. The bill was introduced in the
Commons in January and provided for a three-year interim period
in which foreign corn would not pay more than a 10s. duty, and
thereafter only a 1s. registration duty. Night after night there were
wild scenes not previously paralleled in the history of Parliament.
One night in March when Peel rose to speak the protectionist Tories
howled for five minutes. On another night in May they screamed
and hooted and shouted their contempt. But with Whig help the
measure was sent to the Lords, and the Commons addressed themselves to the Protection of Life (Ireland) Bill. On 25th June, the sixth
night of debate, the member on his feet was interrupted with a
message from the Lords. The Speaker informed members that the
other place had agreed to the Customs Duty and Corn Importation
Bills without amendment. That same night Whigs and protectionist
Tories, who had voted for the first reading of the Irish coercion bill,
combined to oppose the second reading. Peel was defeated by
seventy-three votes and a few days later he resigned.

Peel's character and his conversion to free trade had dramatic and
permanent effects upon the party system. He was not himself what
is called "a good party man". Morley recalls how Sir John Hobhouse, meeting Disraeli at an evening party, expressed a fear lest
Peel, having broken up one party would also be the means of breaking up the other. "That, you may depend upon it, he will," replied
Disraeli, "or any other party that he has anything to do with." Not
long afterwards Wellington told Russell that he thought Peel was
tired of party and was determined to destroy it.[12]

The most obvious beneficiaries from Peel's conversion to free
trade were the Whigs. In the summer of 1845 they had no prospect
of office. Peel's position seemed impregnable, and even in the
winter when his resignation gave them a chance of forming a
minority government their divisions compelled them to renounce it;
the immediate difficulty was the unwillingness of Grey, as Howick
had now become by his father's death, to see Palmerston back at the
Foreign Office. As if in a twinkling Peel's breach with his party had
transformed their outlook. Russell became Prime Minister for the
first time, Palmerston and Grey accepted each other as Foreign and
Colonial Secretaries, and the Whigs were in office with brief exceptions for a period of twenty years.

The other side of the Whig triumph was the Tory disarray. The
United Kingdom had seldom seen a government in an apparently

stronger position than Peel's government in May 1845. Writing of the newspapers at that time, he said:

"They cannot deny that trade is prosperous, that the people are contented, that the labourer has a greater command than he ever had over the necessaries and comforts of life, that Chartism is extinguished—at least fast asleep—that the Church is stronger than it ever was, except for its own internal stupid differences and controversies, that any wish for organic change in the constitution—for addition to popular privileges—is dormant, that the revenue is so prosperous that our calculations of deficiency are constantly baffled, that our monetary system is sounder than it has been, and yet that there has been boundless activity in commerce and in all speculations of gain, and that even land is increasing in value, in consequence of the prosperity of commerce."

Yet even then Peel discerned two sources of discontent among his followers:

"But we have reduced protection to agriculture, and tried to lay the foundation of peace in Ireland; and these are offences for which nothing can atone."

The split, when it came six months later, was comparable in magnitude with the havoc that Burke's secession wrought among the Whigs in 1793. Peel's Cabinet had included seven men who had been or were to be Prime Minister. In the rump of the Tories Stanley, Disraeli and Bentinck were the only men of ability, Stanley distrusted Disraeli, and Bentinck was soon to be taken away. Twenty years of traversing the wilderness—we might almost say thirty—were to be the lot of the Conservatives before they were firmly in power again.

10

WHIGS AND PEELITES
1846–1867

Whig ministers dependent on Peelite support—the collapse of Chartism opens the way for Disraeli to rally working-class support for Conservatism—Palmerston, Russell, Derby and Aberdeen in turn take office—Disraeli's efforts to win Gladstone back to the Conservatives—reform again becomes an issue—Gladstone accepts the Exchequer in a Palmerston government—end of the Peelite group—Russell introduces a new reform bill—the "cave of Adullam"

DESPITE the change of government, Parliament was allowed to run out almost its full course. The Whigs continued to tread Peel's path and Peelite votes kept them safe from defeat. Disraeli was beginning the long process of educating the Conservative party and himself. There is many a bitter irony in political life. Just as Peel had educated the party to acceptance of the Reform Act, so it fell to Disraeli to educate it to the acceptance of free trade in wheat. By 1850 he was proclaiming that "protection is not only dead but damned".[1]

In the meantime the general election of 1847 had taken place. It left the parliamentary situation much as it was before, with Whig ministers still dependent on Peelite votes for their majorities in the Commons. The Peelites lost the support of the Conservative registration societies that their leader had called into being, but Bonham gave his personal support to Peel, and thereafter faded out of politics. He had tried hard to find a seat for Gladstone after his withdrawal from Newark, but it was only gradually, and very reluctantly, that Gladstone accepted the new order of things according to which a candidate in soliciting the leaders of a constituency had to be "prepared to take up bodily their presumed views and opinions upon all leading questions". The decision of one of the Oxford burgesses not to stand again provided Gladstone with a constituency more interested in his Church views than in protection, and he held it for eighteen years.[2] Peel was himself returned for Tamworth, but the number of his followers was reduced from about 120 at the time of the split to fewer than sixty.

This number of Peelites was nevertheless sufficient to turn the voting scales. Added to the Whig–Liberal–Radical members, they provided a large majority for free trade; added to the protectionists, they could just make a majority on other issues—but so long as Peel lived they never did vote as a body with the protectionists. In forming his government Russell told Peel he was willing to include any of his associates. Peel thought such a union inadvisable, but said he would have no cause for complaint if offers were made to his friends. Offers were made to Dalhousie, Lincoln and Sidney Herbert, but were not accepted. The Peelites stayed outside, but with the consequence that only Peelite measures could be passed; and Gladstone was soon reflecting that "the Liberal proceedings of Conservative governments and the Conservative proceedings of the new Liberal administration unite in pointing to the propriety of an abstinence from high-pitched opinions".[3]

There was speculation whether the Peelites would form a new party, but this was never likely, and looked less likely as time went on. In 1846 the Peelites were all free trade Conservatives, and most of them differed from protectionist Conservatives only over the single issue of protection. They looked to eventual reunion with the main body of the Conservatives, and when protection ceased to be an issue many of them drifted back. In this atmosphere there was no incentive to form a party. "We have no party," Gladstone wrote in 1849, "no organization, no whipper-in; and under these circumstances we cannot exercise any considerable degree of permanent influence as a body."[4] There was even less incentive to do so after the death of Peel in 1850, while working and voting with the Whigs had inclined the minds of some Peelites towards a Liberal solution of their dilemma. Pre-eminent among them was Gladstone himself. It was not until 1859 or 1860 that the dilemma was finally resolved, and until that day the Peelites continued to blur the outlines of the two-party system.

While the Conservative party was still struggling to get over Peel's defection, it was embarrassed by the election of Lionel de Rothschild by the City of London in 1847. As a practising Jew, Rothschild could not take the oath as then prescribed by the House of Commons. Disraeli could sit there because he had been baptized a Christian, but he remained a Jew in every fibre of his being and could not be silent when he saw Rothschild kept out. He spoke movingly in favour of Russell's proposal to modify the oath, and out of loyalty Bentinck supported him. The rest of the protectionist Conservatives voted solidly for the retention of the oath, and Bentinck was told that his action was not approved. He resigned the leadership of the party in the Commons. The following year he died of a heart attack.

Fate was edging Disraeli towards the top against all obstacles. Stanley put up a stubborn rearguard action. He offered Disraeli the work but not the title of Conservative leader in the Commons. Disraeli declined. Stanley offered to put the leadership into commission among Granby, Herries and Disraeli. "Sieyès, Roger-Ducos and Napoleon Bonaparte" was the comment of Aberdeen, mindful of what took place on 18th Brumaire.[5] Disraeli tolerated the arrangement, and within a few weeks he stood out as the undoubted leader of the Conservatives in the lower house.

In the confused political situation one source of further confusion was cleared away. The Chartist movement fizzled out. After the failure of 1839 the Chartist forces were regrouped and the movement entered a second phase. In May 1842 a second petition for the Charter, for which over three million signatures were claimed, was brought to Westminster at the head of a long procession. This was the zenith of the movement's influence, and when the petition was rejected it began to decline, but it was to make one further spectacular bid. Feargus O'Connor, who in the early days of the movement proclaimed the need to use physical force against such "moral force" men as Lovett, found his way back to Parliament in 1847, and in the following year he was encouraged by the revolutionary spirit on the continent to promote a third petition, for which no fewer than six million signatures were claimed. A great gathering of Chartists on Kennington Common was arranged for 10th April 1848 with a view to presenting it at the House of Commons. Thinking that O'Connor was really planning revolution, the Cabinet took such military precautions that the procession was abandoned. The petition arrived at the House of Commons in three cabs amid shouts of derisive laughter, and was found to have fewer than two million signatures. O'Connor's loss of self-confidence was increased by the failure of a scheme he had fostered for settling Chartists on the land as smallholders, and eventually he went out of his mind. Ernest Jones tried to get the movement back on to sound foundations, but the times were no longer propitious. The period of high prices and social distress lasting roughly from 1838 to 1842 under which Chartism had flourished had come to an end, and, whether free trade was a contributory factor or not, there began a long period of prosperity such as British industrial workers had not previously known. The Factory Acts also began to have their ameliorative effect. The causes of discontent were removed, the aspirations of the workers for higher wages, shorter working weeks and better conditions were canalized into trade union channels, and Chartism ceased to be a political force. Though it apparently failed and left no political party behind, its indirect influence was not negligible. It was the first working-class political movement of modern times, and even its failures had an educative value for the very inexperienced leaders of the industrial workers; it drew attention to the harshness of the working man's lot under *laisser faire*, preventing unqualified acceptance of Benthamism and Cobdenism; and it helped to compel the mitigation of the harsh Poor Law and the adoption of factory legislation. It stimulated Disraeli in his efforts to ally the working men to the Tory cause and it kept the Liberals from the full rigours of *laisser faire* doctrine.

Unable through dependence on Peelite votes to strike any resolute line in domestic policy, the Whig government won its greatest successes in foreign policy, but this was also its undoing. Palmerston's bombastic conduct of the Foreign Office could be tolerated so long as "the watchful eye and the strong arm of England" were able to protect a Gibraltar-born Jew from "injustice and wrong" in Greece, and it was popular with the nation, but it alarmed the Court. The immediate personal approval of Louis Napoleon's *coup d'état* that he expressed in 1851 to the French ambassador in London, to the embarrassment of the British ambassador in Paris, led to his dismissal. Russell would have made good the loss by an invitation to Graham to join the Cabinet, but his colleagues were too suspicious of the religious views of the Peelites. A militia bill in 1852 gave Palmerston the opportunity for revenge, and after the government had been defeated by eleven votes he wrote cheerfully to his brother, "I have had my tit-for-tat with John Russell, and I turned him out on Friday last."[6]

Thus Lord Derby (as Stanley had become by the death of his father) was called upon against his wishes to form a government based only on a minority in the Commons. It was a painful but useful experience in the re-education of the party. He would have included Palmerston and Lansdowne, but they would not accept without a formal renunciation of protection, and Derby would not give it. In the end he was obliged to form his government entirely from protectionist Conservatives. Hardly any had been in office before; seventeen were sworn of the Privy Council in a single day. Because the Duke of Wellington, on hearing the list read out, kept asking "Who, who?" it is known to history as the "Who, who? government". Disraeli was made Chancellor of the Exchequer with the leadership of the Commons.

The number of Peelites had by this time fallen to about forty, but in a fairly evenly balanced house this was enough to turn the scales; and it was thanks to their tolerance that Derby's ministry remained in office for ten months instead of four. Gladstone detected four shades of opinion among his associates. The Duke of Newcastle, not his old patron at Newark but the heir, Lincoln, was almost alone in the view that they were to lead a new party.

Graham was ready to join the Liberals. He described his position as "Whig and something more". The great bulk of the Peelites from the ex-Chancellor Goulburn downwards, asserting that their only difference with Derby was over protection, looked for reunion with the Conservatives. Aberdeen, Sidney Herbert and Gladstone himself perceived a call to sit on the fence until their course became clearer. There was much discussion about the right name to indicate the Peelite position. Gladstone thought it preferable to be, like Peel, on the Liberal side of the Conservative party rather than on the Conservative side of the Liberal party. The name Liberal-Conservative had some vogue, and Russell observed that Whig had the convenience of expressing in one syllable what Liberal-Conservative expressed in seven, and Whiggism in two syllables what Conservative progress expressed in six. While the question of a name could wait, the Peelites had to make up their mind at once where to sit in the House of Commons. This is a matter of great symbolic importance. After Peel's break with his party in 1846 the Peelites had continued to sit among the Conservatives. When the summons to Derby sent the Conservatives to the Speaker's right, the Peelites had to decide whether to follow them there or to stay on the Speaker's left. After much discussion, they determined to sit as a body on the opposition side, but below the gangway, except for Graham who exercised his Privy Councillor's right to a seat on the opposition front bench.[7]

Their opposition was not factious, but Derby thought it expedient to ask for a dissolution and a general election was held in July. The new prosperity of the industrial workers was attributed to free trade, and Derby's followers found it politic to be protectionist in a county, neutral in a small town and free traders in a big one They gained some voters, and their strength in the House of Commons after the election was variously reckoned to be between 290 and 320. The Peelites suffered some losses, but were still almost forty strong, and once more held the balance. They could have turned the government out immediately had they supported a motion by Villiers advocating free trade in terms which ministers could not accept. On that occasion they preferred to support a face-saving formula,[8] but in December Disraeli's budget, in which tea and beer drinkers were helped at the expense of house-owners, was more than Gladstone could stomach. After a closely reasoned speech late into the night in which he tore the budget to pieces, ministers were defeated and Derby resigned. It was the first of the great oratorical duels between the two men, and their mutual antipathies were to govern the British party system for many years to come. A few nights later revellers at the Carlton, seeing Gladstone quietly reading, told him that he ought to be thrown out of the window into the Reform across the way.

It had been shown that neither the Whigs nor the Tories could govern alone in the nice balance of the time. If Derby would have jettisoned protection, a Conservative government including leading Peelites would have been possible a little earlier, but Gladstone's stripping of Disraeli put this out of the question. The alternative was a coalition of Whigs and Peelites. Russell had made some unsuccessful overtures in that direction in 1851, but the times were now more propitious, and Prince Albert wanted it. Such a coalition, it was agreed, could not be led by Russell, whose Durham Letter and Ecclesiastical Titles Bill were obnoxious to the Peelites, and whose habit of announcing policy without consultation was distasteful to all his colleagues. Aberdeen visited Lansdowne, and the Peelite and Whig patricians each tried to pass the invidious task to the other. In the end Aberdeen reluctantly agreed to take it. Russell found consolation in another Ministry of All the Talents, and, like Fox in 1807, he accepted the Foreign Office and the leadership of the House of Commons. Palmerston, after many hesitations, took the Home Office. The Peelites, such are the rewards of holding the balance of power, though only forty strong in the Commons, were given six places in the Cabinet, the Exchequer going to Gladstone after Graham's refusal. The Whigs were given an equal number, though numbering some 270 in the Commons. One Radical, Molesworth, was included. "The cake is too small," Disraeli commented as news of the struggle for office reached him.[9]

Gladstone had time to produce only one memorable budget before the nation was involved in the calamity of the Crimean War. The Peelite ministers belied in war the reputation for administration they had acquired out of office in peace. At the first sign of parliamentary criticism, Roebuck's motion in 1855, Russell resigned, to the disgust of his colleagues, and the government were defeated. Derby, invited to form a new government, offered Palmerston the lead in the House of Commons with the assent of Disraeli; he also asked Gladstone and Herbert to join. They declined, and Derby gave up the task. Lansdowne next tried, but gave up when Gladstone would not join. In later life Gladstone counted it a major mistake not to have accepted Lansdowne's invitation; if he had done so, he would have been reckoned a Tory, and the party picture in the second half of the century would have been very different from what it was. On such personal decisions does history turn. Russell was next invited to form a government, but he was at this time thoroughly distrusted as an incorrigibly difficult colleague, and no one would join him except Palmerston. A Palmerston administration had at last become inevitable. After first refusing, Graham, Gladstone and Herbert agreed to join it, and a fortnight later resigned. There was great delight in Brooks's, where the Peelites were still objects of suspicion. Of the Peelites, the Duke of Argyll and Canning alone remained. The

Tapers and Tadpoles gave Palmerston a few months as Prime Minister: with one brief interval, he held the office until his death ten years later. Everybody was against him except the people; and with them his prestige was boundless.

Palmerston was then seventy-one. He had been in office for nearly forty years and had served under ten Prime Ministers. Originally a Tory, he had served from 1830 in Whig Cabinets, but he was never accepted by the Whig aristocrats as one of themselves and he was detested by the Manchester school. In the art of managing Parliament and the Queen he was supreme. His long tenure of office was personal and made possibly only by the confusion in the parties.

Defeated over the activities of the lorcha *Arrow* in Chinese waters, he appealed in 1857 to the country, which showed its support by routing his Radical critics (even Bright at Manchester) and giving him a solid Liberal majority. In the following year he was unexpectedly defeated on a proposal, arising from Orsini's attempt to murder Napoleon III, to class conspiracy to murder abroad as felony rather than misdemeanour. This time it was Russell's tit-for-tat. Derby was again called in, and although having only a minority in the Commons he consented. He tried very hard to get Gladstone to join him, but that statesman, so eagerly sought by both sides, and now on the Conservative side of the Liberals rather than on the Liberal side of the Conservatives, had made up his mind to decline even before he received from Bright a persuasive letter arguing that his future lay with the Liberals. An alliance between Derby and Gladstone would have been the most natural thing in the world with their common devotion to the Church of England and their common love of the classics; Derby had resigned office in youth rather than see any part of Irish church revenues secularized, Gladstone risked his political life in his zeal for the Oxford movement, and both were Homeric authors. Protection had divided them, but that was no longer an issue. A more serious obstacle, it may be surmised, was the leading place of Disraeli in Conservative counsels. Yet when Ellenborough's resignation of the Board of Control made a vacancy again, and Derby once more pressed his suit, the reluctant Gladstone was astonished to get a communication from Disraeli in which the leader of the House of Commons drew up a catalogue of his actions to show how "for more than eight years, instead of thrusting myself into the foremost place, I have been, at all times, actively prepared to make every sacrifice of self for the public good, which I have ever thought identical with your accepting office in a Conservative government". He reminded Gladstone that "Mr. Canning was superior to Lord Castlereagh in capacity, in acquirements, in eloquence, but he joined Lord C. when Lord C. was Lord Liverpool's lieutenant, when the state of the Tory party rendered it necessary. That was an enduring, and on the whole, not an unsatisfactory con-

nexion, and it certainly terminated very gloriously for Mr. Canning."[10] There is no reason to doubt that this letter was as sincere as
it was magnanimous, but between Gladstone and Disraeli there was
a deep psychological gulf, and he replied coldly and stiffly. Though
Graham would have approved a union with Derby, he again declined, and Derby was compelled to form a purely Conservative
government.

With Disraeli leading in the Commons, he was able to carry
measures for removing the disabilities of Jews and transferring the
government of India to the Crown, but soon fell on the question of
further parliamentary reform. This question was again becoming
urgent. The reforms of 1832 had been well digested and no longer
satisfied. Russell, who had been nicknamed "Finality Jack" in 1837
for declaring the 1832 Act to be a final settlement, had brought in a
new Reform Bill in 1854, but had been obliged by the war to drop it.
In an effort to win friends, Derby and Disraeli now took up the
cause and would have extended the franchise to graduates, professional men and men having £10 in consols or £60 in a savings
bank, would have extended the £10 household franchise to the
counties, and would have deprived 40s. borough freeholders of their
additional county votes. This "infringement of what passed for a
Liberal patent", as Morley called it,[11] did not prosper. Many Conservatives were restive, particularly at the assimilation of the household suffrage in boroughs and counties; Spencer Walpole, the Home
Secretary, resigned. Even Gladstone made a powerful defence of
nomination boroughs as a nursery of statesmen. Bright poured scorn
on the "fancy franchise". Russell objected that the bill did not go far
enough. An amendment which it was realized ministers could not
accept was put up. It was carried by thirty-nine votes, and although
the Parliament was only two years old Derby asked for a dissolution
on the pretext that the people should be consulted. The Conservatives returned some thirty stronger in the Commons, but were still a
minority in the whole house. There were anxious computations
among the whips whether a combination could be found sufficiently
strong to turn the Derby ministry out. This resolved itself into two
further questions, would Russell and Palmerston agree to serve together, one subordinate to the other, in a Liberal government, and
would Gladstone join it? At Willis's Rooms on 6th June Whigs and
Liberals came together and decided to support an amendment to the
Address to be moved by the Marquess of Hartington. In the
critical division Gladstone gave his vote in favour of confidence
in Derby, but Derby was nevertheless defeated and resigned. After
much coming and going Palmerston returned to No. 10 Downing
Street, while Russell condescended to accept the Foreign Office and
later an earldom. Marvel at the reconciliation of the Whig patricians
was lost in still greater wonder that Gladstone should accept office

H

as Chancellor of the Exchequer. There would have been nothing surprising if Gladstone had agreed to serve under Palmerston on several earlier occasions, but it was found odd that the man who had voted one night to keep Derby in should a few days later become the colleague of the man who had turned him out. Even Gladstone's subtle mind found it hard to explain his action. By acceptance of office under a Whig Prime Minister he had at last crossed the Rubicon dividing the Tory and Whig parties : and he had a hard fight to retain his seat at Oxford. The Peelites as a group now finally passed out of British politics. In 1860 Gladstone resigned from the Carlton.

Acceptance of office gave Gladstone the opportunity to carry a series of outstanding budgets. One of his financial measures, the repeal of the paper duty, has an interest bearing on the party system as it affected the powers of the upper house, which, as we have noted, had been since 1830 a Tory stronghold. It had become the practice to dispose of financial proposals in separate bills, and the repeal of the paper duty, which Gladstone desired as it was "a tax on knowledge", was embodied in such a bill. It was not enthusiastically received even by his colleagues. Palmerston spoke against it in Cabinet, and it passed the Commons by the precarious majority of nine votes. Palmerston told the Queen that the Lords would be justified in throwing it out, and they did. This raised the question of the acknowledged sole right of the House of Commons in matters of taxation, and even Palmerston was obliged to join Gladstone in supporting three resolutions affirming the privileges of the lower house in financial matters. In the following year the repeal of the paper duty and other financial measures was included by Gladstone in a single Finance Bill, which the Lords hesitated to reject for fear of putting the whole financial system of the country in jeopardy. This practice has ever since been followed, and has proved a most effective method of asserting the sole competence of the elected representatives of the people in the all important department of finance, and thereby the supremacy of the dominant party.

One other aspect of the proceedings in Palmerston's last ministry with a bearing on the party system is the rising pressure for further parliamentary reform. Russell had introduced another bill on this subject in 1860. It would have introduced a £6 household franchise in the boroughs. Russell had introduced his bill against the opposition of Palmerston, and concurrently with Gladstone's controversial financial proposals. Both measures were meeting systematic obstruction that threatened their passage, and Russell reluctantly agreed to drop his bill.

In 1863 he told supporters of the measure to "rest and be thankful".[12] Parliament was dissolved in the normal course in 1865, but the balance of parties was left unaltered. Gladstone, now an unmistakable Liberal, was defeated at Oxford, but had taken the precaution of finding another seat in South Lancashire. It is an example of how small things can affect parties that his defeat for the university seat was the result of the introduction of voting by post— Oxford and Cambridge were uniquely accorded this privilege— which gave the country clergy better opportunity to express their suspicion that Gladstone was heading for disestablishment.

Palmerston died a few months later, Russell (now in the Lords) became Prime Minister again and Gladstone led the Commons. The death of Palmerston gave Russell his chance to make a further assault on the citadel of the franchise. His bill, introduced by Gladstone in the Commons, would have reduced the borough franchise from £10 to £7, enfranchised lodgers who paid £10 a year rent, and reduced the county franchise from £50 to £14. The Conservative party opposed it as too advanced, but the strongest opposition came from a Liberal, Robert Lowe, a sceptic on the subject of trusting the people, who rose to unsuspected heights of oratory. He was supported by about thirty other Liberals, called by Bright "the Adullamites" from the distressed and discontented who took refuge with David in the cave Adullam.[13] "You cannot fight against the future," Gladstone told opponents, "time is on our side."[14] He had now identified himself completely with the popular cause. A motion by Lord Grosvenor that the franchise should not be reformed until there had been a redistribution of seats was defeated by only five votes in the Commons. In committee Lord Dunkellin carried by 315 votes to 304 an amendment to substitute rateable value for gross estimated rental on the basis of the new £7 franchise. The change was not so vital in itself, but what was serious was that the majority included forty-four of the government's normal supporters. There was some discussion whether an appeal should be made to the country. Brand, the chief whip, advised against this course (and threatened to take no part in it) as the expense of a new election so soon after that of 1865 would be unpopular with their friends and they could win it only by bringing in extreme men in place of the dissidents, who might be driven permanently to the opposite side. Russell tendered the Cabinet's resignation, was asked by the Queen to withdraw it, and re-presented it when the Cabinet declined to go on. Derby was sent for again, and, when he failed to bring in the Adullamites, formed a purely Conservative administration. By one of the strangest turns in British political history, within a few months this Conservative administration had secured the passage of a Reform Bill going far beyond what Parliament had rejected at the hands of Russell.

11

REFORM ACT OF 1867—BEFORE AND AFTER

Freedom of action of members of Parliament—Whigs and Tories really coalitions of groups—Tory measures carried by Whig governments and Whig measures by Tory governments—Liberal Registration Association, the first national headquarters, formed in 1861—rebuilding of the Conservative organization after 1846— Disraeli's Reform Bill of 1867—stimulus to party organization— National Union of Conservative and Constitutional Associations— Disraeli's declaration of Conservative principles—Gladstone welds the Liberal party into a new unity—and becomes Prime Minister— Disraeli reorganizes the Conservative party—Conservative central office

ON the even of the Reform Bill of 1867 the political struggle was still concentrated in Parliament. Outside the Palace of Westminster party organization was still rudimentary. The franchise was confined to the upper and middle classes, elections were expensive and as often as not uncontested, and Parliaments usually ran their full course of six or seven years. A member of Parliament, while normally giving his allegiance to one of the great leaders, did not necessarily feel under an obligation to vote for all his policies, and the whips could never count on fewer than ten per cent of their normal supporters straying into the opposite lobby. In these circumstances parliamentary debate could still decide the nation's course and the shape of legislation, and there was much interchange among parties. Melbourne, Palmerston, Derby, Disraeli and Gladstone all began on different sides from those on which they ended.

Though the influence of the whips was growing, and they were constantly taken into consultation by their leaders, their main function was that of intelligence. They conveyed to the leaders the opinions of members, and gave their estimates of the way members would vote, but they would not have presumed to tell leaders what policy they should follow or members how they should act. The leaders, regarding themselves as the servants of the state rather than of their party, tended to look upon the party as the instrument for carrying out their policy rather than upon themselves as instruments for carrying out their party's policy. Peel showed his readiness to break his party rather than yield on the policy he believed to be right, Russell and Palmerston frequently announced the policy first and left the party to follow later, Disraeli showed himself remarkably agile in adapting his policy to the parliamentary requirements, and Gladstone acknowledged no master save his conscience. The leaders holding such dominant positions, the course of party history was greatly affected by personal likes and dislikes, and episodes in personal history. If Peel had not snubbed Disraeli's desire for office in 1841, the Conservative party might not have broken in 1846, even if he had thereby deprived himself of the services of Stanley; and if Gladstone had not disapproved of Disraeli even more than of Palmerston, he might never have become "the people's William"; and either the Whigs would have remained in control of the Liberal party for much longer or the Liberal party would have become Radical much more quickly under Bright or someone of his views.

There were two great parties in the field, the Whigs and Tories, when the Reform Bill was passed in 1832, and there were still two great parties in the field, though now usually called Liberals and Conservatives, when the Reform Bill was introduced in 1867. In between the clear-cut lines of the two-party system had been blurred by the secession of the Peelites from the main stream of Conservative tradition and the presence of Irish members more interested in the remedy of Irish grievances than in the battle of Whig and Tory. The Peelite members of the House of Commons declined in numbers from about 120 at the time of the break in 1846 to under forty when they finally disappeared in 1859, merged in one or other of the great parties, and their influence was even greater than their numbers would have warranted, particularly in the years when they held the balance in the house. The Irish nationalists, who wrested a substantial part of the representation of the emerald isle from the Whigs and Tories, became a formidable parliamentary party under O'Connell's leadership, though never counting more than forty and sometimes falling to twelve. After his death the Irish nationalists did not form so distinctive a group, but in the year 1867 Fenian outrages were again forcing Ireland on the centre of the parliamentary stage.

Though there is an undeniable continuity between the Conservatives of 1867 and the Tories of 1832, and between the Liberals of 1867 and the Whigs of 1832, there had been much change in the persons and policies of both parties; and if they are examined closely, they are seen to be coalitions of groups rather than monolithic unities. All through this period the Radicals, in particular, were recognizable as a distinct group, or rather sect, within the Liberal fold; and at the end the Adullamite cave showed that there were malcontents to the right as well as to the left.

In foreign policy Conservatives and Liberals tended to be true to their basic temperamental differences in their reluctance or readiness to change the existing order of things, and in particular Conservatives tended to uphold the settlement reached at the Congress of Vienna and Liberals to champion nationalist movements seeking to upset it. This basic difference, though valid, should not be pressed too far. The Foreign Office was still very much a law to itself, especially during the long reign of Palmerston, and the plenipotentiary powers of ambassadors in those days were not the mere name that they have become today, as "the great Elchi", Stratford Canning, showed by pursuing as ambassador to Turkey a policy of hostility to Russia that was embarrassing to Aberdeen's government and contributed to the outbreak of the Crimean War. The support given to nationalist movements by the Liberals is most notably exemplified by the championship of the Italian *Risorgimento* by Palmerston, Russell and Gladstone, but they had opponents in their own Cabinet, and Gladstone had been exhibiting the same sympathies while still a Peelite Tory. The same Palmerston who so often supported democratic causes abroad gave a hasty welcome to Louis Napoleon's *coup d'état*, thereby earning the displeasure of his sovereign. In those days, and for many years to come, the Crown still claimed in the field of foreign affairs rights that it had already surrendered, or was surrendering, in the domestic field, and the interest of the Court helped to ensure some degree of continuity in the conduct of British relations with foreign powers despite the alternations of parties in office.

Though Durham's report on Canada is now taken as the beginning of the consciously adopted policy of self-government for the oversea territories of the Crown, there is little to distinguish before 1867 in the colonial policies of the major parties. Disraeli's imagination had not yet been caught by the glitter of empire,[1] and the Victorian burst of oversea expansion was still to come. The cleavage between the parties was usually then, as now, along the lines of domestic policy. In 1832 the two great parties were sharply divided on parliamentary reform, and in 1866 they were again sharply divided on this issue, but soon the Conservatives were to be outbidding the Liberals in an auction for votes. The great issue of protection for agricultural interests which had divided the parties so sharply in 1846 had been settled in favour of free trade, and as British agriculture had remained prosperous in spite of the loss of protection there was no disposition to raise it. The Conservatives still remained broadly the party of the land, and the Liberals of the manufacturing and commercial classes, but the deepest-seated di-

vision still remained that the Conservatives were the champions of
the Church of England, and the Liberals of the protestant Nonconformists. It was becoming curious now that the most powerful person in the Conservative party was the Jew Disraeli (baptized a
Christian in his youth), and the most powerful figure in the Liberal
party the High Churchman Gladstone, but such are the inscrutable
ways of Providence and the workings of the party system, and each
threw himself with zest into the rôle for which fate had cast him. In
the early forties Disraeli's imagination had been fired by the country's Catholic past and by the current efforts of the Tractarians to
revive Catholic faith and practice in the Church of England, while
Gladstone's mind had similarly been caught by the vision of the
Catholic mission of the Church of England (oddly enough while
reading the Occasional Offices of the Prayer Book in Rome), and he
was throughout life the intimate friend of Pusey, Newman and
Manning. It was more than could be expected that both Disraeli and
Gladstone should follow where the kindly light of Oxford led.
Disraeli's ardour soon cooled, and the author of *Sybil* became the
champion of "a bill to put down ritualism".[2] Gladstone remained
personally constant in his zeal for the Church of England, but from
1864 onwards such Nonconformist leaders as Dale, Allon and
Spurgeon claimed him as their leader,[3] and he was soon carrying
ecclesiastical measures that dismayed most of his fellow-Churchmen
as much as they warmed the hearts of dissenters.

This reversal of rôles illustrates another curious feature of the
period between the first and second Reform Bills, that Tory measures
were often carried by Whig governments, and Whig measures by
Tory governments. This, as we have seen, was particularly true
when Peel was at the head of the Conservative party; for though the
voice that defended the measures of 1835–41 was Melbourne's the
hand that shaped them was Peel's, and in the years 1841–6 Peel
broke himself and his party in carrying measures commonly associated with the Whigs. Though Disraeli taunted Peel in 1845 with
stealing the Whigs' clothes while they were bathing, his leader
Derby was to boast in 1867 that they had "dished the Whigs" by
carrying reform before the Liberals could do so.[4]

The conditions of a two-party system are such that it is not really
surprising to find Whigs carrying Tory measures, and Tories carrying Whig measures—or, for that matter, Conservatives carrying
socialist measures, and socialists carrying Conservative measures.
The Tory minister could normally count on Tory support, and in a
closely balanced house might get additional support by proposing
Whig measures; the Whig, in turn, could normally count on the
loyalty of Whigs, and could hope for still wider support in fostering
Tory measures. It was only when leaders strained the loyalties of
their supporters too far, as Peel did in 1846, that the system of give-

and-take broke down; and perhaps if Peel had had any other opponent than Disraeli he might still have carried the day.

The two-party system can function properly only if there is an underlying unity between the parties, at least to the extent that great measures passed by Parliament will be allowed to remain undisturbed on the statute book. This basic unity underlying the two-party system has been greatly fostered by a development which began in the middle of the nineteenth century, the rise of an independent and politically neutral civil service. We have seen the confusion that existed in the eighteenth century between the political and administrative work of such departments as the Treasury and the Admiralty. Though there had been some progress in the separation of political and executive functions, in the year 1850 the staff of each department was appointed by the minister in charge of that department, and, in Morley's words, "civil employment under the Crown was in all the offices the result of patronage, though in some, and those not the more important of them, nominees were partially tested by qualifying examination and periods of proba-tion".[5] Gladstone asked Sir Stafford Northcote and Sir Charles Tre-velyan to report on needed reforms. In 1853 they advised that entry to the civil service should be by competitive examination, and that a central board should be appointed for the purpose of conducting these examinations. Russell protested that the proposed Civil Service Commission would take the place of the Queen—by which he meant that members would be deprived of their patronage—but it was set up in 1855. For some years their examinations tested only the quality of candidates nominated to them, but in 1870, when Gladstone was Prime Minister, an open competitive examination was made the doorway to all departments except the Foreign Office. In this way there was built up a body of talented and industrious men recruited solely by merit whose services were at the disposal of ministers irrespective of party. When governments changed, they remained at their desks, and as it was inevitable that the advice they gave to incoming ministers was substantially the same as they had given to outgoing, they tended to be a stabilizing force. This tend-ency became accentuated as political questions became more com-plex and the area of government activity more extensive, inasmuch as the amateur called upon to head a department found himself at a disadvantage in relation to the professional devoting all his life to the study of such questions; and growing emphasis upon the secrecy of state papers worked in the same direction as it became impossible for political leaders in opposition to know all the facts upon which they would have to form a judgement in office. Even Gladstone was obliged to change his tune in office from what it had been in "a position of greater freedom and less responsibility". So powerful a regulator of the party system has the civil service become that sometimes the rôles have been reversed, and instead of civil servants being the instruments for the execution of ministers' policies, ministers become the parliamentary instruments of policy which the higher civil servants have decided.[a] The exact relationship at any moment depends upon the strength of the personalities involved, their knowledge of the facts and their skill in the art of government, but the rôle of the civil service from the time of the Gladstonian reforms in making the party system work is undeniable.

In 1832 there was a large Whig party with some Liberals in it; in 1867 there was a Liberal party with Whigs in it. No precise date can be given when the party ceased to be Whig and became Liberal, for it was as gradual a process as growing up. It was not merely a substitution of one name for another, because Liberal meant more than Whig, as Graham had implied. It meant that the party was ceasing to be dominated by the sacred circle of the great-grand-motherhood. Halévy says the term Liberal was not officially adopted until 1847, but this seems to be a misunderstanding for, as Sir Ivor Jennings justly observes, there is no evidence that the term "Liberal" was officially adopted in that year nor was there then anyone who had power to adopt it. The party that Russell led amid much grumbling in 1852 was still generally called Whig, and after 1859 it is usually called Liberal; this is perhaps as narrow an interval as can be found for the transformation of the Whig into the Liberal party. Bell, in his life of Palmerston, says categorically that the Liberal party was formed at the meeting in Willis's Rooms on 6th June 1859 attended by Whigs, Peelites and "advanced Liberals". Dr. Southgate[b] seems to support this view in saying "there was no point in turning out Derby ... unless the members of Parliament opposed to Tory government agreed, through their several champions, to constitute a Liberal party not only for the purpose of expelling a ministry, but for the purpose of sustaining its successor", and in adding, "When such agreement was made at Willis's Rooms on 6th June, 1859 and ratified by a vote of 323 to 310 for the Marquess of Hartington's amendment to the Address ..." This would make Palmerston the first Liberal Prime Minister, and the editors of the first series of Queen Victoria's *Letters* agree that he was the first Liberal Prime Minister, but date his assumption of this rôle to 1855, when the Peelites left him. It is significant that Gladstone made his passage from the Tories to the Liberals without ever being a Whig; as he had not been born a Whig, he never could be one.[6]

By 1861 the Liberal party must certainly be regarded as in existence,[c] for that year saw the formation in London of a Liberal Registration Association composed of "gentlemen of known Liberal opinions", which was, in effect, the first national headquarters of the party, or of any party, and gradually took over the work previously done unofficially by the Reform Club.

We have seen how the national organization of the Whig-Liberal party had been directed in a loose way under the whips by Joseph Parkes and James Coppock. When Coppock died in 1857, it was decided to follow an example already set by the Conservatives and to appoint a parliamentary, principal or national agent. A leading City solicitor, William Richard Drake, was appointed, and he later described his duties to a parliamentary commission as "advising the leaders of the party, members of Parliament and candidates on matters connected with election law, and communications with candidates seeking seats in Parliament, and with constituencies seeking candidates, and placing the former in communication with the latter through the local parties". He further explained that the parliamentary agent was not paid a salary, and was remunerated solely by his usual professional charges from the conduct or defence of election petitions placed in his hands.[7]

Drake worked under the Liberal chief whip, Henry Brand, and these two were responsible for the formation in 1861 of the Liberal Registration Association, renamed in 1877 the Liberal Central Association, but usually known in the party as "the whips' office". As secretary they appointed Thomas Nicolls Roberts, who had been in charge of the electoral registration office of the Anti-Corn Law League. Its main tasks were to promote the formation of constituency registration societies, to give them guidance, and to ensure that Liberal "outvoters" were brought to the poll. Outvoters were persons entered on the register in a particular constituency but living in some other constituency. In boroughs qualified electors had to reside within seven miles of the constituency, but qualified county electors could vote even if they never resided in the county. Outvoters amounted to some fifteen per cent of the electorate, and it was a matter of no small moment to get them to the poll. Until 1858 candidates frequently paid the expenses of outvoters, and often added something to make their journey worth while. After 1858 only the cost of a vehicle to get the outvoter to and from the polling booth could be met. To make contact with outvoters, persuade them to take the trouble of voting and provide them with the means of doing so was beyond the capacity of constituency registration societies, and the Liberal Registration Association made this a considerable branch of its work. It kept lists of outvoters, and offered them vouchers to travel by rail to and from the poll. The vouchers were always made out for the first class, as electors would have considered it beneath their dignity to have travelled second or third. The vouchers were returned by the railway companies to the Liberal Registration Association, which paid for them and in general recovered the cost from candidates. This practice was made illegal in 1884.

The Conservative organization so carefully nourished by Peel was shattered in 1846 when he broke with the main body of the party. As Bonham and most of the local agents continued to give their loyalty to him, the protectionists had virtually to build a new organization out of nothing. Bentinck appointed William Beresford as chief whip, and he had the general oversight of Conservative organization not only in Parliament but throughout the country. As such he managed the election of 1852 for the Conservatives and fell foul of a House of Commons committee for his indifference to bribery at Derby. A division of functions then took place. Sir William Jolliffe, later Lord Hylton, was appointed chief whip, and Disraeli's solicitor, Philip Rose, a member of the firm of parliamentary agents known as Baxter, Rose, Norton & Co., was made principal agent—this, at least, is how he was often called, and it accurately describes his functions, though the title was not formally conferred until 1871. While Beresford attended to the work in Parliament, Rose had the main responsibility for Conservative organization in the country. Another member of the same firm, Markham Spofforth, acted as his assistant and was given the task of re-establishing a chain of Conservative agents in the constituencies. In 1859 he succeeded Rose as principal agent. Four or five years later a Conservative Registration Association was set up to cater for outvoters as the Liberal Registration Association was already doing. It had a secretary of its own, Henry Smith, but was under the general control of Spofforth.

Disraeli showed an ability in matters of organization that would not have been expected in a statesman of his flamboyant nature, but we may be confident that more of his thought was given to the general character of a Tory or Conservative party. "The Conservative party, unless it is a national party, is nothing"[8] was a later saying of his, but it reflected his beliefs from his first days in the House of Commons. It was his constant endeavour to give the Conservative party such a national character, and especially to win the support of the great mass of industrial and agricultural workers, for whom neither the Whig aristocrats nor the Liberal manufacturers had much concern. He had opposed household suffrage in the boroughs when it was proposed by Russell, but it was the duty of an opposition to oppose; and then there came a series of riots by the disfranchised that assisted his conversion, and powerfully helped to persuade his colleagues. A mob tore down the railings in Hyde Park, processions a mile or more long blocked the streets of great cities from London to Glasgow, ugly meetings attended by hundreds of thousands at Birmingham, Manchester and Leeds recalled the atmosphere of 1830, and showed, in Morley's words, "that even though the workmen might not be anxious to demand the franchise, yet they would not stand its refusal".[9] If the franchise had to be widened, Disraeli argued, let the Conservative party get the credit for it.[d]

As originally introduced by Disraeli in March 1867 the second Reform Bill would have given the franchise in boroughs to all householders paying rates, and in counties to householders paying a rent of £12 a year or more. The vote was to be given to ministers of religion, university graduates, men having £50 in the funds, and men paying £1 a year in direct taxes; and if such persons also had a property qualification they were to be allowed to cast two votes. Cranborne was not comforted by these fancy franchises and resigned his office, along with Carnarvon and General Peel. Gladstone tried to limit the vote to £5 householders, but a tea-room revolt among the Liberal members ensured the defeat of the limitation. He had to admit that "the idea of household suffrage, when the phrase had once been advertised by a government as its battle-ground, was irresistible".[10] Thenceforth the Liberals sought to make the government line up to the profession of household suffrage, and secured the reduction of the qualifying period to one year. Disraeli was equal to the challenge, and not only agreed that £10 lodgers should have the vote, but, while quite alone on the front bench, and being unable to consult any of his colleagues, he blandly accepted a Liberal member's amendment that no person other than the occupier should be assessed to the rates in a parliamentary borough.[11] This was, in effect, to give the vote to the "compound householder", who paid the rates in his rent. Thereafter, there was no point in keeping the fancy franchises, and they were struck out. A modest measure of redistribution was attached to the bill, thirty-five seats being transferred from small towns to great cities; and in constituencies returning three members it was laid down that electors could not give more than two votes. This was a device to try and ensure some representation for minorities.

What had appeared to Derby as a laudable dishing of the Whigs struck Gladstone as "diabolical cleverness", Lowe as an act of tergiversation meriting alike "the contempt of all honest men, and the execration of posterity" and Cranborne as "a political betrayal that had no parallel in our parliamentary annals". Such charges are understandable; but there was a sincerity in Disraeli's philosophy of uniting the aristocracy and the working classes in a single nation. In the outcome almost a million new voters were added to the electorate, far more than the justly celebrated measure of 1832 had enfranchised. Derby called it "a leap in the dark", Carlyle said it was "shooting Niagara".[12]

Such an enlargement of the electorate could not fail to have repercussions in the field of party organization, and the Representation of the People Act, 1867, to use its formal title, is a landmark in the history of the subject comparable with the Reform Act of 1832. It was the Conservative party which first recognized the need, and the immediate development was the grouping of constituency

associations into a national union and the holding of an annual conference by that union. The way in which this development came
about is described in the minutes of a meeting held at the Free-
masons' Tavern, London on 12th November 1867. There were present the representatives of fifty-five urban constituencies and the
newly enfranchised graduates of the University of London under the
chairmanship of John Gorst, M.P. The chairman explained that it
was "not a meeting for the discussion of Conservative principles, on
which we are all agreed, it is only a meeting to consider by what
particular organization we may make those Conservative principles
effective among the masses". The honorary secretary then read a
statement explaining how the meeting, which ranks as the first in
the long series of Conservative party conferences, had come
about:[13]

"The working classes of England some time back commenced
forming themselves into associations to support the present government upon the question of reform, and to maintain the fundamental
principles of our ancient constitution. It was felt that their position
would be strengthened and their influence augmented by the formation of a central union. Conferences were convened in the early part
of the present year to consider the question, which were numer-
ously attended by representatives, especially from the northern districts, and it was there resolved to establish a union for this purpose.
On the present occasion it is proposed to finally settle the name,
rules, and constitution of this society, and to appoint the first
officers. This association will afford a centre of communication and
action between local associations supporting constitutional views.
There is, of course, no intention to interfere in any way with local
action; the object of the union is to strengthen the hands of local
associations where existing in their respective districts, and to encourage the establishment of associations in districts where they are
wanting, and further to organize associations by the holding of
meetings for the general expression and diffusion of constitutional
principles, and the dissemination of sound information upon topics
of general political interest, and to secure the combined action of
all constitutional associations."

After a lively discussion it was decided that the name of the new
organization should be the National Union of Conservative and
Constitutional Associations, and that its object should be to constitute a centre for such bodies. The name Constitutional had been in
the fashion for some years as an alternative to Conservative, with
the scarcely concealed suggestion that opponents were out to sub-
vert the constitution. The Liverpool Conservative Association had
been relabelled the Liverpool Constitutional Association in 1848,
and many other constituency bodies were similarly called. The Constitutional Club was founded in London in 1883 as a Conservative

centre, and as late as 1924 the label Constitutional marked a stage in the return of Winston Churchill to the Conservative party.

The rules as adopted in 1867 provided that every Conservative or Constitutional association subscribing one guinea or more per annum might be admitted to the union; and any branch or affiliated association consisting of not fewer than 100 members might be admitted on a separate subscription. A Central Council of the union was constituted, and H. Cecil Raikes, who had taken a leading part in the formation of the union, became its chairman in 1869 and held the post for five years. In that capacity he made a notable speech in 1873 defining the functions of the union. He is reported as saying[14] that "we had now outlived the time of great family influences, and also that period which succeeded the first Reform Bill, which might be called the period of middle-class influence in boroughs. We were living in a day in which the people were to be applied to in a much more direct, clear, and positive manner than was the case under the older forms of the constitution, and, therefore, any party who wished to retain their hold upon the country must ascertain how far their proceedings were in harmony with the wishes of the people". This emphatic endorsement of the need to consult the people was balanced by a warning that the National Union could not take the place of the party leaders. "Complaints were made that it did not do all that it ought to do; but he pointed out that it was often suggested that it should do things which did not belong to its peculiar line of duty. The union had been organized rather as what he might call a handmaid to the party than to usurp the functions of party leadership."

In some parties the relations between the main party organization in the country and the parliamentary leadership have been to this day a matter of great argument and some delicacy. It says much for Raikes's perspicacity that he saw the problem at the outset and laid down lines that the Conservative party has been content to follow.

For the first few years of its life the National Union did not attract much attention or win much support. It was thought politic to take the second annual conference to Birmingham, where the Conservative Working Men's Association had nearly 3,000 members, but only seven persons attended, including the officers. The third conference, at Liverpool, had an attendance of thirty-six, and the fourth, at York, only thirty-five. The National Union was not placed on the map until 1872, when the conference was accompanied by a banquet at the Crystal Palace, at which Disraeli made one of his best-known speeches. It was then that he declared:[15]

"The Tory party, unless it is a national party, is nothing. It is not a confederacy of nobles, it is not a democratic multitude; it is a party formed from all the numerous classes in the realm—

classes alike and equal before the law, but whose different conditions and different aims give vigour and variety to our national life."

Disraeli's efforts to bring the new working-class voters into the Conservative ranks were not altogether seconded by his colleagues, and there was a deferential attitude about many working-class Conservatives which led *The Times*, in a fine simile, to write of him as discerning in the inarticulate mass of the English populace the Conservative working man as the sculptor perceives the angel prisoned in a block of marble.[16] It was nevertheless a sound instinct. After the Reform Act of 1867 it became essential for the Conservative party to get a substantial measure of working-class support if it was to retain power.

Success did not come immediately, and the newly enfranchised urban householders at first spurned the hand that gave them the vote. Derby's resignation early in 1868, followed by his death the following year, brought Disraeli to the post of Prime Minister which it had been his youthful ambition to attain—at last he had climbed to the top of the greasy pole, he observed. The Irish question, influenced by Fenian agitation, was full of menace. He declared it was essential to deal with Irish grievances. Gladstone, who had been "watching the sky with a strong sense of the obligation to act with the first streak of dawn", agreed, and carried in the House of Commons three resolutions to the effect that the establishment of the Church of Ireland should cease. He found himself the hero alike of Roman Catholics and Nonconformists, and the Liberal party was welded into a unity it had not known for some time. Disraeli, taunted with his speech in 1844 when he described the roots of Ireland's mischief as a weak executive, an absentee aristocracy and an alien church, thought this was going too far.[17] He decided to dissolve in the autumn when the registers under the new act should come into force. He hoped, perhaps expected, to have in the new Parliament what he had not possessed in the old, a majority behind him. His dream was soon dissolved. Out of 2,292,208 votes cast, 1,408,738 were given to Liberal candidates, and 883,470 to Conservative. By this time the party affiliations of candidates were much clearer than they had been, and the Liberals were seen to have a majority of 112 in the new house. Disraeli resigned forthwith, and Gladstone became Prime Minister for the first time.

Profiting from defeat, Disraeli set about a major reorganization of his party. He acted according to the fashion by which a defeated party usually attributes its unpopularity with electors, not to policies, nor to personalities, but to defects in organization. One outcome was a reconstruction of the national party headquarters which is generally regarded as the foundation of the Conservative Central Office, though, as Dr. H. J. Hanham points out,[18] it was not so regarded at the time. We have seen how under the general direction of the chief whip, Spofforth had been made principal agent with the oversight also of the Conservative Registration Association. The arrangements with his firm Baxter, Rose and Norton were not considered adequate to meet the new conditions after the Reform Act, and in the summer of 1868 a committee was set up to take charge of the impending election. Spofforth, thus elbowed out, found also that the new arrangements for the trial of election petitions in the courts had cut away the financial basis of his position. He resigned in 1869, and Disraeli, who had come to the conclusion that "an entirely new system must be set up", began to look about "for a young and ambitious Conservative who would be ready to devote the best years of his life to working out a scheme". He found such a person in John E. Gorst, the first president of the National Union, who was a barrister and had lost his seat at the general election. Gorst made his headquarters in the office of the Conservative Registration Association, and Keith-Falconer, the secretary of that body, became the first secretary of the Conservative Central Office, as it was now called. To ensure harmonious working with the National Union, Gorst and Keith-Falconer were made joint honorary secretaries of that body, and in 1872 the Central Office and the National Union were housed in the same building.

In his penetrating account of politics in the time of Disraeli and Gladstone entitled *Elections and Party Management*, to which reference has already been made, Dr. H. J. Hanham notes the important rôle played by William Nevill, 5th Earl and later 1st Marquess of Abergavenny, in Conservative organization at this time.[19] His name will not be found in the political histories nor even in the *Dictionary of National Biography*, but Dr. Hanham is undoubtedly right in discerning his "enormous influence behind the scenes because of his disinterestedness and ability". Nevill had worked regularly in the party offices until 1868, when he succeeded to the earldom, and was, in effect, the deputy to whom Disraeli left the detailed work of supervision; and until 1902 he was "the confidential adviser of successive party leaders, virtual manager of the Carlton and Junior Carlton Clubs (and founder of the Constitutional), principal trustee of the party funds, a formidable *grand seigneur* and an expert on patronage". It has always been the case in the Conservative party, as Lloyd George was to find at a later date, that great influence is exercised by persons whose names are unknown to the general public.

12

LIBERAL *versus* CONSERVATIVE
1868–1885

*Two well-defined parties—Ireland the main bone of contention—
the Church of England "the Conservative party at prayer" and the
Liberals "the voice of the Nonconformist conscience"—Education
Act of 1870—the Conservatives become the champions of "the
trade", and the Liberals of temperance—the Conservatives become
an imperialistic party—growth of internationalism among Liberals
—the Eastern Question—Conservative returned to power—the Irish
members establish a separate organization—The Birmingham
"caucus" shows Liberals new ways to organize—Lord Randolph
Churchill a Conservative critic—the Queen's partiality for the
Conservatives—she invites Hartington to form a government—but
is advised to send for Gladstone—disappointment of the Radicals—
"Fourth party"—Salisbury and Northcote become joint leaders of
the Conservatives—Cecil family's dominance in the Conservative
party—Randolph Churchill takes up the cause of "Tory democracy"*

IN 1868 the party struggle in Great Britain emerged from the long
period of confusion that had followed Peel's break with his party.
For the next seventeen years it was a ding-dong struggle between
two strong and well-defined parties sharply differing on policy and
principle but with enough underlying unity to make the system
work. The parties became symbolized by their leaders; and the
struggle waged between Disraeli and Gladstone for eighteen years
before 1868 was now continued on a higher plane for another
thirteen until broken off by the death of one of the combatants. The
parties were closely matched, and could hope at any general election to undo the reverses of the previous one. The days of unbreak-
able Whig or Tory dominance were over, and the government of the
country rested in the hands of the Liberals from 1868 to 1874, of the
Conservatives from 1874 to 1880, of the Liberals from 1880 to 1885.
It was in many ways the hey-day of the party system, and when
W. S. Gilbert wrote the *libretto* for *Iolanthe* in 1882 he could make
Private Willis sing with general approval

I

I often think it's comical
  How Nature always does contrive
That every boy and every gal,
  That's born into the world alive,
Is either a little Liberal,
  Or else a little Conservative!

From 1866 this had been substantially true, but in the twenty years before 1866 the division of the country into Conservatives and Liberals had by no means been so clear, and if *Iolanthe* had been written four years later the truth of Private Willis's sentiments would not have been so self-evident.

It was Ireland that was to shatter the simplicity of the British party system, and immediately in 1868 Ireland became a bone of contention between the parties. As Gladstone leaned on his axe after being told to await the Queen's messenger at Hawarden, he announced, "My mission is to pacify Ireland",[1] but the Conservatives had a different idea of what pacification meant. The Irish question sharpened the historic difference between the parties in respect of the Church, and more than ever made the Conservatives the champions of the Church and the Liberals the mouthpiece of the Nonconformists. It was from this time that the Church of England came to be called "the Conservative party at prayer" and the Liberals the voice of "the Nonconformist conscience". Even before Disraeli's government fell Gladstone had removed a Nonconformist grievance by securing the passage of a bill for the abolition of the compulsory collection of church rates, and soon after forming his government he delighted Nonconformists and Roman Catholics by carrying the disestablishment of the Church of Ireland. The Education Act of 1870 also brought out into the open the different attitudes of the parties to the Church of England, but in establishing a dual system of state board schools alongside the Church schools Forster's bill made many concessions to Church opinion and displeased the Radical element in the Liberal party. From 1874 onwards the alliance of Conservatives with the Church and Liberals with dissent was still further heightened by the question of alcoholic refreshment. In the bitterness of defeat at the polls that year Gladstone said the Liberals had been "borne down in a torrent of gin and beer"; and Bright said that in Lancashire publicans and Irishmen had joined together, one for *delirium tremens* and the other for religious education.[2] Though these were grotesque exaggerations, the connexion of the Liberals with the Nonconformist temperance crusades and the link between the Conservatives and "the trade" dates from this time and was to be a feature of British politics until the Liberal decline. Gladstone's son, Herbert, on becoming member for Leeds, experienced the pressure for "local veto".[3]

Another major cleavage between the parties was opened in these years. As we have noticed, there had hitherto been little difference between Conservatives and Liberals in the matter of relations with the oversea territories of the Crown, but in his speech to the National Union at the Crystal Palace in 1872 Disraeli struck a new note that came to be called imperialism.[4]

"Self-government, in my opinion, when it was conceded, ought to have been conceded as part of a great policy of imperial consolidation. It ought to have been accompanied by an imperial tariff, by securities for the people of England for the enjoyment of the un-appropriated lands which belonged to the sovereign as their trustee, and by a military code which should have precisely defined the means and the responsibilities by which the colonies should be defended, and by which, if necessary, this country should call for aid from the colonies themselves. It ought, further, to have been accompanied by the institution of some representative council in the metropolis which would have brought the colonies into constant and continuous relations with the home government."

The reference was, of course, chiefly to the dominions peopled mainly by colonists of British stock—to Canada, Australia and New Zealand—for the great era of acquisition of tropical territories was still to come. Disraeli confessed that he had once thought disintegration inevitable, but opinion was rising against it, and the people had decided that the empire should not be destroyed.

"In my opinion no minister in this country will do his duty who neglects any opportunity of reconstructing as much as possible our colonial empire, and of responding to those distant sympathies which may become the source of incalculable strength and happiness to this land."

It was on this occasion that Disraeli laid down three aims for the Conservative party: "the maintenance of our institutions, the preservation of our empire, and the improvement of the condition of the people".

A clear difference between the parties began to emerge about this time on the treatment of foreign affairs. The settlement of the Alabama claims by arbitration in 1872 produced a sharp collision between the rising nationalism of the Tories and the growing internationalism of the Liberals. There were many Liberals who hoped to see, with Tennyson, "a parliament of men, the federation of the world"; and even the practical Gladstone hoped to establish "a tribunal of paramount authority" in "the general judgement of civilized mankind".[5] The difference over foreign affairs became acute from 1876 owing to the reopening of the Eastern Question. It began with risings against Turkish rule in the Balkans, followed by savage repression in Bulgaria. Several Balkan nations flew to arms, and the three imperial courts of Russia, Austria and Germany agreed upon a

"Berlin memorandum" imposing on the Turks certain reforms to be carried out under European supervision. Great Britain, France and Italy were invited to adhere to this memorandum. France and Italy did so, but Disraeli's government refused. This withdrawal from the Concert of Europe offended the international ideals of the Liberals; and as it implied support for the Turks it offended their championship of small nationalities. The Conservatives showed themselves true to their name and history by seeking to maintain the *status quo*, while Liberals once more showed their readiness in the cause of the oppressed nationalities to overthrow the existing order. It was not, however, simply on the grounds of preserving or changing the existing state of things that the Conservatives and Liberals took up their respective stands. In either case the question was how British interests could best be strengthened. Disraeli had formed the view that Russia was a menace to British interests and that her expansion should be contained. This meant support of Turkey. To Gladstone Turkey was the oppressor of Christian minorities, and he sought in the championship of these minorities a source of strength greater than alliance with an infidel power could provide.

These divergences between the parties on imperial and foreign affairs were accompanied by a differing emphasis on defence. The imperialist and nationalist policies to which Disraeli committed the Conservatives led from time to time to threats of war, as at the Lord Mayor's feast in 1876, and such menaces would have been empty without the means to support them. The Conservatives were gradually drawn into the position of being the party that supported the armed forces and large armaments; the extreme section became known as Jingoists, and their policy Jingoism, from the music-hall song current in 1878[6]—

We don't want to fight, but by Jingo if we do,
We've got the ships, we've got the men, we've got the money too.

Such an attitude was anathema to Gladstone on the grounds alike of ethics and of economy; he was supported by a small but strong and growing body of pacifist opinion in the Liberal party which favoured the abandonment of armed force as an instrument of policy, and the submission of all disputes to international arbitration. Such a Liberal was Henry Richard, member for Merthyr Tydfil since 1868 and secretary of the Peace Society.

The Ballot Act of 1872 played its part in the formation of the party system, for by making the vote secret it freed men from the compulsion to vote as their landlords, employers or customers dictated and so opened them to the persuasion of party propaganda. When the test of a general election came in 1874 the legislative achievements of the previous six years did not avail to prevent a great Conservative reaction. The Liberal majority of 112 in 1868 was converted into a Conservative majority of forty-eight in 1874. The Liberal rout is partly accounted for by Nonconformist and Roman Catholic dissatisfaction with the Education Act, and still more by the onset of a cyclical trade depression, but the superior organization of the Conservative party, to which Disraeli had been addressing himself zealously for the past six years, played its part "Disraeli", as Buckle wrote in his biography, "was thus responsible for starting the first great party machine, and he reaped the harvest in the victory of 1874."[7]

A momentous development in Irish politics made the Tory triumph even greater than the overall majority of forty-eight suggested. The Irish nationalist members had hitherto been reckoned a group among the Liberals, but from this date they became a separate party. This development was led by Isaac Butt,[a] who had first made his reputation as a Protestant Conservative lawyer and as such had been elected to Parliament in 1852. He held his seat until 1865, when his constant need of money took him back to the courts. His views had gradually become more Liberal, and the effect of disestablishment was to drive him into alliance with the nationalists. In 1870 he started the home rule movement in a speech demanding an Irish Parliament for local affairs, and the following year he was once more returned to Parliament. There he was soon recognized as the leader of the Irish nationalists, whose numbers were swelled to fifty-nine in 1874 by the new secret ballots. These fifty-nine home rulers were reckoned as Liberals in computing the Conservative majority, but they established a separate parliamentary organization, and Gladstone wrote that "the weight of the home rulers has clearly told more in favour of the [Conservative] ministry than of the opposition; and the Liberal party would have been stronger, not weaker, had the entire body been systematically absent".[8] From Gladstone's point of view the situation was much worsened in 1875 when Charles Stewart Parnell[b] was elected for Meath. A Protestant landowner of English extraction, cold in his temperament and ill at ease in the company of his fellow men, he would have been discerned by few as the leader of the Irish Nationalist party, but he quickly ousted Butt, and from 1877 induced the Irish members to follow a policy of systematic obstruction in the Commons. Under his leadership the Irish members began to act together as a body and always on the opposition side.[c] This is the origin of the saying that the Irish are "agin the government".

After the Liberal defeat at the polls in 1874 Gladstone, exasperated by the differences in the party, and desiring "an interval between Parliament and the grave", resigned the leadership and his mantle fell on Hartington. He felt himself "to be in some measure out of touch with some of the tendencies of the Liberal party, especially in religious matters",[9] and found additional reasons in his inability to carry all his followers with him in the matters of public economy and education. Retaining his seat in the House of Commons, he listened with anger while Disraeli, supporting Tait's Public Worship Regulation Bill, cheerfully attacked "the mass in masquerade",[10] and he devoted himself to two pamphlets on the newly proclaimed dogma of papal infallibility which endeared him still more to the Nonconformists but widened the gap between him and the Irish members.

The Liberals reacted to the defeat of 1874 as the Conservatives had reacted to the defeat of 1868, and as every defeated party has acted since, by overhauling their organization. It was at Birmingham, ever the leading Radical centre, that a new way to organize parties and win elections was devised by the Liberals.[11]

The Birmingham Liberal Association had been founded in 1865, and its secretary, William Harris, set out to defeat the intentions of the clause in the Reform Bill of 1867 forbidding an elector to cast more than two votes in a three-member constituency. The object, it will be recalled, was to ensure fair representation of minorities, but it occurred to Harris that by a proper organization of Liberal voters all three seats in Birmingham could be secured for Liberal candidates. His plan was that all the Liberals in a ward or polling district should choose delegates to a committee, and that this committee should select the candidates and settle the tactics of the election. As the committee was democratically elected, he argued, it was reasonable to expect that both candidates and electors should abide by its decisions. When the general election of 1868 approached, the three Liberal candidates, Bright, Dixon and Muntz, were assigned to the wards two by two, and Liberal voters in a ward were instructed to vote for the assigned candidates and not for the third one. "Vote as you are told" was the order that went out; it shocked Conservatives, and even offended Radicals who remembered the glorious days of 1832, but it achieved its purpose. Birmingham returned three Liberals, and was the only constituency to defeat the minority clause of 1867.

Under the Education Act of 1870 a cumulative system of voting for school boards had been adopted, that is to say, each elector was given fifteen votes which he could distribute among the candidates as he pleased, even giving them all to one if he wished; this was known as "plumping". When the first elections took place, Harris tried to organize the Liberal votes in favour of Liberal candidates, but the complexity defeated him, and only six seats were secured.

The association nearly collapsed, but in 1873 two men who saw the tremendous potency of Harris's ideas entered upon the scene and made the Birmingham Liberal Association so formidable that it quickly became a model for many other Liberal associations and in the fullness of time set a pattern for all constituency associations in all the major parties in all parts of the country. One of the two men was Francis Schnadhorst, a draper, who was the secretary of the Central Nonconformist Committee set up in Birmingham to oppose Church influence in education; he became secretary of the Birmingham Liberal Association in 1873. The other was Joseph Chamberlain,[d] a screw manufacturer, Unitarian in religion and a Radical in politics, with a reputation for republicanism. He had been a member of the Liberal Association from its formation, but had previously given most of his energies to the National Education League formed to campaign for free, compulsory and secular education. The League had made a point of putting up a candidate at every by-election in which the Liberal candidate would not give a pledge to support their wishes; it was an innovation in British politics that cost Gladstone's government some twenty seats. In 1873 Chamberlain became mayor of Birmingham, but his republicanism did not prevent him from welcoming the Prince and Princess of Wales to the city the following year. When Dixon resigned one of the city seats in Parliament in 1876 Chamberlain was returned unopposed in his place.

As organized by Schnadhorst and Chamberlain, the Birmingham Liberal Association was based upon the ward. Any resident, whether an elector or not, was allowed to join the ward branch of the association so long as he accepted its principles; there was a nominal subscription of a shilling a year, but it was not always extracted. At a public meeting the ward members elected a ward committee of any size they pleased, and the ward committee could co-opt other members to an unlimited extent. The chairman and secretary of each ward committee were *ex officio* members of an executive committee for the whole city, and each ward committee in public meeting also sent three members to the executive committee; as there were sixteen wards, this provided eighty members, and as the eighty were allowed to co-opt another thirty this gave the executive committee a membership of 110. There was also a larger deliberative body called the general committee made up of the 110 members of the executive committee together with thirty members elected to each of the sixteen wards, or 480, so that the total membership of the general committee was 590; for this reason the general committee was usually known as the Six Hundred. Finally the Six Hundred elected four persons to join seven persons nominated by the executive committee as a committee of management. Questions of policy were in principle settled and candidates selected by the Six Hundred, and it was a rule of the association that if the Six Hundred did not select an applicant as a candidate he must submit to its decision.

Superficially this was a democratic organization in which every office-holder and committee member owed his position directly or indirectly to election by the ward members. On closer examination and in practice the democracy was a façade behind which a tight little oligarchy firmly controlled the Birmingham Liberals. Schnadhorst and Chamberlain had taken ample measures to insure themselves against any rash expression of the popular will. Against eighty elected members of the executive committee there were no fewer than thirty co-opted members, and we may feel certain that the more energetic and regular elected members were able to ensure that the co-opted thirty conformed to their own pattern. The executive committee in turn provided no fewer than seven of the eleven members of the committee of management. It is small wonder that critics, with Venetian memories, dubbed it "The Council of Ten". As if this were not enough Chamberlain and Schnadhorst made a practice of sending their friends from ward meeting to ward meeting to ensure the election of the right candidates. Though their firm control of the machine was little disguised, the many meetings held to discuss policy did play a valuable part in the political education of the city.

These tactics gave the Liberals a virtual monopoly of the municipal as well as the parliamentary representation of Birmingham. This was the first entry of party in any systematic way into municipal politics, and the Conservatives were reduced to an impotent minority in the town council. Schnadhorst and Chamberlain then became missionaries for the Birmingham plan in other great towns, many of them still smarting from the electoral reverses of 1874. The reopening of the Eastern Question helped their missionary zeal by giving them a cause for which to fight, and they exploited it to the full.

In 1877 Schnadhorst and Chamberlain went a step farther by inviting all Liberal associations of a representational character to send delegates to a conference at Birmingham with a view to forming a federation. About a hundred accepted, and their delegates were invited by Chamberlain to set up a federation that would be a truly Liberal Parliament outside the imperial legislature. After Harris had also spoken of the need for the rank and file of Liberals to take the initiative in the choice alike of men and of measures, some fears were expressed lest the independence of the constituency associations should be threatened, and doubts were expressed about admitting all Liberals whether they paid a subscription or not, but in the end a decision to set up a National Federation of Liberal Associations was taken. Soon it came to be called more concisely the Liberal National Association.

The organizers had the good fortune to be able to persuade Gladstone to speak at their inaugural meeting in Birmingham, when eighty-three associations were represented. He could do so because he was technically a private member of Parliament, and he wel-

comed the platform offered as he was already filled with a missionary zeal against the Turks and their Tory allies. His support was of
the utmost importance, for his private status could not conceal the
fact that he was still the greatest and most influential personage in
the Liberal party. Before some 25,000 persons, Gladstone com-
mended the principle of free popular choice on which the federation
was based; and was soon whipping his audience into a frenzy on the
subject of Bulgarian atrocities.

Inevitably Chamberlain became president, Harris vice-president
and Schnadhorst secretary of the new federation. The headquarters
was kept in Birmingham. Only fifty-seven borough associations
actually became members of the federation at the outset, but the
zeal of its organizers, the blessing of Gladstone, and the success of
the Birmingham plan soon won many new members. The founders
described their aims in the following words:[12]

"The essential feature of the proposed federation is the principle
which must henceforth govern the action of Liberals as a political
party—namely, the direct participation of all members of the party
in the direction of its policy, and in the selection of those particular
measures of reform and of progress to which priority shall be given.
This object can be secured only by the organization of the party
upon a representative basis: that is, by popularly elected committees of local associations, and by the union of such local associations, by means of their freely chosen representatives, in a general
federation."

As the federation grew in size and influence, the Birmingham
model tended to be copied by new associations and to influence the
older ones. A large general committee—the Six Hundred at Manchester, and so on—preserved the appearance of democracy and
smaller executive management committees kept the realities of
power. There was nothing new in the idea of a national grouping of
associations, for the Conservatives had possessed this in the National
Union since 1867. What was new was the ruthless efficiency of the
Birmingham model based on the centralization of control under the
façade of a representative character. This made the National Union
seem a very amateur organization. The Conservatives retorted by
dubbing it "the Birmingham caucus". Like other words we have met
in the vocabulary of British party politics, the term caucus was
borrowed from overseas as a term of abuse. In the United States it
had for some time been used, according to the *Oxford English Dictionary*, to indicate—"A private or preliminary meeting of members
of a political party, to select candidates for office, or to concert
measures for furthering party interests; a meeting of wirepullers." In
England it was now used pejoratively by Disraeli and his friends to
imply that the National Liberal Federation, and its constituent
associations, were trying to manipulate elections and dictate to

constituencies. It was in vain. Schnadhorst and Chamberlain had initiated something to which even the Conservatives would be bound to pay the flattery of imitation.

It was not only Conservatives who looked askance at the "caucus". There were many Liberals who were deeply suspicious of the innovation, and none more so than W. E. Forster, who had sat for Bradford since 1861. He would have preferred that no one should stand between a member or candidate and the electors, but was persuaded in 1868 to accept a joint electoral committee with Edward Myall, who was the chief opponent in the House of Commons of his Education Bill. When he arrived in Bradford for the 1874 election he found his previous committee would not serve again, on account of Nonconformist hostility to the Education Bill, but with Whig and Tory support he was elected above the two official Liberal candidates. The Liberal Association was thereupon reorganized in accordance with Birmingham ideas, and Forster was asked for an assurance that before standing again he would submit his name to the association and abide by its decision. This he refused to do. "I cannot forget," he said, "that I am member for the borough, and I cannot think it right to make myself the nominee or delegate of any association within the constituency, however important that organization, or however I may agree with it in political opinion."[13] The association capitulated, and Forster sat for Bradford until his death in 1886.

While Schnadhorst and Chamberlain were organizing the "caucus", the Conservatives were meanwhile having more than a little trouble in their own ranks. Lord Randolph Churchill had been elected to Parliament in 1874, but made no mark until in 1878 he suddenly blossomed forth as a savage critic of his own front bench. The chief object of his invective was Sclater-Booth, later Lord Basing, the President of the Local Government Board, whose County Government Bill he denounced as "this crowning desertion of Tory principles, this supreme violation of political honesty";[14] but he did not spare Sir Stafford Northcote, who had become the Conservative leader in the Commons.

The Earl of Beaconsfield, as Disraeli became in 1876 when he left the Commons for the Lords, attributed the Conservative defeat in 1880 to the social distress arising from failure of the crops and "the new foreign political organization",[15] by which he meant the National Liberal Federation. It played a part, but as only sixty-seven English and Welsh borough associations were then affiliated to the federation, and these secured the return of only sixty members, it could not be a decisive part. Agricultural distress also played its part, though due not so much to the failure of the crops as the importation of cheap cereals from the hitherto virgin lands of North America. A third reason was the return of Gladstone to active politics and his success in turning a political campaign into a crusade for righteousness.[e] On a large packet of notes made in 1876 on "Future retribution" he noted later, "From this I was called away to write on Bulgaria", and he does not mince his words:[16]

"Let the Turks now carry away their abuses in the only possible manner, namely by carrying off themselves. Their Zaptiehs and their Mudirs, their Bimbashis and their Yuzbachis, their Kaimakams and their Pashas, one and all, bag and baggage, shall I hope clear out from the province they have desolated and profaned."

To Beaconsfield in the office of Prime Minister such language was the vapouring of "a sophistical rhetorician, inebriated with the exuberance of his own verbosity".[17] The danger of war was averted at the Congress of Berlin, from which Beaconsfield claimed to have brought back "peace with honour";[18] but the occupation of Cyprus, after a secret treaty with Turkey, the annexation of the Transvaal and war with the Afghans marked a new policy of imperial expansion to which Beaconsfield now committed the Conservative party. The rift between the parties was growing deeper.

Gladstone, who had sought the suffrages of Greenwich in 1868 in a justified apprehension that he would lose South-west Lancashire, had decided not to stand again for the southern seat, and in 1879 accepted an invitation to contest the county seat of Midlothian, then held by the Tory Lord Dalkeith, son of the Duke of Buccleuch who had been his colleague in Peel's Cabinet in 1845. He then embarked upon a speaking tour in his new constituency which must rank among the greatest feats in the history of oratory. He denounced every aspect of government policy in terms of unmeasured indignation, and his speeches were fully reported in the national press and reprinted as pamphlets. Queen Victoria was disturbed. No previous Prime Minister had stumped the country in this way, and though he was technically a private person the possibility that he might again be asked to lead a victorious party was not to be ruled out. Gladstone was not unduly perturbed, and though not technically a party leader, and though the country was not yet in an election campaign, and though he confined himself to his own constituency, he foreshadowed the party leader's election tour. The Queen's displeasure marked a new phase in their relationship. She had already succumbed to the flattery of Beaconsfield, who admitted that he laid it on with a trowel and who added new dominions to her empire, and her future relations with Gladstone, who addressed her like a public meeting, were to be cold and hostile. The Queen who had begun as the creature of the Whigs became a partisan of the Tories; and as happened in the reigns of the Georges the Prince of Wales became the friend of the opposition.[f] There was this difference that the partisanship was concealed from the public eye, and as the Sovereign had now surrendered almost all powers it made little difference to the course of events, though as painful to the one as it was gratifying to the other of the party chiefs involved.

Beaconsfield asked for a dissolution of Parliament in the spring of 1880 as it was nearing the end of its life. His election address had the form of a letter to the Lord Lieutenant of Ireland. As Beaconsfield waited at Hatfield, lent to him in the absence of its owner, news came in very different from what he had expected. Instead of being confirmed in power, he found the new House of Commons to be composed of 347 Liberals, 240 Conservatives and sixty-five Irish Nationalists, so that the Liberals had a majority of forty-two over all others combined. He took the result with composure, and Gladstone noted that "the downfall of Beaconsfieldism is like the vanishing of some vast magnificent castle in an Italian romance".[19] Beaconsfield resigned without waiting for defeat in Parliament—this was no longer considered constitutionally necessary—and the question immediately arose, for whom should the Queen send? Gladstone thought she should have sent for Granville, as the leader of the party, but her choice fell on Hartington, in accordance with the advice she had received from the outgoing Prime Minister. Hartington advised her to transfer the commission to Gladstone, without whom no Liberal government could be formed and who could not be expected to serve in a subordinate position. As Gladstone's biographer later wrote, "No minister, not Pitt in 1784, nor Grey in 1831, nor Peel ten years later, nor Palmerston in 1855, was ever summoned by more direct and personal acclaim."[20] The Queen eventually sent for Gladstone and gave him the commission. She tried to influence his nomination for the War Office, but did not press him; the doctrine that the leader of the dominant party must be allowed to choose his Cabinet colleagues could no longer be gainsaid.

Gladstone had assured himself of the support of Granville (for the Foreign Office) and Hartington (for India) before going to Windsor, and the new generation of radicals noticed with some concern that the great posts were all going to patrician Whigs. He behaved, says Morley, as though he were a Grey or a Russell, and in effect told the Radicals that they must be content to have obtained him as Prime Minister instead of Hartingdon. This was not at all to their relish, and Gladstone agreed to give office to one of their number, Sir Charles Dilke, but to his amazement Dilke said he would serve only if either he or Chamberlain were given a seat in the Cabinet. After meditating on this unprecedented demand, Gladstone chose Chamberlain for the Board of Trade; Dilke became Under-Secretary for Foreign Affairs.

The clarity of the two-party struggle in the new Parliament was blurred, and its proceedings greatly enlivened, by two groups following the leadership of Parnell and Churchill.

Of the sixty-five Irish Nationalist members, thirty-five accepted Parnell's leadership, and at his dictation adopted a policy of systematic obstruction of business in the house. This was the parliamentary reflexion of the policy of "boycott" and "moonlighting" followed in Ireland as the result of an alliance between Parnell and the Land League set up by Michael Davitt, a Fenian ex-prisoner. Violence in Ireland led to a Coercion Bill, which Parnell and his followers set out to prevent passing into law. Early in 1881 they kept the debate going for forty-one hours, until Speaker Brand put the question on his own responsibility though not strictly entitled to do so by the rules of the house. Before the year was out Parnell and other leaders of the Land League were lodged in Kilmainham gaol, but he was released under the so-called Kilmainham treaty with Gladstone the following year, and his ability to dictate terms to Gladstone was to prove before many years were out a major disruptive element in the British party system.

In the new Parliament the attempt of Charles Bradlaugh, a professed atheist, first to be allowed to affirm and, when this was refused, to take his seat after repeating words which he described as "sounds conveying no clear and definite meaning", raised a controversy which reverberated throughout the whole life of that Parliament and paralysed parliamentary action whenever it recurred. It was Sir Henry Drummond Wolff who led the opposition to Bradlaugh; he was supported by John Gorst, and at a later stage by Lord Randolph Churchill. The three men discovered an affinity, or rather an identity of interest, that extended beyond Bradlaugh; and they were joined, more sporadically, by Arthur James Balfour, nephew of Salisbury. They harried Gladstone—"the Moloch of Midlothian" as Churchill called him—and other occupants of the Treasury bench—but did not shrink from severely criticizing their own front bench, especially what they regarded as the ineffective leadership of Northcote. They were nicknamed the "Fourth party",[21] because a member who spoke of the *two* parties prompted Parnell to call out "three" and Churchill in turn to make it "four". They were not, of course, a party in the formal sense but what would today be called a ginger group. There was no question of a leader or a common policy; but it was agreed that, whenever one was attacked, the others should come to his defence; and "upon these conditions", Churchill's son wrote, there "was created a parliamentary group which proved, in proportion to its members, the most formidable and effective force for the purposes of opposition in the history of the House of Commons". Before long it became apparent that Churchill was seeking to secure the leadership of the Conservative party for himself, and he attempted to make the National Union the base for his attempt to storm the citadel of power.

Gorst had his own reasons for discontent. He had given up the oversight of the Central Office in 1877 over a disagreement with the new chief whip, Sir William Hart Dyke, who wished to manage all the extra-parliamentary activities of the party from the whips' office (as the Liberals still did). After defeat in 1880 there was the usual demand for an inquest on organization, and Beaconsfield presided over a meeting held for that purpose at Bridgewater House. A committee drawn chiefly from the Carlton Club was set up under the chairmanship of W. H. Smith to make recommendations, Gorst returned to the Central Office and Rowland Winn became chief whip. W. H. Smith's committee became a permanent Central Committee with charge of all extra-parliamentary work, Gorst being its executive officer, and the whips were confined to their parliamentary duties. It was not possible to have two kings in the Central Office any more than in Brentford, and in 1882 both Smith and Gorst resigned. Smith's successor was Edward Stanhope, but the "Fourth party" liked him even less than Smith.

When Beaconsfield died in 1881 Salisbury had taken his place as Conservative leader in the Lords. Northcote was already leader in the Commons, and as neither was disposed to give way to the other they were regarded as joint leaders of the Conservative party. The accession of Salisbury to this position marked the opening of a new era of Cecil dominance in the Conservative party, though no one could have foreseen at the time that Salisbury would be Prime Minister from 1886 to 1902, except for a few years, and would be succeeded by his nephew, Balfour, especially as Balfour was then playing about with the "Fourth party", and, as befitted the apologist for philosophic doubt, was showing only a languid interest in politics. After Balfour, Salisbury's sons were to play no inglorious part in the political life of the country, and the Conservative party was sometimes dubbed "the Hotel Cecil".[22] This rise of the Cecils had the consequence of re-establishing the pre-eminence in the Conservative party of the landed aristocracy linked with the Church, from which Peel, the merchant's son, and Disraeli, the "mystery man" and novelist, had temporarily diverted it—though Disraeli had done his best at Hughenden to make himself look like a landed proprietor.

This long period of Cecilian dominance was still in the future in 1883 when Churchill considered who was fit to wear the mantle of Beaconsfield and came to the conclusion that there was none more fitted than himself.[23] The philosophy that he evolved to meet the needs of the hour he called "Tory democracy",[24] and the instruments he employed were two, the new Primrose League and the old National Union.

Churchill shared the faith of the author of Sybil and the 1867

Reform Act in the inherent Toryism of the working classes. The defiant revival of the name Tory recalled the voice that harried Peel, and "Tory democracy" echoed "Young England"; but the doctrine sounded all the more thrilling to working-class ears when it came from the scion of a ducal house. The ancient slogan, *Vox populi, vox Dei*, Churchill told a Blackpool audience, was for the Whigs only sounding brass and for the Radicals a fetish, but for the Tories a living faith and an immortal truth. There were among Conservatives, he said on another occasion, people who still did not understand that the Tory party could no longer be identified with a small and narrow class of landed proprietors, but must seek its strength in the great towns and rural districts.[25]

The Primrose League was brought into existence in 1883. In sending a primrose wreath to Beaconsfield's funeral the Queen had affixed a card with the words "His favourite flowers, from Osborne, a tribute of affection from Queen Victoria". There is no real reason to think that he had any special liking for primroses, though he did make Lord St. Jerome in *Lothair* commend them as a capital salad; but on the strength of the belief Sir George Birdwood wrote to *The Times* suggesting that primroses should be worn on the anniversary of his death, and when Wolff found all his friends wearing primroses on 19th April 1883 for the unveiling of the statue he conceived the idea of starting a Primrose League. Churchill and Gorst took up the idea with enthusiasm. Every member had to declare on his honour and faith that he would devote his best ability "to the maintenance of religion, of the estates of the realm, and of the imperial ascendancy of the British Empire". The members were given picturesque medieval names, and full play was made with the snobbish appeal of great ladies within its ranks. In the first year there were 747 knights, 153 dames and fifty-seven associates enrolled in forty-six habitations, and by 1891 there were over a million members. The League satisfied the deep-seated need of people for colour and ritual in their lives, and reflected the rise in imperial feeling towards the close of the century.[26]

The older instrument of Churchill's ambition was the National Union. Gorst was a vice-president, Wolff a member of its Central Council from its foundation and Churchill became one by co-option in 1882. In the following year the annual conference was due to be held in Birmingham, for which city Churchill had already announced his candidature. With the support of his friends he resolved to become chairman of the Central Council and to win for the Central Council from the Central Committee[27] the control of the party's organization and finances. He gave his reasons with great frankness to the conference at Birmingham:[28]

"I wish to see the control and guidance of the organization of the Tory party transferred from a self-elected body to an annually

elected body. I wish to see the management of the financial resources of our party transferred from an irresponsible body to a
responsible body. I say that this so-called Central Committee is an
irresponsible and self-elected body and that the Council of the
National Union is a responsible and an annually elected body, and I
wish the control of the party organization to be in the hands of the
National Union and taken out of the hands of the Central Committee. There is no instance in history of power, placed in the hands
of a self-constituted and irresponsible body, being used otherwise
than unwisely at first and corruptly at last . . . I should like all
the finances of the Tory party to be open for inspection for anyone who may wish to look at them, be he friend or foe. Where
you allow secret expenditure you will certainly have corrupt
expenditure."

Possibly through advertising their intentions too much in advance
the "Fourth party" did not succeed in packing the Council with
their nominees, but when additional members were co-opted they
had enough to secure the appointment of an organization committee with Churchill as chairman of it. This broke with a convention that the chairman of the Council—then Lord Percy—was
chairman of any committee. Percy resigned, and Churchill was
elected in his place. There followed a complicated correspondence
with the duumvirate, in the course of which Salisbury gave an
anodyne description of the National Union. After noting the complaint that the Central Council "had not the opportunity of con-
curring largely enough in the practical organization of the party" he
continued: [29]

"It appears to us that that organization is, and must remain, in all
its essential features local. But there is still much work which a
central body like the Council of the National Union can perform
with great advantage to the party. It is the representative of many
associations on whom, in their respective constituencies, the work
of the party greatly depends. It can superintend and stimulate their
exertions; furnish them with advice, and in some measure with
funds; provide them with lectures; aid them in the improvement and
the development of the local press; and help them in perfecting the
machinery by which the registration is conducted and the arrangements for providing volunteer agency at election times. It will have
special opportunity of pressing upon the local associations which it
represents the paramount duty of selecting, in time, the candidates
who are to come forward at the dissolution."

Churchill and his associates wickedly took this harmless letter to
be a charter conferring on the National Union almost all the powers
they wanted, and drafted a report to the Council in this sense. Salisbury protested that he and Northcote had no thought of diminishing
the powers of the Central Committee, but the report was never-

theless presented and adopted. Thereupon Churchill received a letter telling him that the National Union must leave the premises that it shared with the Central Committee. On behalf of the organization committee Churchill sent to Salisbury a strong letter, subsequently published, complaining of "the powerful and secret influences" which might at last "be effectual in reducing the National Union to its former make-believe and impotent condition".[30] He resigned the chairmanship of the Central Council and meditated over his candidature, but there were so many manifestations of sympathy for him among the rank and file that the leaders thought it best to compromise; nor was Churchill, the trial of strength ended in his favour, averse from doing so. At the 1884 conference of the National Union in Sheffield twenty-two of his thirty candidates were elected with himself at the head of the poll. Lord Percy with all the official backing of the party behind him secured the election of only eighteen out of his thirty-six nominations. Salisbury and Churchill soon afterwards reached an amicable agreement. The Central Committee was abolished, but Churchill made no effort to secure for the National Union anything more than a little extra money. The Primrose League was formally confirmed as an ancillary organization of the party and the "Fourth party" dissolved into the mists of history. Though nothing was put on paper, or perhaps even expressed in words, it emerged clearly that Salisbury would be the next Conservative Prime Minister and that Churchill rather than Northcote would be his chief lieutenant;[31] and having secured his place in the succession, Churchill began to see virtues in the Central Office and the whips' organization that he had not previously suspected.

Sir Michael Hicks Beach became chairman of the National Union, and under his soothing guidance it ceased to give any more trouble to the leaders. Certain reforms were carried out. Until 1884 the Central Council had consisted of twenty-four elected and twelve co-opted members; thereafter all thirty-six were elected. In 1885 it was decided that every Conservative association "should be affiliated without the need of any formal action". In 1886 a new set of rules was adopted and ten provincial unions each with a paid secretary were created. The most important changes were, however, two personal appointments. In 1885 Aretas Akers-Douglas was appointed chief whip and Richard W. E. Middleton on his recommendation was made principal agent. Akers-Douglas, then only thirty-three, sat for East Kent, and Captain Middleton, as he was always known, had been for two years Conservative agent in West Kent. They had the benevolent approval of the Marquess of Abergavenny, whose seat was just outside the county, and became known as "the Kentish gang". For the next ten years they worked together in a brilliant partnership which is still looked upon in Conservative circles as the

K

golden age of party organization. Middleton was responsible for some notable innovations such as the Association of Conservative Clubs and the training of party agents, but his chief achievement was to see that his party's principles were convincingly presented to the voters at successive general elections.

13

THE LIBERAL SPLIT
1886

Gladstone's Reform Bill of 1884—"delicate and novel communications"—the bill increases the electorate to five millions—the Irish vote with the Conservatives—Salisbury forms a government based on the abandonment of coercion—the general election of 1885— Conservatives and Parnellites exactly equal Liberals—Chamberlain turns against home rule—to which Hartington is already averse— the "Hawarden kite" reveals Gladstone's acceptance of home rule—the Conservative government reverts to coercion—and is turned out by the Liberals and Irish—Gladstone forms a government pledged to examine the practicability of a Dublin Parliament—Hartington and other Whigs decline to join—the first Home Rule Bill—Chamberlain and Trevelyan resign—ninety-three Liberals vote with the Conservatives against the bill—after the general election the Conservatives are the strongest single party

IT was inevitable that the franchise conferred upon borough householders in 1867 should sooner or later be extended to householders in the counties, and Gladstone took the necessary steps in 1884. That a Conservative government should give the vote to urban and a Liberal to rural householders is a reversal of rôles to which we are becoming accustomed. Though the extension was inevitable, and any opinions of the unfitness of agricultural labourers—at any rate, of English agricultural labourers—were left unspoken, the bill soon ran into difficulties because the Conservatives feared electoral massacre unless the enlargement of the franchise was accompanied by a redistribution of seats. Gladstone, who made it a principle of life to deal with one thing at a time, and was not wholly averse to the result the Conservatives feared, wished to get the franchise settled before dealing with redistribution. The bill passed the Commons by large majorities, but was in effect rejected by the Lords. Gladstone asked the people of Edinburgh[1] to note that of the twelve Parliaments in which he had sat since the Reform Act of 1832 ten had had Liberal majorities, and another—that of 1841-7—had put out the

Conservative government of Sir Robert Peel and supported till it was dissolved the Liberal government of Lord John Russell. Since 1832 there had been only one Tory House of Commons, that of 1874–80, but the House of Lords had always been on the side of the one against the ten. Others used stronger language, and Morley said it was time to "mend or end" the House of Lords. The fact that the struggle between Lords and Commons was deferred was due to the Queen, who suggested that it would be a means of arriving at some understanding if the leaders of the parties in both houses could exchange their views personally. Gladstone had a talk with North-cote at the house of a friend, and a few days later invited Salisbury and Northcote to discuss the deadlock over tea in Downing Street. Noting that "no precedent could be found in our political or party history for the discussion of a measure before its introduction be-tween the leaders of the two sides", Morley observed that Salisbury "proved to be entirely devoid of respect for tradition", while Glad-stone "declared himself to be a strong conservative in comparison". Within a fortnight Gladstone was able to report to the Queen that "the delicate and novel communications" between the leaders had been successfully terminated.[2] There was a brief dispute over the question whether the franchise should be extended to Ireland, but the hesitations were swept aside by Gladstone in a torrent of oratory. Both Commons and Lords passed the franchise bill before the end of the year. The Representation of the People Act, 1884, laid down that "a uniform household franchise and a uniform lodger franchise at elections shall be established in all counties and boroughs throughout the United Kingdom", and that persons who, though otherwise qualified, were neither tenants nor £10 lodgers should have the vote equally with them. It was the virtual com-pletion of the democratic process so far as males were concerned, and it added about two million persons to the existing electorate of three millions. It was the most substantial enlargement of the elec-torate made in any of the three Reform Bills to that date, and natur-ally the need and scope for party organization were correspondingly widened. The accompanying redistribution bill was passed in 1885. It provided that boroughs with a population of less than 15,000 should be disfranchised, and that boroughs with less than 50,000 inhabitants should have only one member. By these provisions and a few minor changes 162 seats were made available for redistribution, and another six were added for England and twelve for Scotland. The boundaries of constituencies were drawn for parliamentary approval by a Royal Commission. Except for a few two-member boroughs, the principle of single-member constituencies was adopted. The net result was an approximation to the principle that each member of the House of Commons should represent the same number of electors, roughly 50,000, but without mathematical exactness in order to respect ancient divisions such as county boundaries.

The manner in which the Representation of the People Act, 1884, and the Redistribution Act, 1885, were obtained is a good example of the working of the party system at its best. The system presupposes an underlying unity, a readiness to put the national interest before party advantage, and a willingness to compromise for that purpose. Gladstone's acceptance of these principles was soon demonstrated. The death of Gordon at Khartoum and the defeat of Colley at Majuba had gravely lowered the standing of ministers in the country and in Parliament. Their majority in the motion of confidence following Majuba was only fourteen. It seemed to the Tory managers that only one more heave was needed to get the Liberals out, and Ireland, where the Crimes Act was soon due to expire, furnished the opportunity. In a speech at the St. Stephen's Club Churchill urged that the Tories should be careful not to be committed to any act or policy which would unnecessarily wound or injure the feelings of their brothers on the other side of St. George's channel; and he told Parnell that if the Tories took office, and he was a member of their government, he would not consent to renew the Crimes Act. "In that case," Parnell replied, "you will have the Irish vote at the elections."[3] The Irish leader had already shown his consciousness of the power that he wielded in the English constituencies through the large Irish immigration. "Beyond a shadow of doubt," he had told a meeting in the Rotunda at Dublin,[4] "it will be for the Irish people in England—separately isolated as they are—and for your independent Irish members, to determine at the next general election whether a Tory or a Liberal English ministry shall rule England. This is a great force and a great power. If we cannot rule ourselves, we can at least cause them to be ruled as we choose." It is probable that the Irish vote would in any case have been thrown on the side of the Tories, for it was then generally expected that the extension of the franchise would benefit the Liberals, and it was in the interest of the Irish to support the weaker of the two great parties so as to ensure that neither gained an absolute majority. The readiness of the Tories to abandon coercion clinched the argument for so doing. It has been disputed whether emissaries did or did not pass between Salisbury and the Nationalists, but no formal compact was needed, only an ability to read the signs of the times. The cabinet was itself seriously divided on the necessity of renewing the Crimes Act, and some members were prepared to court defeat with a view to throwing the responsibility on to other shoulders. A skilfully devised amendment to the Finance Bill condemning the proposed increase of the beer and spirit duties in the absence of a corresponding increase in the duties on wine provided an issue on which much defection was to be expected in the government ranks and on which the Irish could be expected to vote with the opposition. While Parnell led his followers into the same lobby as the Tories, the chief Liberal whip, Lord Richard Grosvenor, made no great efforts to get the Liberals into the other lobby, and the government were defeated by twelve votes. The majority included 219 Tories and thirty-nine Nationalists; but six Liberals voted against their own government and no fewer than seventy-six abstained. Noting in his diary, "This is a considerable event",[5] Gladstone interrupted his reading of Edersheim on the Old Testament to tender the government's resignation. The Queen was surprised that defeat on such an issue should be treated as a vital question, but Gladstone well understood that more was involved than the tax on beer. His biographer perceptively noted:[6]

"The defeat of the Gladstone government was the first success of a combination between Tories and Irish, that proved of cardinal importance to policies and parties for several critical months to come. By a coincidence that cut too deep to be mere accident, divisions in the Gladstone cabinet found their counterpart in insurrection among the Tory opposition. The same general forces of the hour, working through the energy, ambition and initiative of individuals, produced the same effect in each of the two parties; the radical programme of Mr. Chamberlain was matched by the Tory democracy of Lord Randolph Churchill; each saw that the final transfer of power from the ten-pound householder to artisans and labourers would rouse new social demands; each was aware that Ireland was the electoral pivot of the day, and while one of them was wrestling with those whom he stigmatized as Whigs, the other by his dexterity and resolution overthrew his leaders as 'the old gang'."

A dissolution was impossible until the Redistribution Act should take effect, and Salisbury was reluctant to take office without assurances of parliamentary goodwill that Gladstone was unwilling to give; he was also embarrassed by Churchill's refusal to serve if Northcote was given the leadership of the House of Commons, a dilemma which Northcote eventually solved by agreeing to go to the upper house as Earl of Iddesleigh. After a long period of delicate negotiations Salisbury was able to announce a "ministry of caretakers", with Iddesleigh as First Lord of the Treasury and Churchill as Secretary of State for India. The Lord Lieutenant, Carnarvon, himself announced the government's Irish policy, and his words were taken to mean the abandonment of coercion and reliance upon the ordinary law. Many Tories in the ranks of the party were alarmed, and on the other side Chamberlain declared that "a strategic movement of that kind, executed in opposition to the notorious convictions of the men who effected it, carried out for party purposes and party purposes alone, is the most flagrant in-

stance of political dishonesty this country has ever known". Hartington said the conduct of the government had dealt a heavy blow
"both at political morality and at the cause of order in Ireland".[7]
More remarkable still, the Lord Lieutenant invited Parnell to meet
him in a London drawing-room and left the Irish leader with the
impression that he was willing to see a separate legislature conferred
upon Ireland. Fortified by this belief, and assured that the number of
his followers must greatly increase as a result of the Reform bills
passed, Parnell stepped up his demands. Until that time he had been
content to ask for a central administrative council in Dublin; from
that time he declared that the sole work of himself and his friends
must be the restoration of a national Parliament.

We have reached a point of critical change in the British party
system. The general election took place on the new register and for
the newly defined constituencies in the autumn of 1885. Parnell's
triumph in Ireland was complete, and he returned at the head of
eighty-six Home Rulers. There were 335 Liberals and 249 Conservatives, so that the combined forces of the Conservatives and Parnellites exactly equalled those of the Liberals. This was a blow to Gladstone, who had warned the electors of Midlothian, "It will be a vital
danger to the country and to the empire, if at a time when a demand from Ireland for larger powers of self-government is to be
dealt with, there is not in Parliament a party totally independent of
the Irish vote."[8]

In the light of the dropping of coercion by Salisbury's government, there was every reason to think that the Parnellites and Conservatives would in fact work together, and Gladstone was prepared
to support a settlement of the Irish question on home rule lines
initiated by Salisbury. This, as J. L. Hammond has pointed out,[9]
would have been in the tradition of British party politics since 1828

"Wellington and Peel established a tradition that survived for half
a century, the tradition that governed and limited the range and
methods of party conflict. It was agreed that it was the duty of an
opposition, when a controversy reached a certain point or a problem assumed a certain character, to seek to limit the mischief that
might be caused by a reform that was distasteful rather than to
prolong resistance by methods that might provoke revolution."

Matters took a very different course from what was expected. To
take them in chronological order, Chamberlain, who had been the
advocate of an Irish Central Board and the opponent of coercion,
began to change his tune. In June he had declared:[10]

"The pacification of Ireland at this moment depends, I believe, on
the concession to Ireland of the right to govern itself in the matter
of its purely domestic business. Is it not discreditable to us that even
now it is only by unconstitutional means that we are able to secure
peace and order in one portion of her Majesty's dominions? It is a

system as completely centralized and bureaucratic as that with which Russia governs Poland, or as that which prevailed in Venice under the Austrian rule."

Yet only a few months later, in September, after Parnell had come out in favour of an Irish Parliament, Chamberlain announced, "If these are the terms on which Mr. Parnell's support is to be obtained, I will not enter into the compact." It is an illustration of the part played by personal circumstances in party politics that Chamberlain's informant in Irish questions was Captain W. H. O'Shea, and Mrs. O'Shea, as the world was yet to learn, was Parnell's mistress. As Hammond justly observes,[11] "While Chamberlain was being poisoned against Parnell by O'Shea's duplicity, Parnell was learning to hate Chamberlain as the power behind the husband of his mistress."

The residual Whigs in the Liberal party, led by Hartington, already shared the dislike of home rule to which Chamberlain was now moving, but in December the Liberal leader was publicly committed to a policy of home rule by what came to be known as the "Hawarden kite". It was, indeed, far from a kite deliberately flown from Hawarden Castle, but the public at that time can hardly be blamed for interpreting it in that sense. Herbert Gladstone was pressed by Wemyss Reid, editor of the *Leeds Mercury*, and Dawson Rogers, manager of the National Press Agency, to give them guidance in view of intrigues by Chamberlain and Dilke to prevent the formation of a government by his father. He gave them interviews intended to be for private guidance in which he expounded his personal views. What he had said was published as Gladstone's plan for home rule.[12]

Gladstone had indeed become convinced that home rule was essential, but it was highly embarrassing in the state of the Liberal party to have this premature disclosure of his mind. What he did not know was that Salisbury's Cabinet had by this time given up its flirtation with nationalism, had abandoned the idea of home rule and was again proposing to resort to coercion. In January 1886 Carnarvon resigned as Lord Lieutenant, and the government announced a bill to deal with the Land League and the protection of the person, property and public order. Gladstone decided that the government must be turned out, nor was Salisbury anxious to retain office. An amendment to the address by Jesse Collings, regretting the absence of proposals for allotments for agricultural labourers, was carried by 331 votes to 252. Parnell's followers voted with the opposition majority, but eighteen Liberals (including Hartington and Goschen) voted with the government and seventy-four abstained. On Salisbury's resignation the Queen had no option but to send for Gladstone, despite an invincible repugnance to the idea of home rule that from time to time led her to violate the neutrality between parties that had come to be accepted as constitutionally proper. In his invitations Gladstone said he proposed to examine the practicability of establishing in Dublin a Parliament to deal with Irish affairs. Hartington and most of the other Whigs—Shelburne, Northbrook, Carlingford and Derby—declined to join. Of the Radicals, only Dilke was wholeheartedly in agreement with Gladstone over Ireland, and he could not be given office because of the divorce proceedings that wrecked his career. Chamberlain and Trevelyan accepted but with serious misgivings, and Chamberlain could not be given the Colonial Office, as he wished, because Gladstone had already promised it to Granville, whom the Queen would not again have at the Foreign Office. The manner in which Gladstone refused made Chamberlain feel that he had been slighted, and the sense of slight was increased when Gladstone declined to sanction his constructive plans as President of the Local Government Board.

There is an air of great tragedy about these events of 1886. Gladstone framed the home rule bill himself without consulting Chamberlain, and when it was brought before the Cabinet Chamberlain and Trevelyan resigned. Gladstone made no effort to conciliate them; having failed to achieve an all-party settlement, he preferred to rely on his own solution without having to struggle perpetually with colleagues over details. A meeting of Liberals who favoured the establishment of a Parliament in Dublin for exclusively Irish affairs, while reserving freedom on the details of the bill, was held at the Foreign Office in May. Some 220 attended, and Gladstone's readiness to consider amendments in committee seemed to assure the second reading. But the Conservatives set out to harry him, and in the House of Commons he withdrew many of the concessions he had made at the party meeting. In the meantime Chamberlain had held a meeting of fifty-five Liberals who, "being in favour of some sort of autonomy for Ireland, disapproved of the government bills in their present shape".[13] Bright sent a letter saying he intended to vote against the second reading, and the meeting by a majority decided to do so.

The Conservatives were by this date solidly ranged against the idea of home rule. As the result of an unfortunately phrased speech in May, Salisbury was regarded as having placed the Irish on a level with the Hottentots.[14] This was inadvert, but Churchill's policy at this time was the result of deliberate calculation, and his encouragement of violent resistance by the English and Scottish Protestants in Ulster set a grave precedent that bedevilled a solution of the Irish problem for years to come. "I decided some time ago," he wrote to Lord Justice FitzGibbon on 16th February 1886,[15] "that if the G.O.M. went for home rule, the Orange card would be the one to play. Please God it may turn out the ace of trumps and not the two." It was in keeping with this decision that he crossed to Belfast on 23rd February and made an inflammatory speech in the Ulster Hall.[16] While asserting that "we are essentially a party of law and order" and deprecating "any violent action resorted to prematurely or without the most obvious and overwhelming necessity", he promised the "Loyalists" that if they were handed over to "the domination of an assembly in Dublin which must be to them a foreign and an alien assembly", there would "not be wanting to you those of position and influence in England who would be willing to cast in their lot with you and who, whatever the result, will share your fortunes and your fate". In a letter to a Liberal Unionist member named Young[17] a little later he made explicit what was implied in his speech. "If political parties and political leaders, not only parliamentary but local, should be so utterly lost to every feeling and dictate of honour and courage as to hand over coldly, and for the sake of purchasing a short and illusory parliamentary tranquillity, the lives and liberties of the loyalists of Ireland to their hereditary and most bitter foes, make no doubt on this point—Ulster will not be consenting party; Ulster at the proper moment will resort to the supreme arbitrament of force; Ulster will fight, Ulster will be right." The fatal jingle, "Ulster will fight, and Ulster will be right", was taken up everywhere and was to echo for many a dangerous year.

The Irish home rule members were naturally solid for the bill, though many objected to details, after hearing from Parnell that rejection would mean the end of Gladstone's government. It was the attitude of the Liberal members that roused the keenest expectations. Even if there had been no Irish problem, it is unlikely that Liberal unity could have survived the year 1886. The Whigs had gone as far as they were prepared to go in the acceptance of Radical measures. The tragic irony is that the home rule bill forced Hartington and Chamberlain into the same lobby against Gladstone. When the division on the second reading came to be taken in the early hours of 8th June, ninety-three Liberals voted against the bill, as did 233 Conservatives. The bill was lost by 343 votes to 313.

Some ministers advocated immediate resignation, but Gladstone felt that the greatness of the cause demanded an appeal to the people. It is a curious episode in the relation of the Crown to the parties that Queen Victoria had been discussing with Salisbury how best her government could be overthrown and what date for a dissolution would best suit the leader of the opposition.[18] Gladstone's speeches in constituencies other than his own incurred the royal displeasure, but he defended himself with the example of Salisbury and Iddesleigh. His strenuous efforts, remarkable in a man of seventy-seven, were not matched by the results. The main body of the Liberals was reduced from 235 to 194, and the "dissentient Liberals" from ninety-three to seventy-eight. The Conservative strength in the House of Commons rose from 251 to 316. The Irish Nationalists held firm at eighty-five. No party possessed an absolute majority, but the opponents of home rule numbered 394 against 279 supporters. In English constituencies five electors voted against home rule for every two who voted for it, but Scottish voters approved home rule in the proportion of five to two, Welsh electors by five to one and Irish electors by nine to two. After some discussion about whether to resign immediately or to await defeat in Parliament, Gladstone tendered the government's resignation, and Salisbury was again called to office. Except for a few years, the Conservative party was to remain in power until 1905.

14

CONSERVATIVES AND UNIONISTS 1886–1895

The "dissentient Liberals" or "Liberal Unionists"—restraint of the Conservatives—Chamberlain loses control of the Birmingham "caucus"—Salisbury offers to serve under Hartington—Churchill resigns—and the Liberal Unionist Goschen accepts the Exchequer in his place—growing imperialism of the Conservative party—it is shared by Chamberlain—who sees more prospect of achieving social reforms through the Conservatives—the Liberals adopt an advanced programme—the Irish Nationalist party is split by Mrs. O'Shea's association with Parnell—the Liberals get only a small majority—Gladstone fails to carry a new home rule bill— the Queen sends for Rosebery—who finds the "Newcastle programme" a heavy burden—Harcourt's budget—the government, weary of "ploughing the sands", resigns—and the Conservatives are returned

W HEN the "dissentient Liberals" or "Liberal Unionists" parted company with Gladstone in 1886 their position was analogous to that of the Peelites forty years earlier. Most of them hoped for a reunion of the Liberal party when the Irish question was cleared out of the way. It was not foreseen by anyone that the Liberal Unionists would, except for a few individuals, remain permanently alienated from the Liberal party and after a period as a separate group would become a wing of the Conservative party, and in due course fused into it.

Various circumstances brought about this result, and not least the fact that most of the seventy-eight Liberal Unionists returned in 1886 owed their seats to Conservative votes. The self-restraint of the Conservatives at this time was matched only by their self-interest. When Hartington called a meeting of his followers in May, he was able to read to them a message from Akers-Douglas, the Conservative chief whip, giving an absolute undertaking that no Conservative would contest the seat of any Liberal who voted against the home rule bill. This categorical assurance played no small part in ensuring that the number of dissentient Liberals should be so high in the critical division. It is one thing to give such an undertaking, and another to honour it, for the local Conservative associations were under no obligation to abide by the wishes of headquarters. A Liberal newspaper asserted that Akers-Douglas had reckoned without his Primrose League—"They are clamouring for local dispensations and relaxations of the rule that the Conservative Whip has laid down; the letter of the self-denying ordinance is a burden to them." Lord Salisbury even learnt to his dismay that a member of his own front bench was proposing to speak in the Petersfield division for a Conservative candidate against a Liberal Unionist, a case complicated by the fact that the Conservative had formerly sat for the same constituency as a Liberal. It says much for Akers-Douglas's growing control of the party, as well as for Conservative discipline, that in almost all cases such conflicts were eventually prevented.[1]

It was easy enough for some of the Whigs to slide into association with the Conservatives, and the wonder is that they had tolerated Radical pressures and insults for so long. It was not so easy for Chamberlain and his fellow-Radicals. A major element in determining their future is that Chamberlain lost control of the "caucus" he had created. At a meeting of delegates of the associations at the Westminster Palace Hotel in London to consider the home rule bill, veneration for the Grand Old Man and innate sympathy with the aim of self-government for small nations combined with the jealousy of other cities for Birmingham to give Gladstone a great majority. The delegates from Leeds led the attack. The local associations, which had found it difficult to make up their minds while the official party attitude was doubtful, now threw off all hesitations and ranged themselves solidly behind Gladstone and home rule. Chamberlain and his friends withdrew from the federation, and formed a new Radical Union with headquarters in Birmingham for the purpose of fighting the elections. The Gladstonian Liberals in the federation denounced them as traitors. The machine that Chamberlain had created was now turned against him, and before long Goschen and Bright were pleading for the right of individual opinions and protesting that members of Parliament were not delegates.

As the general election showed, Liberals in the country were not so solidly ranged behind the new Irish policy as the proceedings at the Westminster Palace Hotel suggested, and the federation lost many local officers. It retained, however, the services of Schnadhorst, who, alone of the Birmingham chiefs, accepted Gladstone's new policy. This was of crucial importance, for Schnadhorst had control of the machine and was able to put all its influence behind Gladstone.

It would hardly have been practicable for the headquarters of the federation to remain in Birmingham, for Chamberlain's control of that city remained almost unchallenged. A suggestion that it might be transferred to Leeds was rejected by the leading Liberals of that city, who did not wish to arouse the same feelings that Birmingham had stirred. Inevitably the headquarters were moved to London, and Schnadhorst was made secretary of the Central Liberal Association as well as secretary-general of the National Liberal Federation. The danger of a conflict between the leaders and the popular organization was thus minimized, though not entirely extinguished; from time to time complaints were made that the federation was merely a tool of the party chiefs and its annual conference an empty show for ratifying decisions taken in advance.

The gradual acceptance by Liberal Unionists of office in Conservative administrations both symbolizes the breach that had opened with official Liberalism and deepened that breach. Salisbury would have been willing to have served under Hartington in 1886 after Gladstone's fall, but Hartington was not prepared for a coalition, and argued that the government would be all the stronger for receiving Liberal Unionist support from outside. Chamberlain at that time was understandably even more adamant against taking office. With our knowledge of what eventually happened to the two men, it is piquant to read his words to Hartington, "Of course I could not join any coalition: it would be absurd in me, and I need not argue it. With you it is somewhat different. You might join and be perfectly consistent. But if you do you must make up your mind to cease to be, or call yourself, a Liberal. The force of circumstances will be irresistible, and you will be absorbed in the Great Constitutional Party."[2]

The surprising resignation of Churchill in December 1886 reopened the possibility of getting a Liberal Unionist into the Cabinet. Churchill's differences with his colleagues had now been composed and his second position in the Conservative hierarchy recognized by his appointment to the Exchequer. He had welcomed the Liberal Unionist secession, and as befitted one who had played in the Conservative party a rôle analogous to that of Chamberlain in the Liberal he made it his special business to smooth the way of the Birmingham demagogue among his new friends. His resignation, ostensibly because he could not concur in the naval and military estimates, was an act of political suicide. No doubt he expected to return with enhanced power, but in his own classic phrase he "forgot Goschen",[3] and this is the interest for the history of party. Salisbury again offered to serve under Hartington, but Hartington again declined, and Salisbury then turned to the man whom Churchill had overlooked. He should not have forgotten him, for Goschen had been a Liberal member for the city of London, who had disagreed with Gladstone's policy long before home rule finally broke his connexion—notably over the extension of the franchise. He had declined the speakership of the House of Commons and the vice-royalty of India. Churchill's only valid excuse for forgotting him is that he was then out of the House of Commons, having lost his Edinburgh seat at the general election; and he was defeated by seven votes in Liverpool before another seat was found for him at St. George's. At the Exchequer he destroyed "the sweet simplicity of the Three per cents" by a notable conversion operation. His importance in the history of party is that his acceptance of office prepared the way for the fusion of the Liberal Unionists with the Conservatives; and the social and commercial ideas he brought with him helped to transform the character of the Conservative party.

Both the major parties went through a process of transformation in the remaining years of the century. It was during the reign of Salisbury that the Conservative party became an imperialist party. The note had been sounded by Beaconsfield. In his younger days, as we have seen, he had considered the colonies "millstones round our necks", but his second government acquired nearly half the shares in the Suez Canal for the United Kingdom, had the Queen proclaimed Empress of India, annexed the Transvaal, added Cyprus to the British dominions overseas, penetrated the Sudan, kept the ambitions of Russia in check and made war upon Afghans and Zulus. Perceiving that Great Britain was no longer a mere European power, he proclaimed her mission to be the metropolis of a great maritime empire.[4] Though his party was rejected at the polls, he had struck a responsive note among many of his countrymen, and even Gladstone was led against his own judgement to bombard Alexandria and occupy Egypt. It needed the threat of the secession of Ireland from the union to convert the whole Conservative party to a sense of its imperial mission. Alarmed at the possibility of finding the island in their rear occupied by a hostile power, and disturbed by the reproaches of the people of English and Scottish stock settled in Ulster, Conservatives awoke to the consciousness of an imperial destiny. Burma was annexed by Salisbury's government in 1886; the Royal Niger Company, the East Africa Company and the British South Africa Company were formed with government support for the development of Africa; and Heligoland was ceded to Germany in return for the abandonment of German claims to Uganda and the Upper Nile, and recognition of a British protectorate over Zanzibar. The new imperial sentiment found its bard in a young man, Rudyard Kipling, who had been born in India and spent no small part of his life in the Queen's dominions oversea; and though much of what he wrote now seems bombast, in one noble hymn he reminded his countrymen by whose awful hand they held "dominion over palm and pine" and warned them against "Such boasting as the gentiles use, Or lesser breeds without the law". The new imperialism was soon to have its music as well as its poetry; and for many years to come Conservative audiences with tears in their eyes would chant the words "Land of hope and glory", praying fervently that their country's bounds might be set "wider still and wider", to the throbbing music that Elgar composed in 1901 for King Edward's coronation the following year.[5]

Though there was poetry and music in the new imperialism, it owed most to a man who had little poetry or music in him. Joseph Chamberlain shared Beaconsfield's desire to combine a sense of imperial destiny abroad with a policy of social justice at home. As a Liberal minister in 1885 he had put forward the "unauthorized programme", in which he demanded free education, small holdings, graduated taxation and local government as the "ransom" that property must pay for its security;[6] but the department for which he asked when Gladstone next had to form a ministry was the Colonial Office.[7] In secret he probably shared the view of Alexander Macdonald, the miners' leader, expressed during Beaconsfield's ministry, "The Conservative party have done more for the working classes in five years than the Liberals have in fifty."[8] Macdonald's remark was justified by some remarkable legislation, of which Richard Cross was the main author—a Public Health Act putting into legal language Disraeli's dictum, *Sanitas sanitatum, omnia sanitas*,[9] an Artisans' Dwelling Act, an Employers and Workmen Act which gave trade unions virtual freedom of action, and a Sale of Food and Drugs Act. This was dismissed by most Liberals as "a policy of sewage", but it was congenial to Chamberlain, and after his breach with Gladstone he began to wonder whether his real allies were not the Conservatives. He accepted, it is true, an invitation to a "round-table conference" of leading Liberals held at Harcourt's house early in 1887. It was attended by Trevelyan, Morley and Lord Herschell as well as by Harcourt and Chamberlain, but no further meetings were held after a truculent article by Chamberlain in the *Baptist Times* warned readers that England, Wales and Scotland must go without needed legislation because some eighty delegates, representing the policy and receiving the pay of the Chicago convention, were determined to obstruct all business until their demands were conceded.[10] Chamberlain had by now come to the conclusion that he would be able to achieve more of his domestic ideals through the Conservative party than had been possible in the Liberal. The Coal Mines Regulation Act, the Allotments Act, the Housing of the Working Classes Act, the Free Education Act and the Agricultural Holdings Act were all in accordance with his own philosophy; but he derived special satisfaction from the Local Government Act, 1888, which substituted elected county councils for administrative purposes in place of magistrates nominated by Lords Lieutenant. Chamberlain had been conducting a campaign to this end from his earliest days in Birmingham politics. The act brought about a further decline in the influence of the great landowners in their counties. Though the Conservative party was to remain attached to the land, the influence within its ranks of the commercial classes symbolized by Goschen and Chamberlain[a] was increasing. It could not be long before Chamberlain would be willing to accept office, as Goschen had already done.

There was first to come a short interlude of Liberal government without real power. The Liberal party was undergoing its own transformation. Though its representation in Parliament was seriously weakened in 1886, the simultaneous departure of Whigs and Radicals freed it from internal conflict and gave it a new unity of purpose on which an eventual return to power could be based; but the process was long and painful. It now became without question "the Gladstonian Liberal party", with the Grand Old Man venerated in many thousands of simple homes throughout the land, but the inexorable advance of old age made it increasingly difficult for Gladstone to control it, and before long it passed beyond the positions that he was prepared to defend.

It was one of Gladstone's traits to become absorbed in one political topic at a time to the exclusion of everything else. From 1885 that topic was Ireland, and the gibe was made that in his attention to the condition of Ireland he forgot the condition of England. Under the new household franchise his followers were not allowed to forget it, and adopted attitudes towards state interference in economic processes, public expenditure and disestablishment of the Church, at any rate in Wales, that he could not approve.

The Irish Nationalist party suffered convulsions of a more violent order. The adoption of home rule by Gladstone and the resumption of a policy of coercion by Salisbury made it inevitable that the Irish members should again ally themselves with the Liberals. A Tenants Relief Bill introduced by Parnell was thrown out, and the Irish Nationalists devised their "plan of campaign" for dealing with the problem in their own way. The tenants of an estate were to agree on what they considered just half-yearly rents, and were to offer this in a body to the landlord. If he refused to accept it as payment in full, they were to hand the money to a managing committee, and the committee was to hand it to some person who could be trusted to use it for the purposes of the struggle. The government denounced the plan of campaign as illegal, and although agreeing to a bill rectifying rents, introduced a Criminal Law Amendment bill which would have permitted accused persons to be tried in England. This was dropped, but not the provisions which made the new act part of the permanent law of Ireland to be brought into force whenever the

L

executive wished. The bill was made the occasion for the introduction into parliamentary proceedings of the "guillotine", or time-
table by which the clauses of a measure were required to be disposed of in a specified number of sittings. Though Gladstone regis-
tered a formal objection, the great majority of Liberals abstained
from opposing this innovation. When the guillotine was employed
on the report stage of the Criminal Law Amendment bill, the
Liberals withdrew from the chamber and the Irish Nationalists dis-
dainfully looked down from the gallery. Arthur Balfour, Chief
Secretary from 1887 to 1891, and the principal author of the
measure, enforced it with a rigour curiously alien to his easygoing
temperament, but only exacerbated Irish discontent. The Pope,
whose love for Ireland was balanced by his desire for the conversion
of England, condemned the plan of campaign as contrary to national
justice and Christian charity, and received the retort from the Irish
Catholic members that they took their religion from Rome but their
politics from home.

In 1887 *The Times* published a series of articles "Parnellism and
Crime" in which a letter purporting to be signed by Parnell, and
justifying the murder of Burke in Phoenix Park, was reproduced
facsimile. It was a forgery and Parnell was vindicated by a tribunal
of three judges against all the personal accusations, but at the height
of his power he was destroyed by one of those incalculable proceedings that make prophecy in politics a hazardous occupation.
Captain O'Shea, who had for years turned a blind eye to his wife's
illicit association with Parnell, sought a divorce and named Parnell
as the co-respondent. The suit was not defended and a decree of
divorce was given in 1890. Three days later a resolution that Parnell
possessed the confidence of the Irish nation passed with acclamation
in Dublin. But the Nonconformist conscience in the Liberal party
would not tolerate a breach of the seventh commandment. On the
same day as the Dublin meeting the National Liberal Federation's
annual conference opened at Sheffield, and the whisper that Parnell
must go ran round. While refusing to make himself a censor of
morals, and insisting that it was for the Irish members alone to
choose their leader, Gladstone was driven to the conclusion that if
Parnell remained leader of the Irish party, the Liberal party would
no longer work in alliance with the Irish and the cause of home rule
would be doomed. He asked an Irish member and Morley to com-
municate this message to Parnell, if Parnell was not disposed himself
to resign, before a meeting of the Irish party fixed for 25th November for the purpose of choosing their leader for the session. Parnell
avoided the emissaries and was re-elected by a party meeting ignorant of Gladstone's ultimatum. Gladstone thereupon had his letter to
Morley published. The Irish members read the fatal sentences:[11]
"Notwithstanding the splendid services rendered by Mr. Parnell to

his country, his continuance at the present moment in the leadership would be productive of consequences disastrous in the highest degree to the cause of Ireland. . . . The continuance I speak of would not only place many hearty and effective friends of the Irish cause in a position of great embarrassment, but would render my retention of the leadership of the Liberal party, based as it has been mainly upon the prosecution of the Irish cause, almost a nullity." Dumbfounded, the Irish members demanded to meet again, and a long series of meetings marked by eloquence, passion and high tragedy ended on 5th December with forty-five members walking out and leaving twenty-five in the room with Parnell. The forty-five retired to another room and declared his leadership at an end. Before the meetings in Committee Room Fifteen Parnell had declared that Ireland could achieve her independence only through a united Nationalist party free of alliances with any English party, and when he was deserted by most of his followers he sought the help of the Fenians to this end. But the Roman Catholic authorities hardened against him, and before 1891 was out he had died, having made Mrs. O'Shea his wife a few months earlier. The division in the Irish party continued for several years.

Until Parnell's disgrace, the Liberals had been faring successfully at by-elections, and there seemed a reasonable prospect that after the next general election Gladstone might have a sufficient majority to carry a measure of home rule concerted with the Irish leader. It was not to be. The revelation of Parnell's double life, and the rift in the Irish party, damaged the Liberal cause in England, as the by-elections immediately began to show. The falling away in popular support was not made good in other ways.

The exasperation of many Liberals with their leader's Irish preoccupations found expression in the "Newcastle programme" adopted by the conference of the National Liberal Federation in that city in 1891. As founded by Chamberlain, the federation had for its basis "the participation of all members of the party in the formation and direction of its policy, and in the selection of those particular measures of reform and progress to which priority shall be given". When it became an official organ of the party, this basis could have proved embarrassing to the leaders for it would have made the conference and not the parliamentary leaders the framers of policy. Various devices were employed to mitigate this conclusion. The general committee in 1888 asked that there should be sent in for the conference only resolutions of a practical character for which there was a general consensus of opinion in the party; and it was ruled from the chair that no amendments could be moved from the floor but must be sent by associations in writing for the next conference. In 1890 the rules were altered so as to vest in the general committee the compiling of the agenda, and in practice this meant that the

general purposes committee sifted the hundreds of resolutions received and framed resolutions for debate. Despite these precautions,
the Newcastle conference in 1891 passed a large number of resolutions favouring such diverse subjects as home rule for Ireland, disestablishment for Wales and Scotland, local option in the matter of
licences to sell drink, public control of Church schools, limitation of
the hours of labour, the creation of parish councils, reform of the
magistracy, compulsory registration of tithe, security for tenants'
improvements, allotments for agricultural workers, the protection
of commons, triennial Parliaments and abolition of plural voting.
Even if the House of Lords could have been relied on to acquiesce,
there would have been enough work to occupy a Liberal government to the end of the century. It is true that the party leaders were
not committed to the resolutions, and would not have admitted that
it constituted a programme, but Gladstone gave it a vague blessing
and increased the confusion by adding the evacuation of Egypt to it.

The Liberal success in by-elections had been checked by Parnell's
divorce and fall, and the Newcastle programme failed to recover the
lost ground. While it offered many sections of the community what
they wanted, it also offered them what they did not want, and its
electoral value is dubious. Parliament was dissolved towards the end
of its natural life in 1892, and at the ensuing general election 268
Conservatives and forty-seven Liberal Unionists were returned, a
total of 315. The number of Liberals was 273, but the eighty-one
Irish Nationalist members could be trusted to vote with them on all
crucial issues, a total of 354. Salisbury resigned, and Gladstone
formed his fourth administration, with Lord Rosebery again at the
Foreign Office, Sir William Harcourt at the Exchequer and Morley
as Chief Secretary for Ireland. It was a gifted government that included Henry Campbell-Bannerman as Secretary for War and
Herbert Henry Asquith as Home Secretary, while among the newer
members (he had first been returned at a by-election in 1890) was a
young Welshman, David Lloyd George, who showed himself a
wizard in debate. Gladstone's mind was set on the problem of Ireland, and with the help of the Irish members he carried a home rule
bill through the Commons by a majority of thirty-one. Unlike the
earlier bill, it provided for two chambers in Dublin and the continued representation of Ireland at Westminster. But the House of
Lords was by this date a Conservative stronghold, and at Salisbury's
instance the peers threw out the bill by 419 votes to forty-one.
Though Salisbury regarded his action as ratified by the next general
election, it was a move full of danger for the upper house as well as
for Ireland. The remedying of Ireland's grievances was delayed by a
generation, and the eventual price paid was civil war and partition;
while the House of Lords became for great masses of Liberal voters
a purely Tory instrument whose powers must be curbed.

The Lords may have hoped to force a dissolution, but Gladstone denied any obligation to dissolve and tried to carry out as much as he could of the Newcastle programme. Little could be done with a majority of only forty in the Commons and a solidly hostile House of Lords. Only one major achievement is recorded, the legislation setting up urban, rural district and parish councils, and this was a complement to the Conservative act of 1888.

Gladstone finally gave up office in 1894. It was not only that he was now eighty-five, hard of hearing and with failing eyesight. He was finding himself increasingly out of sympathy with the new trends in Liberalism, and when he broke the news of his resignation to the Cabinet—thus enabling Harcourt to take from his pocket the paper, "yellow with age",[12] prepared for that occasion—it was because he would not agree to heavier taxes for increased armaments deemed necessary by the Service chiefs in the international situation. Later in the same day in his final speech in the House of Commons, possibly casting his mind back to the day sixty-two years previously when he had first sat there by the grace of the Duke of Newcastle, he animadverted on the changes made by the Lords in the Parish Councils Bill. Raising his voice, he warned the nation that the question "which is raised between a deliberative assembly, elected by the votes of more than six million people, and a deliberative assembly occupied by many men of virtue, by many men of talent, of course with considerable diversities and varieties, is a controversy which, when once raised, must go forward to an issue".[13]

The question who was to be Gladstone's successor had naturally occupied the minds of Liberal ministers for a long time, and two camps had formed round the Foreign Secretary and the Chancellor of the Exchequer, less out of enthusiasm for the one than out of distrust for the other. Rosebery's foreign policy, and particularly the decision to assume the administration of Uganda from the British East Africa Company, had roused strong criticism among his colleagues, and not least in the breast of Gladstone himself, who subsequently wrote of him that he was "imbued with the spirit of territorial grab".[14] Rosebery had been caught up in the expansionist mood of the close of the nineteenth century, and this was the beginning of what later came to be known as Liberal imperialism. Though damaging to him in his relations with some of his immediate colleagues, his championship of empire probably did him no harm in the country at large. The national stature he gained from the Foreign Office was matched by the prestige he had won as the first chairman of the new London County Council. "It seemed to me," he wrote later,[15] "that the public was not aware of the magnitude of this experiment, and that the men of thought, leisure, and business capacity—with whom London abounds to an extent disproportionate even to its vast population—should come forward to

give their best energies to so noble a work, and make it a success."
The Progressives, who had won a decisive victory in the first elections, announced their intention to take all nineteen aldermanic
seats, and Rosebery, elected as an independent, protested in a speech
of such good sense that he was immediately proposed for the
chairmanship and elected after a long debate by an overwhelming
majority. In his period of office he helped to make the government
of London worthy of the chief city in the world; and according to
his biographer, his "work as chairman of the L.C.C. was in many
respects the most important single factor in his advance to the
premiership".[16] If Mr. James's assessment is correct, Rosebery
blazed a trail that has led many others, not indeed to No. 10 Downing Street, but to high positions in the state. In his case his chances
were enhanced by the prestige he had gained by acting as a mediator
between the mine-owners and the mine-workers in the bitter strike
of 1893. There had by this time grown up in the Liberal party some
prejudice against the idea of a Prime Minister in the Lords—it was
noted that Melbourne had been the last Liberal Premier in the upper
house. Those to whom the idea was anathema turned to Harcourt,
whose position at the Exchequer gave him some claim on the succession, and Harcourt's son "Lulu" intrigued with remarkable
assiduity to bring about this result; but Harcourt's aggressive manner and biting tongue had created too many enemies for these
manoeuvres to succeed, and "Lulu" damaged rather than assisted his
father's cause.

Estranged from Rosebery by his imperialist foreign policy, and
sensitive to the defects of Harcourt, Gladstone went to Windsor for
his final audience of the Queen prepared, if asked for his advice, to
recommend her Majesty to send for Spencer.[17] It would have made
no difference to the outcome for Spencer, like Kimberley, had resolved that if summoned he would advise the Queen to send for
Rosebery. As it happened, the Queen did not seek her outgoing
Prime Minister's advice, but of her own volition commissioned
Rosebery to form a government. At a later period in the history of
the Liberal party it might have roused concern that the sovereign
should select the Prime Minister without reference to the party, but
at that date only a minority even of Liberals would have contested
the Queen's right to select her chief minister, the relief at not getting
Harcourt was so great that Rosebery's own defects were overlooked, and at that time Rosebery seemed to possess many qualities
as the Liberal leader. He was elected as such at a party meeting in
the Foreign Office on 12th March. "The meeting today was very
near freezing point, except when one name was mentioned," Acton
told Gladstone, "but there was no hitch."[18]

In the meantime Rosebery had persuaded Harcourt to overcome
his objection to having a peer, Kimberley, at the Foreign Office as

well as a peer at No. 10 Downing Street, and the other ministers continued in their places; but the Harcourts remained sullenly hostile, and Morley was consumed with anger at not being allowed to succeed to the Foreign Office. Marjoribanks also agreed to remain as chief whip, but had to return ten minutes later to say that he was no longer a member of the House of Commons as his father, Lord Tweedmouth, had died; he had been a good whip, and was succeeded by another skilful whip, the Welshman Tom Ellis, but Ellis was of a more radical cast of mind and never achieved the same cordial relations with Rosebery.

This was an unpropitious setting for Rosebery's administration, and the new Prime Minister created consternation in the party by admitting that home rule could not be carried until there was a majority for it in the English constituencies. If nothing could be done about home rule, plenty of domestic problems were clamouring for solution, but Rosebery found the Newcastle programme a heavy burden to carry. It was necessary, he explained, for the Cabinet to sift the policies advocated by the National Liberal Federation, and while this was being done ministers found themselves bombarded with correspondence. Some of the appeals were menacing, some coaxing and cajoling, but all were earnest and all correspondents agreed in asking that their particular hobby should be made the first government bill. "Any delay in pushing forward each measure that has been recorded in what is called the Newcastle programme implies, we are told, the alienation of all the earnest and thoughtful members of the Liberal party—in fact, the backbone of the Liberal party. And I have come to the conclusion that the Liberal party is extremely rich in backbones."[19]

The changing character of the Liberal party was indicated in the spring of 1894 by Harcourt's famous budget, which made increased provision for naval expenditure on the basis that a "two-power standard" must be maintained for the British Navy and imposed death duties on a graduated scale ranging from one to eight per cent according to the value of the estate. Gladstone's ideas that all taxation was an evil, that money was best left to fructify in the pockets of the people, and that public expenditure, especially on armaments, must be minimized were abandoned. The new death duties, modest as they were at first, were immediately recognized as fraught with the most dangerous potentialities for owners of property; and it was they that led Harcourt to declare, "We are all socialists now."[b]

A government with Rosebery as Prime Minister and such men as Harcourt and Morley in his Cabinet could not have held together for long, even if the House of Lords, heedless of warnings that they would "fill up the cup", had not frustrated most of the government's plans. The government, observed Asquith, were simply "ploughing the sands", and in 1895 they took the opportunity of a snap defeat on the cordite vote in the Army Estimates to resign. Salisbury, called back to office, immediately advised a dissolution. The general election showed that the electors had not been alienated by the action of the House of Lords in rejecting or emasculating legislation sent up from the Commons. No fewer than 340 Conservatives and seventy-one Liberal Unionists, a total of 411, were returned, against 177 Liberals and eighty-two Irish Nationalists, a total of 259. From the party point of view it had proved well worth while to allow the Liberals three years of ineffective office. Rosebery made known that he would never again serve with Harcourt. He need not have troubled. Ten years were to pass before the Liberals were again called upon to form a government, and by then Harcourt was dead and Rosebery out of touch with his party.

15

UNIONIST DOMINANCE AND DISSENSION
1895–1905

*Chamberlain becomes Liberal Unionist leader in the Commons—
Goschen joins the Conservatives—the election of a new Speaker in
1895 made a party issue—Chamberlain agrees to serve in Salisbury's government as Colonial Secretary—brilliant Tory organization—Liberals in disarray—Rosebery resigns leadership—and is
eventually succeeded by Campbell-Bannerman—the Boer War con-
solidates the Tories and throws the Liberals into further confusion
—split in the Irish Nationalist party healed—Liberal League
founded by Rosebery's supporters—resignation of Salisbury—who
is succeeded by Balfour—Church schools give the Liberals a rallying cry—Chamberlain decides to go for protection—resignation
from the government—Conservative unpopularity increased by
proposals for using Chinese labour in South Africa—and by the
Licensing Bill of 1904—Balfour resigns—and Campbell-Bannerman
forms a Liberal government*

T HE summons to office in 1895 raised once more in an acute
way the relations between Conservatives and Liberal Unionists.
In form their relation from 1885 had been that of an alliance, each
forming a separate party with its own officers and organization.
There were still many Conservatives who were suspicious of
Chamberlain, and personal jealousy of his gifts mingled with fears
that he would push the Tory party too far in the direction of social
reform. The Midland Conservatives were particularly irked by the
pre-eminence of Chamberlain in their area, and there was always
relief when the Irish question cropped up and gave Tories and
Liberal Unionists a chance of demonstrating their identity of
view.

The death of Hartington's father in 1891 had made the relationship still more delicate, for his elevation to the House of Lords as the
8th Duke of Devonshire left Chamberlain as the leader of the Liberal
Unionists in the Commons. This was not at all to the taste of

Goschen, who solved the problem in his own way early in 1893 by joining the Carlton (proposed by Salisbury, seconded by Balfour) and sitting in the Commons with the Conservatives. The question again became acute just before the fall of Rosebery's government in 1895 when Mr. Speaker Peel expressed a wish to resign. This had party implications, because Liberals had been elected to the chair for sixty years, and Conservatives felt it was their turn. There was a tradition that a sitting Speaker should not be disturbed even if a general election put his former party into a minority, and in accordance with this tradition the Conservatives had not opposed Brand's re-election in 1874. As Salisbury wrote in a letter to Akers-Douglas,[1] "ever since John Russell carried the chair by storm in 1835, every Speaker has resigned at a moment when his party was in a majority: and consequently each successive Speaker has been a Liberal". If Lefevre and Denison had waited only twelve months, their resignations would have been dealt with by Tory governments. "Now if every Liberal Speaker resigns to a Liberal majority," argued Salisbury, "and the rule is laid down that a Speaker once elected must not be disturbed—it follows mathematically that the speakership belongs permanently to the Liberal party."

The Liberal Unionists considered that they rather than the Conservatives had the right to contest Mr. Speaker Peel's seat, Warwick and Leamington, when he resigned, and they put up his son, George Peel. The Conservatives threatened to put up their own candidate, but in the end agreement was reached on Alfred Lyttelton, a more acceptable Liberal Unionist. There was a Liberal Unionist candidate in the field for the speakership, Leonard Courtney, but as Chamberlain disliked him he withdrew. No accommodation could be reached between Liberals and Conservatives, and after a sharp contest the Liberal nominee, Gully, beat the Conservative by eleven votes. The local Conservatives in Carlisle, supported by Akers-Douglas, wished to oppose him at the next election, and the Conservative members of the House of Commons were restive at the idea of re-electing him as Speaker after the election, but they did so and he sat in the chair till 1905.

Chamberlain had been upset by the revelation of his unpopularity with some sections of the Conservatives, and talked with apparent sincerity of retiring from politics, but in the end a still closer association with the Conservatives came about. He agreed to serve in the government that Salisbury was forming, and obtained the office that he had asked for in vain at the hands of Gladstone in 1886—that of Secretary of State for the Colonies. This caused some surprise as it was not then regarded as a political prize, but Chamberlain knew what he wanted, and through it soon made himself the second man in the government. His acceptance of office necessitated the vacation of his seat, and the seeking of the writ for the vacancy by a Tory whip was noted in the press as a dramatic act symbolic of his final passage to the Conservative ranks.

Among these government changes Akers-Douglas accepted the post of First Commissioner of Works and ceased to be chief whip. Though his advice on party organization did not cease to be sought, this broke the unique combination that had existed between himself as chief whip since 1885 and Captain R. W. E. Middleton, who had been styled principal agent of the party in 1885 and was made honorary secretary of the National Union in 1886. Thanks to their single-minded devotion to the efficient working of the party machine, their lack of interest in policy and absence of personal ambition, their mutual understanding and complete loyalty to the leader of the party, they achieved a perfection in party organization which remains the ideal of party managers. It was in marked contrast with the years immediately before 1885 when Lord Randolph Churchill was trying to use the National Union as his instrument in the control of the party; nor indeed could the technical skill of Akers-Douglas and Middleton have availed if Salisbury had not established an unchallengeable position in the party. His daughter, Lady Gwendolen Cecil, has given a memorable picture of their relationships.[2]

"That was the classic period in Conservative electioneering. Under Mr. Akers-Douglas as whip, and Captain Middleton as chief agent, the organization attained a completeness which could hardly have been improved upon. The accuracy with which Captain Middleton, whether by intuition or from experience, could calculate his 'co-efficient of error' in the returns of his local workers, became proverbial. He would send forecasts to Lord Salisbury on the eve of a by-election which would be almost exactly reproduced in the numbers polled the following day. Apart from their efficiency, both party officials had a straightness, loyalty and simplicity of outlook which made them very pleasant to work with, and their chief's relations with them were intimately easy. A then junior member of the staff recalls how often, after the close of a House of Lords sitting, his brougham would draw up at St. Stephen's Chambers and, seating himself at Captain Middleton's table, while subordinates withdrew to a discreet distance, he would go through the last reports from the constituencies, weigh the qualifications of proposed candidates, or discuss with whip and agent the latest tea-cup storm among some section of his supporters."

This golden age of Conservative organization lasted from 1885 to 1902, when Salisbury resigned the premiership and the leadership of the party; and the following year Middleton resigned his dual posts as principal agent and honorary secretary of the National Union. As Mr. R. T. McKenzie points out,[3] the pattern of relationships between the three principal organs of the party then established has survived virtually unchanged to the present day. "The party in Parliament has preserved its autonomy; the Central Office has continued to function in effect as the personal machine of the leader and has fulfilled most of the executive functions of the National Union; and the latter organization has, with varying degrees of docility, fulfilled its function as an electoral machine and a channel of communication between the parliamentary leaders and their followers in the country." Conservatives would cavil only at the word "docility" and for "varying degrees of docility" would probably substitute "complete harmony and loyalty".

While the Conservative organization was running like a well-oiled machine, the Liberals were in a sorry state of disarray. Game to the end, Gladstone thundered in 1896 against the Turkish massacre of the Armenians, lamenting that he no longer had the years of 1876. Rosebery was horrified at the idea of breaking off relations with the Sultan and running the risk of war single-handed; but Gladstone was at any rate in retirement, and Rosebery was more harassed by his colleagues in Parliament. Before 1896 was out he threw his hand in and announced to Tom Ellis, the chief whip, his resignation of the Liberal leadership. No leader of the Liberal party in the full official sense was elected in his place, but the leadership of the Liberals in the Commons devolved on Harcourt and of the Liberal peers on Kimberley. By 1898 Harcourt also had had enough, and in a letter to Morley he announced his resignation. Morley also, in effect, retired from politics at this time to write the life of Gladstone, who had at length yielded up his fiery soul to his maker. The leadership in the Commons fell to Campbell-Bannerman,[a] and early in 1899 a meeting of members of Parliament held at the Reform Club established him as leader of the Liberal party in the same full sense in which Rosebery had been. The nominations of Henry Fowler and Asquith were withdrawn.

The harmony was short-lived. The swelling theme of British imperialism rose to a crescendo in 1897 upon the diamond jubilee of Queen Victoria's accession to the throne. As the captains and the kings assembled to pay their homage with men of every colour from every zone of the inhabited earth, the British people felt a consciousness of their mission to rule such as no other people had known since the ancient Romans. This was the moment for which Chamberlain had sought the Colonial Office, and when the Boers in the Transvaal invaded Natal in 1899 he took up the challenge with alacrity.

The Boer War consolidated the Tories but threw the Liberals into even greater confusion. The British forces, ill-prepared for such a struggle in a distant land, began with a series of disasters, and the appeal to patriotism rallied all Conservatives behind the government whatever views may have been held privately. "My country right or wrong" became the watchword. The Liberals did not feel the same compelling need to support the government. They became sharply divided between the "Liberal imperialists" and the "Pro-Boers" Rosebery was naturally in the former camp; more surprisingly, he was joined by Asquith. Campbell-Bannerman was opposed to the war, and so naturally were Harcourt and Morley. But the most virulent of the pro-Boers was Lloyd George, who at this time established his growing reputation by the brilliant impudence of his attacks on Chamberlain.

In 1900 better news began to come from the front, and the Conservatives thought it opportune to take advantage of their own unity and their opponents' disunity to hold a general election two years in advance of the statutory limit. Devonshire amiably explained the reason: "We all know very well that the captain of a cricketing eleven, when he wins the toss, puts his own side in, or his adversaries, as he thinks most favourable to his chances of winning." By reason of the background of war against which it was held the contest became known as "the khaki election", and with some exaggeration Mr. Frank Owen has written: "The khaki election was, in fact, a one-man show, and that man was not the Prime Minister, or even the leader of the party. The event was dominated by Joseph Chamberlain, the Colonial Secretary. He, almost alone of the ministers, was popularly held not to blame for the early military defeats and the muddle over medical supplies." Following the advice of Labouchère, "Go for Joe," Lloyd George pursued Chamberlain relentlessly.[4] The calculations of the Tory managers proved correct, and the Unionists had a net gain of six seats. In the new Parliament there were 349 Conservatives and sixty-eight Liberal Unionists, a total of 417; there were 171 Liberals and eighty-two Irish Nationalists, a total of 253, giving the government a clear majority of 164.

At this time the split in the ranks of the Irish Nationalists was healed. On Parnell's death in 1891 John Redmond had become the leader of his faction, while from 1896, on the expulsion of T. M. Healey from the Irish National Federation, John Dillon had been the leader of the larger section. In 1900 both sections agreed to unite under Redmond's leadership, but a new threat to Irish unity appeared with the foundation in the same year by Arthur Griffith of Sinn Fein (Ourselves Alone). Griffith held it to be useless to wait upon the British Parliament and demanded that the Irish members should cease to attend at Westminster and constitute an Irish National Council in Dublin.

Defeat in the general election did not induce the Liberals to settle their differences. In 1901 Rosebery's followers formed the Liberal Imperial Council to promote his aims. The rival dinner-parties of the Liberal leaders were dubbed "war to the knife and fork".[5] Their dissensions were not confined to private gatherings. In June 1901

Campbell-Bannerman roused the Liberal Imperialists to fury by a speech in which he asked, "When was a war not a war?", and answered himself, "When it was carried on by methods of barbarism in South Africa." Rosebery replied with a speech in which he made two enigmatic statements that stuck in the minds of his hearers. "You start with a clean slate as regards those cumbersome programmes with which you were over-loaded in the past," he told them. "I must plough my furrow alone. That is my fate, agreeable or the reverse: but before I get to the end of that furrow it is possible that I may find myself not alone." Before the year was out in a speech at Chesterfield, largely justifying his views on the Boer War, he again asked for "a clean slate" and demanded that the "fly-blown phylacteries of obsolete policies" should be put aside. Campbell-Bannerman used it as an excuse to open negotiations, but was disconcerted to be told that Rosebery would no longer have anything to do with Irish home rule. The only outcome was the formation of the Liberal League by friends of Rosebery who supported his policies and desired to restore him to the leadership. From its platform Rosebery explained the doctrine of the clean slate as meaning the abandonment of the Newcastle programme, repudiated the vision of an Irish Parliament, and urged Liberals to concentrate on education and efficiency.[6]

It appeared as though the Liberals must be condemned to the wilderness for ever by their internal dissensions and that the Unionists were set for a further long spell of office when the situation was reversed with startling and dramatic rapidity.

It seemed at this time that all things had come to an end. The end of the century was quickly followed by the death of Queen Victoria (January 1901) and the resignation of Salisbury (July 1902). It is rarely that the end of a century so neatly coincides with the end of an age. By virtue of the length of her reign, the Queen maintained to the end a personal line in party politics that had already become unconstitutional in the sixty-four years of her rule. She was almost openly partisan, a Whig when Melbourne was her adviser, a Tory after she fell under the spell of Disraeli. Her eldest son, the future King Edward VII, true to the tradition of the Hanoverian heirs-apparent, was thrown into the other camp and, without going to the length of setting up a rival court, cultivated at Marlborough House the friendship of Gladstone and the Liberals. It was only with the Queen's death that the doctrine of the Sovereign's detachment from party politics could become a reality. Today the idea of the Sovereign as above the party struggle, accepting her ministers with equal readiness from any party with command of the House of Commons, and served by her Majesty's opposition no less than by her Majesty's government, is regarded as central to the party system; but it was not shared by the aged Queen whose frail body was at length laid to rest at Windsor in 1901. Salisbury, Prime Minister with only a brief break from 1886, was almost as much a part of the age as his Queen. He had permitted himself to be deprived of the office of Foreign Secretary in favour of Lansdowne after the election of 1900, and peace in South Africa in May 1902 gave him an honourable opportunity to vacate also the post of Prime Minister. He did so the more readily as the succession passed almost automatically to his nephew, Balfour, who was first commissioned by the King to form a government and two days later elected leader of his party by a meeting of Conservative peers and members of the House of Commons.

Then the troubles of the Conservatives began. Even before he had become Prime Minister, Balfour had introduced into the House of Commons an Education Bill which is now recognized as among the most constructive acts of statesmanship in modern British history, but at the time fanned the flames of sectarian bigotry to a frightening extent. The Education Act of 1870 had created the dual system with two sets of schools, one wholly provided and maintained by religious authorities, the other wholly provided and maintained by elected school boards. The former schools had been mainly provided by the Church of England while the state was still indifferent to the education of the masses, but there were some Methodist schools and a growing number of Roman Catholic schools to meet the needs of a population continually increasing by immigration from Ireland. Church people and Roman Catholics began to find it hard that they should have to find money to maintain and improve their own schools and also to contribute like all other taxpayers to the cost of building and maintaining board schools. The problem was resolved in a bold manner in the 1902 measure, which swept away school boards; made the county, county borough and in some cases borough and urban district councils the local education authorities; required church school managers to keep the school premises in good repair and to provide them free of charge to the local education authority; and required the authority to pay the salaries of the teaching staff and other costs of maintenance.

At once the cry of "Rome on the rates" was raised by a vocal section of Nonconformists led by Dr. Clifford. Chamberlain, the old advocate of free and secular education, was deeply embarrassed, and the veteran churchman Salisbury would have preferred not to see the issue raised, but there were many Tories who felt that the Conservative party had again found its soul in alliance with the Church. The Liberals were delighted to find a new rallying cry that enabled them to forget their recent dissensions. Asquith and Lloyd George shared a common platform at the Queen's Hall under the chairmanship of Rosebery. Once more Conservatives and Liberals were aligned on the historic dividing line between Tories and Whigs, the championship of the Church by the one party and the defence of dissent by the other; and they threw themselves into the contest with zest. But in truth this was not something the Conservatives had sought. The measure was the product of a group of able civil servants, in particular Sir Robert Morant, indifferent to party, who realized that such a reform was needed. It was supported by one prominent Liberal, Lord Haldane, whose experience of Germany had taught him the shortcomings of our own educational system in an increasingly competitive world. Balfour showed courage in taking up, despite his uncle's misgivings, a proposal so dangerous politically. There was a further difference from the old historic struggle. There were now over eighty Irish Nationalist members in the House of Commons whose votes would be guided by the wishes of their fellow Roman Catholics in Britain; and in this matter the wishes of the Roman Catholic body in Britain, which was by this time a force in the land, were virtually identical with those of the Church of England and opposed to those of the Protestant dissenters. The Irish Nationalists gave their support to the Conservatives and helped the passage of the bill, but only after bitter and protracted debates. The fight did not end with the Royal assent. Nonconformists organized a "Passive resistance" movement by which they refused on grounds of conscience to pay the education rate. In not a few cases their goods were distrained in lieu of payment, and the comparison with Hampden's refusal to pay ship money was often on Nonconformist lips. The Welsh Nonconformists, whose natural militancy was heightened by Lloyd George's oratory, were specially troubled by the large number of single-school areas, where their children were obliged to attend Church schools. They made a determined and highly successful effort at the ensuing local elections to secure control of the municipal and county councils, and once in control they resolved to levy no education rate until they secured complete control over the spending of the money. Some authorities refused to administer the Education Act at all. The reply of the government was to pass the Local Education (Local Authority Default) Act, 1904, which empowered the Board of Education to make payments direct to school managers and to deduct the amount from the Exchequer grants payable to the defaulting authorities.[6a]

The revolt was broken, but the cost to the Conservative party in electoral popularity was heavy. The election of a Baptist Liberal candidate in a by-election in 1902 in North Leeds, which had returned a Conservative at the five previous elections, was an omen; and before the Conservative party could surmount these difficulties it was weakened by a still more serious division within its own ranks.

Joseph Chamberlain, who had split the Liberals in 1886, was now fated to split the Unionists, and that by raising another historic controversy, the question of free trade. It came about through his devotion to imperial unity, which had become the dominating passion of his life. The first imperial conference associated with Queen Victoria's diamond jubilee in 1897 had been followed by a second in 1902, and it there became clear to Chamberlain that the only union to which the Prime Ministers of the oversea territories would agree was one based on imperial preference. There had been introduced in the 1902 budget a small duty of a shilling a quarter on imported corn which did not conflict with the principles of free trade as it applied to corn from all countries and was so small as to be only a registration duty. (It had been kept until 1869 and its removal then had been regarded as a piece of economic pedantry.) Chamberlain hoped to abolish this tax for the colonies and to keep it for foreign countries as a start in the policy of imperial preference, but while he was away in South Africa trying to reach an agreed settlement with the Boers the Chancellor of the Exchequer, Ritchie, abolished the tax altogether. This was a bitter blow to Chamberlain, and led to an estrangement within the Cabinet between the rigid free traders and the advocates of imperial preference. The divergence was unperceived by the general public until Chamberlain made a speech to his constituents in May 1903 in which he sketched a plan for raising more revenue by rearranging the tariff with the dual object of granting a preference to imports from the colonies and financing social reform at home. It was a carefully framed and not unattractive policy, but in proposing to tamper with free trade Chamberlain touched a sensitive political nerve; and a fortnight later in a speech to the House of Commons he frankly admitted, "If you are to give a preference to the colonies, you must put a tax on food."[7]

Throughout the Liberal ranks, already profiting from the Education Act, there rang the cry, "The Lord hath delivered them into our hands." It was not Chamberlain's habit to let his actions fall behind his words, and in July he founded the Tariff Reform League. Salisbury's death in August removed the one man with sufficient authority to have held the party together. Balfour,[b] knowing that he had colleagues who were as wedded to free trade as Chamberlain was to imperial preference, had laid down that particular opinions on economic subjects should not be made a test of party loyalty, and had talked of an inquiry into the facts, but this only delayed the day of decision. On successive days in September there appeared Balfour's Cabinet paper *Economic Notes on Insular Free Trade*, the Board of Trade's blue book *British and Foreign Trade and Industry*, and the resignations from the Cabinet of Ritchie, Lord George Hamilton and Chamberlain. Ritchie and Hamilton resigned because of their belief in the inviolability of free trade, Chamberlain to be free to conduct a campaign for imperial preference. Austen Chamberlain, son of Joseph, was significantly put at the Exchequer

M

in place of Ritchie. It was taken as a hopeful sign by free traders that Devonshire remained in the Cabinet, but he also was soon to go. The occasion was provided by a speech of Balfour to the party conference in which the party leader declared that he "intended to lead".[8] While holding that a tax on food was not within the limits of practical politics, he asked for a reversal of the fiscal tradition of the past two generations so that the power of negotiating on fiscal questions might be resumed. This did not go far enough for most members of the conference, now swinging round to Chamberlain's views, but it went too far for Devonshire, who resigned his Cabinet post the following day. He concluded that he and Balfour did not mean the same thing by free trade. Balfour, who had only just rearranged his ministry to meet the earlier defections, and had made the Duke's nephew Secretary of the Treasury, was taken aback.

Chamberlain opened his campaign at Glasgow on 6th October 1903, when he argued that the figures of British trade from 1872 showed a relative decline compared with that of such protectionist countries as Germany and the United States, and asked for no tax on raw materials, a small tax on food other than colonial, and a general tax of ten per cent on the price of imported manufactures. He concluded the series with a meeting at the city of London Guildhall in January 1904 when he called on his audience to "learn to think imperially".[9]

After taking a rest in Italy and Egypt, Chamberlain resumed the campaign in the autumn. In the meantime a young Conservative, Winston Churchill, son of Randolph Churchill and a descendent of Marlborough, who had been elected for Oldham in 1900, had broken with his party on account of his free-trade convictions. When he rose in the Commons to advocate free trade, the occupants of the government front bench walked out and were followed by almost all the Conservative members, who then jeered at the speaker through the glass doors. Two months later the rebel Churchill crossed the floor and took a seat near to Lloyd George on a bench below the gangway. The Welsh agitator and the young aristocrat had taken a fancy to each other since their first meeting in the house, when Lloyd George had cut his own remarks short so that Churchill might have a free run for his maiden speech. It was the beginning of a long and momentous friendship between two men who, more than any others, are entitled to the name of saviours of the state; but of this there could be no inkling in 1904, when neither had yet held office.

When he resumed campaigning in the autumn of 1904, Chamberlain encountered trouble from the Duke of Devonshire, with whom he had walked in an uneven partnership since 1886. The duke, in resigning from the government, had remained president of the Liberal Unionist organization, and objected to the subsidization of local Liberal Unionist associations supporting tariff reform. If this departure from neutrality continued, he argued, it would be "almost impossible with any advantage to maintain, under present circumstances, the existence of the Liberal Unionist organization".[10] Chamberlain was willing to see all associations subsidized so long as they supported the government, but, knowing that they were mostly in favour of his campaign, decided to call the duke's bluff. On his own initiative he summoned a party conference where a new constitution was adopted. Devonshire and the other free traders thereupon withdrew from the organization, and founded the Unionist Free Food League and the Unionist Free Trade Club. Among the old Whig's active supporters were Goschen and Lord Hugh Cecil, son of the late Prime Minister and cousin of Balfour. Chamberlain was quite content with this outcome, and reorganized the Liberal Unionist organization with himself as president and Lords Lansdowne and Selborne (both Cabinet ministers) as vice-presidents.

As if Church schools and fiscal reform were not enough to fill the cup, the Unionists exposed themselves to further damaging attacks by their proposals for dealing with the labour problem in South Africa and the evil of drunkenness at home. The Kaffir labour force employed in the mines had been dispersed during the Boer War and could not be reassembled at the wage rates offered afterwards. Though Chamberlain dreamed of white immigrants, this was not a practical solution; and in the end 50,000 Chinese coolies were brought in to work in the deep, hot mines for periods of three years. What was officially known as "Chinese indentured labour" soon became travestied on Liberal platforms as "Chinese slavery". The Licensing Bill of 1904 was an honest and statesmanlike effort to deal with the great social evil of drunkenness by making better provision for the granting and extinguishing of licences to sell liquor. The bill transferred the power to grant licences from justices of the peace to quarter sessions, and provided that if a licence were withdrawn there should be compensation save in cases of misconduct from a fund assessed on the trade itself. This was a constructive method of dealing with a great social problem, but since 1874 the Tories had become identified with "the trade", the Liberals with "temperance", and the opportunity of representing the Tories as the paid lackeys of the brewers was too good to be missed. "The Licensing Bill," said Lloyd George, "is a party bribe for gross political corruption—an act which Tammany Hall could not exceed."[11]

Such tribulations would have taxed the ablest of the Tory party managers, but the combination of Akers-Douglas and Middleton had now been broken up, the new Conservative officials were not of the same calibre and the reunited Liberals were exploiting their opportunities to the utmost. Asquith found in the tariff reform controversy an opportunity to put himself right once more with the main body of the party. The controversy, turning so largely on the correct presentation of figures, suited his analytical mind, and he trailed Chamberlain round the country in a series of memorable speeches. Lloyd George, who used "figures as adjectives", was devastatingly effective in the education and licensing debates.

The Unionist government was doomed, and it was only a question when the bell should toll. The need to avoid a change during the Russo-Japanese war, with Russian naval vessels searching British ships and in one hour of panic firing upon a British fishing fleet, delayed the end till 1905. In November of that year Balfour appealed for unity in the party and the sinking of differences, but his speech had precisely the opposite effect. Chamberlain, now assured that he had the majority of Unionists behind him, demanded the adoption of his whole policy of fiscal reform. Early in December Balfour resigned, and the King sent for Campbell-Bannerman. Rosebery, antagonized by the inclusion of Irish home rule in the new Prime Minister's policy, continued to plough his lonely furrow, but with this single exception Campbell-Bannerman was able to draw on all sections of the party.[12] The Liberal imperialists were represented by Asquith at the Exchequer, Grey at the Foreign Office and Haldane at the War Office. The Radical element provided Morley for the India Office and Lloyd George for the Board of Trade. All in all, it was the most brilliant Cabinet that had sat round the long table in No. 10 Downing Street for many a year; and even the minor figures of the government would have formed an illustrious Cabinet. Among them a place was found for the new recruit, Winston Churchill, as Under-Secretary for the Colonies. The one thing the government lacked at that moment was a majority in the House of Commons, and Campbell-Bannerman promptly set out to obtain it by a dissolution. Before we study the general election of January 1906, it is first necessary to notice a new phenomenon, hardly appreciated at the time, that had appeared over the horizon of British party politics.

PART THREE
ORGANIZED PARTIES IN THE
TWENTIETH CENTURY

16

ENTRY OF THE LABOUR
PARTY
1900–1906

Earlier history of the labour movement—the Social Democratic Federation—the Socialist League—the Fabian Society—Keir Hardie founds the Scottish Labour party—the Independent Labour party founded in 1893 "to secure the collective ownership of the means of production, distribution and exchange"—the Labour party is born in 1900 as the Labour Representation Committee—the Taff Vale judgement—the big unions join—and the Social Democratic Federation withdraws—Labour candidates required to abstain from identifying themselves with the Liberal or Conservative parties—a levy made on affiliated organizations—Liberal pact with Labour for the 1906 election

THE Reform Act of 1832 had given the vote to a large section of the middle classes, but the labouring masses remained without the franchise until it was conferred on householders in two stages in 1867 and 1884; and when they did secure the right to take part in elections to Parliament, many manual workers felt that they were not adequately represented by either the Conservative or the Liberal party. To them the contests of Conservatives and Liberals was a strife between their masters over matters in which for the most part they had no interest. The course eventually adopted, to found a new Labour party, took a long time to win acceptance and still more to realize; but when it was realized it dramatically altered the character of the British party system.

From the Peasants' Revolt of 1381 onwards there had from time to time been stirrings in favour of higher wages, shorter working days and better working conditions which it is not fanciful to describe as a labour movement. In the Industrial Revolution these stirrings had taken the form of trade unions, and although they were declared at common law and by a statute of 1800 to be unlawful combinations in restraint of trade they nevertheless grew and were given exemption from some of the penalties by acts of 1824 and 1825. Attempts to get the workers of many trades to combine, of which the most alarming to employers was the Grand National Consolidated Trades Union in 1834, failed. For a time the labour movement was diverted to political aims by the Chartists, but after the collapse of Chartism the movement again confined itself to economic objectives, and efforts were specially made to get the various societies catering for a single trade to join in one national trade union. In 1868 the Trades Union Congress with a permanent organization was established, and a year later it set up a parliamentary committee mainly for the purpose of watching legislation that affected unionists. A firm legal basis for trade unions was at last provided by acts of 1871, 1875 and 1876.

Neither the Trades Union Congress nor any of its affiliated unions showed any strong disposition at this time to press for the election of working-men candidates to Parliament, though the question was discussed at the congresses of 1869 and 1874. The first effort to secure the election of manual workers to Parliament—after the Chartist candidatures of the forties and fifties—was the formation of the London Working Men's Union in 1866. Owing to lack of funds it did not actually sponsor any candidates when the general election took place on the enlarged franchise in 1868, but three working men—George Howell, W. R. Cremer and E. O. Greening—stood unsuccessfully as Liberal candidates. It was the beginning of an alliance between working-class candidates and the Liberal party that was to last until 1906. The addiction of the Liberal party to the principles of *laisser faire* weighed less in the eyes of such "Lib-Lab" candidates—so they came to be dubbed—than the hierarchical character of the Conservative party; and the eloquent exposition of Tory democracy by Beaconsfield and Churchill counted for less than the fact that the Liberals were prepared, as the Tories were not, to finance a few Labour candidates and to give them a straight fight.

The initiative of the London Working Men's Union was taken up on a wider scale by the Labour Representation League formed in 1869 "to secure the return to Parliament of qualified working men: persons who by character and ability command the confidence of their class, and who are competent to deal satisfactorily with questions of general interest as well as with those in which they are specially interested".[1] It took the occasion of a by-election in Southwark in 1870 to promote the candidature of George Odger, a shoemaker, against both the Liberal and the Conservative candidates. Odger was unsuccessful, but at the general election of 1874 the League supported thirteen working-men candidates and was successful in securing the return of Thomas Burt and Alexander Macdonald for Morpeth and Stafford respectively. Burt was a miner and Macdonald an ex-miner who had become a teacher. They were both given straight fights by the Liberal party. They are usually regarded as the first Labour members of Parliament, but they took the Liberal whip and for all practical purposes were Liberal members. On re-election in 1880 they were joined by Henry Broadhurst, who had been secretary of the League; as a stonemason he had taken part in the rebuilding of the Palace of Westminster after the fire, and a hammer and chisels that he used are still shown in one of the rooms where members may receive visitors. The Labour Representation League died soon afterwards, but in 1885 no fewer than eleven "Lib-Lab" candidates—six of them miners—were elected, and after the general election of 1886 there were still nine. At the Trades Union Congress of 1886 it was agreed to set up a Labour Electoral Association; but the association broke away from the control of the T.U.C. and allied itself openly with the Liberals.

As Sir Ivor Jennings points out,[2] the position of the "Lib-Lab" members was markedly altered in 1886. Until that date Dilke and Chamberlain were pushing the Liberal party hard in the direction of Radical reforms, but Dilke's disgrace and Chamberlain's defection left the "Lib-Lab" members isolated. The resulting temptation to look outside the Liberal party for political salvation was strengthened by the formation of two new bodies. The Social Democratic Federation was the name adopted in 1884 by the Democratic Federation founded in 1881 by an old Etonian with a flowing beard, Henry Mayers Hyndman, who was said by his enemies to have become embittered against society because his father had left most of his wealth for the building of churches. Despite the innocence of its name it was committed to the creed of Karl Marx, which Hyndman had espoused—without due acknowledgement, thereby giving lasting offence to the German Socialist. William Morris and others seceded in 1884 and founded the Socialist League, which came to repudiate parliamentary action and before it expired in 1890 became imbued with anarchism, but Hyndman continued to disseminate Marxist Socialism through the Social Democratic Federation, and despite his haughty and disdainful manner had a considerable influence upon many individuals who later became Social leaders. The Fabian Society founded about the same time—in the winter of 1883–4—by Edward R. Pease and others was also committed to Socialist views, but was a body of a more empirical and practical character, and took its economics more from Mill and Jevons than from Marx. It was soon joined by George Bernard Shaw and Sidney Webb, and a phrase coined by the latter at a later date, "the inevitability of gradualness", characterized the Fabians from the outset. Though they set before themselves the lofty aim of "reconstructing society in accordance with the highest moral possibilities", they proposed to do so by "permeating" the older parties with their principles. In the creation of elected local authorities under the act of 1888 they saw an opportunity of carrying their principles into effect by instalments through municipal enterprise, and became the advocates of "gas and water socialism". The publication of *Fabian Essays* in 1889 made a deep impression by the well-written argument for a socialism more congenial to the British character than Hyndman's imported variety.[a]

The process of forming a new working-class party was accelerated by one of those personal incidents that have so often been decisive in British party history. In 1888 James Keir Hardie tried to get himself selected as the Liberal candidate at a by-election in mid-Lanark. He failed, a London lawyer being preferred. Thereupon he stood as a "Labour and Home Rule" candidate, was placed at the bottom of the poll, and promptly founded the Scottish Labour party "to educate the people politically, and to secure the return to Parliament and all local bodies of members pledged to its programme".[3] In the next few years Labour unions with similar objects were founded in Bradford, Colne Valley and several other places in Yorkshire and Lancashire. At the general election of 1892 all five candidates nominated by the Scottish Labour party were defeated, but Keir Hardie won West Ham South and John Burns won Battersea, both with Liberal support, J. Havelock Wilson won Newcastle in a three-cornered fight, and Ben Tillett was only just beaten in Bradford; and it was in Bradford that a conference was held early in 1893 to consider the formation of a Labour party independent both of Conservatives and of Liberals. It came about because Joseph Burgess, editor of the *Workman's Times*, invited all readers who wished to join such a party to write to him, and over 2,750 did so. The Bradford conference decided to form such a party and to call it the Independent Labour party.[b] Though prepared to work for a series of immediate reforms, the new party adopted for its ultimate object "to secure the collective ownership of all the means of production, distribution and exchange". The fateful phrase committed the Independent Labour party to a socialist policy from the outset, but it was a non-Marxist socialism.

The historian of the Labour party has made a pertinent comment on the Bradford conference. Mr. Pelling writes:[4]

"The most interesting feature of the gathering was the presence of a new type of political delegate—the intelligent, respectable, working trade unionist of the new labour clubs. Men of this type, young and friendly, their countenances gleaming with good humour above their loose red ties, dominated the scene. They were not politicians for politics' sake; they were the working class in earnest, the product of the new education and the widening franchise. Their enthusiasm and discipline impressed the observers in the gallery and the reporters who crowded at the press table. They were the tangible evidence of a new factor in British politics."

Among the "new men" whom the I.L.P. attracted into politics

two were to play major rôles in their country's destiny, one a Scot and the other a Yorkshireman. Both joined in 1894. Ramsay Mac-Donald was already a member of the Fabian Society and from 1894 to 1900 he was on the executive committee of that body, but he was ill at ease in it and Webb regarded him as a visionary and intransigeant. It was the refusal of the Liberals to adopt a trade union candidate for a by-election at Attercliffe that impelled him to write to Hardie an application to join the I.L.P. The flat in Lincoln's Inn Fields where he and Margaret MacDonald kept a modest open house after their marriage in 1896 became a great meeting-place for international socialists. His presence, his voice, his manner put him despite his humble birth in the grand tradition of political leaders. The Yorkshireman, Philip Snowden, was a dour fighter with a bitter, rasping tongue, having none of MacDonald's imagination but with a far firmer grasp of figures. Hardie, MacDonald, Snowden and Bruce Glasier were the main spokesmen of the I.L.P. in its early days, and worked tirelessly in its cause. MacDonald was made its secretary.

By 1895 the I.L.P. had 10,000 members, and it fought twenty-eight seats, all except four against Conservative and Liberal candidates, but it did not win any; MacDonald and Snowden were among the defeated, and Keir Hardie even lost West Ham through estranging his former Liberal supporters.

The founders of the Independent Labour party had hoped to get trade union backing and money, but this was not forthcoming, partly because the attractiveness of the party's title did not disguise its socialist aims. The Fabian Society, while prepared to use the Conservative and Liberal parties for its own purposes, had long been urging the trade unions to set up their own party. The labour disputes in the years before 1890—strikes of match-girls, gas workers and dockers—all helped to increase the pressure. The resignation in that year of Henry Broadhurst as general secretary of the Trades Union Congress helped, for he had been a main architect of the alliance with the Liberals. The Conservative triumph in 1895 and the weakness of the Liberals contributed. A series of judicial decisions, some in the House of Lords, depriving trade unions of rights that they thought they had long possessed, brought exasperation with the existing parties to a head.

The Trades Union Congress at last capitulated. In 1899 the Amalgamated Society of Railway Servants submitted a resolution instructing the parliamentary committee "to invite the cooperation of all the cooperative, socialistic, trade union and other working [-class] organizations to jointly cooperate on lines mutually agreed upon in convening a special congress of representatives from such of the above-named organizations as may be willing to take part to devise ways and means for securing the return of an increased number of labour members to the next Parliament".[5] The language of the resolution was inelegant but discreet. It is said to have been drafted in Hardie's office, perhaps with MacDonald's help. Even so, the miners, who were strong enough in certain constituencies to force their own candidates upon the Liberals, strongly opposed. Much of the support came from the new unions of unskilled workers who were only just beginning to be organized. The resolution was carried by only 546,000 votes to 434,000; but carried it was, though it was by no means certain that all who voted for it understood what it meant.

Hardie and MacDonald knew exactly what they wanted, and took advantage of the scepticism of the parliamentary committee about the project to ensure that the arrangements for the conference were remitted to a special body on which the parliamentary committee (still soaked in Liberalism) had only four representatives and the Independent Labour party, the Social Democratic Federation and the Fabian Society had six. The Cooperative movement, still very Liberal in outlook, refused on this occasion to be cooperative. The six representatives of the Socialist societies included Hardie, MacDonald and Shaw, and they may be regarded as the chief architects of the new party, though the natural antipathy of MacDonald and Shaw for each other had been sharpened by the Boer War. The I.L.P., like the S.D.F., denounced the war as capitalist exploitation, but the Fabian Society refused to do so, and MacDonald resigned his membership along with George Barnes, Mrs. Pankhurst and others. The special committee decided to call a conference for 27th and 28th February 1900 in that gloomiest of all buildings in the city of London, the Memorial Hall in Farringdon Street. MacDonald drafted eight resolutions for the conference and won acceptance for them from the organizing committee. There was no mention of socialism, as that would have frightened the T.U.C. When the conference met, the S.D.F. demanded a new party that should be "based upon the recognition of the class war" and should "have for its ultimate objective the socialization of the means of production, distribution and exchange". This was rejected, as was a proposal from the other fringe that the new organization should work for the return to Parliament of working-class Liberals sympathetic with the aims of the Labour movement. The way was open for Hardie to move MacDonald's formula that there should be a "distinct Labour group in Parliament who should have their own whips and agree upon their policy, which must embrace a readiness to cooperate with any party which for the time being may be engaged in promoting legislation in the direct interests of labour, and be equally ready to associate themselves with any party in opposing measures having an opposite tendency".[6] In order to secure this object the conference decided to set up a Labour Representation Committee to which affiliated organizations were to pay ten shillings a year for each thousand members. The Labour Representation Committee was to have an executive consisting of seven trade unionists, two representatives from the I.L.P., two from the S.D.F. and one from the Fabian Society.

In this way the Labour party was born, though it was not to be so called until 1906, and in form the Labour Representation Committee did not differ from the Labour Representation League of 1869 or the Labour Electoral Association of 1886. It was given no directions with regard to policy. It differed from the older parties in that they had begun in Parliament and had created an extra-parliamentary organization to support their parliamentary activities, whereas the Labour Representation Committee started outside Parliament with the object of securing representation therein. This difference has had consequences that have endured to the present day. It differed from the older parties also in that they consisted entirely of individuals, whereas the Labour Representation Committee had no individual members but only affiliated organizations. This difference also has persisted, though since 1918 the Labour party has had individual members' sections. It differed yet again from the older parties in being openly based upon a class concept, but the distinction cannot be pressed hard. Though in theory membership of the Conservative and Liberal parties, and candidature for the highest offices in them, were open to anyone in the land, in practice they were dominated by the upper and middle classes; and although the Labour party was brought into existence to secure greater representation for the labouring classes, not a few members of the upper and middle classes lent it their support or used it as an instrument for achieving their personal ambitions. The Fabian Society from its inception was composed almost entirely of middle-class intellectuals.

It is an interesting question why the advocates of greater representation for the labouring classes founded a new party instead of trying to capture or transform an existing one—which, in the light of the "Lib-Lab" story, could only have been the Liberal party. The Liberal party had itself been transformed almost out of recognition from the old Whig party. The question is both asked and given a plausible answer by Mr. Henry Pelling:[7]

"If its socialist enthusiasm was not strong, why did not the newly enfranchised 'working class', with its growing homogenity, not infiltrate and capture the bastions of an existing political party, and in particular the Liberal party? Certainly the Liberal party seemed likely to be open to some such infiltration, for it was already a coalition of political forces whose relative strength varied from time to time, and it contained a radical wing which had made a strong appeal for working-class support. Unfortunately, however, in the 1870's and 1880's its structure had become rather rigid, and its leadership lacked both the power and the will to alter the situation.

The local Liberal associations, largely in the hands of business and professional men and Nonconformist ministers, would rarely adopt working men as candidates, partly because they would have to take on the burden of paying the election expenses and upkeep of a poor man, and partly because their own special interests would suffer if the 'labour question' were thrust to the fore. The ageing Gladstone, obsessed with his 'mission' to 'pacify Ireland', would not take up the questions which seemed so vital to young labour leaders, such as the state payment of M.P.s; and it was against his principles to venture into the vast field of social legislation if he could possibly avoid it."

If we add the check to radicalism in the Liberal party after 1886 owing to the loss of Chamberlain and the eclipse of Dilke we have a sufficient answer to the question.

Thanks to MacDonald's skill in negotiating, the socialist societies (the I.L.P. being included in that term) had secured a voice in the Labour Representation Committee out of all proportion to their membership or financial contribution; and the strength of the socialist element was increased still further by the choice of MacDonald as secretary. There was not much competition for the job, which was virtually unpaid for four years, but it was offered to a certain Brocklehurst and declined before MacDonald was unanimously elected. The office was a back room in MacDonald's flat in Lincoln's Inn Fields, and after twelve months he was voted the sum of twenty guineas "as an acknowledgement of his past services".

The Labour Representation Committee had to contest its first general election within six months of being formed, and it is hardly surprising, when we consider the short time available, the lack of resources and the atmosphere of the "khaki election", that the achievement was minimal. Fifteen candidates were endorsed, but the Labour Representation Committee, whose total expenditure came to £33, could give them no more than a small supply of leaflets. The trade unions and socialist societies who sponsored these candidates gave more help. Of the fifteen, only two were elected. Keir Hardie was lucky to get in at Merthyr in company with a Liberal, because the South Wales miners opposed the Boer War and the other Liberal candidate did not. Richard Bell, secretary of the Amalgamated Society of Railway Servants, was elected at Derby, also in the company of a Liberal, but he was himself a Liberal in everything except name and in 1904 was treated as a Liberal member. As eight "Lib-Labs" were returned at the election, and the two Labour members were far from seeing eye to eye, the claim of the Labour Representation Committee to represent the labouring classes was not obvious.

The outlook for the Labour Representation Committee was transformed by the Taff Vale judgement of 1901. After a strike on the Taff Vale railway in that year, the general manager of the railway company brought actions for damages against the secretary of the Amalgamated Society for picketing the railway stations at Cardiff. The House of Lords not only upheld a case known as Lyons v. Wilkins which seriously restricted picketing, but held that the funds of the union were liable for torts committed by its officials; and the Taff Vale Railway Company did, in fact, collect £23,000 in damages.

The dismay and indignation of the trade union movement at this decision found expression in a resolve that what the lawyers had proclaimed to be the law must be undone by act of Parliament; and this led not only to the revival in the fortunes of the Liberal party but to much stronger support for the Labour Representation Committee. The affiliated membership of the committee, which was only 376,000 in 1901, rose to 469,000 in 1902 and to 861,000 in 1903. At the outset, apart from the new unions of unskilled workers, only a few unions had affiliated, and they for special reasons—the Railway Servants because of the large volume of railway legislation in Parliament, and the Boot and Shoe Workers and printers' unions because of the technological changes through which their industries were passing. The Engineers joined in 1902 and the Textile Workers in 1903. Among the big unions only the miners continued to stand aloof, and that mainly because of their power to compel the Liberal party to support their candidates. There had in the meantime been one loss, which was really a gain. Failing to get the 1901 conference, as it had failed to get the inaugural conference, to base the new party on the class war, the Social Democratic Federation withdrew. Its two seats on the executive were filled by trade unionists, and as Pease, the Fabian representative, generally sided with them against the I.L.P., the trade union element in the party was strengthened. Attempts to expel the socialist societies were, however, defeated as regularly as attempts to commit the new party to socialism.

Increasing membership permitted modest expansion, and in 1902 MacDonald was given £25 for the use of his back room as an office and allowed thirty shillings a week for an assistant. He chose J. S. Middleton, who was to serve the Labour party faithfully as an unassuming official for many years. In 1904 two rooms in Victoria Street were rented as an office, and MacDonald was paid £250 a year, out of which he had to find £100 for his assistant.

In the meantime there had been significant successes at by-elections. At Clitheroe (North-east Lancashire) in 1902 Snowden had been chosen by the I.L.P., but he withdrew in favour of David Shackleton, secretary of the Cotton Weavers, who stood as a Labour candidate under the auspices of the Labour Representation Committee and received the support of the former Liberal member for the division. The Conservatives did not put up a candidate and Shackleton was returned unopposed. Before the year was out Will

Crooks, with Liberal support, won Woolwich, and Arthur Henderson, a Wesleyan and Ironfounder who had been a Liberal agent, was induced to stand at Barnard Castle and increased the Labour representation at Westminster to a total of five—or four if we omit Bell, for he angered his former colleagues in 1904 by sending a telegram of congratulations to the Liberal who had defeated the committee's candidate at Norwich. Bell's action was regarded with special disapproval as the 1903 conference had decided that in future members elected to Parliament with the support of the Representation Committee should "abstain strictly from identifying themselves with, or promoting the interests of, any section of the Liberal or Conservative parties". Endorsed candidates were required to "accept this pledge or resign", and were directed to "appear before their constituencies under the title of Labour candidates only". The sanction for these requirements was provided by another resolution of the same conference, which decided to make a levy of one penny a member annually on all affiliated organizations for the purpose of maintaining its members of Parliament in the House of Commons and meeting their election expenses. No drawings were to be made until £2,500 had been accumulated, after which all members of Parliament sponsored by the Labour Representation Committee were to receive £200 a year.

These decisions were momentous in the history of the British party system as they formally and finally committed the Labour movement to the building up of a new party distinct from the two historic parties. At that date no one could discern how successful the new Labour party was going to be; but if it continued to attract the organized workers at the rate at which it was then drawing them in, it was bound, as we can now see, to lead either to the realignment of the British party system on a tripartite basis or to the destruction of the Liberal party.[c]

If Herbert Gladstone, then Liberal chief whip, could have foreseen these consequences in 1903 he would hardly have entered into negotiations with MacDonald for an electoral pact by which each would use his influence to ensure that so far as possible Liberal and Labour candidates would not oppose each other. At that time the necessity of persuading a small number of Liberal associations not to run a candidate in order to give a straight fight to a Labour man seemed a small price to pay for the assurance of Labour votes in other constituencies, constituting the great majority, and Labour support in the new House of Commons. To MacDonald, ever conscious of the poverty of his resources, the deal offered a prospect of more seats than the Labour Representation Committee could possibly obtain by its own efforts; and once a solid group of Labour members was returned to Parliament, this would be something on which to build. Long before the negotiations with Gladstone, in an

article in the *Echo* in 1901, MacDonald had written of the cooperation between the I.L.P. and the Radicals in the Liberal party in
opposing the Boer War and had urged "some arrangement for
mutual help, not so much by speaking or working for each other as
by securing for each other opportunities of contesting seats un-
hampered by third candidates".[8]

The Unionists made the alliance easier by their choice of issues. In
supporting the Education Act of 1902 the Fabian Society was the
odd man out as it had been over the Boer War, and Webb as a civil
servant had a hand in drafting it; but Henderson was typical of the
Nonconformists now flocking into a party which one of its later
secretaries claimed to owe more to Methodism than to Marxism,[9]
and most Labour voters took the Liberal view of the measure. The
cry of "Chinese slavery" roused an instinctive opposition among
trade unionists for it threatened the standards of white immigrants
and might presage an attack on labour standards at home. As for the
new fiscal ideas, a socialist society would have more affinities with
protection than with free trade, but few Labour voters were socialists at that time, and the trade unionists were more conscious of the
danger of dearer food. The deal was struck, and although the general
election did not take place so soon as was then expected it was big
with consequences.[d]

N

17

THE NEW LIBERALISM
1906–1910

Huge Liberal majority—Balfour accepts "fiscal reform"—Liberal abandonment of laisser faire—significance of the twenty-nine Labour members—increased party bitterness—measures dropped because of opposition by the Lords—Liberal dilemma—an independent socialist's victory at a by-election—Asquith becomes Prime Minister and Lloyd George Chancellor of the Exchequer—"People's budget"—the Lords reject the Finance Bill—Asquith obtains a dissolution—Liberals and Unionists returned in almost equal numbers —the Liberal government now dependent on the Irish Nationalist and Labour parties

IN throwing the responsibility for dissolution upon Campbell-Bannerman towards the end of 1905, Balfour was suspected by friends and opponents alike of playing a master card, but in truth he was throwing his hand in. If we leave out the rather different case of the break-up of the coalition in 1922, he was the last Prime Minister to resign in advance of a defeat at the polls. The dominant theme of the campaign was the fiscal question—the "big loaf" *versus* the "small loaf"—but "Chinese slavery" played its part and Church schools and licensing had left their memories. Home rule for Ireland was muted, through realization that nothing could be done until means were found to overcome the opposition of the House of Lords. As the results began to come in during January 1906 it became evident that this was no ordinary victory but a landslide. Only 132 Conservatives and twenty-five Liberal Unionists were returned, and among the defeated was Arthur Balfour himself in Manchester. The Liberals numbered no fewer than 377. In addition there were fifty-three Labour members, of whom twenty-four were "Lib-Labs" supported by the Liberals and twenty-nine were nominated by the Labour Representation Committee. There were the usual eighty-three Irish Nationalist members. The Liberals and "Lib-Labs" together numbered 401, and all other parties together could muster only 269, giving the Liberals a clear majority of 132 over all others; but normally the Irish Nationalist and Labour members could be expected to vote with the Liberals, giving the government a voting strength of 513 against the 157 Unionists, a normal majority of 356. Nothing like it had been known since the first Reform Parliament of 1832.

The election of 1906 marked the end of an age, for though the labels on the old party bottles remained the same, the contents were markedly different; and a new bottle of unknown quality had been added to the shelf.

An immediate consequence of the election was to commit the Conservative party to protection once more after more than half a century in which the question had been allowed to remain practically dormant. Though the fall in the Liberal Unionist membership of the house between the general elections was proportionately almost the same as the Conservative fall, what people noticed was that Chamberlain had triumphed in West Birmingham and every other Birmingham division had returned a tariff reformer; and of the 132 Conservatives returned, no fewer than 109 had declared themselves in favour of tariff reform. Chamberlain had clearly won his campaign inside the party, and in the "Valentine letters" exchanged between him and Balfour—so called because they were written on 14th February 1906—the latter acknowledged :[1]

"I hold that fiscal reform is, and must remain, the first constructive work of the Unionist party.

"That the objects of such reform are to secure more equal terms of competition for British trade, and closer commercial union with the colonies.

"That, while it is at present unnecessary to prescribe the exact methods by which these objects are to be attained, and inexpedient to permit differences of opinion as to those methods to divide the party, though other means may be possible, the establishment of a moderate general tariff on manufactured goods, not imposed for the purpose of raising prices or giving artificial protection against legitimate competition, and the imposition of a small duty on foreign corn, are not in principle objectionable, and should be adopted if shown to be necessary for the attainment of the ends in view or for purposes of revenue."

At that time Balfour was out of Parliament and Chamberlain was leading the Unionists in the House of Commons. The agreement between the leaders was ratified a few days later by a party meeting, a seat was found for Balfour by the resignation of a city of London member, and he was confirmed in his leadership of the party. A few months later, with dramatic suddenness, Chamberlain was removed from the public scene. Immediately after enthusiastic celebrations in Birmingham of his seventieth birthday he was incapacitated by a paralytic stroke and, though he survived almost to the outbreak of war in 1914, he never spoke in public again. It so happened that the annual Conservative conference was held in Birmingham the year after Chamberlain's seizure, and in his speech after the conference Balfour committed the party even more firmly to protection.

While the Conservative party returned after 1906 to its ancient ways, the Liberals went forward to the new and little-trodden paths of social reform and state intervention. To understand the reason for its swift conversion from *laisser faire*, it is necessary first to appreciate the significance of the new Labour party.

The Labour Representation Committee had put fifty candidates into the field. All except one were of working-class origin. Forty of them were sponsored by trade unions, trades councils or local Labour representation committees and ten by the Independent Labour party. Only eighteen were opposed by Liberal candidates, and some of those Liberal opponents were not backed by their parties. There were ten two-member divisions in which one Liberal and one Labour candidate fought together against Conservatives. As we have noted, twenty-nine of the fifty were returned to Parliament. Twelve of them came from Lancashire where cooperation with the Liberals had been close in view of the previous Tory domination of the county; in Wales the Liberals felt less need to make concessions to Labour, and in Scotland none at all. Only five secured election against Liberal opponents. The Independent Labour party had sponsored seven of the new Labour members, including Hardie, MacDonald and Snowden; the others were sponsored by trade unions, trades councils or local committees, but some of them were also members of the I.L.P. and one (Will Thorne, secretary of the Gasworkers' Union) belonged to the Social Democratic Federation.

Immediately after the new Parliament met, the Labour Representation Committee took the name of the Labour party, by which it has since been known. (It is usual in the history books to give the Labour party a continuous history from 1900, and this is proper, but the name dates only from 1906.) The twenty-nine members proceeded to elect officers and whips, just like the older parties, but with a significant difference. The chief officer was not called "leader" but "chairman" of the Parliamentary Labour party, and he was made subject to annual election. This came about because at the first election there were two candidates, Hardie (sponsored by the I.L.P. and a socialist) and Shackleton (sponsored by the Cotton Weavers and not a socialist). On a show of hands they obtained an equal number of votes, MacDonald as secretary of the party abstaining. In a ballot MacDonald again abstained, and the two candidates again obtained the same number of votes. In a second ballot MacDonald voted and Hardie was elected, but he had to promise that he would not make his chairmanship permanent. He was succeeded in 1908 by Henderson (hitherto the party whip), and Henderson was succeeded in 1910 by Barnes. When Barnes fell ill in 1911, MacDonald agreed to stand, and he at length assumed the post to which his parliamentary abilities entitled him. Henderson took MacDonald's place as secretary of the party, and MacDonald remained chairman until the outbreak of war in 1914. He had been doubtful about giving up the (modestly) paid post of secretary for the unpaid office of chairman with an assurance of only two years' tenure, but by 1914 he had established his pre-eminence among his colleagues, and it seems likely that but for the war he would have become "leader" in the full sense, even if not in name.

These early incidents illustrate the mutual suspicions of socialists and non-socialists, intellectuals and trade unionists, with which the Labour party has at all times in varying degrees been affected. Most of the Parliamentary Labour party in 1906 were anything but revolutionaries, and Elton aptly notes that a photograph of the twenty-nine taken on the terrace of the house makes them look "less like a set of revolutionary malcontents, than an excursion of non-conformist lay-preachers".[2] So Ben Tillett felt in 1908 when he exploded with a pamphlet *Is the Parliamentary Labour Party a Failure?* which described Henderson, Snowden and Shackleton as "sheer hypocrites", "liars at five and ten guineas a time", "cruel hoaxers", "softly feline in their purring to ministers and their patronage", "betrayers of the class that willingly supports them", and "press flunkeys to Asquith".[3]

"Flunkeys to Asquith"—yes, but most of the twenty-nine members knew that they would not be sitting in Parliament if it had not been for the goodwill of the Liberal party. In a real sense the creator of the Labour party was Herbert Gladstone. The Liberals on their side knew that but for the Labour votes given to Liberal candidates in constituencies where there was no Labour candidate there would have been many more Tory faces in the House of Commons; and the existence of a Labour party making a powerful new appeal to the working masses was a potent influence in driving the Liberal party into social and economic reforms that would have been anathema to Herbert Gladstone's father. The significance of the Labour party was not lost upon shrewd observers. Balfour was guilty of partisan exaggeration in describing Campbell-Bannerman as a "mere cork" on the socialist tide,[4] but did not err in writing to Lord Knollys:[5] "We have here to do with something much more important than the swing of the pendulum or all the squabbles about free trade and fiscal reform. We are face to face (no doubt in a milder form) with the socialist difficulties which loom so large on the continent. Unless I am greatly mistaken, the election of 1906 inaugurates a new era."

The significance was appreciated also on the other side of the Atlantic by Balfour's correspondent, Senator Lodge, who wrote to him:[6]

"With us such violent changes have usually been followed by equally violent and quick reactions; but the more significant feature of your election seems to be, not the size of the Liberal majority—that will come and go—but the appearance of a large and compact body of Labour members. I think it was certain to come, but I believe it portends a very radical alteration in your politics and the adjustment of parties."

Driven by Labour pressure and by its own new men into social reform and state interference with industry, the Liberal party became still further alienated from the Conservative. Even before the new Parliament met, the differences over Church schools, licensing laws, Irish home rule and tariffs had made the party conflict more acute than it had been for a generation. The need to raise money by taxation for the social reforms to which the Liberal government was now committed introduced a new element of discord by making the Liberals appear the enemies, and Conservatives the champions, of property in all its forms, but particularly in the form of land, which still possessed a mystical appeal to Tory hearts. State intervention in economic processes and championship of the trade unions against employers still further exacerbated the conflict by appearing, according to the economic ideas of the time, to strike at the sources by which taxable wealth was created. The fiery radical from Wales was the chief instigator and pilot of government legislation in these matters; and the name of Lloyd George became more hated among men of property and birth than that of any foreign despot. In desperation at finding all they stood for threatened, Conservatives used the one weapon left to their hands; and when the House of Lords insisted on its right to throw out radical legislation and even a radical budget, a constitutional crisis of the greatest magnitude was precipitated. Into a cauldron already seething the Irish problem was thrown. Party differences reached a point of bitterness not known since the agitation that led to the first Reform Act. They found expression in disaffection among army officers, and it is not unlikely that there would have been civil war in Ulster if the outbreak of a world conflict had not silenced domestic discord.

Yet the King's government was somehow carried on, and Great Britain even reached new levels of prosperity. Despite the bitterness of party strife, there was an underlying unity between the parties, so much so that Hilaire Belloc, a member of Parliament from 1906 to 1910, combined with Cecil Chesterton to write a book[7] maintaining that the party system was an "organized imposture", in which a pretence of party differences concealed the collusion between the two front benches. Those front benches, connected in not a few instances by ties of blood and marriage, were at one in their determination to keep in existence the same type of society, a type of society from which they both benefited. Belloc, who was temperamentally unsuited for the routine work of the House of Commons, and Cecil Chesterton failed to recognize that the party system will work only if men are prepared to cooperate in a friendly way in private while differing sharply on policy in public. The element of truth in their views must not conceal the gravity of the bitterness between Conservatives and Liberals in the years before 1914. Real though that bitterness was, it was not allowed to interfere with the conduct of foreign policy which about the turn of the century had assumed a menacing importance. The "rattling of the sabre" by the Kaiser Wilhelm II made it necessary even for the friends of imperial Germany, such as Chamberlain among the Unionists and Haldane among the Liberals, to accept the need for new alignments in foreign policy and greater preparedness in defence. The *entente cordiale* with France in 1904 and the conclusion of the alliance with Japan in 1905 were outward signs of the new defensive measures, while Balfour later explained his delay in resigning till the end of 1905 by the need to see the new 18-pounder gun in service Campbell-Bannerman tactfully invited Grey to take the Foreign Office largely because Grey would be more acceptable to the Conservatives than Morley in a department which was peculiarly liable to attract Tory criticism; and whatever criticisms may justly be levelled at his conduct of that great office in the next eight momentous years, they are criticisms more from his own side than from the opposition. The main charge is that for some years he concealed even from members of his own Cabinet, except Campbell-Bannerman, Asquith and Haldane, the fact that he had agreed to military conversations between British and French experts which created a presumption that in the event of war British troops would be found at the side of French; but the whole Cabinet was informed in 1912, when questions had begun to be asked. It can be claimed on behalf of Grey that when war came his country entered it as a virtually united nation; but it can be claimed against him, though not proved, that if foreign policy had been made the subject of normal party processes, with all the attendant publicity, Germany would not have been left in doubt about British intentions and might have more effectively restrained the Austrian moves that set Europe in flames.

The related subject of defence was kept largely but not wholly out of the party conflict. There was a continuity between the creation of the Committee of Imperial Defence by Balfour in 1904, though Balfour felt nervous about leaving the new and delicate mechanism in Liberal hands, and the Army reforms of Haldane in 1907, but in 1909 the maintenance of the "two-power standard" for the Royal Navy brought about sharp exchanges between the parties. German naval expansion led the Admiralty, through its First Lord, McKenna, to demand provision for six new Dreadnoughts in the estimates. The Chancellor, by then Lloyd George, and the President of the Board of Trade, Churchill, were willing to agree to four. Asquith suggested that four should be laid down at once and preparations made for another four. "The Admiralty," wrote Churchill in later life, "had demanded six ships; the economists offered four, and we finally compromised on eight." This "curious and characteristic solution" might not have come about if the Conservatives, apprised of the facts, had not made it the subject of agitation throughout the country. "We want eight and we won't wait" was the chorus that spread from Wigan to Croydon and Glasgow.[8]

On the domestic front the party struggle began almost immediately in 1906 over an Education Bill to amend the act of 1902 in a manner acceptable to the Nonconformists. There were now some 200 dissenters in the House of Commons, a phenomenon not known since the days of Cromwell. Augustine Birrell, the President of the Board of Education, proposed that voluntary schools should be compulsorily transferred to the local authority with facilities for the giving of "denominational" instruction in transferred schools out of school hours by persons other than the regular teachers; and that in populous districts upon the demand of sufficient parents there should be schools maintained out of public funds in which "denominational" teaching could be included in the curriculum. The bill passed the House of Commons by a large majority, but the Lords introduced amendments to which the Commons refused to agree, and after all attempts at compromise had failed the measure was dropped.

Better fortune attended a bill for the provision of meals in schools. Promoted by the Labour party, it received very wide support and was the beginning of a formidable volume of social reform. The Education (Provision of Meals) Act, 1906, enabled local education authorities to help voluntary agencies in providing meals for children attending public elementary schools and in the case of necessitous children permitted them to defray the cost.

The House of Lords was equally circumspect when the government introduced legislation to rectify the decision of the law lords in the matter of the Taff Vale strike, partly because the bill restored to trade unions rights they had previously enjoyed and partly because a royal commission had endorsed the need for remedy. The bill was one in which the Labour movement was specially interested, and it is not without significance that Campbell-Bannerman accepted a Labour member's proposal, giving direct protection to trade union funds, in place of a roundabout method of protection devised by his law officers. The Trade Disputes Act of 1906 freed trade unions from all liability to actions for conspiracy if their acts were done in furtherance of a trade dispute;[9] authorized peaceful picketing; and forbade the courts to entertain any civil action against a trade union. The opposition did not divide against the measure either on second or on third reading in either house, and in the Lords not even an amendment was moved.

Both these measures showed the influence of the small group of Labour members, for although they were numerically weak in the House of Commons they were rightly felt to represent something powerful outside. The Unionists showed no such inhibitions when the government introduced a bill to abolish plural voting, and the Lords rejected it cavalierly after the briefest of debates.

For a time in 1907 the grant of responsible government to the Transvaal and Orange River colonies and the creation of the British Expeditionary Force and Territorial Army diverted attention from the coming struggle. Not a few useful measures even reached the statute book, including a Deceased Wife's Sister Act particularly dear to Liberal hearts—for had not a Liberal been defined as a man who believes in free trade and hopes to marry his deceased wife's sister? But a Scottish Small Holdings Bill and a Valuation Bill were dropped because of opposition in the Lords; a new Education Bill and an Irish Councils Bill (a tame substitute for home rule but providing some devolution of administrative powers) were abandoned without even getting so far; and a Licensing Bill, announced from the Throne, was not even introduced. Members of the Cabinet brooded on how best they could cope with an upper chamber that would reject or emasculate their most cherished legislation. The simplest course would have been to have gone to the country with a plan for reform of the House of Lords. In 1906, or even 1907, this would not have cut deeply, if at all, into the massive Liberal majority, but there was no unanimity on the reform needed, even the rejection of the Education Bill was not thought a sufficiently serious justification, and most members, at that time unpaid, did not relish the expense of another election. Campbell-Bannerman contented himself with getting the House of Commons to pass a resolution "that in order to give effect to the will of the people, as expressed by their elected representatives, it is necessary that the power of the other house to alter or reject bills passed by this house should be so restricted by law as to secure that within the limits of a single Parliament the final decision of the Commons shall prevail".[10]

The tempo quickened in 1908. It may have been accelerated by the astonishing victory in a Colne Valley by-election the previous year of Victor Grayson, a young Socialist from Owens College, Manchester, despite the fact that he was disowned by both the Labour Party and the I.L.P. Although he took the Labour whip in Parliament, raising the number of Labour members to thirty, Grayson was too flamboyant a character to accept party discipline, and found the pleasure of attacking his colleagues on public platforms no less intoxicating than the liquors to which he quickly succumbed; but the Liberal leaders may well have seen some significance in the fact that he, and not Hardie or MacDonald, was the idol of working-class and unemployed audiences.

Illness compelled Campbell-Bannerman to resign in the spring of 1908 and he died within a month. He was succeeded by Asquith, and Lloyd George took Asquith's place at the Exchequer. The new Prime Minister himself introduced the budget and the Finance Bill he had prepared as Chancellor, in which for the first time a distinction was drawn between "earned" and "unearned" income, and he has rightly received his share of the credit for drafting an Old Age Pensions Bill giving a pension of five shillings a week, wholly paid for out of taxation, to persons over seventy without other means exceeding ten shillings a week.

The Old Age Pensions Bill was the first of the measures in which monetary benefits are given to correct the inadequacies of economic processes. It proved the thin end of a very big wedge. The House of Lords did not like it, and one peer had described it as "so prodigal of expenditure as likely to undermine the whole fabric of the Empire".[11] Nevertheless, their lordships did not reject it on second reading but contented themselves with amending it in Committee. The Commons regarded this as a breach of privilege, treating the measure as a money bill, and the Lords grudgingly gave way.

Two more education bills were introduced in this session and both came to nothing. Each was based on the principle of "contracting out". The former, introduced by Reginald McKenna, provided that in single-school parishes Church schools were to be compulsorily transferred to the local education authority subject to the right to give "denominational" teaching out of hours; in other places voluntary schools might "contract out" of the system and become state-aided schools on the basis of a grant of 47s. a head. It was allowed to lapse after second reading, and when the government was reconstructed McKenna's successor, Walter Runciman, introduced another bill on the same general lines but providing a right of entry to give "denominational" teaching in all council schools. It had been drawn up in consultation with the Archbishop of Canterbury, Davidson, and represented a genuine effort to break the deadlock, but agreement could not be reached on the financial basis of "contracting out" and it was withdrawn in committee.

Frustrated in their efforts to amend Balfour's Education Act of 1902, the Liberals at length produced their Licensing Bill to amend his measure of 1904. The object was to reduce the number of public houses by laying down that in any area they must not exceed a certain ratio to the population. Compensation for licences extinguished was to be raised by a levy on the trade, but payments were to cease after fourteen years. Salisbury observed that he no more felt inclined to sleepiness at Hatfield, with twenty bedrooms, than at some seaside villa with a dozen. Balfour, according to his niece, was "furious" about a bill that to his mind was against every interest of public decency and morality.[12] The brewers threatened to withdraw their support from the Unionist party if the Lords did not throw out the bill. The King, with the approval of the Prime Minister, took the unusual action of trying to persuade Lansdowne that the peers should not do so. Lansdowne reminded the King of their "bitter experience" over old-age pensions. He summoned a meeting of Unionist peers at his house, and by a large majority it was decided to oppose the bill, which was duly rejected after a three-day debate. For the government Lansdowne's brother, Lord Fitzmaurice, mournfully observed:[13] "We have a great number of noble lords here who may have been seen walking about in the streets of the city, but have not very frequently attended your lordships' debates." These were the "backwoodsmen", of whom Lloyd George was to complain bitterly.

So the third session of the Parliament elected in 1906 came to an end. The enormous majority in the Commons given to the Liberal party had so far proved almost entirely useless. Mr. Roy Jenkins pertinently observes:[14]

"As in the two previous sessions, no measure, other than a money bill, had passed on to the statute book in anything like its original form unless, on third reading in the Commons, it had secured the acquiescence of Arthur Balfour. For three years the smallest opposition within living memory had effectively decided what could, and what could not, be passed through Parliament. In the language of the day, the cup was full, and the sands were exhaustively ploughed."

The crunch came in 1909 when Lloyd George introduced his first budget. It has often been suggested that he deliberately framed it with the object of provoking the peers to reject the accompanying Finance Bill, and that he had to overcome much opposition from his Cabinet colleagues, but the evidence, carefully assessed by Mr. Roy Jenkins,[15] is against the attribution of such Machiavellian subtlety to the Welsh wizard. The salient facts are that Lloyd George was under the necessity of raising more money to pay for the old-age pensions and increased expenditure on the Navy; and that new measures of reform calculated to catch the public imagination were needed if the sudden crumbling away of popular support for the government, as shown by the by-elections since the beginning of 1908, was to be arrested. If such measures were introduced in the ordinary way they were certain to run up against the veto of the House of Lords; but if they could be incorporated in the Finance Bill, it was to be expected that the Lords would not dare reject them. On balance it seems probable that by including all his proposals in the Finance Bill Lloyd George hoped to avoid a conflict with the House of Lords rather than to provoke it.

The main features of the "People's Budget" were an increase in death duties, the introduction of a differential tax between earned and unearned incomes, a children's allowance for small incomes, the introduction of super-tax on incomes of £5,000 a year or more, a tax on the unearned increment in land values to be paid when the land was sold or when it passed at death, a capital tax on the value of underdeveloped land and minerals, a reversion duty on any financial gain to a lessor at the end of a lease, increases in the tobacco and whisky duties and in the licenses for selling tobacco and alcoholic drinks, the setting up of a Road Fund to be fed by taxes on motor vehicles, and the setting up of a Miners' Welfare Fund out of the proceeds of a tax on mining royalties and way-leaves. Of these proposals the super-tax (later called surtax) has proved the most potent instrument in smoothing out irregularities in wealth, but at the time the proposed taxes on land values roused the fiercest controversy. Even though the revenue to be raised, and the scale of the taxes, were trivial by the standards to which we have since become accustomed, the range and novelty of the proposals made the "People's Budget" the most formidable challenge to old ideas, and Lloyd George struck a challenging note in declaring it to be a "war budget". "It is," he continued, "for raising money to wage implacable warfare against poverty and squalidness." Balfour said it was "arbitrary and unjust . . . a shock to confidence and credit". To Lansdowne it was "a monument of reckless and improvident finance". Carson saw in it "the beginning of the end of all rights of property". Even Rosebery, still describing himself as a Liberal, though he resigned the presidency of the Liberal League, called it "inquisitorial, tyrannical and socialistic". Lloyd George's language in the House of Commons, where the bill was fought line by line for seventy days and nights with 554 divisions, was moderation itself, but when he realized that nothing was to be gained by moderation he made a speech at Limehouse that added a new word for vitupera-tion to the English language. Though today it seems no more start-ling than the budget itself, it provoked the Duke of Beaufort to wish to see "Winston Churchill and Lloyd George in the middle of twenty couple of dog hounds".[16]

The country waited anxiously to see whether the Lords would swallow the budget. More than 250 years had passed since the House of Lords had rejected a Finance Bill, and it had come to be accepted as one of the fundamentals of the constitution that money bills were the prerogative of the House of Commons. The argument for the right to reject was that the land-tax proposals involved a land-valuation bill which it was improper to insert in a Finance Bill.

The King, fearful of the outcome of a collision between the two houses, obtained Asquith's consent to invite Balfour and Lansdowne for talks with a view to discovering some middle way. Nothing came of these conversations, and it is probable that both men had already decided that rejection was desirable. They knew that rejection must be followed by a general election in which the Liberals would seek power to override the veto of the House of Lords Whether their success at by-elections had deluded them into thinking that they could wipe out the great Liberal majority at such a general election, or whether they were merely borne along by irresistible pressure from their followers, cannot be certainly known. After five days of debate the second reading of the bill was lost by 350 votes to seventy-five. The King's private secretary told the Clerk to the Privy Council "very gravely and emphatically that he thought the Lords mad".[17] Lloyd George, though he had hoped to the last, if so sober a witness as Lord Crewe is to be believed, that the bill would pass, accepted the challenge with alacrity. "At last," he declared, "the cause between the peers and the people has been set down for trial in the grand assize of the people, and the verdict will come soon."[18]

In discussing Unionist tactics for dealing with Liberal legislation, Balfour had written to Lansdowne in 1906:[19]

"It is, of course, impossible to foresee how each particular case is to be dealt with, but I incline to advise that we should fight all points of importance very stiffly in the Commons, and should make the House of Lords the theatre of compromise. It is evident that *you* can never fight for a position which *we* have surrendered; while, on the other hand, the fact that we have strenuously fought for the position and been severely beaten may afford adequate ground for your making a graceful concession to the representative chamber."

Lloyd George could not have known of this correspondence, but it amply justified him in saying in 1908:[20] "The House of Lords is not the watchdog of the constitution, it is Mr. Balfour's poodle." It was not a tolerable situation that the leader of 157 members of the House of Commons should be able to thwart the will of the great majority of the members sent to that chamber by the electorate, even though it may be readily conceded that, owing to the British electoral system, party strength in the House of Commons was not necessarily an index of party strength in the country.

The situation in which the House of Lords had become an instrument of the Tory party was of fairly modern growth. To gather together points of which some have already been noted in their places, at the beginning of the eighteenth century in an upper house of 150 members there had been a small Whig majority which Queen Anne in 1711 turned into a small Tory majority by the creation of twelve peers for the express purpose of ratifying the Treaty of

Utrecht. In the long period of Whig dominance following the death of Anne new creations restored the small Whig majority, and the Whigs kept this small majority until the advent of the younger Pitt. In his seventeen years as Prime Minister Pitt raised no fewer than 140 commoners to the peerage, and gave the Tories a predominance in that chamber which for the first time made it a party assembly and raised a grave constitutional issue in 1831. It was Pitt's peers or their sons who provided the bulk of the vote against the Reform Bill. While Peel led the Tories they did not abuse their strength in the Lords, and his break with the party meant that the Tories found themselves almost evenly balanced by the Whig and Peelite lords. This did not last. As the Liberal party evolved in a radical direction, more and more peers gravitated towards the Tory benches, and in 1886 the balance was fundamentally disturbed by the Liberal Unionist secession from the Liberal party. The effect of the split was even greater in the upper house than in the lower. According to a memorandum written for the Queen by Rosebery in 1894[21] it "threw the great mass of the Liberal peers into the arms of the Conservative majority", and the Liberal vote in the Lords was reduced to little more than thirty. When a critical test came in 1893 with the Liberal government's home rule bill there were only forty-one votes for it and 419 against; and soon Gladstone uttered his Parthian warning that the conflict between the houses, once raised, "must go forward to an issue". In the memorandum already cited Rosebery analysed the dilemma with complete clarity while failing to offer any remedy:

"It is easy to understand how galling this house is to the party to which it happens to be opposed. When the Conservative party is in power, there is practically no House of Lords: it takes whatever the Conservative government brings it from the House of Commons without question or dispute; but the moment a Liberal government is formed, this harmless body assumes an active life, and its activity is entirely exercised in opposition to the government."

In 1906 there were eighty-eight peers who described themselves as Liberals, 124 as Liberal Unionists and 355 as Conservatives; together with thirty-five who avoided any party label, they made a house of 602, in which the Unionists had a majority over all others of 356, and over the Liberals of 391. The Unionist majority over all others in the Lords was thus exactly the same as the normal government majority in the Commons; and, for one reason or another, the Unionists were in a far stronger position in the Lords than the Liberals in the Commons. They behaved exactly as Rosebery had described, and in 1910 the issue that Gladstone had prophesied was fairly joined. As it happened, the question was twice put before the electors in that year, and they twice returned the same answer.

As the Lords had refused provision for the public service, a dissolution was the only possible course, and Asquith asked for it immediately. In a speech at the Albert Hall on 10th December 1909 he laid down the lines on which the Liberals would fight. They were "the absolute control of the Commons over finance, the maintenance of free trade, and the effective limitation and curtailment of the legislative powers of the House of Lords". In addition, he reserved the right to re-introduce home rule for Ireland into the party programme.

For the Conservatives, Balfour played down the constitutional issue and sought to get attention concentrated on the details of the budget. He alleged that the attack on the House of Lords was the culmination of a conspiracy to make the Commons independent of the people as well as of the peers, and claimed that the Lords were within their rights to force an election on such a budget.

The Conservative rout in 1906 had been followed by the establishment of the Junior Imperial and Constitutional League (the "Junior Imps") for the purpose of catching the new voters young and by a reorganization of the party machinery. The whips had been given an advisory committee, certain duties had been transferred from the Central Office to the National Union and the Council of the National Union had been enlarged. The Conservatives started with the comforting knowledge that they could not fail to improve their position. The by-elections had shown that they were bound to make a great inroad into the Liberal majority. The question was, could it be turned into a minority?

The Liberal Unionists were so closely allied with the Conservatives as to be virtually indistinguishable. They had been present at the meeting that elected Balfour as leader, and both Balfour and Chamberlain habitually spoke of "the Unionist party" in the singular. They shared the same whips in Parliament. Nevertheless, in 1910 the Liberal Unionists in the country were still technically a separate party. Joseph Chamberlain had to content himself with sending letters to candidates, and Austen Chamberlain took the task of leadership upon himself. He sought to make it an election for or against tariff reform.

The Irish Nationalists had not shared the Liberal enthusiasm for the "People's Budget" as it seemed to them that a budget levying higher taxes on whisky and tobacco did not deserve that name; but Redmond saw in the proposal to curb the powers of the House of Lords a prospect of getting round the main obstacle to home rule. For this reason the great majority of the Irish Nationalists were prepared to swallow the tax along with the whisky, to urge Irishmen in Great Britain to vote Liberal, and to promise their support to the Liberals in the new Parliament; but nine remained obdurate and fought the election as Independent Nationalists.

The Labour party in the House of Commons at the dissolution

was forty-five strong, for the Miners' Federation had eventually decided to affiliate, and its fifteen "Lib-Lab" members then accepted the Labour whip. But all was not happy in the new party. The necessity to work within a parliamentary time-table fixed by the major parties, and the need to avoid antagonizing the Liberal party by provocative actions in the house or reckless candidatures at by-elections were galling to the militant socialists, who regarded both "capitalist" parties as equally bad. The refusal of the I.L.P. conference to endorse their censure of Grayson's theatricalities led MacDonald, Hardie, Snowden and Glasier to resign their membership of its council. Overshadowing all else, the Osborne judgement of 1909 jeopardized the very existence of the party. It will be recalled that since 1903 the Labour party had made a levy of a penny a member on all affiliated organizations. In 1907 Osborne, who had been a member of the Amalgamated Society of Railway Servants since 1892, sought from the courts a declaration that the union's rule levying contributions towards the payment of members of Parliament pledged to observe the conditions imposed by the Labour party was *ultra vires* and void. The King's Bench decided against him, but the Court of Appeal reversed the judgement, and at the end of 1909 the House of Lords upheld the Court of Appeal. The decision of the law lords, given eleven days after Asquith and Balfour had opened their campaigns, produced consternation in the Labour camp, and inevitably made the Labour leaders hope for a Liberal victory, as it was only through a Liberal majority in Parliament that the judgement could be rectified. There was no electoral pact on this occasion, but means were somehow found to put seventy-eight candidates into the field. Elsewhere, the bulk of the Labour vote must have gone to Liberal candidates.

The question of votes for women was successfully kept out of the election. Thanks to the militant action of the suffragettes, this had become a burning issue. Though some Conservatives and more Liberals were in favour of extending the parliamentary suffrage to women, the party leaders on both sides and the main bodies of the parties were resolutely opposed. The Labour party was theoretically in favour of the extension, but divided on the manner of so doing. Fortunately, the suffragettes themselves did not press the issue, and the fact that the polling took place in the month of January may have helped to cool their ardour.

Polling was spread over the latter half of January 1910. So far as the main parties were concerned, the election turned out to be "the closest-run thing" since the battle of Waterloo. The electors returned 275 Liberals and 273 Unionists (of whom 242 were Conservatives and thirty-one Liberal Unionists). In England taken alone, the Unionists fared better, with 239 successful candidates, than the Liberals, with 226; but in the Celtic fringe the Liberals emerged with only four seats less than in 1906. The overall result was a Unionist gain of 116 seats compared with their 1906 figure; and they achieved this result although all the seats lost by the government at by-elections were regained by the Liberals, an illuminating commentary on the value of by-elections as a pointer to the next general election. If the Liberals had no allies, they would have found it difficult to remain in office, but they did not stand alone. The Irish Nationalists had suffered by the defection of the nine Independent Nationalists led by William O'Brien, all of whom were elected, and they lost one seat, but Redmond was able to lead seventy-three members into the government lobby of the House of Commons. The Labour party, fighting on its own and crippled by the Osborne judgement, secured the return of forty members, which was an increase of eleven on its 1906 figure though a reduction of five on its numbers at the dissolution; and as the main concern of Labour members was to secure legislation reversing the Osborne judgement their support in the lobbies could be counted on by the government. Grayson lost his seat, and disappeared from the parliamentary scene as suddenly as he had entered it. If all the Irish Nationalists (including the nine Independents) voted with the government, the Liberals had a majority of 124; but the Independent Nationalists could certainly not be counted upon to do so, and even the support of Redmond's followers was conditional. A temporary alliance of Unionists and Irish Nationalists could defeat the combined forces of the Liberals and Labour by forty. The Liberals were dependent on the Irish vote as they had not been in the previous Parliament. It was a situation calling for new tactics; but in this precarious and delicate position the Liberal government was able to carry major constitutional changes which it had been impotent to bring about in the period of its unassailable majority.

18

PARTIES AND THE CONSTITUTION 1910–1914

King Edward's attitude to the creation of peers—the Finance Bill carried and Parliament Bill introduced—death of King Edward—discussions between the Liberal and Conservative leaders—Lloyd George's proposal for a coalition—the second general election of 1910—Liberals and Tories returned in equal numbers—Redmond again master of the situation—the Unionist peers divided into "hedgers" and "ditchers"—Parliament Bill passed—"Balfour Must Go" campaign—Bonar Law succeeds—creation of the post of Chairman of the Party Organization—Conservative and Liberal Unionist parties fused—changes in the Conservative outlook—Welsh disestablishment carried—Home Rule Bill introduced in three successive sessions—Bonar Law's support of armed resistance —the Curragh incident—an inter-party conference

IN his Albert Hall speech at the opening of the election campaign Asquith had said: "We shall not assume office and we shall not hold office unless we can secure the safeguards which experience shows us to be necessary for the legislative utility and honour of the party of progress", but in fact he had failed to obtain from King Edward in advance a "guarantee" that if the Lords continued to prove obstructive the Crown would create enough peers to ensure the passage of a bill removing their veto. The King, regarding the Liberal policy as "tantamount to the destruction of the House of Lords", thought that before a large creation of peers was threatened there should be another general election in which the measure for curbing the upper house would be specifically placed before the electors.[1]

While there were many Liberals who wished to destroy the House of Lords, this was not true of all. Grey led those who sought to reform the second chamber and leave it with real powers. In Asquith's mind veto and reform were perceived as two separate issues, and this was the point of view that eventually prevailed.

On 21st March three resolutions were introduced into the House of Commons as a prelude to a Parliament Bill. The first made it clear that the Lords could not constitutionally amend or reject a money bill, and it was left to the Speaker, acting in accordance with certain rules, to certify whether a bill came into that class. Any other bill sent up from the Commons in three successive sessions was to pass into law without the assent of the peers if in the third session the peers failed to agree to it without amendment (other than amendments agreed to by the House of Commons) within twenty-eight days. This vital resolution destroyed the absolute veto of the House of Lords, and reduced its obstructive power to a delay of two years and one month; and the resolution was so worded as to allow the three sessions to be spread over more than one Parliament, thus ensuring that a government disliked by the House of Lords need not be reduced to impotence during the last two years of a Parliament. The third resolution reduced the maximum life of Parliament from seven years to five. With an increasing sense of democracy it was felt that members should submit themselves to re-election more frequently, but through the outbreak of war the next Parliament was, in fact, to last for eight years.

The Cabinet's plan was first to secure approval of the general purpose as expressed in the resolutions, then to give a first reading to a Parliament Bill based on them, and then re-introduce Lloyd George's Finance Bill which had started the trouble. Failure to secure the passage of the Finance Bill in 1909 had not been as embarrassing as it might have been because, whether legally or illegally, most of the taxes had been collected and the deficiency was made good by a Treasury (Temporary Borrowing) Bill to which the Unionists for tactical reasons made no objection. Still, the Finance Bill had some time to be obtained, and it was tricky because the Irish Nationalists were insisting as the price of their support that the government should ask for the "exercise of the prerogative", that is, for the creation of sufficient peers, if the Lords should reject the resolutions. This was a pledge that Asquith at that time was unable or unwilling to give, and when a Unionist member asked him what he would do if the Lords should refuse assent to the resolutions he replied: "We had better wait and see." It was advice he repeated on other occasions, once possibly hissed out in the imperative as "Wait and see", and in the heat of party conflict it was years later to be used most unfairly against him.[2]

The resolutions were exhaustively debated in the Commons and passed by handsome majorities as the Liberals were supported not only by the Labour party but by almost all of Redmond's Irish Nationalists. This was interpreted by the public as proof that Asquith intended to ask for the creation of peers. He was ready to announce the government's intentions during the consideration of the second resolution, but in a curious scene the Unionists refused him the general consent that was needed, and he waited until the Parliament Bill had been introduced. He stated that if ministers could not ensure that statutory effect were given to their policy in that Parliament, they would either resign or recommend a dissolution. "Let me add this," he said in deliberately complex terms whose import would not be mistaken,[3] "that in no case will we recommend a dissolution except under such conditions as will secure that in the new Parliament the judgement of the people as expressed at the elections will be carried into law." The die was cast, and party strife entered upon a period of bitterness seldom known before or since.

There was a brief period of deceptive calm. When the Finance Bill was re-introduced, the Independent Nationalists remained adamant in their opposition, but Redmond, reminding O'Brien that landlords and distillers were not the only people in Ireland, gave firm support to Lloyd George, and the second and third readings were carried by majorities of eighty-six and ninety-three. The bill was immediately taken to the Lords, and there to the general astonishment it was allowed to pass with little debate and without a division. The Lords accepted the general election as a decision in favour of the "People's Budget" and reserved their forces for the constitutional issue. It was exactly twelve months since Lloyd George had stood at the dispatch-box to unfold it.

The next stage in Asquith's programme was to produce the text of the Parliament Bill, and this meant resolving the issue between those who wished to confine it to the ending of the veto and those who would reform. The bill was confined to the veto and the length of Parliament, but as a sop the reformers were given a preamble expressing an intention some day of reconstituting the second chamber on a popular instead of hereditary basis. Though attempts have from time to time been made, the preamble has not been given effect.

The peers suddenly began to take an interest in reforming their own house, and a series of resolutions by Rosebery, based on the principle that the possession of a peerage should no longer of itself give the right to sit in the House of Lords, was carried despite a heavy douche of cold water from Lansdowne and an open onslaught from Halsbury.

At this point a difficult situation was made still more complex by the unexpected death of King Edward VII. His successor, King George V, did not move among high political questions with the ease of the dead monarch. In his long reign he was to develop great political sagacity, but in the spring of 1910 it was felt unfair to involve the new sovereign in a bitter party conflict over a grave constitutional issue. When the King suggested some understanding with the opposition with a view to preventing a general election, Asquith agreed to offer a two-party constitutional conference. The suggestion was readily accepted by the Unionists, not so readily by the government's own supporters. O'Brien's Independent Nationalists had no objection, but Redmond's followers found it irksome, and would have been even more irritated if they had heard Asquith tell the King that "he would not pay attention to what Mr. Redmond said".[4] The Labour party was suspicious of what might be concocted behind closed doors by the two "capitalist parties". There was even a small Liberal revolt under Josiah Wedgwood, but for a period of six months public controversy ceased and discussion was conducted confidentially between Asquith, Lloyd George, Crewe and Birrell for the Liberals and Balfour, Lansdowne, Austen Chamberlain and Cawdor for the Unionists.

The task of reconstructing from the often conflicting accounts of the participants' biographies what took place in these secret discussions has been skilfully undertaken by Mr. Roy Jenkins.[5] Left to themselves, Asquith and Balfour would probably have been able to reach agreement, but Lansdowne proved a stubborn champion of the Lords' prerogatives, and he was stoutly supported by Cawdor and more weakly by Austen Chamberlain. Though Lloyd George's budget had set these events in train, there can be no doubt that he was willing to reach agreement, for he was the chief actor in an extraordinary play within the play that took place at this time.

This was no other than a proposal for a coalition government. In view of the ferocity of his attacks upon the existing social system in general and the Conservatives in particular, Lloyd George was the last person from whom such a proposal would then have been expected; but in retrospect it is not so surprising, for he was later to show an indifference to parties amounting almost to contempt. According to his own later account,[6] the accession of the new King seems to have played no part in his plan, and the constitutional crisis only a subordinate one. Though formerly regarded as a pacifist, he had become alarmed by the worsening international situation and "growingly concerned with the precariousness of our position in the event of our naval defence being broken through". In the year 1910, he wrote, "we were beset by an accumulation of grave issues—rapidly become graver ... It was becoming evident to discerning eyes that the party and parliamentary system was unequal to coping with them". In the peace of Criccieth he wrote a memorandum "urging that a truce should be declared between the parties for the purpose of securing the cooperation of the leading party statesmen in a settlement of our national problems—second chamber, home rule, the development of our agricultural resources, national training for defence, the remedying of social evils, and a fair and judicial inquiry into the working of our fiscal system". He submitted it to Asquith, who was not displeased and agreed that it might be put to Balfour. Crewe, Grey, Haldane and Churchill were also brought into consultation on the Liberal side; and Lloyd George himself showed the memorandum to F. E. Smith and Garvin on the Conservative side. Balfour consulted Lansdowne, Cawdor, Curzon, Walter Long and Austen Chamberlain. They could hardly believe that Lloyd George was prepared to accept a measure of tariff reform, which they had hitherto demanded in vain, and was offering them a form of conscription, for which they had not dared to ask. The first reaction among the Conservative leaders was not unfavourable, but after Balfour had sounded a little more deeply he was obliged to tell Lloyd George that too many wounding things had been said by him for any coalition of which he was a member to have much chance of acceptance. Lloyd George promptly offered to stand down and give his support from the outside. Balfour said there was still one other person whom he would have to consult, and added: "You will be surprised when I give you his name." Lloyd George was. It was that of Akers-Douglas, then Lord Chilston, who had faded out of the public eye but whose great experience as Conservative chief whip made him a good judge of what the rank and file of the party would stand; and he told Balfour plainly that the party would not stand for such a sacrifice of principle as would be involved in coalition. Balfour had to tell Lloyd George sorrowfully that he could not become another Peel in the party, and the plan was dead. "It was not rejected," Lloyd George commented, "by the real leaders of the party, but by men who, for some obscure reason best known to political organizations, have great influence inside the councils of a party without possessing any of the capabilities that excite general admiration and confidence outside." Chilston's grandson and biographer thinks this "does Akers-Douglas both too much honour and not enough"; it is likely that his assessment of the party reaction reinforced Balfour's own, and anyway he never claimed to be more than a party man. The country had to wait until war came for a coalition government, and, as Mr. Roy Jenkins pertinently observes, when it was torpedoed in 1922 the men who remained loyal to Lloyd George to the end were Birkenhead (as F. E. Smith had then become), Churchill and Austen Chamberlain who had been his chief backers in 1910.[7]

The failure of Lloyd George's plan for a coalition was soon followed by the breakdown of the constitutional conference. The early meetings had taken place in the Prime Minister's room at the House of Commons, and it was a sign of the way things were going when Landsdowne advised rejection of Crewe's invitation to meet at his country house during the recess lest it should be said that they had been softened by the excellence of his champagne. No further meetings were held until October. The Conservatives were apparently prepared to agree that the Lords should not be permitted to reject money bills if the "tacking" of other measures on to money bills were prevented; and it was proposed by Lloyd George that a joint committee of both houses presided over by the Speaker should decide whether a bill was a money bill. It was agreed that the fate of an ordinary bill which had been twice passed by the Commons and twice rejected by the Lords should be decided by a joint sitting, but no agreement could be reached on what numbers the two houses should respectively contribute to such a joint sitting. The greatest difficulty was raised by "organic", that is constitutional, bills. The Unionists argued that such bills, having been twice passed by the Commons and twice rejected by the Lords, should be submitted to a referendum. The very word referendum, according to Sir Harold Nicolson, would cause Asquith's "usually tolerant features to writhe into an expression of contemptuous disgust",[8] but he was prepared to exempt certain constitutional bills from the operation of the Parliament Act. The organic measure in which everyone was specially interested was home rule, and the fertile mind of Lloyd George suggested that if the next home rule bill was rejected by the Lords there should be an immediate general election. If the government won, they should proceed with the measure as an ordinary bill; if they lost, they would of course resign, but the next Liberal government would be able to proceed with another home rule bill under the Parliament Act. Balfour summarized this as meaning that "since the people on three separate occasions had expressed their hostility to home rule, it was high time to withdraw the subject from their cognizance and to hand it over to the unfettered discretion of the House of Commons and the joint sitting".[9] At this point the two sides became deadlocked, and on 10th November the conference was declared at an end without agreement. A Cabinet was called and was in favour of an immediate dissolution.

The centre of interest now shifted to the King at Sandringham. It was a heavy responsibility to have thrust upon him so early in his reign, and he was not helped by receiving contradictory advice from his two private secretaries, Lord Knollys and Sir Arthur Bigge (later Lord Stamfordham). It was still the King's wish that he should not be asked to give a guarantee to create peers until after a bill for the abolition of the veto had been submitted to the electors, but on 15th November the Cabinet formally minuted:[10] "His Majesty's Ministers cannot, however, take the responsibility of advising a dissolution, unless they may understand that, in the event of the policy of the Government being approved by an adequate majority in the new House of Commons, His Majesty will be ready to exercise his constitutional powers which may involve the Prerogative of creating Peers), if needed, to secure that effect shall be given to the decision of the country." They added that the understanding should not be made public unless the occasion should arise; though this was done to protect the King from unnecessary involvement in the party struggle, he resented it as an imposition.

Knollys strongly urged that the King should accept what the Cabinet proposed as being safe and constitutionally correct. Bigge was adamantly opposed to acceptance, taking the line that it would make the King a partisan and place "a powerful weapon in the hands of the Irish and Socialists".[11] The King returned to London on the 16th. At some point he was assured by Knollys that "Mr. Balfour would in any event decline to form an administration".[12] This was decisive, and the King followed his advice. It was perhaps well for the peaceful evolution of the British constitution, but Knollys does not appear to have had any firm basis for this assurance, and it conflicts with his own record of a secret meeting attended by himself and Balfour at Lambeth Palace in April, when Balfour "made it quite clear that he would be prepared to form a Government to prevent the King being put in the position contemplated by the demand for the creation of Peers".[13] Three years later, when the King first saw this record, he felt some justifiable indignation at having been kept in ignorance of it. Knollys had by then given up his post. After a long talk with Asquith and Crewe on 16th November, the King wrote in his diary:[14] "I agreed most reluctantly to give the Cabinet a secret understanding that in the event of the Government being returned with a majority at the general election I would use my Prerogative to make Peers if asked for. I disliked having to do this very much, but agreed that this was the only alternative to the Cabinet resigning which at this moment would be disastrous. Francis [Knollys] strongly urged me to take this course & I think his advice is generally very sound, I only trust & pray he is right this time."

The election was quiet, despite the efforts of Lloyd George, so soon forgetful of his plans for coalition, to repeat at Mile End his performance at Limehouse. "An aristocracy is like cheese, the older it is the higher it becomes", was a sample of his gibes. In answer to the Unionist emphasis on the collections being made in North America for the home rule cause, he asked since when had the British aristocracy started despising American dollars: "Many a noble house, tottering in its fall, has had its foundations underpinned, its walls buttressed, by a pile of American dollars." In a different vein Asquith spoke in all parts of the country with eloquence and dignity and provoked Balfour in a long-remembered meeting at the Albert Hall into saying that he would not have the slightest objection to submitting the principles of tariff reform to a referendum. When Austen Chamberlain read the announcement he felt he had received a slap in the face and later complained of "referendum sickness".[15] The electors who had gone to the polls so recently as in January found it hard to work themselves up to any great pitch of excitement in December, and one million fewer votes were cast. A large number of individual seats changed their party colour, but the overall result was much as before. In the new house Liberals and Tories, at 272 exactly balanced each other. (The Liberals lost three seats and the Unionists one on balance.) Labour gained two seats on balance, bringing its representation to forty-two. Though O'Brien and Healy poured their scorn on Redmond for selling the Irish vote to the government, the Irish Nationalists (official and Independent together) rose to eighty-four, a net gain of two. Once again Redmond was master of the parliamentary situation.

The philosophical Balfour was ready to accept the decision of the electorate, and over dinner he told Esher and Knollys, for transmission to the King, that "his Majesty could not well ultimately refuse to comply with Mr. Asquith's demand, should it be made, for a promise to create peers". He was then and for some months unaware that such a promise had already been given. The King, still uneasy, said he would like to see Lansdowne. Asquith reluctantly agreed, after reminding the King that "it is not the function of a constitutional sovereign to act as arbiter or mediator between rival parties and policies; still less to take advice from the leaders of both sides, with the view to forming a conclusion of his own". From Lansdowne the King received no assurance of accommodation on the part of the Unionist peers. Lansdowne was hoping against hope that something would turn up to improve the prospect.[16]

The Parliament Bill was re-introduced in the same form as in the previous Parliament, and was given a first reading on 22nd February by 351 votes to 227, and a second reading on 2nd March by 368 to 243. The Lords occupied their time while waiting with further talk of reform. Over nine hundred amendments to the Parliament Bill were tabled in the Commons during the committee stage, but few changes were made, and on 15th May it received its third reading by 362 votes to 241 and went to the critical test of the upper house.

There the Unionists decided to give it an unopposed second reading but to seek amendments in committee. The approaching coronation, fixed for 22nd June, may have been one reason for this display of benevolence, but when the six-day committee stage was opened on 28th June the bill was altered beyond recognition. The most far-reaching amendments substituted a joint committee for the Speaker in certifying money bills and introduced the referendum.

The Cabinet told the King that the bill might just as well have been rejected on second reading, and that ministers would have to advise the Crown to exercise its prerogative so as to secure the passing of the bill in its original form. The King agreed, requesting only that the Lords should first be given an opportunity to pronounce on the rejection of their amendments by the Commons. Just a week earlier Balfour had been informed by the palace of the pre-election pledge given by the King. The King had always resented the obligation of secrecy which made him, the most straightforward of men, seem to himself to be guilty of duplicity in dealing with the opposition. It was desirable that the seal should be broken, for many Unionist peers were being encouraged to resist the Parliament Bill in the belief that the King would not create peers. What Balfour had heard, probably from Knollys or Esher, was formally but still secretly confirmed by Lloyd George a little later. At once a division opened in the Unionist ranks between those who wished to give way rather than see the House of Lords swamped by new peers (the "hedgers") and those who wished to die in the last ditch (the "ditchers" or "die-hards"). The "die-hards" were organized by the young Lord Willoughby de Broke and the aged Earl of Halsbury; they made Grosvenor House, the London residence of the Duke of Westminster, their headquarters; and their strategy was to adhere to such amendments as "would have the effect of securing to the second chamber the powers at present exercised by the House of Lords, notwithstanding the possible creation of peers, or the dissolu-tion of Parliament". The division became publicly manifest in the third reading debate in the Lords on 20th July, when Halsbury made an inflammatory speech insisting on the need to retain the Lords' amendments, while Lansdowne gave signs of retreating by announc-ing that the opposition would not withdraw some of their amend-ments "so long as we remain free agents".[17]

That same day Asquith sent to Balfour and Lansdowne identical letters indicating that when the bill returned the Commons would be asked to disagree with the Lords' amendments; that if the neces-sity should arise the King would be advised to exercise his preroga-tive to secure the passing of the bill into law in substantially the same form in which it left the Commons; and that his Majesty had been pleased to signify that he would consider it his duty to accept and act on that advice. When members of the Unionist "shadow Cabinet" met the next day they did so with this letter before them and the knowledge that the threat to swamp the House of Lords with new peers was no idle one. This made such men as Curzon cross over to the "hedgers" from the "ditchers". ("It was all snob-bishness on Curzon's part," said George Wyndham, "he could not bear to see his order contaminated by the new creation."[18]) Those present were asked to declare themselves for or against resistance. A deep rift appeared. Those favouring resistance were Halsbury, Sel-borne, Salisbury, Austen Chamberlain, F. E. Smith, Wyndham, Car-son and Balcarres. Those for yielding were Balfour, Lansdowne, Curzon, Midleton, Londonderry, Derby, Ashbourne, Bonar Law, Walter Long, Alfred Lyttleton, Henry Chaplin, Robert Finlay and Arthur Steel-Maitland. Chilston, the party's bell-wether, was for the "die-hards" but voted with the majority only out of loyalty to his leader.

From the "shadow Cabinet" Lansdowne went to a meeting of Unionist peers, which he appears to have regarded with Olympian detachment. In a masterpiece of understatement his friend Lord Newton observed that for once in a way "Lord Lansdowne showed some slight deficiency in the art of leadership". Balfour was even worse, and wrote a memorandum criticizing the "music hall attitude" of the resisters which would have provoked fury if his colleagues had not induced him to suppress it.[19]

By this time feeling was running high, and when the Prime Minister rose in the House of Commons on the motion to consider the Lords' amendments with the object of announcing the government's intentions he stood for half an hour at the dispatch-box unable to make a single complete sentence heard above a bedlam of organized interruptions. It was a disgraceful scene, unmatched before or since in British parliamentary annals, and it is piquant to reflect that the ringleaders were a future Lord Chancellor and a future Provost of Eton, F. E. Smith and Lord Hugh Cecil. After Asquith, "declining to degrade himself further", had sat down, Balfour was heard in silence and Grey made some cloudy remarks, but when Smith rose to continue the debate this was more than the government supporters could stand, and the Speaker suspended the sitting on the ground that grave disorder had arisen.

The "die-hards" were not abashed, and as a demonstration organized a Halsbury banquet at the Hotel Cecil, after which the diners would have drawn the aged peer's carriage from the Strand to his Kensington home if his family had not intervened. Wyndham even talked, and Willoughby de Broke wrote, of resort to armed resistance and personal violence; and Lansdowne took it sufficiently seriously to disown it in the Lords. Halsbury almost boasted that his supporters were a separate party. "We have our meetings now not at Lansdowne House but at Lord Leith's and the Duke of Westminster's, and we have our whips."[20]

The Unionists temporarily restored unity in the party by the old device of attacking the enemy, and almost identical votes of censure on the government for the advice given to the Crown were moved in the Commons and the Lords. Simultaneously with the vote of censure in the Lords, the Lords' amendments to the bill were taken into consideration by the Commons on 8th August. As there was to be no immediate creation, the fate of the bill in the Lords was likely to depend upon the number of Unionist peers prepared to vote for it, and this made the government take a conciliatory line over the amendments. Several concessions were offered, but this did not placate Lord Hugh Cecil, who wished to see Asquith punished for high treason. The Lords received the Commons amendments to their amendments the following day, and a two-day debate was opened with a general discussion before they were considered *seriatim*. At that point, despite much convassing of Liberals, "hedgers", "ditchers" and prelates, no one had the slightest idea how the vote would go. It was one of those rare occasions when votes were turned by speeches, and was mainly a contest between the two factions in the Unionist party. When the first day's debate ended after midnight, Stamfordham feared that a statement by Crewe, that the King had given his November undertaking with natural and legitimate reluctance, might be encouraging the "die-hards" to think that even now the government was bluffing. After consulting the King he was authorized to ask Morley to dispel it, and in the resumed debate the following afternoon Morley said:[21] "If the Bill should be defeated tonight his Majesty would assent to a creation of peers sufficient in number to guard against any possible combination of the different parties in opposition by which the Parliament Bill might again be exposed a second time to defeat." After the general debate, the amendments were taken in turn. The first two concerned money bills, and Morley's motion "that this House do not insist upon the said amendment", was in each case carried without a division. The next amendment was the crucial one, as it would have excluded certain categories of bills. Morley moved the same motion, "that this house do not insist upon the said amendment", and after two hours of debate the division was called. After what seemed an age of suspense, the clerk announced: "Contents, 131; Not contents, 114." The government had won, and the 249 persons listed in one of Asquith's more secret papers would not need to be asked to wear the ermine. Eighty-one Liberals had been joined by thirty-seven Unionists, preferring to see the House of Lords clipped rather than swamped, and by thirteen prelates, determined not to repeat the error of their predecessors at the time of the Reform Bill. "We were beaten by the bishops and the rats," said Wyndham; Lord Hugh Cecil suggested excluding the former from a reformed House of Lords, and the latter were hissed in the Carlton Club. There were nine dukes in the "die-hard" lobby, none among the "hedgers". The King confided to his diary his great relief and went to Bolton Abbey. Asquith, nursing laryngitis, was able to delay his return from the country by an hour. Balfour, disgusted with the course of events, heard the news in Paris on his way to Bad Gastein to meditate on the injustice of political life.

Following the universal rule of defeated parties, the loss of the election in December 1910 had led to recrimination among the Unionists against their leader and complaints of defects in organization. It was pointed out that Balfour had lost three elections running—although it may have been unfair to lump together the two elections held in one year the argument told—Balfour's ineffective handling of the Parliament Bill increased the discontent, and Leo Maxse, editor of the *National Review*, caught the party mood when he wrote for the September number an article on the theme "Balfour Must Go", which was soon abbreviated to "B.M.G." and became the slogan of a campaign. According to Balfour's niece, the slogan neither hastened nor retarded anything, and he made his own decision to retire early in September on his return from Bad Gastein when reports from the party managers confirmed his feelings of dissatisfaction. To Balcarres and Steel-Maitland he gave as his reasons "the length of time he had been in harness, his age and the argument that when the party returned to office he would be too old to survive a long ministry". (He was, in fact, only sixty-three, and eleven years later he was still in high office.) He suggested Austen Chamberlain in the Commons, Curzon in the Lords, for the succession; Walter Long he thought too discursive, too quick-tempered, too changeable and too complimentary. The next day he received a letter from Long, severely critical of himself and the party management and policy, which he stigmatized as "a bold and brutal invitation to retire". On 7th October the Halsbury Club was founded by such "die-hards" as Milner, Carson, Selborne, Wyndham, F. E. Smith and Willoughby de Broke. Though they protested that they did not want to create a separate party or organization, but only to ensure that by working together their views should have a fair chance, the formation of the club was a direct challenge to Balfour's leadership and he saw that it could not be ignored. He made the public announcement of his resignation to the City of London Conservative Association on 8th November, and observed afterwards: "I really think I must ask Leo Maxse to dinner tonight, for we are probably the two happiest men in London."[22]

As a former Prime Minister Balfour had been accepted as leader of the whole Unionist party, but on his resignation, as he had himself indicated, the Unionist peers would elect their leader, the Unionist members of the Commons would elect theirs, and neither would automatically become leader of the whole party. He would have to earn the title either by becoming Prime Minister or by winning for himself general acceptance. Lansdowne's first thought was to retire with Balfour, but he was persuaded to remain as leader of the Lords, and Curzon had to wait. In the Commons there was a contest for the leadership which had no previous parallel in the history of the party, if only for the reason that the party had usually had its leader chosen for it by the prior designation of one of its members as Prime Minister; it so happens that 1911 was one of those rare occasions when the Conservative leadership has changed hands while the party was in opposition. Austen Chamberlain and Walter Long were the obvious candidates, and the former stated their merits and demerits with great objectivity:[23]

"I think it is true to say that my colleagues in the late government, including the whips, the keener tariff reformers, and many of the younger men thought that I was the better fitted to fill the vacancy, but I still called myself a Liberal Unionist, I had only joined the Carlton Club a little time before, and the part which I had taken in recent events had certainly aroused some passing antagonism. Long, on the other hand, was a lifetime Conservative, a typical country gentleman, and senior to me both in length of service in the house and in Cabinet rank, and he aroused none of the jealousies or doubts which were inseparable from my position."

Long's superiority in Cabinet rank was a technicality as Chamberlain had been Chancellor of the Exchequer and Long only Chief Secretary for Ireland. It is a typical paradox of British politics that Chamberlain, the representative of Birmingham business, should have been a tariff reformer and "die-hard" champion of the privileges of the Lords, while Long, the Tory squire, was opposed to taxes on food and could not ultimately defend the Lord's veto. It is not wholly surprising that their political differences had left them on bad terms, and this helps to explain the course of events.

The arrangements for the election were in the hands of Balcarres, the chief whip, and he called a meeting of all Unionist members of Parliament for Monday, 13th November at the Carlton Club.[24] It was necessary to have a leader before the Conservative conference met at Leeds that same week. In the meantime there was furious canvassing by the supporters of Chamberlain and Long. In the interests of the party's public image Balcarres wanted to avoid a contest and if private canvassing showed that one of the candidates had a lead, to induce the other to withdraw; privately he hoped to keep Long out as fervently as he hoped to get Chamberlain in. His plan was upset on Thursday, 9th November, when it was learnt that Andrew Bonar Law would also be a candidate. This fifty-three-year-old businessman, born in New Brunswick of Presbyterian stock, had been brought to Scotland by his mother's sister after his mother's death, had been a Conservative member of Parliament only since 1900 and had not held higher office than that of Parliamentary Secretary to the Board of Trade. Though a strong advocate of tariff reform he had not joined the "die-hards" in opposition to the Parliament Bill. In 1911 his candidature seemed presumptuous. To Chamberlain it may have seemed worse, for Law had promised not to contest first place with him, but this was at a time when Law thought Chamberlain would have no rivals for the leadership. Long's candidature altered circumstances in his eyes and made him receptive when his fellow-Canadian, Max Aitken, later to become Lord Beaverbrook, suggested that he should stand. The Chamberlain camp was troubled, for any votes that Law could take would probably have gone to their candidate, inasmuch as Chamberlain and

Law were men of the same stamp, both tariff reformers, the one with a background of Unitarianism and Birmingham, the other of Presbyterianism and Glasgow. The prospect was complicated by the absence of any rules for the conduct of the election. It was not known whether the candidate who secured most votes would be declared elected or whether (as Law himself supposed) the candidate with the lowest number of votes (presumably himself) would first be eliminated and a straight fight allowed between the other two. Much persuasion was used to get Law to withdraw, but Aitken screwed up his resolution to remain in the field. On the Friday Balcarres warned Chamberlain that Law's entry had injured his chances and that the lobbying was all on Long's side. Chamberlain convinced himself that even if he won Long would never be loyal to him. He took the painful decision to withdraw in favour of Bonar Law if Long would do the same. Balcarres, after failing to dissuade Chamberlain, agreed to convey the message to Long. At a meeting on the very day of Balfour's resignation Long had agreed with Chamberlain that neither would concede a walk-over to the other unless a trial ballot showed a conclusive majority, but that both would withdraw if there should appear a third candidate with a substantial backing who was reasonably acceptable to their supporters. That contingency had now arrived, and Long honoured the agreement and consented to withdraw. Balcarres went off to inform Law, only to find that with the prize in his grasp he had scruples about accepting and felt he must consult Chamberlain. Living up to Sir Winston Churchill's epitaph "He always played the game and always lost it", Chamberlain told Law he could not now withdraw; but Law's conduct left a feeling of grievance long afterwards. Before the meeting took place at the Carlton Club on Monday, Aitken told Law, "You are a great man now, you must talk like a great man, behave like a great man." Henry Chaplin, as the senior Conservative ex-minister, presided over the meeting, and Law's election as leader was proposed by Long and seconded by Chamberlain. Carson was sent to bring in Law, and so, as his biographer relates : "A Presbyterian of Canadian origin, who had spent most of his life in business in Glasgow, had become leader of the party of Old England, the party of the Anglican Church and the country squire, the party of broad acres and hereditary titles. Not since the days of Disraeli had so strange a choice been made; and certainly no choice more strange has been made since."[25]

Though Bonar Law had successfully thrust himself into the saddle, he had a perilous ride for a year or two. The tariff reform controversy again became acute. A large number of Conservatives in Scotland and the north of England, particularly in Lancashire, regarded the whole tariff reform crusade as a mistake, and the proposed taxes on food, however light, as a disastrous liability that would make it impossible to win an election. They had the powerful support of the great families of Cecil and Stanley. The tariff reformers were not prepared to abandon taxes on food because they regarded it as essential for political reasons to give a preference in the British market to colonial foodstuffs. It was a struggle between Birmingham Toryism and Manchester Toryism. The tariff reformers were disturbed by the Albert Hall pledge given by Balfour during the second election of 1910 to submit tariff reform to a referendum, and made it their aim to get it repudiated. In 1912 the "shadow Cabinet" at last agreed that food taxes must be kept in the programme and the idea of a referendum dropped. This accorded with Bonar Law's own predilections, and at an Albert Hall meeting in November the pledge of a referendum was publicly repudiated by Lansdowne on the platform from which it had originally been made by Balfour. At once there was an outcry from the free fooders, as the Conservative opponents of taxes on food had become known. Under criticism, Bonar Law explained at Ashton-under-Lyne that food taxes would be imposed only if the colonies wanted them.[26] This did not satisfy Lancashire Tories, and a hostile resolution was avoided at a meeting of the Lancashire Conservative Association only by an adjournment. Bonar Law and Lansdowne agreed that they would resign rather than abandon their policy. This caused consternation in the party, and at the instance of Carson a memorial was signed by all Unionist back-benchers except six urging Bonar Law and Lansdowne to remain in office, while accepting a change in the party's tariff policy. After much hesitation they agreed to do so in the interests of party unity.

Discontent among the Unionists had not been confined to the leadership, but extended also to organization. This was reflected in three long articles in *The Times* in January 1911,[27] which led the chief whip, then Sir Alexander Acland-Hood, to comment that it would "have shown a very poor spirit in the party if, after they had been beaten twice, they had not said there must be something wrong with their organization". He added that he "liked the idea of a committee to inquire into their organization, and he himself strongly advised Mr. Balfour to have such a committee".[28] One consequence was that he himself was succeeded as chief whip by Balcarres. A more important change was the creation in July of the office of Chairman of the Party Organization to take over the duties at the Central Office previously carried out by the chief whip. This meant that in future the work of the whips would be confined to Parliament, and supervision of the organization of the party in the country would be entrusted to the Chairman of the Party Organization, who has, however, always been a member of one of the Houses of Parliament. It was laid down that the Chairman of the Party Organization would be appointed by the leader of the party, and would be responsible to him. Supreme authority in the party, both in Parliament and outside, continued to be vested in the leader, as being in control both of the whips and of the Chairman of the Party Organization, but in practice, as Balfour had found and Bonar Law was soon to find, his authority could be exercised only with consent. The first appointment to the office of Chairman of the Party Organization was Sir Arthur Steel-Maitland. These changes did not extend to Scotland, which had its own organization, and where the Scottish Unionist whip continued to be responsible for extra-parliamentary activities until 1950.

Steel-Maitland found much to criticize in the organization of the party, and especially in the relations of the National Union and Central Office. In a long memorandum to Bonar Law[29] he expatiated on the waste of money, the lack of adaptation of means to ends, the failure to select the most suitable men for the various committees and the need to put the whole organization under one head. He alleged that the Central Office could not tell within £10,000, probably not within £20,000, what the year's expenditure had been. The raising of funds, especially by Lord St. Audries, had been more satisfactory. Starting without any invested funds, he left a nest egg of over £300,000—a very fine performance, even if "a year's peerages are hypothecated". The admission that peerages were sold would not have startled anyone in the inner circles of the parties at the time, and is worth recalling only because of the later charges against Lloyd George.

To this point the Conservatives and the Liberal Unionists had formally been separate parties, though their working together was so close that they were regarded as one party, and as often as not were simply called the Unionist party. This is not to deny that from time to time inherited prejudices found expression in mutual suspicions, as we have seen even at the highest level in the contest of Chamberlain and Long for the leadership; but the alliance was so mutually advantageous that these prejudices were usually suppressed. In numbers and financial contributions the Conservatives were much the predominant partner, but the Liberal Unionists provided abilities and driving force out of proportion to their numbers. It was decided in 1912 to put the practical union on to a formal basis, and after many meetings had been held and memoranda exchanged the Conservative party and the Liberal Unionist party were fused as the Conservative and Unionist party. The name Liberal was retained in the title of the National Union which became the National Unionist Association of Conservative and Liberal-Unionist Organizations, a cumbrous title simplified in 1924 to the present name of the National Union of Conservative and Unionist Associations. From 1912 onwards the normal official designation of a candidate, member or organization has been "Conservative and

P

Unionist", but for historical reasons some candidates, members and organizations have preferred to call themselves "Unionist" and others "Conservative".

These changes, and the accession of Bonar Law to the leadership, were the outward signs of a change that had come over the character and policy of the old Tory party. Though the party was soon to give one last demonstration of its devotion to the Anglican establishment, it was ceasing to be the party of the Church of England. Though Conservative glasses were still fervently raised to "The King", it was a shock to find the King on the Throne, however reluctantly, acting on the advice of his Liberal ministers instead of regarding himself as an instrument in the Tory organization; and George V had a much higher regard for Asquith than he ever achieved for Bonar Law. Though the squires, so far as they continued to exist, were still normally to be found in the Conservative ranks, the Tories were no longer almost exclusively the party of the land but were beginning to be dominated by businessmen; and even the squires were rapidly getting into business themselves. Though the Tories fought the Parliament Act, there was a decisive element not prepared to fight for the veto to the last ditch and still more prepared to concede that birth and rank were not in themselves qualifications for the legislature. The fall of Balfour marked not only the end of the long rule of the house of Cecil, but the end of a stage in the evolution of the Tory party.

It marked also an epoch in the history of Great Britain. While the storm over the Parliament Bill raged within the Palace of Westminster, the protagonists were puzzled that so little interest was taken in it by the great public outside. It was the hottest summer within memory, and the public were distracted by the Tonypandy riots, the Clapham Common murders, the Sidney Street siege and the appearance of a German gun-boat off Agadir, but these were not sufficient explanations. The fact was that the centre of political interest was shifting from religious and constitutional to social and economic questions. Syndicalist theories, circulated by the *New Age* and in other ways, were taking hold of the industrial workers, and a railway strike which disorganized the economic life of the country for several days made statesmen apprehensive about the growing power of the trade unions. This apprehension was increased in 1912 when a strike of miners revealed a disturbingly bitter spirit on both sides of the industry. These labour troubles gave a significance to the small Labour party in the House of Commons not to be measured by its numbers, for its members were concerned with the new realities of the political situation. It was a main interest of the Labour party to persuade the Liberal government to undo the Osborne judgement, and this was eventually achieved by the Trade Union Act, 1913, which allowed political action financed by a political levy to trade unions on condition that there was a prior ballot in a favour, and that members who did not approve of political action were given the opportunity of "contracting out" from paying the political levy. The numbers of trade unionists, which stood at 2,565,000 in 1910, rose to 4,145,000 in 1914. A daily newspaper, the *Daily Herald*, was founded in 1911 to promote the aims of the Labour movement, but the workers obstinately continued to read the capitalist papers and it had to struggle for existence.

The passage of the Parliament Bill opened a new chapter of bitterness in the relations of Unionists and Liberals which was further exacerbated by Bonar Law's accession to the leadership of the Conservative party. He was a man of blunt speech who introduced what Asquith called "the new style" into parliamentary oratory. Asquith was pained to read that Law, speaking in Belfast, had accused the Liberals of selling the constitution to remain a few months longer in office. In the House of Commons he asked if this meant that he and his colleagues were selling their convictions, and Law replied: "You have not got any."[30] It was a debasing of the parliamentary coin, but Law's followers immensely preferred such fighting charges to the ambiguities and qualifications of Balfour.

There were to be plenty of opportunities for exercising such gifts in the next few years, when party bitterness rose to alarming heights and might easily have broken into civil war if the nation had not become involved in a struggle for its very existence. Redmond and his Nationalists demanded the price of their support for the "People's Budget" and the Parliament Bill in the shape of home rule for Ireland. Lloyd George within the Cabinet and the Welsh Nonconformists outside demanded the disestablishment of the Welsh Church as the price of Welsh loyalty to the Liberal party in successive elections. Both these measures were pushed through Parliament under the new procedure of the Parliament Act in three successive sessions in the teeth of fierce opposition. This procedure was not necessary in the case of the National Health Insurance Bill of 1911, but it roused the same animosities as the "People's Budget". To cap all, the so-called Marconi scandal gave the opposition a wonderful opportunity, used to the full, to blacken the reputation of leading ministers.

The National Insurance Act, 1911, is now recognized as the greatest step forward in British social history and the true foundation of the modern welfare state, but it was seen at the time in a less favourable light. It was a scheme for insurance against sickness and unemployment by contributions from the state, employers and employed, drafted in the light of German experience. Though Lloyd George claimed to be offering the workers "ninepence for fourpence" (the state contributed 2*d.* a week, the employer 3*d.* and the worker 4*d.*), they were suspicious and would have preferred ninepence for nothing. Medical men were hostile to the idea of panel patients to be treated alongside their private patients. Duchesses protested against the idea that they should lick stamps, and ten thousand domestic servants pledged themselves in the Albert Hall not to pay. In the end all opposition was silenced. Lloyd George made the friendly societies and trades unions approved societies for the purpose of administering benefits, though it could have been done more cheaply through the Post Office. A deal was made between Ramsay MacDonald and the Master of Elibank, the Liberal chief whip, to the effect that the Labour members would support the Insurance Bill if the government would promote a bill for the payment of members of Parliament. The government carried out their share of the bargain, and the payment of £400 a year towards the expenses of members was carried; the measure was of special help to the Labour party, though far from unwelcome to many Liberals. The Irish Nationalists gave their support to the Insurance Bill, as they had done to the "People's Budget", with an eye on home rule. In the end the Unionists thought it politic to give an unopposed third reading to the bill, and some even suggested that they had up their sleeves a Conservative insurance bill which would be far better.

The Marconi scandal was exploited to the uttermost. In 1912 the Postmaster-General, Herbert Samuel, provisionally accepted a tender from the English Marconi company for the building of radio stations throughout the Empire. This led to a steep rise in Marconi shares. There was also an American Marconi company, in which the English company had a majority holding. The managing director of both companies was Godfrey Isaacs, brother of Sir Rufus Isaacs, the Liberal Attorney-General. He offered his brothers Henry and Rufus a block of shares in a forthcoming issue by the American company, and though Rufus declined to do a direct deal he eventually bought from Henry 10,000 shares at a price well below their market value, though he seemed not to know this. On the same day he disposed of 1,000 to Lloyd George, and 1,000 to the Master of Elibank at the price he had paid. When the new issue was floated, the price rose to nearly double what had been paid. All three sold a large part of their holdings, but subsequently bought more, and in particular the Master of Elibank bought 2,500 for the Liberal party fund.

Rumours began to circulate, and in the House of Commons on a motion to appoint a select committee to inquire into the Marconi contract Lloyd George and Isaacs denied having had any dealings in the shares of "the Marconi company"; in the context this meant the English Marconi company, but it was taken to cover the American company also. The truth came out when Herbert Samuel—an entirely innocent party—and Isaacs brought a libel action against Le Matin, and engaged Carson and F. E. Smith to represent them. These

Tory lawyers ran into severe criticism in their party for accepting the briefs and so depriving themselves of the right to criticize their clients in the House of Commons, for most Unionists saw at once the possibility of making party capital out of the transactions and seized it as a heaven-sent opportunity. Lloyd George and Isaacs were summoned before the select committee; the Master of Elibank had conveniently gone off to Bogota, which soon became a familiar word on every Tory platform. The merits of the dispute were now forgotten, and it became a trial of strength between the major parties. The Liberal majority on the select committee exonerated the ministers, the Conservative minority censured them. When the committee reported, this procedure was repeated in the house, and Bonar Law's amendment regretting the transactions and the want of frankness with the house was rejected by 346 to 268. Nevertheless, much harm had been done to the Liberal party and to the personal reputations of the three ministers. The most astonishing episode in the miserable business was yet to come. Barely four months later Rufus Isaacs was made the Lord Chief Justice of England.

The disestablishment of the Church of England in Wales could be defended on the same grounds as the disestablishment of the Irish Church at the hands of that great churchman Gladstone in 1869. It was the Church of a minority, and at that time it was to some extent an alien Church. If disestablishment of the four Welsh bishoprics had alone been proposed it would have been difficult to resist, and in particular it is unlikely that the Presbyterian Law and the Unitarian Chamberlain would have resisted. But disestablishment alone would not have satisfied the Welsh Liberal members, on whom the government depended, and the Welsh Nonconformists, on whom they in turn depended. It was coupled with disendowment —the confiscation of all endowments prior to 1660—and this attack on property allied the whole Unionist party in opposition to the bill. "Whatever hesitation I may have had about the question of disestablishment," Chamberlain told a West Bromwich audience,[31] "I have none about the question of disendowment. . . . Unless you preserve the legal rights of property, no man's property and no trust property and no church's property is safe." Even for F. E. Smith, no pillar of the Church, it was "a bill which has shocked the conscience of every Christian community in Europe".[32]

The Established Church (Wales) Bill was introduced in April 1912, and after fierce debate was passed in the House of Commons by large majorities, only to be thrown out in the Lords. Passed once more in the Commons in 1913, it was again thrown out in the Lords. Every stage was contested with bitter but wearisome iteration. Passed once more in the Commons in 1914, it automatically became law under the Parliament Act in the summer of 1914, but by that time the shadow of war was over the land, and with general consent its operation was postponed. It did not come into effect until 1920. Welsh Churchmen have surmounted the consequences of disendowment and most are not ungrateful for disestablishment, though neither result seemed likely during the heat of the struggle.

The third home rule bill, like the first (1886) and the second (1893), was a measure to separate the whole of Ireland from the United Kingdom, but in the three sessions during which it was acrimoniously debated between the parties the question of Ulster, or more strictly the northern counties, sometimes reckoned as four, sometimes as six, became of paramount importance. The arguments for freeing southern Ireland from alien rule and an alien church could be used to show that the Anglo-Scottish Protestant population in the northern counties should not be subjected to the domination of Irish Roman Catholics. It was an argument whose force was felt by the Nonconformist members of the government, such as Lloyd George, but at that time the necessity for the integrity of Irish territory was assumed by almost everyone, and they suppressed any doubts they may have felt. Bonar Law had no need to suppress his, and the fact that he was the son of a Presbyterian minister who had been born in Ulster and died in Ulster played its part in sharpening the conflict.

The Irish home rule bill followed a parallel course to the Established Church (Wales) Bill. It was passed by the Commons in the 1912–13 session, and rejected by the Lords on second reading, again passed by the Commons in the 1913 session and again rejected by the Lords. Only one episode from the ding-dong story need be recalled. During the first committee stage of the bill, the government were defeated as the result of a snap division on a financial amendment. Asquith said that he would introduce a resolution to rescind the amendment. When he did so, on 13th November 1912, some Unionist members wished to shout him down, as they had done the year previously. Bonar Law restrained them, but when Asquith's resolution was put disorder broke out and the Speaker adjourned for an hour. When the sitting was resumed, the uproar was just as bad, and after ten minutes the Speaker adjourned till the following day. The Unionists cheered loudly, and as Churchill and Seely rose to leave they hissed "Rats" at them. Good-humouredly Churchill waved his handkerchief, and this so provoked an Ulster member, Ronald McNeil, that with deadly accuracy he hurled a copy of the Standing Orders at the minister's head.

If passed in the same form by the Commons in 1914, the home rule bill would soon afterwards become law despite the Lords, but the centre of interest had in the meantime shifted outside Parliament. Carson, who had become the leader of the Ulster Unionists in 1910 in succession to Walter Long, told a great gathering at Craigavon in 1911 that the Ulster Unionist Council would set up a provisional government to take over the province as soon as the home rule bill (not then introduced) was passed. Soon afterwards the Orange lodges and Unionist clubs began military drills, a movement which led to the Ulster Volunteer Force in 1913. This was ominous enough, but worse was to come at a great Tory demonstration at Blenheim on 29th July 1912. After describing the government as "a revolutionary committee which had seized upon despotic power by fraud", Bonar Law warned them that there were things stronger than parliamentary majorities, and added: [33]

"Before I occupied the position which I now fill in the party I said that, in my belief, if an attempt were made to deprive these men of their birthright—as part of a corrupt parliamentary bargain—they would be justified in resisting such an attempt by all means in their power, including force. I said it then, and I repeat now with a full sense of the responsibility which attaches to my position, that, in my opinion, if such an attempt is made, I can imagine no length of resistance to which Ulster can go in which I should not be prepared to support them, and in which, in my belief, they would not be supported by the overwhelming majority of the British people."

Men recalled how in 1886 Randolph Churchill had said, "Ulster will fight, and Ulster will be right," and the words were repeated on many lips in no light spirit. In September Ulster Unionists began signing a document, known as the Covenant, asserting the right of Ulster to resist. Over half a million signatures were obtained. Asquith meditated legal action against Carson, F. E. Smith and Craig, but could hardly do so without taking action also against Bonar Law; and his own sense of the rule of law made him doubt whether the struggle would in fact be carried to arms.

At this point the attitude of the King became of crucial importance, for the only hope of avoiding the passage of the home rule bill that the Unionists could see was a dissolution, and efforts were made to persuade the King that he still possessed the power to dissolve and ought at the appropriate time to use it. On 3rd May 1912 in an astonishing conversation after dinner at Buckingham Palace Bonar Law gave the King "the worst five minutes that he has had for a long time", as he told Austen Chamberlain that same evening. According to Chamberlain's record, Law said to his Sovereign: [34]

"Our desire has been to keep the Crown out of our struggles, but the government have brought it in. Your only chance is that they should resign within two years. If they don't, you must either accept the home rule bill or dismiss your ministers and choose others who will support you in vetoing it—and in either case half your subjects will think you have acted against them."

The following September Bonar Law was invited to Balmoral, and in a memorandum that he drafted for the King he made his meaning quite clear: [35]

"If the home rule bill passes through all its stages under the Parliament Act and requires only the royal assent the position will be a very serious and almost an impossible one for the Crown. . . .

"In such circumstances Unionists would certainly believe that the King not only had the constitutional right but that it was his duty before acting on the advice of his ministers to ascertain whether it would not be possible to appoint other ministers who would advise him differently and allow the question to be decided by the country at a general election."

The argument was reinforced by the contention that the constitution was in suspense until the preamble to the Parliament Act was carried out, and by calling the government supporters "the Radical party". In the summer of 1913 the King again sought to ascertain the Unionist position, and he received from Law and Lansdowne a memorandum arguing that the constitution was in a state of suspense, that dissolution was the only way of avoiding civil war and that if the Prime Minister would not recommend a dissolution the Sovereign had the right to dismiss him and send for someone who would give that advice. The King, schooled by Asquith, saw the flaws in such dangerous advice. When Lansdowne went to Balmoral the following September the King told him that according to Asquith a constitutional monarch was bound to follow his ministers' advice; if he personally disagreed, the most he could do would be to put his views on record. As the British constitution had developed in the reign of Queen Victoria there can be little doubt that Asquith's advice was right and Bonar Law's wrong. The last time a sovereign had claimed the right to dismiss his ministers was in 1834, when William IV dismissed the Melbourne ministry, and it was not a happy precedent, for Melbourne, confirmed by a general election, was soon back in office.

The King also told Lansdowne something that was of greater practical consequence. Asquith had suggested that a compromise might be possible by giving separate treatment to Ulster. The King not only passed on this hint but several times urged that meetings between the party leaders might be useful. Bonar Law, who followed Lansdowne at Balmoral, met Churchill there, and in conversation with him the idea of separate treatment for Ulster came to attract him. He wrote to Carson, "As you know, I have long thought that it might be possible to leave Ulster as she is, and have some form of home rule for the rest of Ireland,"[36] and Carson readily agreed.

There followed two secret meetings between Asquith and Bonar Law, held on 14th October and 6th November in Aitken's house at Cherkley. It is a remarkable commentary on the working of the British party system that such meetings, originally prompted by the King, could take place at the height of the controversy when men's hands were already reaching for their guns. The talks broke down over what was meant by the exclusion of Ulster. Bonar Law told Stamfordham that he now despaired of any agreement between the parties, and said the government "must either submit their bill to the judgement of the people, or prepare to face the consequences of civil war".[37] The King, warned by Asquith that an election forced by him against the advice of ministers could be fought only on the issue "King against the people", dropped any idea of requiring a dissolution.

The Unionist leaders now toyed with a novel and dangerous method of forcing a dissolution. This was to amend the annual Army Act in the House of Lords so as to exclude the use of the Army in Ulster. If *per impossibile* the Cabinet accepted the amendment, Carson and his provisional Ulster government could not be hindered. If the Cabinet rejected the amendment, as they were bound to do, the Lords could throw out the Army Act and so prevent the use of the Army anywhere until the measure could be forced through under the Parliament Act in three successive sessions. This would be intolerable in the international situation, and Asquith would be forced to dissolve. As Mr. Robert Blake comments:[38] "On any view such tactics were reckless in the extreme, and it is an astonishing revelation of the extent to which the Irish problem had dazzled, almost blinded, the leading politicians of the Conservative party, that they should have even considered such a perilous course; although in the end, it is only just to add, they did not adopt it." The gravest aspect of the matter was perhaps that Sir Henry Wilson, the Anglo-Irish Director of Military Operations at the War Office, was privy to the idea and approved.

Fortunately for his reputation, Bonar Law dropped the plan only a few hours before he became aware of the incidents at the Curragh, which made it clear that the government could not in any case rely on the Army to coerce Ulster. It is still impossible to unravel with complete assurance[39] the tangle of events that led the Commander-in-Chief in Ireland, General Sir Arthur Paget, to send the following telegram to the War Office on 20th March: "Regret to report Brigadier and 57 officers, 3rd Cavalry Brigade, prefer to accept dismissal if ordered north." The government had become alarmed at the possibility of attacks on ammunition stores and other violent action, and resolved to strengthen their forces, but Brigadier-General Hubert Gough and the other officers at the Curragh were only exercising a choice which they had been invited, indeed ordered, to make. John Seely, who had been made Secretary of State for War in 1912, resigned on account of criticism of some "peccant paragraphs" that he had added to a Cabinet memorandum, pledging that the forces of the Crown would not be used "to crush political opposition to the policy or principles of the home rule bill", and

Asquith took the War Office under his own control. The Curragh incident was in no sense a mutiny as it is commonly called, but it made clear that, if given the same choice, a very high percentage of officers would make the same decision, and no reliance could be placed on the Army to fight the Ulster Volunteers. The successful landing at Larne of 35,000 rifles and 3,000,000 cartridges from Hamburg for the use of the volunteers increased the apprehension.

Compromise had now become essential, and compromise meant the exclusion from the home rule bill of the Protestant part of Ulster. Asquith announced that the third reading of the bill would be taken (for the third session) in the Commons before Whitsun, and that an amending bill would be introduced in the Lords. When the bill was produced on 23rd June, it was seen to provide for an option for each county of Ulster to remain outside the provisions of the home rule bill for six years, with automatic inclusion at the end of that period. It was drastically altered by the upper house. The murder of the Archduke Ferdinand at Sarajevo on 28th June gave new urgency to the efforts to reach a compromise, and the former Liberal chief whip, now Lord Murray of Elibank, took a hand but with no result. Asquith then suggested that the King should call a conference, and without optimism the Unionists agreed. It was attended by Asquith and Lloyd George, Bonar Law and Lansdowne, Redmond and Dillon, Carson and Craig, and was presided over by the Speaker after the King's opening address. The conference broke down after three days without agreement on the area to be excluded and with no discussion of the time-limit for exclusion. A few days later gun-running into Howth was followed by shooting between British soldiers and a Dublin crowd.

The international situation was now very dark, and on the morning of the day 30th July, when the amending bill as altered by the Lords was due to be taken in the Commons, Asquith received an urgent message asking him to go round to Pembroke Lodge. It is not often that the leader of the opposition summons the Prime Minister to attend on him, and a desire for secrecy was no doubt the reason. Carson was with Bonar Law, and they suggested that in the interests of national unity the amending bill should be postponed. Asquith gratefully agreed, and the bill was never in fact brought before the House of Commons.

19

WAR AND COALITION
1914–1918

Unionist support for war—Redmond pledges Irish support—Mac-
Donald strikes a discordant note—but Labour supports the supple-
mentary estimates and Henderson takes his place—Fisher refuses
to serve under Churchill—Asquith agrees to a coalition—the Con-
servatives demand an equal share and the exclusion of Haldane—
the Labour party agrees to Henderson joining—Lloyd George and
Bonar Law become reconciled—and Lloyd George forms a coali-
tion—a predominantly Unionist government—Lloyd George's per-
sonal magnetism destructive of party lines—he succeeds in bring-
ing Churchill back—the "doormat incident" offends the Labour
party—Henderson resigns, but Labour still remains in the coalition
—attempt by the military and political opposition to overthrow
Lloyd George—his triumph in the Maurice debate—the Liberals
who vote with Asquith become marked men—Bonar Law and
Balfour agree to fighting the election as a coalition, and Lloyd
George accepts imperial preference—coalition candidates receive
the "coupon"

THE outbreak of war led to dramatic and permanent changes in the British party system.

The Unionists had supported Sir Edward Grey's foreign policy. On 2nd August Bonar Law sent Asquith a letter saying on behalf of Lansdowne and other colleagues as well as himself that "it would be fatal to the honour and security of the United Kingdom to hesitate in supporting France and Russia".[1] There was no suggestion that British intervention depended on the invasion of Belgium. Asquith's reply made it clear that the government would not declare war unless Belgium were invaded. In the end it made no difference as Belgium was invaded, and at eleven of the clock in the evening of 4th August Great Britain was at war with Germany. By violating the neutrality of Belgium, and so bringing into play British treaty obligations, the German government enabled Asquith to take an almost united Cabinet into the war. Despite the strong pacifist element among the Liberals, only Morley and Burns resigned from the Cabinet. If Belgium had not been invaded and Great Britain had nevertheless gone to the aid of France, a serious split in the Liberal party and in the Cabinet would have been certain.

In the historic debate in the House of Commons on 3rd August Redmond followed Grey and Bonar Law and pledged the support of the Irish Nationalists in the event of war. He urged the government to remove all troops from Ireland and said the Nationalist Volunteers would join with the Ulster Volunteers in keeping the shores of Ireland free from invaders. It was a noble gesture that greatly enhanced Redmond's standing in the House of Commons, but within two years in Ireland itself the influence of the Nationalists members was drowned by the rising tide of Sinn Fein.

In the debate on 3rd August a discordant note was struck by Ramsay Macdonald, who, in pursuance of a decision by the Parliamentary Labour party that morning, said Great Britain ought to remain neutral. In an appeal to the Liberals he said that only neutrality "was consistent with the honour of our country and the traditions of the party that are now in office". The invasion of Belgium transformed opinion in the Labour party as in the country at large, and only the leaders of the Independent Labour party remained opposed to intervention. The British Labour party followed the example of the German and French Socialist parties in voting the credits needed for the war, and the Second International, which had pledged itself at Stuttgart in 1907 to exploit any war for revolutionary purposes, collapsed before the greater forces of nationalism and patriotism. When the British Parliamentary Labour party decided on 5th August not to oppose the supplementary estimates made necessary by the war, MacDonald resigned as chairman and Henderson was elected in his place. Before long Henderson and his colleagues were actively supporting the prosecution of the war.

On the last day of July Bonar Law had received through F. E. Smith a message from Churchill asking if he would be willing to enter a coalition government in the event of war. Bonar Law had no relish either for the proposal or its source, but when war broke out he readily agreed to a suspension of normal party activity both in Parliament and in the country. He regarded it as the breach of a pledge when Asquith decided to put the Irish home rule bill on the statute book (along with the Welsh Church bill), while at the same time introducing a single-clause bill postponing their operation till the end of the fighting; but Asquith could do no other in view of Redmond's determination to see the measure formally enacted. When the bill postponing home rule was introduced in the Commons, Bonar Law made a bitter speech comparing the Prime Minister's bad faith with that of the Germans in invading Belgium, and the Unionists then walked out. Asquith thought them "a lot of prosaic and for the most part middle-aged gentlemen, trying to look

like early French revolutionists in the tennis court".[2] The Independent Labour party felt under no restraint in its propaganda, and
MacDonald joined with four Liberals opposed to the war—Norman
Angell, E. D. Morel, Charles Trevelyan and Arthur Ponsonby—in
forming the Union of Democratic Control to work for democratic
control of foreign policy, no annexations of territory, an international organization to keep the peace and disarmament.

Though the Unionists would not have been prepared to enter a
coalition in 1914, Balfour, as a member of the Committee of
Imperial Defence since 1904, was invited to meetings of the War
Council. Field-Marshal Earl Kitchener, appointed to the War Office,
was technically not a party man but was more than acceptable to
the Unionists. Admiral Lord Fisher, whom Churchill misguidedly
brought out of retirement to be First Sea Lord when Prince Louis of
Battenberg was made a victim of Germanophobia, maintained the
frankest correspondence with Bonar Law and had no scruple in
revealing to him the grave departmental dissensions. These particularly concerned the Dardanelles expedition, the darling child of
Churchill's fertile mind to which Fisher was vehemently opposed.

The rumpus came to a head in May 1915 when Fisher flamboy-
antly resigned and, though ordered back to his desk by the Prime
Minister in the name of the King, refused to serve any longer under
Churchill. He laid down six conditions of an unparalleled insolence
on which alone he would be prepared to return. Bonar Law told
Lloyd George that if Churchill remained as First Lord, the opposition would attack the government irrespective of the consequences.
"Of course we must have a coalition," said Lloyd George, "for the
alternative is impossible,"[3] and he took Bonar Law to Asquith.
About this time there was much concern among those who knew
about the shortage of shells. They were being fired on the western
front at a prodigal rate not previously known in warfare, and
although all munition works had been requisitioned and placed
under a new Ministry of Munitions the supply of shells was as yet
far short of the demand. The shell crisis, though not yet known to
the general public, reinforced the demand provoked by Fisher's
resignation for a reconstruction of the government, and Asquith saw
that he must yield to it. The day after Bonar Law's call with Lloyd
George, 18th May, Asquith sent him a letter saying that all the
members of the administration had placed their resignations in his
hand and offering to form a coalition government in which the
Unionists would be fully represented. With Bonar Law and Lansdowne's acceptance the long period of Liberal rule—nine years
extending over four Parliaments—came to an end. In all the long
history of the British party system, there has been no period more
crammed with men of political genius or more productive of bene-
ficent constitutional, social and economic changes. Few would then

have predicted that they would never again see a purely Liberal government.

The next few days were not edifying. Bonar Law made no requests for a change in policy but demanded for his party an equal share with the Liberals in all the chief posts and in all patronage. Asquith conceded the demand in form but set out to give as little away as possible, and in particular not to have Bonar Law at the Exchequer (on the ground that it would not do to have a tariff reformer there) or at the Ministry of Munitions (as he had made up his mind to give the Admiralty to Balfour, and to retain Kitchener at the War Office, and could not have all the service departments in Unionist hands).[4] Asquith's obstinacy was heightened by the petty insistence of the Unionists on the exclusion of Haldane, because he had once said, in a philosophical context, that Germany was his spiritual home,[5] and their insistence on the inclusion of Carson. Lloyd George talked Bonar Law into accepting the Colonial Office, a subordinate department in time of war, and took the Ministry of Munitions himself. McKenna went to the Exchequer, to which Austen Chamberlain had patriotically waived any claim.

The coalition was not limited to Liberals and Unionists. In view of the need to maintain good relations on the industrial front, Asquith thought it politic to invite Arthur Henderson to be President of the Board of Education. Henderson referred the invitation to the Parliamentary Labour party, which by a small majority was opposed to acceptance, and to the national executive, which favoured it. The Independent Labour party was more strongly represented in Parliament than on the national executive. At a joint meeting of both bodies the opponents were outvoted, and Henderson entered the Cabinet, and two Labour members were given junior office. The office was not one for which Henderson's talents were suited, nor very important in time of war, though it would become important as peace drew nearer, but Labour had after fifteen years put one foot in the door that led to the arcana of power.

In the Cabinet of twenty-two members twelve were Liberals, eight Unionists, one non-party (if Kitchener may be so called) and one Labour. Churchill, who had moved great fleets, had to console himself with the Duchy of Lancaster, but the Liberals as a party retained their hold on the governmental machine. Only one of the major wartime offices, the Admiralty, was held by a Unionist. Austen Chamberlain was given the India Office, and Walter Long, so recently a contender with him for the highest place, after saying that he also would like to be a Secretary of State, contented himself with the Local Government Board. It may have been from a desire to divide the Conservative leadership that Curzon was given the high-ranking post of Lord Privy Seal, and Curzon himself advanced the theory that the coalition placed all ministers on the same level, owing allegiance to the Prime Minister but to no one else. This theory was put to the test when Asquith omitted Bonar Law's name from a Cabinet committee to study conscription, nor was Law mollified when told that Curzon had been consulted. It would have been natural in a coalition for Bonar Law to have led the House of Commons in Asquith's absence, but even that satisfaction was denied him.

The mode of its formation did not augur well for the coalition, and it was put to severe strain by the evacuation of Gallipoli, the introduction of conscription, the Easter rebellion in Dublin and the death of Kitchener. Though the office of Secretary of State for War had lost much of its significance by a decision to give the Chief of the Imperial General Staff direct access to the Cabinet, it still loomed large in the public eye, and clearly must be filled either by Lloyd George or Bonar Law. At that time neither man could see much good in the other, but Aitken brought them together at his house and it was agreed that Lloyd George should get the job. It is disputed in what circumstances Asquith received the news of this agreement from Bonar Law at his country house,[6] but from that time Bonar Law began to turn away from Asquith and to think more kindly of Lloyd George.

There was at this time much dissatisfaction with the conduct of the war. Haig's great counter-offensive launched on the Somme in 1916 had spent itself with a terrible loss of life, and from Dublin to Bucharest the news was uniformly depressing. Asquith, shaken by the death in action of his brilliant son Raymond, was at last beginning to show the strain of nine years in office. Carson was hammering the government from the opposition benches of the House of Commons, Northcliffe in the pages of *The Times* and the *Daily Mail*. Some, like Northcliffe, wished to give the soldiers more power; others, like Lloyd George, wished to give them less. So long as Lloyd George and Bonar Law distrusted each other, Asquith's position was safe, but their reconciliation opened new possibilities.

The curtain-raiser for the dramatic events of the end of 1916 was a debate in the House of Commons on 8th November, when Carson, who had resigned the post of Attorney-General out of discontent with the conduct of the war, moved a seemingly innocent resolution that confiscated enemy properties in Nigeria "should be sold only to natural-born British subjects or companies wholly British". It was, in fact, a heavily loaded resolution, calculated to bring the maximum number of Conservative protectionists into the lobby with Carson against the government, which wanted a free auction. The government won easily, but sixty-five Unionists voted with Carson against seventy-three who voted with Bonar Law. As Bonar Law had declared when the coalition was formed that he would resign the moment the party lost confidence in him, he was disturbed.

Aitken,[7] who had no confidence in Asquith's administration, would have had Bonar Law resign at once, and when this advice was not taken he set out to bring Bonar Law, Carson and Lloyd George together. He soon found that Lloyd George and Carson were already working in close concert with the object of creating a small War Cabinet freed from departmental duties, of which Asquith should not be a member. Bonar Law was more difficult to bring into line, and at first he talked angrily of going to the country with Asquith against Carson. While desiring to see a small War Cabinet, he was anxious to be loyal to Asquith and still distrusted Lloyd George. Nevertheless, "the triumvirate"—Lloyd George, Bonar Law and Carson—began to meet, and on 25th November at Pembroke Lodge Aitken drafted and Bonar Law amended a statement which was to be offered to Asquith for announcement. It asked for a War Cabinet consisting of the Prime Minister and three other members whose names were left blank, except that Lloyd George was designated as chairman in the absence of Asquith.

When Bonar Law took these terms to Asquith, the Prime Minister's first reaction was not unfavourable, but after reflecting at Sutton Courtenay he wrote to Bonar Law that the plan could not be carried out without fatally impairing the confidence of loyal and valued colleagues, and undermining his own authority. Bonar Law's reply was to suggest that Asquith and Lloyd George should discuss the plan.

At this point for the first time Bonar Law put the proposal to his Unionist colleagues. Their old hatred of Lloyd George was matched by their new dislike of Carson, and their hostility was undisguised. To Bonar Law it seemed that Asquith would be supported not only by almost all the Liberal ministers but by nearly all the Conservative, and that the support for Lloyd George and himself would be extra-parliamentary, or at any rate extra-Cabinet.

When Lloyd George saw Asquith, he handed him a memorandum which went one step farther in that the Prime Minister was excluded from the War Committee, and he nearly antagonized Bonar Law by asking for the supersession of Balfour. On 1st December Bonar Law dined alone with Aitken to try and clear his mind, and Aitken, who knew that Lloyd George was dining at another hotel, brought the two men together for a momentous midnight interview. They then decided, in Lloyd George's words, to "go forward with our plan of reorganization, whatever the consequences".[8]

That same day Asquith had written a letter to Lloyd George making counter-proposals which were, in effect, a rejection of Lloyd George's plan. At this point, thanks to Aitken, circumstantial details of the crisis began to appear in the press. Bonar Law summoned a meeting of his Unionist colleagues for Sunday, 3rd December, and after an angry and confused discussion the following resolution was passed:[9]

"We share the view expressed ... by Mr. Bonar Law some time ago that the government cannot continue as it is. It is evident that a change must be made, and in our opinion the publicity given to the intention of Mr. Lloyd George makes reconstruction from within no longer possible. We therefore urge the Prime Minister to tender the resignation of the government. If he feels unable to take that step, we authorize Mr. Bonar Law to tender our resignations."

That afternoon Bonar Law saw Asquith, who had with difficulty been persuaded to return from the country. For some reason he never showed the Unionist resolution to Asquith, but he communicated the gist of it. Asquith was shaken, perhaps by the demand for resignation rather than reconstruction, perhaps by the suspicion that the Unionist minister had now gone over to Lloyd George. He decided to compromise, and in an interview with Lloyd George a little later he agreed that the Prime Minister was not to be chairman of the War Committee, though entitled to attend its meetings and to have a right of veto on its decisions. Still later that same day the agreement was confirmed in the presence of Bonar Law, who went to bed happy.

At breakfast the next morning the compromise so hardly reached was shattered when Asquith opened *The Times*. There he saw an article describing in detail the plans for reorganization, revealing that Lloyd George, Bonar Law and Carson had been working together to secure them, suggesting that Asquith's powers would be nominal, and observing that his qualities were better fitted to preserving the unity of the nation than to forcing the pace of a War Council. He attributed the article to Lloyd George—though the offending passages had, in fact, been suggested to Geoffrey Dawson by Carson[10]—and sent him a letter repudiating the compromise and insisting that the Prime Minister must be chairman of the War Committee. It is possible that the leading article in *The Times* was not the only reason for his change of front. That same morning Liberal ministers who had been ignorant of Sunday's proceedings hastened to assure him of their support, and some Unionists appear to have told him that they had acted, not to oust him, but to strengthen his hand. Possibly Asquith realized he had more backing than he thought when he made the compromise. When Lloyd George received Asquith's letter on the Tuesday, he saw that he could agree only at the cost of admitting defeat and promptly sent in his resignation. On seeing Asquith's letter, Bonar Law made up his mind that he must back Lloyd George. From the other Liberal ministers Asquith received an assurance of unanimous support, but from Curzon, Lord Robert Cecil and Chamberlain he heard the unpleasant news that if both Lloyd George and Bonar Law resigned they would feel bound to do likewise.

Q

At the request of the Unionist members Walter Long asked Bonar Law to meet them in Austen Chamberlain's room at the India Office. Bonar Law angrily refused, thinking erroneously that Long and the three "Cs" wished to depose him as leader. Instead, he summoned a meeting himself at the Colonial Office, and convinced his colleagues that he had not misrepresented their wishes to Asquith. After the meeting Bonar Law sent the following letter to Asquith:[11]

"Lord Curzon, Lord Robert Cecil and Mr. A[usten] Chamberlain have reported to a meeting of all the Unionist members of the Cabinet, except Mr. Balfour, who was unable to be present, the substance of their conversation with you. After full consideration we are of opinion that the course which we urged upon you on Sunday is a necessity and that it is imperative that this course should be taken today. We hope that you have arrived at the same conclusion, but if this is not so we feel that we have no choice but to ask you to act upon our resignations."

Asquith did not delay but that evening tendered his resignation and that of the whole government to the King, and in accordance with the custom of the constitution the King first sent for Bonar Law as the leader of the largest party in the House of Commons. In anticipation of the summons Lloyd George and Bonar Law had met, and had agreed that if Asquith would serve under either of them, the other would accept a subordinate post, but that if Asquith would not do so Lloyd George should be Prime Minister. To this latter part of the bargain Lloyd George agreed with sincere reluctance, for at that time it seemed he had all the Liberal ministers against him and most of the Conservative, but Bonar Law overbore him. Accordingly, Bonar Law asked the King for time to consult Asquith, but Asquith refused to serve under him or Balfour. Night fell with no decision.

The following morning Bonar Law, Lloyd George, Carson and Aitken met and decided to seek Balfour's advice. The advice was that the King should call a conference of political leaders, and Asquith, Balfour, Lloyd George, Bonar Law and Henderson met at Buckingham Palace that afternoon. The object was still to see if there was anyone under whom Asquith would serve. On Balfour's proposal it was agreed to recommend Bonar Law if Asquith would serve under him, if not to recommend Lloyd George. Asquith consulted the Liberal ex-ministers and replied:[12]

"They are unanimously of opinion—and I agree with them—that I, and probably they, can give more effective support from outside. They also think that we could not carry the support of the Liberal party for any such arrangement."

The King bowed before the unavoidable and sent for Lloyd George, but it was still far from certain that the dynamic Welshman would be able to form a government. It was his intention to abandon the previous system of a Cabinet and War Council, and to have a small War Cabinet of four or five members, but at the moment of the royal commission the only persons on whom he could count were the other members of the "triumvirate", Bonar Law and Carson. His first approach was to offer the Foreign Office to Balfour; it was a move as delicate as it was ironical, for Balfour knew that Lloyd George had demanded his removal from the Admiralty, but he accepted, protesting gently that Lloyd George held a pistol to his head, and his acceptance ensured that of others. Asquith had not expected him to capitulate to Lloyd George's charms, and was visibly shaken; for the first time he realized that he was not indispensable.

Nevertheless, the Liberal ex-ministers remained solidly loyal to Asquith with the single exception of Lloyd George's own Parliamentary Secretary at the Ministry of Munitions, Christopher Addison, whom he promptly placed at the head of that department. Addison quickly proved his worth in the lobbies, and before the day was out he was able to assure his chief of 126 Liberal members' votes, about half of the parliamentary party.

Lloyd George's next approach was significantly to Labour, which he decided was entitled, in view of the complete engagement of the nation's resources in war, to a bigger share in the government than it had enjoyed in the previous coalition. To a deputation from the Parliamentary Labour party and the National Executive he offered state regulation of the coal mines and shipping, the rationing of food, a place in the War Cabinet and the oversight of two new ministries of special interest to their supporters, Labour and Pensions. MacDonald, Snowden and Webb were not impressed by Lloyd George's appeals, but J. H. Thomas, an opponent of Asquith's coalition, came out in favour, and by a majority of seventeen to fourteen the deputation decided for entry. Henderson was given the post in the War Cabinet, John Hodge became Minister of Labour, George Barnes the Minister of Pensions and several Labour M.P.s obtained junior posts.

Lloyd George now felt strong enough to engage the Tory leaders —Walter Long and the three "Cs"—who had been most hostile to himself and Bonar Law, and whose absence from the government could destroy it. He first approached Walter Long, who would not go in without the others. Judging his man, Lloyd George then offered a place in the War Cabinet to Curzon, who accepted with indecent alacrity and without consulting the others. He had assured Asquith that no Tory minister would join a Lloyd George–Bonar Law Coalition. This weakened the position of Chamberlain and Cecil, and by the evening all four were closeted with Lloyd George to discuss the terms on which they would enter. At this point, as Asquith's biographers observe, there were not enough pistols to go round.[13]

Lloyd George made no difficulty about accepting their ban on Churchill as Bonar Law had made the same condition.

The other Tories raised no problems, and with surprising speed Lloyd George was able to announce his government. The permanent members of the War Cabinet would be himself and three other ministers without departmental responsibilities—Curzon, Henderson and Milner. The South African proconsul was unexpectedly substituted at the last moment for Carson. Bonar Law, as Chancellor of the Exchequer and leader of the House of Commons, was not normally expected to attend but had the right to do so. The permanent members thus consisted of one Liberal, two Unionists and one Labour member, and although Lloyd George angrily told C. P. Scott "half the *acting* Cabinet is 'Lib-Lab' ",[14] to most people it seemed to be a predominantly Tory body. The ministry as a whole left this impression even more strongly. Whereas Asquith's senior ministers included twenty-two Liberals, thirteen Unionists and one Labour, Lloyd George's numbered twenty-one Liberals, twenty-one Unionists, three Labour and one non-party. The shifting of the balance was even more dramatic than these figures suggest, for most of the Liberals occupied subordinate posts, and all the key positions except that of Prime Minister were in the hands of Unionists. With the help of Lloyd George from within, the Unionists achieved in a few weeks that control of the administration that they had failed to secure by ten years of direct assault. Asquith and his Liberal followers now transferred themselves to the opposite benches and constituted themselves the official opposition. The Liberal party has never since played more than a balancing rôle in the British party system, and a deep cleavage opened between the Asquithian and Lloyd George factions.

The overthrow of Asquith and the formation of the new coalition could not have taken place if Lloyd George at the height of his powers had not exerted a personal magnetism over those around him such as few leaders have ever achieved. To find the like we have to go back to Chatham in the eighteenth century; and years afterwards so great a war-leader as Churchill could not speak of his old chief save in tones of awe. Like other magnetic forces, the personality of Lloyd George repelled those whom it did not attract, but the spell he cast over men so outstanding in their diverse ways as Balfour, Bonar Law, Austen Chamberlain, F. E. Smith and Churchill himself shows that we are not dealing with any ordinary phenomenon of politics.

Such a personality played havoc with the old party lines, and led to something like personal government. The strength of Lloyd George's position was put to the test in July, when at last he felt sufficiently secure to bring Churchill into the administration. Press rumours that he intended to do so had caused a flurry among the

Tory leaders. Long, Curzon and Derby entered their separate pro-
tests, and Sir George Younger, chairman of the Conservative Party
Organization, conveyed to Lloyd George a resolution of the National
Unionist Council to the effect that Churchill's appointment would
be "an insult to the Navy and the Army".[15] Nevertheless, Lloyd
George not only made Churchill Minister of Munitions (creating the
new post of Minister of Reconstruction for Addison), but did so
without consulting Bonar Law, and sent Lord Beaverbrook (as Max
Aitken had now become) to tell him that the news had already been
given to the press. There were angry recriminations, but Lloyd
George weathered the storm. At the same time he gave the India
Office to Edwin Montagu, who had shown his eagerness to leave the
Asquithian ranks, and he tried to solace Carson for depriving him of
the Admiralty by giving him a place in the War Cabinet as originally intended.

The balance of the coalition was nearly upset about the same
time by the "doormat incident" jeopardizing the continued participation of the Labour party. It arose from the outbreak of revolution in Russia in March. The Scandinavian and Dutch socialists had
proposed a conference of socialists from belligerent as well as
neutral countries to be held at Stockholm with a view to laying
down conditions of peace that national parties would try to get
accepted by their governments, and after the revolution the Russian
Workers' and Soldiers' Councils took up the cry. The Labour party
decided to send MacDonald and two others to Russia to investigate,
but the deputation never got beyond Aberdeen as the Sailors' and
Firemen's Union refused to convey MacDonald. In the meantime
Henderson had visited Russia at the suggestion of Lloyd George,
whose first anxiety was naturally to keep the Russian armies in the
field; and on his return, "with more than a touch of malarial fever"
as Lloyd George complained,[16] he came out in favour of sending
delegates to the Stockholm conference. The National Executive of
the Labour party was still divided in its views on the wisdom of so
doing, and it decided that he, MacDonald and Wardle should go to
Paris to discuss the issue with the French socialists. There he secured
agreement that the Stockholm conference should be regarded as
consultative, not binding upon participating parties, and he determined to go ahead, whatever might be said by his colleagues in
the Cabinet, if he could get the backing of an emergency conference
of the Labour party.

These doings were not at all to the liking of Henderson's colleagues in the War Cabinet, and even Lloyd George, who had at first
favoured Stockholm, had become hostile. When Henderson returned
from Paris on 1st August Lloyd George had some sharp words with
him, but asked him nevertheless to attend the War Cabinet that
afternoon. On arriving at No. 10 Downing Street he found that the

other members first wished to discuss his conduct privately, and he was asked to wait for a little while in the private secretary's room. The "little while" turned out to be nearly an hour, and when he was admitted he was in no mood for conciliation and invited the Prime Minister to dismiss him. This Lloyd George was reluctant to do, and even nine days later when Henderson persuaded the Labour party conference by a large majority to support the Stockholm meeting he shrank from dismissal but laid down that Henderson was not to be summoned to Cabinet meetings. At this point Henderson himself resigned, but both he and Lloyd George still hesitated to force matters. The Labour party did not withdraw from the coalition, Henderson's place in the War Cabinet was given to Barnes, and Wardle was made a minister.

It is no part of this work to study the prosecution of the war by the Lloyd George administration, but differences between the Prime Minister and the military leaders on the way the war should be fought had permanent consequences for the party system. In February 1918 the War Cabinet decided to reduce the powers of the Chief of the Imperial General Staff to what they were before Robertson's appointment, and when Robertson would neither accept the reduced position nor the alternative offered to him Sir Henry Wilson was appointed in his place. A few months later Wilson removed General Sir Frederick Maurice from the post of Director of Military Operations at the War Office. The military and political opposition to Lloyd George thereupon combined in a resolute effort to overthrow his government.

The operation began with a letter from Maurice in the *Morning Post* of 7th May stating that certain answers given in the House of Commons by Lloyd George and Bonar Law were untrue. It was a gross act of insubordination and a breach of the Official Secrets Act, for which Maurice could properly have been tried in the military and civil courts, but he knew that he had powerful friends. Among them was Asquith, who asked Bonar Law in the House of Commons what action the government proposed to take to deal with the charges. Bonar Law, indignant at the attack on his honour, said they proposed to appoint two judges to hold an inquiry. Asquith refused a judicial inquiry, and moved for a select committee—though he must have realized in the light of the Marconi inquiry that a select committee would divide along strictly party lines. Lloyd George's blood was now up, and on his advice the Cabinet decided that if Asquith would not have an inquiry by judges he should have no inquiry at all. The Prime Minister, it was made known, would oppose Asquith's motion in the house, treat it as a motion of confidence, and hand in the resignation of the whole government if defeated.

Thus was the stage set for the momentous debate on 9th May. The

Asquithian Liberals and their supporting newspapers were confident that the hour of justice had come, but were disappointed when Asquith opened the debate with a faltering speech. Still, there were the disclosures of the Maurice letter. Lloyd George, who followed Asquith, tore it to shreds within ten minutes, and soon his excited followers, beside themselves with enthusiasm, were shouting: "Divide, divide." He was able to show from the minutes of the Supreme War Council that Robertson had been mistaken in his charges against Bonar Law and that the information he had himself given to the House of Commons had been supplied by Maurice's own department while Maurice was still Director of Military Operations, and was correct. It was a devastating parliamentary performance, and Asquith would have been wise to accept Carson's invitation to withdraw his motion. When the lobbies were cleared, only ninety-eight of his followers voted with him and seventy-one Liberals voted with Lloyd George. The motion to appoint a select committee was lost by 293 votes to 106. The bitter feelings roused by this debate did not subside easily, and the Liberals who had voted with Asquith became marked men in the sight of Lloyd George, as was to be shown in the general election which took place seven months later.

For several months before the armistice, as soon indeed as the last German offensive had been rolled back, there had been much discussion behind the scenes about the next general election, the time when it should be held and the manner in which it should be conducted. There was general agreement that it should be held soon, for Parliament had already exceeded by two sessions the limit laid down by itself in 1911; and the Representation of the People Act, 1918, had transformed the basis on which elections would be fought. This revolutionary measure, which finally assimilated the borough and county franchises, gave the vote to all males of the age of twenty-one or over with residential or business qualifications, and to all women of the age of thirty or over who were householders or married to householders or graduates. It limited plural voting to one residential vote and one business or university vote. By this sweeping measure the electorate was increased from a little under 7,500,000 to nearly 20,000,000, and the percentage of the population over the age of twenty with a vote was raised from thirty to seventy-four. The principles of the bill were drafted by an all-party conference under the Speaker's chairmanship, and so rapidly had opinion moved under the stress of war that it went through both houses almost unopposed. The bill included provisions for the redistribution of seats, and a later bill permitted women to sit in the House of Commons. Such a large extension of the electorate was bound to affect the outlook and fortunes of all parties, and their methods of presenting their appeal, but the great question in the summer of 1918 was whether there should be a separate appeal by parties, that is to say, whether the coalition should continue.

As early as mid-July the Liberal ministers had set up a committee under the chairmanship of Addison on the assumption that the coalition would go on after the war. They asked that a form of agreement with the Unionists should be prepared immediately, that a common programme should be drawn up for joint signature and that a general statement of policy should be made by the Prime Minister at a favourable opportunity. At this time a wartime election was more than a possibility, especially as the fighting seemed likely to continue into 1919, but it was opposed by the King and eventually ruled out by the early collapse of Germany. While the results of the "khaki election" of 1900 inclined some of the more partisan spirits in the coalition to work for a wartime election, a powerful body of non-party opinion was determined that the precedent should not be followed. It was natural that the Liberal ministers should seek a continuance of the coalition, for Lloyd George was bound to be leader, and in a resumption of party strife they would find it difficult to make common cause with the Asquithians. It was more doubtful whether the Unionists would wish to keep the coalition in existence. One of them at any rate knew the conditions that he would require. In August Beaverbrook's *Daily Express* declared that if the Prime Minister sought re-election on a basis of a coalition government which was to endure he must satisfy those who were to vote for him that his views and theirs were the same, and it asked particularly about tariff reform and imperial preference, Irish policy and the Welsh Church. Lloyd George was indignant with his Minister of Information, as Beaverbrook then was, but he was quite willing to make concessions over free trade, and so powerful a solvent of old ideas had the war proved that few Conservatives were still prepared to quarrel with him over the Welsh Church. Early in October Bonar Law put his own thoughts before Balfour. He inclined to the view that an early election was desirable, and that the Asquithians could have no complaint as they had seized every opportunity of attacking the Prime Minister, but that the responsibility for dissolution should be left to Lloyd George. The Conservatives should support him for the duration of the war, but thereafter be free to act as they thought best in controversial issues. In a remarkable analysis he continued:[17]

"It would indeed be entirely against my own personal ambitions, if I were thinking of that, for obviously the probable result of it would be that, if an election were fought in this way, Lloyd George as the leader of the fight would secure a greater hold on the rank and file of our party and he would also be so dependent on that party after an election that he would permanently be driven into the same attitude towards our party which [Joseph] Chamberlain was placed in before, with this difference—that he would be the leader of it. That would, however, I am inclined to think be not a bad thing for our party, and a good thing for the nation ... Our party on the old lines will never have any future in this country."

Balfour approved of Bonar Law's way of thinking. By the end of October Bonar Law had agreed with Lloyd George to fight the forthcoming election as a coalition, and Lloyd George wrote him a letter suggesting the policies in which they could cooperate. He accepted the policy of imperial preference as defined in the resolutions of the Imperial Conference and would look at problems without any regard to theoretical opinions about free trade or tariff reform. Irish policy must be governed by the fact that home rule was already on the statute book, but no one would attempt to force the rule of a Dublin parliament upon an unwilling Ulster. He could not contemplate the repeal of the Welsh Church Act, but would reconsider some of the financial details.

Bonar Law called a meeting of Conservative members of Parliament for 12th November, but before it could be held rumours of what was proposed brought to Lloyd George's room two deputations of Liberals who saw the danger of extinction and urged him to reach an agreement with Asquith. According to his own account he was not averse from seeing Asquith and some of his friends in the government, but he would not commit himself until he had consulted Bonar Law. The Unionist leader was equally agreeable, and, following a suggestion made by a member of one of the deputations, Lloyd George offered Asquith the Woolsack. The offer was declined. It was a fatal error for the Liberal party. Asquith seems to have suspected that he would be required to sacrifice his friends, but it is more likely that he could not bring himself to take third place after two men whom he regarded as having done him great injury and whose policies he profoundly distrusted.

When the Unionist meeting was held on 12th November the armistice had already been signed, and no one was disposed to challenge Bonar Law's decision, endorsed by all the Conservative ministers, that the party should go to the polls in alliance with the coalition Liberals under the leadership of Lloyd George. He dwelt on the need to maintain unity in the post-war period, to solve controversial subjects in a non-revolutionary manner and to give the government a strong mandate in negotiating the treaties of peace. In seeking to reconcile his Unionist followers to Lloyd George's continued leadership, he significantly said:[18]

"By our own action we have made Mr. Lloyd George the flag-bearer of the very principles upon which we should appeal to the country. It is not his Liberal friends, it is the Unionist party which has made him Prime Minister, and made it possible for him to do the great work that has been done by this government."

Bonar Law developed the analogy with Joseph Chamberlain that he had used privately with Balfour, and left no doubt that he was working for the absorption of the coalition Liberals by the Unionists rather than for the end of his party's identity when he used words that, as his biographer notes, gained their full significance four years later: [19]

"What I propose does not mean that our party is going to cease to exist. We go into this election—at least if I have my way—as a Unionist party forming a portion of a coalition, I should be sorry if it were otherwise. From the time that my colleagues in the House of Commons did me the honour of electing me to be their leader I have felt that I was in the position of a trustee; and even throughout the war one thing that I have aimed at constantly has been to preserve, if it could be done, the unity of our party. That does not mean, of course, that if at any time that interest had conflicted with the national interest I should not have readily sacrificed the party interest."

Two days later, as leader of the House of Commons, Bonar Law announced that polling would be on 14th December and that the votes would be counted on 28th December. The same evening a special emergency conference of the Labour party met to decide Labour's attitude. Barnes was enjoying his place in the War Cabinet and Clynes his work as Food Controller, and a majority of the parliamentary party wished to remain in the coalition; but the National Executive under Henderson's influence was opposed. The conference decided in favour of withdrawal, and Clynes obeyed; but Barnes, Wardle, James Parker and G. H. Roberts remained with Lloyd George and technically lost their membership of the Labour party.

The stage was thus set for an election in which a coalition of Unionists and Lloyd George Liberals would be principally opposed by Asquithian Liberals and Labour. Two things still remained to be done. One was to distinguish Lloyd George Liberals from Asquithian Liberals, and so far as sitting members were concerned a rough-and-ready test was soon devised. The division lists in the Maurice debate[a] were brought out, and those Liberals who had voted with Asquith in that division were regarded *prima facie* as opponents of the coalition and those who had voted with Lloyd George as supporters. The other problem was more difficult, namely, to ensure that supporters of the coalition did not fight each other. This would have been even more intractable if Lloyd George had been able to find more than about 150 Liberal candidates. He had nearly 100 sitting members available, but it was all that he and his chief whip, Captain F. E. Guest, could do in the available time to muster half as many again. This left the Conservatives free to field some 450 candidates, but even so Younger had the utmost difficulty in restraining Conservative associations from putting up candidates against approved Lloyd George Liberals. It says much for the self-discipline of the Conservative party that he was as successful as he proved. Those candidates who were accepted as supporters of the coalition received a letter from Lloyd George and Bonar Law commending them to the electors, and in the language of wartime rationing this piece of paper was stigmatized by Asquith as "the coupon".

In the circumstances in which the election was fought possession of the coupon was the most valuable asset that any candidate could possess. Though hostilities had ceased, it was in fact a "khaki election", and the main issue before the electors was whether they were for or against Lloyd George. Never before nor even since has the personality of a leader counted for so much in an election, and the Unionists were content to have it so. The man who had won the war, so the argument ran, should be allowed to win the peace, and those who opposed him should be given short shrift; but the argument was soon overlaid with the baser themes of "Hang the Kaiser" and "Make Germany Pay". The war had caused suffering on a scale unknown before, and the electors were in no mood for rational argument. It was Sir Eric Geddes who coined the fateful pledge, "We will squeeze the German lemon until the pips squeak,"[b] and Lloyd George in his early speeches contented himself with asking that Germany should pay to the limit of her capacity; but he was ever susceptible to atmosphere, and after declaring at Bristol that the Germans would be made to pay to the uttermost farthing he slipped in the pungent threat, "and we shall search their pockets for it" [20]

20

COALITION CONTINUED
1918–1922

Coalition triumph—Asquithian Liberals routed—Labour representation increased, but leaders defeated—Irish Nationalists almost eliminated—and Sinn Fein members refuse to take their seats—change in the character of the Conservative party—bitterness between the Asquithians and Lloyd George Liberals—rise in importance of the Labour party—the new constitution of 1918—Labour and the New Social Order—the Cooperative Representation Committee—fusion of coalition supporters proposed and dropped—the Labour party chooses social democracy—formation of the Communist party of Great Britain—Bonar Law succeeded by Austen Chamberlain—home rule brought about with separate Parliaments in Dublin and Belfast—Tory dissatisfaction with the treaty fatal to the coalition—danger of war with Turkey—Bonar Law re-enters politics—Baldwin and Bonar Law persuade the Carlton Club meeting to withdraw from the coalition—Lloyd George resigns

THOUGH a big victory for the coalition was a foregone conclusion in the circumstances in which the election was fought, the result in terms of seats in the House of Commons far exceeded the wildest expectations. Out of 707 seats about 600 were contested by some 1,500 candidates. Almost every candidate who had received the coalition "coupon" was elected, and the government's avowed supporters numbered 478; of these 330 were Unionists, 133 were Liberals, four were Coalition Labour, one described himself as a Coalition Radical and ten were members of the National Democratic party, an organization formed earlier in the year by dissentient members of the Labour party who strongly supported the war effort. There were only 229 members who had not received the "coupon", and of these forty-eight were Unionists who might normally be expected to vote with the government. The Asquithian Liberals were utterly routed, only thirty-three being successful; even Asquith himself lost his seat at East Fife, though the coalition leaders had delicately refrained from giving the coupon to his Unionist opponent, and every one of the Liberal leaders went down to defeat with him. The Labour party increased its representation to fifty-nine, but in view of the far larger number of candidates placed in the field compared with previous elections this was not encouraging; and all the Labour leaders were defeated except Clynes, who was given an unopposed return as a reward for his reluctance in leaving the coalition. In addition three unendorsed Labour candidates were successful, and one candidate for the newly founded Cooperative party to be described shortly. Yet so much greater was the Liberal rout that Labour found itself in the position of being the numerically strongest party opposed to the government.

This would not have come about but for the startling results of the Irish elections. So strongly had the cult of violence taken possession of Ireland that the old Nationalist party, which had so often and for so long held the balance of power at Westminster, could secure the return of only seven members; Sinn Fein rode to triumph with seventy-three successful candidates, including the only woman to be elected, Countess Markiewicz, but they declined to take their seats at Westminster and soon set up a constituent assembly of their own in Dublin. There were five Independents to make up the total. In all, even if the Sinn Fein members had taken their seats, the successful coalition candidates had a majority of 249 over all others, twice as much as Lloyd George had dared to hope for; in practice the majority was in excess of 400, and the Conservatives alone had a clear majority over all others. It was an overwhelming triumph, but even in the hour of victory shrewd observers noted that the number of seats gained at Westminster was out of proportion to the votes cast in the country. Coalition candidates had received 5,091,528 votes, but candidates without the "coupon" had polled 4,589,486. In round figures nine electors had voted against for every ten who had voted for it. This was a narrow and deceptive basis for so great a parliamentary majority.

When Parliament met on 4th February 1919 there was much speculation about the question whether, in the absence of the Irish, the Liberals or Labour would be recognized as the official opposition. Neither was disposed to yield to the other, but it was seen that Sir Donald Maclean, as the senior Liberal who had survived, took the seat of the leader of the opposition, while Adamson sat next to him with other Labour privy councillors. After Mr. Speaker Lowther —with whom this question of precedence must have been settled in advance—had been re-elected, Maclean was the prior of the two to offer congratulations, but Adamson, when his turn came, did not fail to point out that Labour was the largest party in opposition in attendance in the house. When members made their procession to the House of Lords, Maclean and Adamson walked on either side of Bonar Law—the Prime Minister being away in Paris for the peace conference. It fell to Maclean to put each Thursday the question about the business of the next week, but the Labour privy councillors sitting around him, with their followers behind, could feel that they had arrived almost at their destination. Within nineteen years of the party's foundation only the width of the table separated the cloth-capped workers from the seats of power.

Thanks not only to the eclipse of the Liberals, the rise of Labour and the disappearance of the Irish but also to the changing character of the parties, the British political scene was never again to be the same as before the war. Among the Conservatives the war accelerated changes that had already begun to take effect. Throughout its long history the Conservative party had been the party of Church and King and the party of the land. Though the rise of the Unitarian Chamberlain and the succession of the Presbyterian Law to the leadership were an omen for the future, the fidelity of the Tory party to the Church of England was still unshaken in 1914, and Conservatives fought Welsh disestablishment to the last schedule. In 1918, when Lloyd George made it clear that he could not drop the enforcement of Welsh disestablishment from the coalition programme, no resistance was offered; only Lord Robert Cecil felt strongly enough about it to resign his office. Though outward attachment to the Crown remained strong, the Conservatives had been pained to find that King George V was not prepared to be used to thwart the will of a popularly-held government, and some tension developed; but because the Tory *mystique* demanded a Throne, and King George's instincts were conservative, and because at that time he disliked the more radical elements in Lloyd George's policies and feared still more the unknown forces in the world of Labour, the King remained, as Lord Beaverbrook has described him, "a powerful influence in the ranks of the Tory party".[1] It was in relation to finance, commerce and industry that the character of the Tory party changed most in the war years. Though the penetration of the party of the land by commercial elements had begun at least as early as the Liberal Unionist alliance, and was underlined when Bonar Law stepped into Balfour's shoes, the war and the ensuing general election brought about in a few years what might otherwise have taken a generation. The resignation of the patrician Lansdowne from the leadership in the Lords on the formation of the Lloyd George coalition symbolized the movement, and the new men swept into the Commons by the electoral tide of 1918 were not such as he would have approved. They were, said Stanley Baldwin bitingly to the rising economist, John Maynard Keynes,[2] a lot of hard-faced men who looked as though they had done well out of the war.[a] Though the Conservative party remained more than any other the party of the land, industry began to pay a bigger contribution to its funds and to play a preponderating rôle in the shaping of its policies.

The two wings of the Liberals together numbered a bare 166 and were torn apart by personal differences that not even time could assuage, differences that have descended to their children and even to their children's children. The Asquithian Liberals, soon dubbed the "Wee Frees", raged impotently at the traitor within the camp, for so they regarded him, who had done them injuries such as no Conservative had been able to inflict, and they reserved for Lloyd George a venom that even the die-hard Tory escaped. Two of their leaders were to return at by-elections in 1919—Simon for the Spen Valley and Asquith for Paisley, with the added satisfaction of making the Conservative coalition candidate lose his deposit—but they were powerless to influence the course of events. Lloyd George's status, though he seemed to have an impregnable position, was far from satisfying. Most of his Liberal followers still hankered after a Liberal reconciliation and still thought of Asquith as a potential occupant of No. 10 Downing Street. Lloyd George himself had sat loosely to party since 1910, and by the end of the war party meant nothing to him except as an instrument for furthering his personal policies and personal ambitions. The war had placed him in a position of supreme authority, and he could not bear to contemplate the thought of surrendering that power which his hands wielded so readily. It was widely believed that he was indispensable, and he had come to believe it himself. So long as the great mass of Tory members calculated that they owed their seats to his name, Lloyd George was safe; but as that belief evaporated, the logic of numbers made it inevitable that he should become the prisoner of the Tories, who would cast him out as soon as he ceased to serve their purpose.

From 1918 the Labour party had to be taken seriously as a major force in British politics, independent of Conservatives and Liberals and opposed to both. It is manifest that many of the votes which the Liberals lost in 1918 were transferred to the Labour party, and that the Liberal party would never again be able to present itself convincingly as the party of the working class.[b]

The Labour party had been equipping itself for this rôle by a major process of reorganization and rethinking. When Henderson left the Cabinet in 1917 he addressed himself almost entirely to the reorganization of the party and the rethinking was largely done by Sidney Webb. They more than any others must be regarded as the architects of the modern Labour party. MacDonald was too much out of favour on account of his pacifism, and his many talents did not include the precision of thought needed for constitution-making.

Until 1918 the Labour party was an alliance of trade unions and socialist societies. It had no constituency branches and no individual members. It was able to act in the constituencies only through the local trades councils—federations of trade union branches, mainly for industrial purposes—or through the local branches of the Independent Labour party. Henderson and Webb set out to transform the Labour party into a nationally organized party with a local party in every parliamentary constituency under the effective control of the national headquarters. While retaining the principle of affiliated societies, they sought to give the Labour party an individual membership also by creating individual members' sections of local parties. These aims were embodied in Clause 2 of a new draft constitution which read:

"The Labour party shall consist of all its affiliated organizations, together with those men and women who are individual members of a local Labour party and who subscribe to the constitution and programme of the party."

In a footnote "affiliated organizations" were listed as "trade unions, socialist societies, trades councils and local Labour parties". Though local Labour parties were thus technically affiliated to the national party, sets of draft rules were devised to ensure as far as possible conformity to a single pattern.

These individual sections of local Labour parties might have been regarded as rivals to the local branches of the Independent Labour party, and so they were to prove, but at the time the I.L.P. felt confident of its ability to use them rather as recruiting grounds for its own membership. It was more disturbed by the proposal in the new constitution that in future the members of the national executive committee, though nominated by sections, should be elected by the whole party conference, for this meant that the trade unions with their massive card votes would be able to determine the elections for each section.

The Independent Labour party was partly reconciled to these changes by the fact that the new constitution, while still avoiding the term socialism, committed the Labour party to common ownership. This was in the third section defining party objects which in the course of subsequent revision has become notorious in controversy as Clause Four. As drafted in 1918 the fourth paragraph of this section read:[3]

"To secure for the producers by hand or by brain the full fruits of their industry, and the most equitable distribution thereof that may be possible, upon the basis of the common ownership of the means of production and the best obtainable system of popular administration and control of each industry and service."

The final words about popular administration were a sop by Webb to the demand for "workers' control" which had gathered force since the syndicalist movement of 1911. It could not be ignored, but Webb was personally contemptuous of the idea, Snowden and others were openly hostile, and nothing has ever been done to give effect to it. "Common ownership" was taken much more seriously, and was later extended to include "distribution and exchange" as well as "production". Although it was theoretically wider than nationalization inasmuch as municipal or cooperative ownership could be brought within the formula, in practice it meant chiefly "the nationalization of the means of production, distribution and exchange". In this form it became a sacred formula, an incantation to be chanted upon a thousand platforms, a refuge when any Labour speaker was running short of ideas, a test of orthodoxy and a shibboleth. The magic words which would have made pre-war audiences recoil with horror now brought a gleam to the eye. The trade unions had moved far from the days of their association with the Liberal party; except in name, they had become socialist.

Simultaneously with the new constitution the Labour party was presented with a lengthy policy document entitled *Labour and the New Social Order*. Drafted by Webb, it struck a new note in party literature. It was much more philosophical and theoretical than the old party programmes, even to the point of being apocalyptic, and it encouraged the gibe that the Labour party was dominated by "intellectuals", a designation awarded as a term of abuse. The forerunner of many such documents, *Labour and the New Social Order* defined the party's main objectives as the universal enforcement of the national minimum, the democratic control of industry, the revolution in national finance and the surplus wealth for the common good. Though Webb's draft, like Clause Four, shrank from the term socialism, the party conference insisted on writing in the words "the socialization of industry". The new constitution was adopted in February 1918 and twenty-five resolutions based on *Labour and the New Social Order* were passed the following June. The Labour party was thereby committed to a capital levy, the immediate nationalization of railways, mines and electricity production, the ultimate nationalization of many other industries and services, and the common ownership of land as suitable opportunities occurred.

The Labour party as it emerged from the war was thus a very different party from the one that entered it. At that time there was no Communist party in Great Britain, and many of the then members of the Labour party would at a later date have been called Communists. The Labour party was sharply divided in those days from the two older parties by its attitude to the revolution in Russia. When the Tsarist régime was overthrown, that great event had been hailed in Great Britain with a considerable measure of sympathy, but among all Conservatives and many Liberals admiration turned to detestation and fear as the Bolsheviks seized power, made peace with Germany and raised the banner of world revolution. A man's attitude to the Bolshevik revolution became a touchstone in politics.

R

Conservatives were uniformly hostile. The Liberals were divided, and a rift opened between Lloyd George, who thought that the revolution must be accepted as an accomplished fact, and Churchill, who would have strangled it in infancy. Only in the Labour party was there still uncritical enthusiasm for the Russian revolution, and its members were soon dubbed by their opponents not only "Socialists" but "Bolshies".

It had been Henderson's aim to get Cooperators and Labour to work together in one big party, and he had toyed with the notion of calling it the People's party. In this aim he was unsuccessful, partly because Cooperators drew back as the Labour party began to embrace socialism. The Cooperative movement had long pursued the practice of neutrality between the parties, but in 1917 the Cooperative Congress was so irritated by the application of the excess profits tax to cooperative societies and similar alleged injustices that it voted in favour of setting up a Cooperative Representation Committee "to secure direct representation in Parliament and on all local administrative bodies".[4] An emergency conference later in the year set up such a National Cooperative Representation Committee and authorized the formation of local Cooperative political councils. A joint committee was set up early in 1918 by the parliamentary committees of the Cooperative and Trades Union Congresses to avoid electoral clashes, but the Cooperative Congress in that year laid down that its candidates must be described solely as "Cooperative" and not as "Cooperative and Labour". Ten Cooperative candidates were nominated at the general election; only one was elected, and he joined the Labour party soon afterwards. This led to further fruitless talks, but in practice the Cooperative party has always acted in Parliament as a wing of the Labour party, though not without occasional tension.

As the peace conference had been convened for 18th January it was necessary for Lloyd George to settle the new administration immediately, and the distribution of offices between the parties soon brought home the realities of power in the coalition. The Unionists, as was inevitable in view of their preponderance in numbers, received the most numerous posts and almost all the key positions save that of Prime Minister. As Bonar Law, while remaining leader of the House of Commons and continuing to occupy No. 11 Downing Street, wished to give up departmental responsibilities, Austen Chamberlain was able to resume the post at the Exchequer to which he had been advanced as far back as 1903; but he was piqued when told he could not occupy the Chancellor's residence and mortally offended when informed that he was not to be in the Cabinet, indeed, that there was to be no Cabinet while Lloyd George and Bonar Law were away in Paris. In the end the difference was resolved by keeping the War Cabinet, of which Chamberlain was already a member, in existence for another ten months. Balfour remained Foreign Secretary and Curzon Lord President; in October, when the peace conference was over, they exchanged offices. Despite the initial reluctance of the King, F. E. Smith was given the Woolsack and the title of Lord Birkenhead. Milner was made Secretary of State for the Colonies. Walter Long obtained the Admiralty. Sir Eric Geddes was made a Minister without Portfolio. Among such a galaxy of talent, few noticed that Stanley Baldwin remained Financial Secretary to the Treasury. These appointments did not leave much for the Liberals. Winston Churchill became Secretary of State for War and Air, Montagu remained in charge of India; the Home Office went to Edward Shortt; Fisher stayed at the Board of Education, with which his name will always be imperishably connected; Addison as Minister of Health had the unenviable task of making good the shortage of houses; and a brilliant advocate in the courts, Gordon Hewart, was appointed Attorney-General. The fidelity of the Labour members of the coalition had to be rewarded, and Barnes was made a Minister without Portfolio. Stephen Walsh, who had been elected as an endorsed Labour candidate, was persuaded to join the government but felt obliged to resign a few days later when the Lancashire and Cheshire miners, who had sponsored his candidature for Parliament, called upon him to do so. Outside the ranks of party but avid for power Northcliffe did not particularly seek office, but he had counted on being a delegate to the peace conference, even to the extent of taking a house in Paris; and when he was not included he began a vitriolic campaign against the Prime Minister which led Lloyd George to describe The Times as "merely a threepenny edition of the Daily Mail".[5]

When the Treaty of Versailles was signed and Lloyd George was able to survey the benches behind him in the House of Commons, he had no illusions. He was a man without a party and at the mercy of the great Tory majority. He set about remedying this situation in characteristic manner, early in 1920, by proposing a fusion of coalition supporters into a single party. The idea was not without its attractions to Bonar Law, and it was supported among the Liberals by Churchill and among the Conservatives by Balfour, Austen Chamberlain, Birkenhead and Younger. The last-named insisted only that the political fund which Lloyd George had been building up, and which he believed to amount to several million pounds, should be handed over to the new party; he called it "gate money".[6] Urgency was given to the discussions by Lord Salisbury's advice to Stockport Conservatives not to support the coalition Liberal candidate in a by-election then pending. Ninety-five members of Parliament, gathered together by Captain Colin Coote, sent to Lloyd George and Bonar Law a message "that this group, believing in the national necessity for the coalition, expresses the hope that it may develop into a single united party". Balfour drafted for his constituency chairman a letter, intended for publication, strongly advocating fusion. He showed it to Bonar Law, who consulted Lloyd George, and with Bonar Law's agreement Lloyd George decided to test the feelings of coalition Liberal members. To his surprise he found that they were anxious to keep their identity and the Liberal name. The lead in opposition was taken by minor figures—T. J. Macnamara, Ian Macpherson and Alfred Mond—but it was decisive. If the response had been favourable, Lloyd George would have hinted at the need for amalgamation at a meeting of the coalition Liberal M.P.s, but as it was he could speak only of cooperation. Bonar Law was on the whole relieved, and as the months passed the feeling in favour of fusion disappeared and the idea was dropped. The coalition Liberal ministers had killed the one scheme that could have saved themselves from extinction.

When these proposals were made the country was still prosperous and Lloyd George was still at the zenith of his popularity and power, but there followed "two cruel years", as Lord Beaverbrook calls them, in which "his structure of self-confidence and success came tumbling down".[7] His chief aim seemed to be to retain the driver's seat in the car of state which he believed to be his rightful place. To that aim parties and principles were alike subordinated.

"To keep the seat of power, the place of patronage [Lord Beaverbrook says], he was prepared to stand out as the leader of Empire-minded men—or appear as the Liberal Apostle of Free Trade : as the Man of Peace in Europe—or the Man of War against Turkey and France : as the hammer of the Russian Bolsheviks—or their noble conciliator : as the Tribune of the British working classes—or the Champion of the Tory landlords against Labour : stern enemy of the Irish—or their tender friend spreading his covering wings about another Celtic race ground under the heel of the oppressor. He took up each position in turn during those tragic years of 1921 and 1922."

The greatest of the problems that beset the government was industrial unrest, at first political in its aims and later a reaction to massive unemployment in part brought about by the government's own policies. The miners were then the most militant section of the Labour movement and were resolved not only to secure better working conditions for themselves but to ensure that the mines should never revert to private ownership and control. At their Southport conference in January 1919 they threatened to strike for these objects, and demanded that the mines should be run by a council to which they would nominate half the members. The following month there was formed the "Triple Alliance" of miners, railwaymen and transport workers pledged to support each other. The government staved off a miners' strike by a commission under the chairmanship of Mr. Justice (later Lord) Sankey, which immediately awarded the miners higher wages and a working day of seven hours, but was so divided over the issue of nationalization as to enable the government to avoid action. In 1920 there were several threats of direct action—that is, strikes for industrial or political purposes—and London dockers refused to coal the *Jolly George* until munitions intended for the Polish campaign in the Ukraine were removed.

In 1921 there was a dramatic change in the industrial scene. By that time millions of workers had been released from the forces, many of the demands left by the war had been satisfied and a surplus of labour began to appear. As demand dropped, prices fell, and the pressure for the lower wages was intensified. A situation that would have been difficult to handle in any case was aggravated by the deliberate pursuit of a deflationary policy by the government. The working of economic forces was hardly better understood in 1918 than in 1815, and despite the grim example of the years following Waterloo a similar policy was followed. Sir Eric Geddes with his "axe"—he was appointed chairman of a committee to cut down national expenditure by £100 million—symbolized a policy which restricted credit at the very time when expansion was needed. The industrial workers, instead of having all power in their hands, suddenly found themselves thrown on to the defensive and were cowed into acceptance of lower wages and longer working hours.

By February 1921 the number of unemployed had risen to over one million. The government, seeing that the collapse in prices no longer made the mines profitable, hastened to return them to their private owners. To make the mines pay, the owners were obliged to reduce wages or increase hours of work, and as the miners refused the proffered terms they were locked out. The other unions in the Triple Alliance voted to strike in support, but after some confusion about whether the miners would refuse a reasonable offer, on "Black Friday", 15th April 1921, the railwaymen and transport workers decided to let the miners settle their own affairs. By May the number of unemployed was over two millions. The miners struggled on alone until June, and then went back to work at greatly reduced wages under district settlements. Decontrol of the mines was followed by decontrol of the railways, and the ending of agricultural and housing subsidies. The unemployed became a great national problem and were to remain the greatest national problem for many years. George Lansbury and his fellow-councillors in Poplar refused to meet the London County Council's precept and went to prison to draw attention to the problem of maintaining the unemployed in East London. There was such a bitterness throughout the land as had not been known since the days of Sidmouth.

This is the background to the actions of the Parliamentary Labour party of those days. Small in numbers, bereft of all its leading figures and dominated by trade unionists in a period when industrial rather than parliamentary action was in vogue, it was throughout the whole of this Parliament only a pale reflection of the trade union movement outside. Of its sixty members or thereabouts, no fewer than forty-nine had been sponsored by trade unions, and of these twenty-five had been mining candidates. Only three of the Independent Labour party's fifty candidates had secured election, and all were new to Parliament, though one of them, William Graham, was later to show no mean abilities. William Adamson, who had led the party since Henderson's withdrawal in 1917, continued to do so even when Henderson found a seat at Widnes in a by-election in 1919, for Henderson realized there was more important work to be done in the country. Adamson continued as chairman until February 1921, when Clynes was elected in his place.

The Labour party inside Parliament was naturally ineffective in these years, and outside it was preoccupied with its relations to international socialism. An international Labour conference was convened at Berne in 1919 and was attended by Henderson, Mac-Donald and Mrs. Snowden on behalf of the British Labour party. The conference was largely taken up with a debate between supporters of the British thesis that socialism could be achieved by democratic methods and supporters of the Bolshevik thesis that it would not come about except through a "dictatorship of the proletariat". The former view was embodied in the "Branting" resolution, so called from the Swedish socialist, the latter in the "Adler-Longuet" resolution, so named from its Austrian and French proposers. In view of the composition of the conference, it was inevitable that the "Branting" resolution was carried by a large majority. It was the beginning of the division of socialists into social democrats and communists. The British Labour party came down firmly on the social democratic side. The Independent Labour party, though having much sympathy with the "Adler-Longuet" stand and not wishing to sever all connexions with the Bolsheviks, was fundamentally at one with the Labour party in aiming at socialism by democratic processes.

The work of the Berne conference amounted to a reconstruction of the Second (or Labour and Socialist) International. In March 1919 the Bolsheviks called a world conference which laid the foundations of the Third (or Communist) International. An attempt to create a Communist party of Great Britain linked with the Third International soon followed. The Independent Labour party having opted for social democracy, the most likely elements out of which a Communist party could be formed were the British Socialist party, the Socialist Labour party, Miss Sylvia Pankhurst's Workers' Socialist

Federation and such local bodies as the South Wales Socialist Society. Differences revealed themselves, and in particular it became clear that the Workers' Socialist Federation was more anarchist than communist, being opposed to all parliamentary action. Eventually a provisional joint committee was set up and called a Communist Unity Conference for July 1920. A few days before the conference met the provisional committee received the following authoritative guidance over the signature of Lenin.[8]

"I consider the policy of Comrade Sylvia Pankhurst and of the Workers' Socialist Federation in refusing to collaborate in the amalgamation of the British Socialist party, Socialist Labour party and others into a Communist party to be wrong.

"I personally am in favour of participation in Parliament, and adhesion to the Labour party on condition of free and independent Communist activity. This policy I am going to defend at the Second Congress of the Third International on 15th July at Moscow. I consider it most desirable that a Communist party be speedily organized on the basis of the decisions and principles of the Third International, and that the party be brought into close touch with the industrial workers of the world and the shop stewards' movement in order to bring about their complete union."

Fortified by advice from such a source, the Communist Unity Conference set up a Communist party of Great Britain and voted by 115 to eighty-five in favour of seeking affiliation to the Labour party. The application, the first of a long series, was truculent, denouncing, for example, the idea that a social revolution could be achieved by the ordinary methods of parliamentary democracy. Henderson blandly replied that "the basis of affiliation to the Labour party is the acceptance of its constitution, principles and programme, with which the objects of the Communist party do not appear to be in accord".[9]

In these years the Labour party, though ineffective at Westminster, was preparing itself for its future rôle as one of the two great parties of the state. The collapse of industrial action made Labour men and women look to the parliamentary party as the instrument by which their aspirations would be carried into effect; and the firm decision to be a social democratic party, and the unhesitating rejection of the Communist overtures, began to convince many voters, especially those disheartened by the fission among the Liberals, that the destinies of the country could at any rate experimentally be entrusted to Labour hands. So long as the coalition hung together, such voters could only wait for a dissolution in the normal efflux of time; but from the beginning of 1921 the increasing strains among the government parties made it doubtful whether the coalition would survive.

The partnership of Lloyd George and Bonar Law on which coalition had rested since 1916 was disturbed in March 1921 when quite suddenly Bonar Law resigned all his offices on account of the state of his health and went to France to recuperate. There was genuine apprehension for his health at that time, but in fact he made a good recovery, and by September he was back in England. Thereafter as a private member he was carefully watched for any sign that he was prepared to break with Lloyd George and end the coalition, but for a long time no such sign came. In that period the expectation grew that he would once again lead the Conservative party, but in the spring of 1921 his career seemed to be over, and other arrangements had to be made. Austen Chamberlain was appointed by the Prime Minister to succeed him as leader of the House of Commons, and at a meeting of Conservative and Unionist members of Parliament held in the Carlton Club soon afterwards he was unanimously elected to the leadership of the Unionist party in the House of Commons. The motion was proposed by Captain Ernest Pretyman. This time there was no rival, and messages supporting his election were read from Balfour, Walter Long, Carson and Horne. His speech of acceptance contained a passage significant in the light of later events: [10]

"I am not going here and now to attempt to forecast the future of our party or even of the coalition; but there are moments when insistence upon party is as unforgivable as insistence upon personal things, when the difficulties which the nation has to confront call for a wider outlook and a broader union than any that can be found even within the limits of a single party, and when the traditions of more than one party, the ideas of more than one party, need to be put into the common stock so that the country may be safely piloted through hours of crisis and danger."

These words must have surprised many of his hearers, for at the time he was regarded as a more zealous partisan than Bonar Law. Chamberlain himself recorded[11] how Lloyd George, when told that the party would certainly choose him, threw up his hands and cried, "He's an awful Tory," and added that the party "appears to share the view that I am more of a Conservative than Bonar". He was at last able to move into No. 11, and the daily contact with the Prime Minister turned his earlier criticisms into a deep affection. The wizard still had power to cast his spell over the men immediately around him.

He did not, however, endear himself to Churchill at this time, for that ambitious minister considered himself the rightful successor to Chamberlain at the Exchequer and was grievously estranged when Lloyd George gave the post to Horne. Perhaps Lloyd George did not want another king in Brentwood; but it is a sufficient explanation that the party balance would have been upset by Churchill's appointment. Only a month or so before, on Milner's resignation after completing the negotiations for Egyptian independence, he had been transferred to the Colonial Office. His time at the War Office was of crucial importance in his personal career and has no little relevance in the history of party, inasmuch as the responsibility for aiding Koltchak, Denikin and Yudenitch in their efforts to reverse the Russian revolution brought him face to face with the grim realities of Bolshevism and made him the avowed opponent of socialism in all its forms. The scion of the Marlboroughs began to question whether the Liberalism which he had embraced could be an effective barrier against the revolutionary levelling doctrines he discerned all around him; and if he still found fault with the Conservatives, it was partly because their subservience to Lloyd George made them blind to the danger that he perceived so vividly. Before accepting his new office he had demanded, and obtained, the creation of a Middle East Department under his control as Colonial Secretary. This made him, with Lawrence of Arabia as his counsellor, the arbiter of the former Turkish domains in that region, but brought him into conflict with Curzon as Foreign Secretary.

Of the other changes made consequent upon Bonar Law's resignation it may be noted here, though scarcely noticed at the time, that Stanley Baldwin moved up to be President of the Board of Trade and for the first time took a seat in the Cabinet.

Personal relationships bedevilled the coalition and were sharpened by party considerations. There are never enough loaves and fishes to go round when governments are formed, and in a coalition there are twice the usual number of claimants. The dismissal of two Liberal ministers and the promotion of a third were notable events in the disintegration of the coalition.

Christopher Addison as Minister of Health had been given the task of providing "homes fit for heroes", and in the opinion of his Conservative critics, not altogether fairly, he failed dismally. Few of his coalition Liberal friends were disposed to leap to his aid, and in March 1921 he was relieved of his office; but dismissal was made acceptable to him and anathema to the Tories by the offer of a seat in the Cabinet and a salary of £5,000 a year. Tory indignation was all the greater because the change was made while Parliament was not sitting. In view of the current demand for economies in government, the salary was made a special object of criticism. Addison reacted with greater vigour than he had shown in the building of houses, and in a press interview declared that the attack on himself was the prelude to excluding all Liberals from the coalition. Chamberlain, meeting his first test as leader of the Conservatives, wrote to Lloyd George to complain that Addison was attempting to turn what was in part a genuine movement for economy and in part an attack on his own administration into a revolt of Unionists against coalition Liberals. He warned the Prime Minister that he could not promise a sufficient number of votes to secure victory in a debate on Addison's appointment due to take place in the Commons. Lloyd George already knew that he would not get Labour support. Lord Salisbury, pursuing his dislike of Lloyd George and the coalition, took the opportunity to write a letter to *The Times* urging Unionist members to leave the coalition. Attempts to get Bonar Law to come out against the coalition failed, but the merits of a Churchill and a Birkenhead administration were canvassed. Lord Beaverbrook was active in these manoeuvres, which he later dubbed "The Plot".[12] Lloyd George at one point thought of resolving the issue by a general election, but in the end decided to sacrifice Addison. He sacrificed his friends, notes Lord Beaverbrook, as the ermine sheds its coat.[13] When the debate came, he coolly announced that the appointment of the Minister without Portfolio was only for the rest of the session, a matter of a few months, and asked that the salary should be reduced by £500 more than the £2,000 demanded by the critics. There was no division. The coalition survived, and so did Addison; he resigned within a month, and later began a new career as an elder statesman in the Labour party.

Edwin Montagu as Secretary of State for India had to bear the responsibility for the removal of Brigadier-General Dyer, who had suppressed a riot at Amritsar in 1919 with what he regarded as exemplary, and critics as ruthless, severity. He was censured by the Commander-in-Chief and deprived of his command. Montagu was already suspect among many Tories for his eagerness to grant political advancement to Indians, which before the end of 1919 found expression in the Montagu–Chelmsford reforms, and when the Dyer case was debated in the House of Commons in July 1920 criticism of the Secretary of State was sharp, and was not unmingled with anti-Jewish prejudice. Austen Chamberlain's biographer notes that "the debate was the first step in the break-up of the coalition", for the critics of Montagu "began to act together on other questions than those relating to India".[14] If Montagu and his wife later that same year voted against the Coalition Liberal candidate in a Norfolk by-election, as a report made to the Conservative Central Office asserted, it is to be explained by antipathy to Lloyd George rather than by affection for the Tories. He had annoyed Lloyd George by claiming the right as a plenipotentiary for India to send a pro-Turkish memorandum to the San Remo conference, which drew up the terms of the Treaty of Sèvres imposed on Turkey. He gave way then, but two years later repeated the offence in aggravated form by authorizing publication of a pro-Turkish telegram from the Viceroy without consulting his colleagues. Lloyd George and Curzon were equally furious, and Montagu resigned in bitterness. According to Chamberlain, the house cheered the news savagely.

The Viceroy at this time was none other than Lord Reading, the former Rufus Isaacs, and his appointment had made it necessary to find another Lord Chief Justice. Birkenhead urged that the proper and traditional successor was the Attorney-General, but Lloyd George did not wish to deprive himself of the services of that able Liberal colleague. He put Hewart in the Cabinet by way of compensation and promised to make him Lord Chief Justice on the eve of the next dissolution. This meant finding a Lord Chief Justice who would be willing to place his resignation in Lloyd George's hands on demand, and after suggesting the aged and failing Lord Finlay he found a suitably compliant candidate in the equally aged but still active Sir Alfred Lawrence, soon made Lord Trevethin. In 1922, while travelling to London to complete the hearing of an adjourned case, Trevethin read the news of his own resignation and obligingly took his pension. These proceedings scandalized the Tory party and the legal profession.

Though the coalition could hardly have survived its personal animosities much longer, certain issues of policy were even more powerful solvents. Inevitably one of them was the Irish question.

In 1920, when the government came to consider how the home rule act could be given effect, a new measure provided for separate Parliaments in Ulster and southern Ireland. It became, and still is, the legal basis for the government of Northern Ireland, but it was not accepted by the south. Lloyd George then fell back on repression, and the hideous struggle of Black and Tans *versus* Sinn Fein was fought till both sides were sickened before negotiations were resumed. A truce was made in July 1921, and the Irish negotiators arrived in London, but Lloyd George found that "negotiating with De Valera is like trying to pick up mercury with a fork". (De Valera asked why he did not use a spoon.)[15] In October the astute mind of Lloyd George found the solution. He saw that he must make an ally of Birkenhead, whose influence in the Conservative party was then at its height. If Birkenhead remained faithful to the cause of Ulster which he had championed so vigorously as "galloper Smith", his eloquence could kill any plan that the south would be likely to accept; but if he backed Lloyd George's proposals, he could swing enough Conservative support to ensure its passage at Westminster. Birkenhead, says Lord Beaverbrook, was reluctant. "He was asked to put his whole future with the Tory party to the hazard, and in partnership with a man who up till then had shown him little trust or confidence."[16] He made his conditions, which were that Churchill, who was then estranged from Lloyd George, should be brought in also as a principal adviser, and that Sir Robert Horne, Sir Eric Geddes and Sir Hamar Greenwood, who were then the Prime Minister's confidants, should be excluded from his counsels. They did not understand the Tory mind, he complained, and were misleading the Prime Minister. Lloyd George, again recalling the habits of the ermine, agreed, and from that moment the coalition became a triumvirate, or perhaps a quadrumvirate as Austen Chamberlain's voice in council remained substantial.

Birkenhead showed his ability to do what Lloyd George hoped. A special problem was created for him by the fact that the Conservative annual conference was to be held in November in Liverpool, that great Anglo-Irish city linked by many bonds both with Dublin and with Belfast. He made a sudden and secret journey to Liverpool to win the support of Sir Archibald Salvidge, the brewer who had become the leader of the Liverpool Tories, and who was reputed to be threatening to smash the Irish conference and the coalition. Though he had to bear the indignity of gibes about "Salvidging Ulster", the Liverpool leader swung the conference in favour of continuing negotiations.[17] There were still many obstacles to be cleared, but in the early hours of 6th December an Irish treaty based on partition was signed. From the time of its coming into force no member from southern Ireland has been eligible to sit in the Parliament of the United Kingdom. With the exodus of the Irish Nationalist members the House of Commons lost much of its colour, zest and eloquence; and the British party system was radically simplified by the disappearance of a closely knit body of members who had for long periods held the balance between Tories and Liberals. As he put his signature to the treaty, Birkenhead observed to Michael Collins that he might be signing his political death-warrant,[18] and although he was still to hold office he did not greatly exaggerate. The concessions to the Irish republicans were anathema to the more extreme elements in the Conservative party, who never forgave Lloyd George or Birkenhead. Carson, newly made a law lord, delivered such a scathing attack on his old friend, the Lord Chancellor, as had never before been heard in a maiden speech in the upper house; nor were Curzon and Chamberlain spared. "The Irish treaty," says Mr. Robert Blake,[19] "was in the end fatal to the coalition. If it had been an immediate success, if the Sinn Fein leaders who signed it had been able at once to establish order in the south, perhaps the Conservative party would have acquiesced. But it was not an immediate success." The indignation of Tory critics of the treaty reached its height when Sir Henry Wilson, wearing the uniform of a British field-marshal, was shot dead by two Irish fanatics on the doorstep of his London house. When Austen Chamberlain visited Wilson's widow to offer sympathy, she greeted him with the word "Murderer", and asked that no member of the government should attend the funeral, until it was pointed out that this might be interpreted as a slight to the Crown.

Lloyd George's instinct had been to go to the country immediately after the signing of the Irish treaty, when the government enjoyed a brief spell of popularity, but he failed to persuade his partners in the coalition. Over dinner at Birkenhead's house the coalition Liberal whip, Charles McCurdy, and the Prime Minister expounded the arguments for consolidating the government's position by an immediate election, but Chamberlain opposed it as unnecessary and unjustified, Churchill was indecisive and Birkenhead kept silent. Lloyd George decided to defer a decision until after his return from the conference of the allies at Cannes fixed for January 1922.

By that time the prestige gained by the Irish treaty had already evaporated. While Lloyd George was abroad, Younger, the chairman of the Conservative party, launched a newspaper campaign against an early election, and announced that he and other Conservatives would decline to stand as coalition candidates. This was open rebellion, and Lloyd George protested to Chamberlain that Younger had behaved disgracefully in disclosing "the most intimate and secret information which would never have been imparted to him unless we had depended upon his being gentleman enough to keep counsel".[20]

Lloyd George still had one card to play. If Bonar Law could be persuaded to rejoin him, all Tory opposition would be silenced. At Birkenhead's hotel in Cannes he told Bonar Law of his intention to dissolve and offered him the Foreign Office. Curzon, only a short distance away in another hotel, was blissfully ignorant that his department was being given away, but Bonar Law did not accept. Back in London, Lloyd George abandoned his plan and with sublime assurance asked a huge meeting of coalition Liberals: "Who started this talk about a general election?"[21] He then toyed with the idea of reuniting the Liberal party and returning to Parliament at the head of a Liberal majority. By March he saw this was a forlorn hope, and made up his mind to stick to coalition with the Tories.

While the government was still reeling from the Irish troubles, it was shaken even more violently by the "honours scandal" that followed the inclusion among the birthday honours in June 1922 of peerages for Sir Joseph Robinson, a South African financier of dubious reputation, and for Sir Archibald Williamson and Sir Samuel Waring, whose wealth was more obvious than their public service. The practice of recommending honours for persons who had made large contributions to party funds seems to have arisen in the last years of the nineteenth century.[22] The growing cost of elections made it tempting to party leaders to raise funds in this easy way, and both the main parties made use of it. For a wealthy man to support with his purse the principles in which he believed was justified as a form of public service. The dangers are obvious, but so long as the persons honoured were otherwise meritorious, and so long as the conferment of such honours was discreet and limited, no great harm was done. Nevertheless, anxiety among those aware of the practice was sufficiently great to provoke debates in the House of

Commons in 1894 and 1907, and on a more extended scale in the House of Lords in 1914 and 1917. The Earl of Selborne obtained the agreement of his fellow-peers in 1914 to a motion that contributions to party funds should not be a consideration in the assessment of claims to honours. The practice did not cease, and in Lloyd George's administration greatly increased.

At the end of the First World War there were many "new rich" anxious to establish themselves in the social scale and fully prepared to testify to their zeal for the public welfare by making substantial gifts to party funds, especially as many of them feared the rise of socialist beliefs and honestly believed that a continuation of coalition government was desirable. Both the Conservative and the Liberal leaders of the coalition were prepared to gratify this form of service to the advantage of the party coffers, but Lloyd George easily outdid his Conservative colleagues. After his break with Asquith control of the independent Liberal funds naturally remained with the Asquithians, and he was obliged to raise large sums of money for the running of what was in effect a separate party if he was not to become wholly subservient to the Tories. Being contemptuous of the whole system of honours, he had no scruple in profiting from the weaknesses of aspirants; but he may not personally have been responsible for, or known much about, the most discreditable feature of the sale of honours, the existence of touts with a tariff of rates at which any honour from a knighthood to a barony would be offered. He probably told his minions to raise the money and left the details to them. This pollution of the fount of honour offended the King and outraged a powerful section of the Conservative party not normally squeamish in such matters.[23]

The birthday honours of 1922 therefore triggered off a great deal of barely suppressed discontent. In the House of Lords the Duke of Northumberland said that the record of the coalition government in the award of honours differed from that of all previous governments by reason of the immense scale on which honours had been lavished, the utterly reckless disregard of the services and character of the recipient, the systematic attempt made to get control of the press by selling honours in return for newspaper support and the extent to which the Liberal element in the coalition had benefited out of all proportion to its members. On the same day in the House of Commons a motion asking for a select committee, which had obtained 300 signatures, was debated. Asquith significantly asked that contributions to party funds should not disqualify the donor from being honoured, and argued that it was the duty of wealthy men to support the political causes in which they believed. Lloyd George denied that payment to party funds played any part in recommendations for honours and offered a royal commission. Out of this there emerged the Political Honours Scrutiny Committee consisting of three privy councillors. The immediate crisis was over, and Lloyd George was still in the saddle, but shaken.

The growing discontent among Conservatives found expression in the "revolt of the under-secretaries". In July the junior Conservative ministers had a conference as a body with Austen Chamberlain, and in August a further conference with all the Unionist members of the Cabinet. Birkenhead was given the task of replying to them, and according to Leo Amery, one of their number, he "began by rating them for their impertinence in having asked for a meeting at all, when they had already been informed of the Cabinet ministers' views, and then went on in the most astonishingly arrogant and offensive manner to lecture them for their silliness and want of loyalty".[24] Far from quelling the revolt, he drove another nail into the coffin being prepared for the coalition, and destroyed his own chances of being accepted as Conservative leader.

It was the Near East that eventually brought down the coalition. The Turkish government at Constantinople had accepted the humiliating Treaty of Sèvres, but in the meantime Mustapha Kemal had risen in Anatolia and he announced his intention of repudiating the treaty. The Greek Prime Minister, Venizelos, offered the Greek army for the purpose of crushing the Kemalist rebellion, and Lloyd George persuaded the allies to accept the offer, which in effect meant backing Venizelos in his plans for expansion in Asia Minor. Within a few months King Alexander of Greece died of a monkey bite, Venizelos was overthrown and ex-King Constantine, no friend of the allies, returned to the Throne. The French withdrew from the enterprise, Kemal pursued the Greeks to the coast, laid Smyrna waste and massacred its Christian population. He turned towards the neutralized zone of Chanak on the Dardanelles, and there was every prospect of further massacres if he should cross the straits.

The British Cabinet was divided in its counsels, and divided along the historic line that had separated Gladstone and Disraeli. Lloyd George had become enthusiastically pro-Hellene, but Curzon had no appetite for a war with the Turks. The Foreign Secretary was not so anxious, however, as to stay in London over the week-end, and in his absence and at the Prime Minister's request Churchill and Birkenhead drafted a statement for the press. It was the first intimation the British people had received that they again stood on the edge of war.

That same week-end the Cabinet, assured that the Conservative conference in November would vote for withdrawal from the coalition, determined to strike first by an immediate dissolution, but owing to the Turkish crisis the decision was postponed. Sir Leslie Wilson, the Conservative chief whip, warned Chamberlain that 184 constituencies had declared their intention of running independent candidates. This was the state of affairs when Bonar Law re-entered the front line of the political battle by sending a letter to *The Times*.

He began by supporting the government's resolve to defend Chanak, but went on : "Clearly the British Empire, which includes the largest body of Mohammedans in any state, ought not to show any hostility or unfairness to the Turks. . . . We cannot alone act as the policemen of the world. The financial and social condition of this country makes that impossible."[25]

There was no mistaking the import. The former Conservative leader, who had left the country to avoid being implicated in any intrigue against Lloyd George during the attack on Addison, who had voted for the Irish treaty almost against his deepest convictions, and who had refused to be drawn into the honours debate, was now serving public notice that his support of the coalition was not unconditional. Though he did not say that he was ready to resume the Unionist leadership, that was the implication which the Conservative opponents of the coalition drew from the letter, and they were correspondingly heartened.

Despite all the warnings Chamberlain was still convinced that he could carry the Unionist party with him in abiding in the coalition. At a meeting of the Cabinet held on 10th October, with Wilson in attendance, the decision to go to the country as a coalition was reaffirmed; of the Conservative members only Baldwin dissented. Chamberlain reckoned that he was more likely to carry a meeting of Conservative M.P.s in this policy than a full party conference, and he wrote to Birkenhead a letter displaying that sublime belief in one's own indispensability so often found at the top and so often the prelude to a fall : [26]

"I am not sure that it may not now be necessary to call a party meeting and to tell them bluntly that they must either follow our advice or do without us, in which case they must find their own chief and form a government *at once*. They would be in a d—d fix!"

This and other evidence makes clear that it was Chamberlain and not the malcontents who wanted the fateful meeting of Conservative M.P.s at the Carlton Club which was eventually summoned for Thursday, 19th October. Originally the meeting was fixed for the Wednesday of that week, but the date was changed so that those present would know the result of a by-election at Newport in Monmouthshire. The seat had been held by a coalition Liberal, and a Liberal who supported the coalition (and was himself being supported by the coalition Liberal headquarters) was being opposed by an independent Conservative and by a Labour candidate. In these circumstances Chamberlain seems to have expected the Labour man to win, and he proposed to argue that to end the coalition would be to let the socialists in.

The days before the meeting were a period of feverish activity. Of the Conservatives in the Cabinet, it was known that Chamberlain,

Balfour, Birkenhead, Worthington-Evans and Horne were in favour of the continuance of the coalition under Lloyd George's leadership. Only Baldwin and Griffith-Boscawen had consistently supported withdrawal. Curzon had been in favour of the coalition, but in the last few days he changed sides, partly through annoyance with Lloyd George's pro-Hellenic policy. The party machine controlled by Younger and Wilson was against the coalition. The under-secretaries, still smarting from Birkenhead's tongue, were against, and so were those die-hards who recognized Lord Salisbury as their leader. Such patricians as the Earl of Derby and the Duke of Devon-shire were expected to favour withdrawal, but they would not have a vote at the Carlton Club meeting, which was confined to members of the House of Commons. A more important rôle was played by a group of back-benchers headed by Ernest Pretyman and Samuel Hoare who were canvassing for withdrawal.

As men studied the lines of the opposed forces, it was clear that Bonar Law's attitude would be decisive. He alone could give the malcontents a prestige equal to that of the Conservative ministers in the Cabinet. If he attended the Carlton Club meeting and spoke, it could be only against the coalition, but would he attend? All Beaverbrook's arts were used to persuade him, and his newspapers were thrown into the cause. So was *The Times*, at last once more, owing to Northcliffe's illness and eventual death, under the control of its editor, Wickham Steed, who strongly believed in the need to revive the normal functioning of the party system; he saw Bonar Law on each of the three nights preceding the meeting. Salvidge also went to Bonar Law's house to spy out the land; he informed Bonar Law that Lloyd George had the support of all of his Conservative colleagues in the Cabinet, and was disconcerted to be told that Curzon was waiting in an adjoining room. The night before the meeting, Bonar Law sent for Beaverbrook and showed him a letter addressed to the chairman of his Glasgow constituency declining to stand again at the next election, with a copy for the newspapers. "The letter is too long" was Beaverbrook's irrelevant comment; but when he saw that Bonar Law wanted to hear him he plied all the arguments for breaking the coalition. At the end Bonar Law said simply: "I am going to the meeting." Asking only if he could re-lease the news to the press, Beaverbrook fled; he made sure that Bonar Law would not be able to change his mind.[27]

Next morning the 274 members of Parliament who made their way to the Carlton Club knew not only that Bonar Law would be there, but that at Newport the independent Tory, Reginald Clarry, was in by 2,090 votes with the Liberal supporter of the coalition at the bottom of the poll. The malcontents were beside themselves with delight, seeing in association with Lloyd George the kiss of death and in freedom the prospect of undiluted Tory rule. At the

S

meeting Chamberlain urged that the old issues of Conservative and Liberal were no longer relevant and that the real challenge was provided to both of them by Labour, now demanding a capital levy, nationalization of the chief industries and the right of work or maintenance. Baldwin, following him, accepted Birkenhead's recent description of Lloyd George as a dynamic force; that dynamic force had smashed the Liberal party and in time would also smash the Conservative party. It was an extremely effective speech, decisive in swaying opinion among the waverers, and it marked out Baldwin for the first time in the eyes of the party as a future leader and potential Prime Minister. Pretyman—the same Pretyman who had nominated Chamberlain as leader the previous year—then proposed and Lane Fox seconded a motion in favour of contesting the next election as an independent party. At this point there was a general cry for Bonar Law, and after some hesitation he came out strongly in support of Pretyman's motion: [28]

"I confess frankly that in the immediate crisis in front of us I do personally attach more importance to keeping our party a united body than to winning the next election.

"The feeling against the continuation of the coalition is so strong that if we follow Austen Chamberlain's advice our party will be broken and a new party will be formed; and not the worst of the evils of that is this, that on account of those who have gone, who are supposed to be the more moderate men, what is left of the Conservative party will become more reactionary, and I, for one, say that though what you call the reactionary element in our party has always been there and must always be there, if it is the sole element, our party is absolutely lost.

"Therefore if you agree with Mr. Chamberlain in this crisis I will tell you what I think will be the result. It will be a repetition of what happened after Peel passed the Corn Bill. The body that is cast off will slowly become the Conservative party, but it will take a generation before it gets back to the influence which the party ought to have."

Balfour spoke in favour of continuing the coalition but ineffectively, and the vote was taken. Bonar Law's speech had made the result certain. There were 187 votes for Pretyman's motion and eighty-seven against. The minority included members of the government, most Welsh members and some Scottish members. In the subsequent mythology of politics, which Lloyd George himself did no little to create, the Carlton meeting was represented as an intrigue in a West End club by a group of politicians unable to see beyond party against Conservative statesmen who put their country first. In fact, as we have seen, it was Chamberlain who asked for the Carlton Club meeting because he thought he could get a better result than from a party conference. He wished to lead the Conservative party in a direction in which it was no longer willing to go. The vote was a democratic decision fairly taken.

Chamberlain hastened with the news to Lloyd George, but was preceded by the telephone. A Cabinet was summoned for that afternoon, and later Lloyd George drove to the Palace to submit the resignation of his government. He advised the King, who had by this time grown genuinely fond of him and regretted his departure, to send for Bonar Law. In accordance with custom he made some recommendations for honours. Curzon did not get the coveted and half-promised dukedom by reason of his last-minute switch of sides, but the faithful Birkenhead was advanced to be an earl. An earldom was recommended also for Farquhar, treasurer of the Conservative party; there were reasons for this apparent piece of magnanimity which did not become clear for a few months.

Once more it had been demonstrated that "England does not love coalitions".

21

UNIONIST INTERLUDE
1922–1923

Bonar Law will not accept office until elected party leader—a "government of the second eleven"—great Unionist victory in the general election—Labour becomes the official opposition—Liberals begin to support proportional representation—Conservative finances and the Lloyd George political fund—character of the Labour party—MacDonald elected chairman—Bonar Law's illness and resignation—Baldwin chosen by the King as Prime Minister in preference to Curzon—and is elected Conservative leader—Baldwin's record as a party manager—he comes out in favour of tariffs—thereby uniting both the Conservatives and the Liberals—the election gives no clear majority

KING GEORGE V, as advised, sent for Bonar Law immediately after his parting with Lloyd George, but Bonar Law asked Stamfordham to visit him first at his private residence. There he explained to the King's private secretary that he was not the leader of the Conservative party, that the party was for the moment broken up and that until he knew he could count on its undivided support he would not accept office. With constitutional correctness Stamfordham replied that the King had sent for him independently of these party considerations, into which his Majesty did not enter. He pointed out the need to have a government which would ratify the Irish treaty by 6th December if it were not to lapse. Bonar Law remained adamant that he would not accept office until the party had elected him as leader, but he agreed to attend Buckingham Palace for an audience and to call a party meeting as soon as possible. It was, in fact, held four days later, on 23rd October, and for the first time prospective candidates for Parliament were invited to attend the meeting as well as Conservative peers and members of Parliament. Mr. R. T. McKenzie is probably correct in saying[1] that the reason was the imminence of a general election, but it is not clear who took the decision or who could have been authorized to take it. Like so many other constitutional developments in Great Britain it just happened, and although the precedent was not followed on the next occasion it has been followed on all later occasions. Curzon took the chair and made it clear at the outset that the purpose of the meeting was to re-elect its old leader. Though technically it would have been open to any person present to have moved someone other than Bonar Law, it would have been inconceivable for the meeting to select any one other than the person on whom the King's choice was already known to have fallen. Curzon himself moved from the chair the resolution: "That this meeting extends a hearty invitation to the Right Honourable A. Bonar Law to resume the leadership of the Unionist party, and in the event of his acceptance it desires to assure him of its loyal support in maintaining the high traditions of the party in the best interests of the nation as a whole." The resolution was seconded by Baldwin and carried unanimously—as was a vote of thanks to Austen Chamberlain for his work as leader of the party in the House of Commons. Thus fortified, Bonar Law immediately went to Buckingham Palace and kissed hands as Prime Minister.

There has been much speculation why Bonar Law insisted on submitting himself to a party meeting before accepting the King's invitation to form a government. His action did not set a precedent, and no other Conservative invited by the Sovereign to form a government has felt such scruples; indeed, all subsequent Conservative Prime Ministers have kissed hands before their election to the party leadership, and the party meeting has ratified the choice already made by the Sovereign. The situation was unusual in that, if the party had not been divided, Austen Chamberlain would certainly have been called to Buckingham Palace, and with equal certainty would have been elected leader. At that time Bonar Law had no formal standing in the party. He was chosen over the heads of Conservative ministers, and he had been an irregular attender at the House of Commons. He may have felt that he needed some party authority for his attempt to form a government, especially in view of the substantial minority vote at the Carlton Club meeting.

Bonar Law's biographer, Mr. Robert Blake, considers that his hesitations were not entirely due to constitutional niceties.[2] He recalls Bonar Law's hesitation over taking the leadership in 1911, when ambition was strong within his breast as it was not in 1922, and suggests he was hoping that even now something might occur that would save him from the supreme responsibility being thrust upon him. It must also be remembered that Bonar Law was, more than any other Conservative leader, a party man. As his speech at the Carlton Club meeting had showed, the unity of the party was a prime consideration with him, and the antithesis between national interests and party interests is not one that would have readily occurred to him. Keynes may have gone a little too far in saying he was "before everything a party man, deeply concerned for his party, obedient to its instincts, and at each crisis the nominee of its machine",[3] but Bonar Law came nearer to the ideal party man than any other Conservative leader has been. It is a sufficient reason why he did not accept the King's invitation until the party had pronounced.

He had been obliged, however, by a stream of callers in the intervening days to behave as though he were a Prime Minister forming a government. It was no easy task. Thirteen ministers in the coalition government headed by Austen Chamberlain, Birkenhead, Balfour, Horne and Worthington-Evans issued a statement immediately after the Carlton Club meeting defiantly announcing: "Other men who have given other counsels must inherit our burden and discharge its consequent responsibility."[4] They confidently expected that Bonar Law would fail and that they would soon be in control again. Curzon obviously had to be kept at the Foreign Office, but so limited was the supply of Cabinet timber that Bonar Law went outside Parliament and outside the Conservative party to offer the Exchequer to McKenna; and only when McKenna declined to leave the well-padded chairmanship of the Midland Bank did he give it to Baldwin, with some misgivings about his lack of experience.

It was ironical that through force of circumstances the first Conservative Prime Minister drawn directly from the middle classes had to include seven peers along with one baronet and three knights in his Cabinet. Salisbury as Lord President, Devonshire at the Colonial Office and Derby at the War Office showed that landed influence was still powerful in the Conservative party. Yet despite the limitations of the field of choice, Bonar Law's ministry was to set the stamp of Conservative governments for the next generation. Sir Philip Lloyd-Greame (later Viscount Swinton) and the Hon. E. F. L. Wood (later Earl of Halifax) inside the Cabinet, Sir Douglas Hogg (later Viscount Hailsham) and Sir Samuel Hoare (later Viscount Templewood) outside it, were to develop their own brand of Conservative thought. In retrospect, the most significant of Bonar Law's recruits was Austen Chamberlain's younger brother Neville, who became Postmaster-General. Neville Chamberlain had his own reasons for rejoicing at the fall of the coalition, for Lloyd George in 1917 had appointed him Director of National Service, a post requiring "a man of exceptional gifts", only to find that he was "a man of rigid competency". Chamberlain resigned in frustration before the end of the war, and Lloyd George later said: "It was not one of my successful selections."[5] It was nevertheless astonishing that Neville should join Bonar Law's administration while his devoted brother was staying with Lloyd George, and Austen commented: "I was not surprised by Neville's decision, but it *hurt* awfully."[6] The echoes were still to be heard in 1935 when Neville Chamberlain, then Chancellor of the Exchequer, had the pleasure of cross-examining

Lloyd George in a Cabinet sub-committee about his proposals for a New Deal and turning them down.

Churchill dismissed Bonar Law's Cabinet as a "government of the second eleven", and Birkenhead declared himself frightened by the mediocrity of the "second-class brains" of the new ministers. He likened Younger to "the cabin boy who had tried to seize the political ship".[7] As the "first-class brains" stayed with Lloyd George, Bonar Law's choice of a second eleven was not deliberate, but in fact he inaugurated a long period, closed only by the Second World War, in which intellectual abilities fell to a discount, and were indeed regarded with suspicion, in the Conservative party. Though the Conservative party had often been dismissed by Liberals as "the stupid party", and had to some extent cultivated the description itself, the party of Peel, Disraeli, Salisbury and Balfour was not markedly inferior in intellectual brilliance to that of Gladstone and Asquith; but the party of Bonar Law, Baldwin and Neville Chamberlain made no attempt to coruscate, and took pride in qualities of character rather than of mind as though the two were incompatible.

When Bonar Law formed his government he felt no confidence that it would survive the general election for which it was clearly his duty to ask. Polling day was fixed for 15th November. It was a confused election. The Conservatives put 442 official candidates into the field, and Bonar Law led them in a policy of "Tranquillity",[8] uninspiring in itself but acceptable to many after the dynamism of Lloyd George. Derby and Salisbury had made it clear that if food taxes were proposed, they would retire, and Amery acquiesced. Bonar Law accepted the recommendation that there should be no taxes on food, and in the course of the campaign he undertook, like Balfour in 1910, that before any fiscal change another general election making it a specific issue would be held.[9] The hopes that Beaverbrook had entertained from his old friend's accession to power were dashed to the ground, and to his further chagrin he found that Bonar Law was discouraging contests against members of Lloyd George's ministry, not only the Conservatives who remained loyal to him but even the Liberal. Younger supported this arrangement, hoping to get in return as much coalition Liberal support as possible in constituencies where Conservatives were opposed by Asquithian Liberals. Beaverbrook thereupon launched a number of independent Conservative candidates in constituencies where supporters of Lloyd George were being given a free run, in some cases paying their election expenses. When Birkenhead and Guest tried to reach an agreement, and asked him if he really meant to run a candidate against Churchill, Beaverbrook said the public interest overruled friendships, which brought from Guest the retort: "You don't deserve any friends."[10]

The name Liberal "without prefix or suffix" being appropriated by the Asquithians, Lloyd George's followers stood as National Liberals. No love was lost between the two sections of the Liberals. "Don't believe a word about reunion," Mrs. Asquith wrote to Bonar Law,[11] and Asquith himself opened his campaign by alleging that the downfall of the coalition had been brought about, not in Belgravia and the Carlton Club but in Downing Street. The independent Liberals made a great effort to regain power, putting 339 candidates into the field. Lloyd George could muster only 138, but it was his confident hope that Bonar Law would be forced to rely on National Liberal votes in the new Parliament.

The Labour party had long been preparing for the election and contested 408 seats, not only far more than it had ever contested before but more than any other party except the Unionists. At its Edinburgh conference that same year the Labour party had adopted a new rule carefully designed to admit such Cooperative candidates as the party accepted, while excluding Communists and Liberals. The new rule laid down that "no person shall be eligible as a delegate who is a member of any organization having for one of its objects the return to Parliament or to any local governing authority of a candidate or candidates other than such as have been endorsed by the Labour party, or have been approved as running in association with the Labour party". The Edinburgh conference declared specifically against "any alliance or electoral arrangement with any section of the Liberal or Conservative parties".[12] At the same conference the Labour party agreed to share with the Trades Union Congress financial responsibility for the *Daily Herald*, then on the point of collapse. Four Cooperative candidates were put into the field with the backing of the Labour party. The Communists put up five candidates, all in Scotland.

The doubts that Bonar Law had felt were swept away as the results flowed in. The Newport by-election had not been a false portent. Bonar Law found himself at the head of 344 Unionists, or 347 if three independent Unionists are included, which gave him a clear majority of seventy-nine over all others. It was the first election the Unionists had won standing as a separate party in that century. Despite their formidable list of candidates, the independent Liberals obtained only sixty seats. Asquith and Simon got through safely. The National Liberals with a smaller number of candidates secured almost the same number of seats—fifty-seven—but their losses were heavy. Chief among them was Winston Churchill, who never sat again in the House of Commons as a Liberal. This was the occasion when, as he himself said, he found himself "without an office, without a seat, without a party and without an appendix".[13] It increased his mortification that the poll was headed by a fanatical teetotaller, Scrymgeour. Guest was also defeated by a Beaverbrook candidate in what had been a traditional Liberal seat, East Dorset. So successful was Beaverbrook's spoiling policy that out of fifty-six seats where Conservative candidates were standing against Lloyd George men, only two Lloyd George candidates were successful. Lloyd George's hope of forcing Bonar Law to rely on him was killed. Even in the midst of his own misfortunes Asquith was elated. His Roman calm for once deserted him and in a letter he wrote:[14]

"For the moment the thing that gives me the most satisfaction is to gloat over the corpses which have been left on the battlefield, Winston, Freddie Guest, Montagu, Kellaway—all of them renegades —and among the lesser fry Harry McLaren."

The Labour party, with 142 victorious candidates, including four Cooperators, nearly doubled its representation. It was easily the second largest party in the new House of Commons, and larger than both sections of the Liberals combined. Meditating on the results, Mr. Speaker Whitley saw that he must recognize the Labour party as the official opposition with all the rights and duties appertaining to that position.[15] The Labour party within a single generation had come within sight of power, and the opposition between Conservatives and Labour as the two main parties in the state, which was henceforth to be the chief feature of the party system, was finally established.

Of the ten National Democratic members elected in 1918, one had joined the Labour party and the other nine were defeated by official Labour candidates. One Communist candidate was successful—J. T. Walton Newbold at Motherwell. Two Irish Nationalists, one Sinn Fein and five Independents made up the total of 615 members to which the house had been reduced by the exclusion of representatives from the Irish Free State.

Those gifted with the faculty for reducing politics to mathematics soon realized that there were considerable disparities between the votes cast and the number of seats obtained. The Unionists obtained their 347 members for 5,383,896 votes, but 4,236,733 votes gave the Labour party only 142 seats. The independent Liberals and the National Liberals were almost equally successful—sixty against fifty-seven—but 2,507,204 votes were cast for Asquithian and 1,678,088 for Lloyd George candidates. The remaining 375,510 valid votes secured the return of only nine members. Such was, and is, the British system, but some began to calculate that with a different system their party's fortunes might fare considerably better. The Liberals began to display an interest in proportional representation that they had never shown when in a position to carry it through the House of Commons.

Soon after the election the Conservative party was involved in a delicate question about its finances. In January 1923 Farquhar, the treasurer, refused to sign a cheque for £20,000 for the payment of salaries and bonuses arising out of the election. He seems to have argued that the money had been collected for the coalition and could not be used by one party alone. This led to a suspicion that he had handed over to the Lloyd George political fund gifts intended for the Conservative party. Younger set out the facts as he knew them in the following letter to Bonar Law : [16]

"I am not in a position to state definitely that he did collect money for the election expenses and handed the money to the Lloyd George executive, but I have every reason to believe that he did so, and hope to be able to prove this one of these days.

"The salient points of the position are :

"(1) That he was treasurer of our party and had no right to collect funds for any other than our own central fund so long as he retained that position.

"(2) That there has never been any fusion of funds during the existence of the coalition, and that collections made by Farquhar either for elections or ordinary expenditure were paid into our own central fund, just as Lloyd George's fund was used by his treasurer and executive.

"(3) When any joint financial responsibilities were undertaken the costs were halved and each party paid by a cheque on its own fund.

"(4) In any case the coalition had come to an end before the general election and Farquhar's reported statement that he had collected money for the coalition does not hold water."

Bonar Law called Farquhar for interview, and then wrote to the former chief whip, Lord Fitzalan of Derwent : [17]

"You have noticed the trouble there was with poor old Farquhar. I have seen him twice and there is now no question of his hesitating to sign the cheques for the actual party funds but I still have a strong suspicion that he has handed sums, and perhaps large sums, to L.G. for his party while he was acting as our treasurer. He is so 'gaga' that one does not know what to make of him but among the many statements he made to me was one which he repeated several times—that he had given no money to L.G. funds which was not ear-marked for that purpose. Hicks, the accountant, has been seeing him and he has become sane enough to realize that that was not a wise thing to say so that he has said to Hicks that he has given no money at all to L.G. except £80,000 from Astor. He spoke to me also about this and said that at the same time he handed over £80,000 to you. This he did, so he tells me, on the ground that Astor had left him a perfectly free hand to deal with it as he liked."

William Waldorf Astor, who had been made a baron in 1916 and a viscount in 1917, died in 1919, and Farquhar told Fitzalan (then Lord Edmund Talbot), according to the latter's recollection, that about a year before his death Astor had given him £200,000 to use exactly as he liked. He gave, so he said, £50,000, or perhaps it was £40,000, to some war charity in which the King was interested and divided the balance between the Conservative and Lloyd George funds. He may or may not have been entitled to do so, but Talbot told Bonar Law that the £80,000 had not been handed to him. Whether in fact the Conservatives received £80,000 out of Astor's gift is still shrouded in mystery.

In March Farquhar was asked to resign as Conservative treasurer, and when he refused Bonar Law dismissed him. The Tory ex-ministers took his side, and over dinner at Birkenhead's house Chamberlain, Balfour and Horne along with Birkenhead himself tried to persuade him to regard themselves as the true Conservative leaders and to place the funds under his control at their disposal. He declined, but it did not matter for by that time there were no such funds. They had all evaporated in Farquhar's fingers. He died in August, leaving princely bequests to members of the royal family which could not be paid because he was penniless.

The parliamentary Labour party in the new Parliament was markedly different in composition from its predecessor. Of the fifty-seven Labour members elected in 1918, no fewer than forty-nine were nominees of trade unions, twenty-five of them ex-miners. The Labour members sponsored by trade unions rose in 1922 to eighty-five (forty-two of them backed by the Miners' Federation), but proportionately they were a smaller element in the party. The I.L.P. secured the election of thirty-two members, and the Fabian Society and Social Democratic Federation had one each; divisional Labour parties had sponsored nineteen; and there were the four sponsored by the Cooperative party. Those pacifists who had lost their seats in 1918—MacDonald, Snowden, Lansbury and Jowett—now re-inforced Clynes, Adamson, J. H. Thomas, Graham and others who had sat throughout. Of the old leaders only Henderson failed to secure election, and he soon came in at a by-election at East Newcastle in January. These veterans were joined by two who had formerly sat as Liberals, Charles Trevelyan and H. B. Lees-Smith, and by Sidney Webb now entering Parliament for the first time. Among the new entrants there were many destined to play a big part in shaping Labour party policy in the future—Arthur Greenwood, A. V. Alexander, James Maxton, Emanuel Shinwell among them. Few at that time, or for many years to come, would have recognized on the back benches a nervous lecturer from the London School of Economics as the man destined to be at the head of the party during its greatest triumphs; but this was the year when Limehouse first send Clement Richard Attlee to Parliament.

On 21st November the Labour members of Parliament met in Room Fourteen for the purpose of electing officers. It was a momentous occasion, and made more momentous than anyone could have realized at the time by the decision then taken. The most important choice before the meeting was whether to continue with

Clynes as chairman, or to allow MacDonald to resume his old place. No speeches for or against would have been in order, and one of those present, Mr. L. MacNeill Weir, thinks the outcome may have been determined by a preliminary question of seemingly little importance.[18]

Clynes, as the retiring chairman, presided at the outset, and said that he and such other members of the policy committee as had been re-elected had been in consultation with the Speaker about seating when the house met for the first time that afternoon. They were gratified to learn that he proposed to give precedence in all important debates to the leader of the Labour party, and that on the leader of the Labour party would devolve the duty of questioning the government as to the course of business. The Speaker proposed to allocate three out of every four supply days to the Labour party, which would thereby be able to choose the subject for discussion on those days, the fourth being given either to the Asquithian or to the Lloyd George Liberals. He could not agree, however, to the Labour party's proposal that it should occupy the major portion of the opposition front bench, leaving to Asquith and his friends only four or five seats between the gangway and the dispatch-box.

Clynes told the meeting that he had expressed strong disapproval of the proposed arrangement, but he left the impression in his quiet way that he did not regard the matter as worth bothering about and did not intend to press it. At once MacDonald leapt up and with flashing eyes denounced the proposal; let the Liberals join the Tories on the other side of the house where they belonged. The more militant members warmed to him, and the meeting turned to the business of elections for which it had been summoned. In the last Parliament the parliamentary party had decided that it would be more sensible to choose its officers at the end of a session rather than at the beginning of a new one, so that they could get to work in the recess, and in accordance with this decision it was moved that the party should carry on with the old officers. This would have confirmed Clynes in office, and an amendment was promptly moved, and carried, that all officers should be elected then and there both for the current session and for the session beginning in the following year.

At last nominations were invited for the post of chairman and leader. The terminology is significant. Hitherto the chief officer had been called "chairman" of the party, which fairly accurately described his functions. The additional description of "leader" was no doubt added because the person chosen would automatically and for the first time become "leader of the opposition", but in retrospect it makes an important stage in the evolution of leadership in the Labour party and shows how the Mother of Parliament was quietly assimilating the new party to the pattern of the old.

In response to the request from the chair MacDonald was immediately nominated by—the pen falters to record it—Emanuel Shinwell,[19] who was later to give his nominee the bitterest election fight of his career. Clynes was also nominated, and Henderson took his place in the chair. The voting was close. According to Macneill Weir and Shinwell, the figures were MacDonald sixty-one, Clynes fifty-six. Dalton and Snowden, who were also present, later gave the majority as four and two respectively.[20] It mattered not how small it was. MacDonald, not Clynes, would confront the Prime Minister from behind the dispatch-box.

In retrospect it was seen that the votes of the Clydesiders were decisive.[21] They were then the most militant section of the Labour movement, and they thought that MacDonald would be a more militant leader than Clynes. They were later to regret their action bitterly, but at the time it seemed right. Both MacDonald and Clynes were members of the I.L.P., but MacDonald had been chairman and seemed to convey the mood of the I.L.P. more than Clynes, who was regarded as a typical trade unionist. There may have been an element of nationalism. MacDonald was a Scot, whereas Clynes was of Irish extraction; this may have helped the Clydesiders in their choice, and even to sway the English members. MacDonald looked and spoke like a leader, which Clynes did not. When all the factors are considered, it is perhaps surprising that MacDonald's majority was so small.

Clynes accepted defeat with great magnanimity[22] and agreed to be deputy chairman. It was resolved to have two vice-chairmen as in the previous Parliament. Stephen Walsh was elected the senior, and when two nominations were made for the second post Josiah Wedgwood, the former Liberal, beat J. H. Thomas by fifty-three votes to forty-four.

Just over three weeks later, on 13th December, a joint meeting of the National Executive committee and the General Council of the Trades Union Congress voted its "complete confidence in Mr. J. Ramsay MacDonald, M.P., as leader of the Parliamentary Labour party".[23] The description of "chairman" was quietly dropped, and henceforth it became customary to call MacDonald simply the leader of the party, just like the leader of one of the older parties. Moreover, although he was strictly only leader of the parliamentary party, from this time onward it became accepted that he was leader of the Labour party as a whole, in the country as well as in Parliament, even though elected only by the votes of his colleagues in the House of Commons.[24]

MacDonald was not averse to being described as leader, and behaved as though to the manner born. The afternoon after his election he took his seat on the front bench next to Asquith. With uncanny prescience he picked out C. R. Attlee to be his parliamentary private secretary. The Lloyd George Liberals sat on the opposition benches below the gangway. Austen Chamberlain took the corner seat on the third bench below the gangway on the government side, a seat which has come to be regarded as indicating a degree of detachment from the government not amounting to formal opposition. The stage was set for the drama.

The main business of the short session before Christmas was to pass the Irish Free State Bill ratifying the treaty and providing the southern part of Ireland with a constitution. Bonar Law successfully kept the temperature low. The Labour party was anxious to keep unemployment in the forefront, and taunted Bonar Law with refusing to see a deputation of hunger-marchers; with more constitutional propriety than a sense of public relations he thought the deputation should be received by the Minister of Labour. The ex-coalition ministers thought they had an opportunity of assailing the government when Gounaris and five other former Greek ministers were shot, but by an extraordinary piece of "collective amnesia"[25] Birkenhead and his colleagues forgot that they had seen documents circulated to them in print. The most important business was a settlement of the British debt to the United States—far exceeded by the allies' debt to Great Britain. Baldwin committed the British government to a settlement which Bonar Law regarded as disastrous, and informed the press before any counter-action could be taken. Bonar Law would have resigned, but was persuaded by his colleagues to stay on.

He was, however, a sick man, and in May he was diagnosed as suffering from an inoperable cancer of the throat. Though he did now know this himself, he could not live more than a few months, and those who did refrained at length from persuading him not to resign. On 20th May his letter of resignation was conveyed to the King, and it was arranged that if his advice about a successor should be sought the King should be told that owing to ill-health he would prefer not to be consulted and was unwilling to take the responsibility for making a recommendation.

Though unwilling to name his successor, Bonar Law expected him to be Curzon, and his reluctance appears to have been in part due to an overbearing letter he had recently received from that lofty statesman. That it should have been the commoner Baldwin and not the patrician Curzon on whom the King's choice fell is one of the high dramas of British political life in the twentieth century; and as the Prime Minister chosen by the King almost automatically became the leader of the Conservative party, the manner in which it came about is of some interest in a study of the party system.

Contrary to a belief held for a long time, the Labour party made no representations against selecting a peer from the upper house, and the arguments against so doing, now regarded as decisive, did not have the same weight in 1923. It would nevertheless have been anomalous if the Prime Minister sat in a house which did not contain—at that time—a single representative of the official opposition, and this thought must have been present to the minds of the King and his private secretary. Curzon had been presiding at meetings of the Cabinet in Bonar Law's absence, but it was usual for the leader of the Lords to do so in the absence of the Prime Minister, and in itself this gave Curzon no title to the succession.

Deprived of the counsel of Bonar Law, the King naturally sought the advice of elder statesmen held in respect by the Tory party. Salisbury, dressed in a frock-coat, boarded a milk train to London to catch Bonar Law before seeing Stamfordham, and came out in favour of Curzon. Balfour, who had no love for the Foreign Secretary, journeyed to London despite phlebitis to urge that a Prime Minister in the upper house would not be acceptable. "And will dear George be chosen?" inquired one of the house party when he returned to his sick-bed at Sheringham. "No," he replied, "dear George will not."[26]

Though Bonar Law had no counsel to offer, the King may very well have been led to believe that he wished to see Baldwin succeed. Mr. Robert Blake has made out a strong case[27] for believing that a decisive intervention was made by Colonel (later Sir) Ronald Waterhouse, a civil servant drawn from the regular army and then serving as private secretary to Bonar Law. He had been found by Bonar Law's most trusted secretary, J. C. (later Lord) Davidson, as a deputy in 1919. He must have had abilities, for though Bonar Law disliked many of his qualities, on becoming Prime Minister he asked for him as principal private secretary. Waterhouse suggested that he might bear Bonar Law's letter of resignation to the King, then at Aldershot. It is significant that Bonar Law's family insisted on his being accompanied by Sir Frederick Sykes, son-in-law of the retiring Prime Minister. At Aldershot Waterhouse appears to have handed to the King or to Stamfordham, without the knowledge of Sykes, a memorandum (unsigned but composed, in fact, by Davidson) which, he said, "practically expressed the views of Mr. Bonar Law". The paper was a well-reasoned plea against Curzon and for Baldwin, partly on personal grounds and partly on the ground that "the time, in the opinion of many members of the House of Commons, has passed when the direction of domestic policy can be placed outside the House of Commons". It would appear that the memorandum was intended as an *aide memoire* for Waterhouse in case he should be asked for his own opinion, but Waterhouse left Stamfordham with the impression that it embodied Bonar Law's own views.

The advice to send for Baldwin, which the King believed he would have been given by Bonar Law and which he was given emphatically by Balfour, agreed with his personal judgement. He made up his mind in favour of the commoner. A telegram from Stamfordham brought Curzon in haste from Montacute, confident that his abilities were now to be recognized by the highest office in the gift of the Sovereign, and it was a cruel blow to him to learn that the Prime Minister was to be Baldwin—"a man," as he moaned, "of the utmost insignificance."[28] Though the immediate shock was great, he was soon behaving with the greatest magnanimity. Despite his first impulse to resign, he agreed to continue as Foreign Secretary; and at the party meeting it was he who proposed Baldwin as leader. On this occasion only Conservative peers and members of the House of Commons were present; and the party unanimously accepted the choice that the King had already made for it.

Baldwin's move to No. 10 made a few changes in the government inevitable. He offered the Exchequer, as Bonar Law had done before him, to McKenna, and on this occasion the old Liberal was prepared to accept if he could do so without the necessity of fighting a contested election. It was hoped to give him a city of London seat, but Sir Frederick Banbury saw no reason why he should resign, the project was dropped, and McKenna stayed at the Midland Bank. The incident is significant in the history of party, not only as showing the disintegration of the Liberals but because McKenna still was, and always remained, a free trader. At that time Baldwin could have had no thought of embracing protection; and this impression is confirmed by the fact that Robert Cecil, who had won his election as a free trader, was brought into the government. The post of Chancellor of the Exchequer was given to Neville Chamberlain, who had risen rapidly in Tory estimation at the Ministry of Health.

Stanley Baldwin resembles one of those stars that after a long period of quiescence suddenly flares into prominence in the sky only to sink again into obscurity. Of his merits as a statesman there will be long dispute; of his genius as a party leader there can be none, though it is a rôle that he did not study and for which he did not consider himself cast. He was, Sir Winston Churchill has observed, "the greatest party manager the Conservatives had ever had".[29] With seemingly effortless ease he overcame a brilliant opposition within his party and a stubborn newspaper campaign without. Though he lost two general elections, he did so at the right time and won (alone or in association) three general elections that effectively kept the Tories in power for a generation. He had taken the lead in recovering the independence of the Conservative party, yet he found his own ideals mirrored not in any Tory statesman but in Asquith and after him in Grey.[30] He placed the stamp of his moderate Conservatism indelibly upon his party's thought; yet his beginnings, as it appeared at the time, were disastrous. He abandoned the caution which had prevailed in the Conservative party since 1850 on the subject of free trade, fought an election to get a mandate for protection, lost it and let in the socialists for their first period of office.

It was, as his biographer, G. M. Young, says,[31] "a bold stroke for a leader who was not yet quite sure of his followers"—a bold stroke, even though there is nothing like a general election for uniting a divided party. Himself a "little Englander", with a distrust of "abroad", he had long been intellectually convinced of the case for tariffs; and the reason he gave for seeking to commit the Tory party once more to protection was the magnitude of the problem of unemployment. He confided his thoughts to the Cabinet, which was nervous, and asked him to confine any public remarks to a personal statement not committing the government. This accounts for his choice of words in his address at the close of the party conference at Plymouth on 26th October. After noting Bonar Law's pledge that there should be no fundamental change in the fiscal arrangements of the country, he accepted the pledge as binding him for that Parliament, but he went on to say:[32]

"To me, at least, this unemployment problem is the most critical problem of our country ... I can fight it. I am willing to fight it. I cannot fight it without weapons. I have for myself come to the conclusion that ... having regard to the economic environment, having regard to the situation of our country—if we go on pottering along as we are we shall have grave unemployment with us to the end of time. And I have come to the conclusion myself that the only way of fighting this subject is by protecting the home market."

There were delirious cheers from the audience at this acceptance by their leader of the old Tory faith in tariffs, and when reported to Onslow Gardens it may have comforted the last days of Bonar Law, who died on 30th October. ("It is fitting," said Asquith, after seeing his body laid to rest in Westminster Abbey, "that we should have buried the Unknown Prime Minister by the side of the Unknown Soldier.")[33] From Plymouth Baldwin took the gospel to Manchester, and in the Free Trade Hall of all places, and despite warnings from Derby[34] about the dangers of making tariffs an election issue in Lancashire, he developed the argument for protection. In that critical atmosphere there was one important concession that he permitted himself to make. He agreed that wheat and meat should not be taxed, so that protection would in practice be confined to domestic manufactured goods. The concession lost him the support of Beaverbrook without gaining that of Lancashire. Salvidge was invited to join the Prime Minister over a week-end luncheon at Knowsley in an effort to discover his intentions, but for most of the meal Baldwin discoursed on how to grow the raspberry—"a jolly little fellow".[35] Salvidge formed the impression that he did not contemplate an election until the new year, but from the comments

T

made by his opponents on his Plymouth declarations Baldwin realized that an election would have to take place before very long. On
behalf of a group of ministers called together by Salisbury, Edward
Wood urged the need to give Parliament and the country an opportunity of examining the question, but "all this in great deference,
recognizing that fixing these matters is your special perquisite".[36]
Baldwin soon made up his own mind, but he had some difficulty in
persuading the King that a dissolution was necessary. The King said
he had implicit confidence in his Prime Minister and in the Conservative party then in power; and it would be a pity if the country
were to be plunged into the turmoil of a general election on a question of domestic policy which would arouse all the old bitterness of
the battles between protection and free trade. He shrewdly warned
Baldwin that his majority might be reduced, or that he might not
get a majority at all; and that his action might unite the Liberal
party. Baldwin's answer was that he had now gone too far and the
country expected a dissolution. The King gave way, and on 13th
November Baldwin told the House of Commons that the election
would be on 6th December.

For the Conservatives the next few days were an anxious time.
Baldwin's decision might easily have increased the disunity in the
party, but Salisbury, Robert Cecil, Edward Wood and Sidney Herbert
received satisfactory assurances, and even Chamberlain and Birkenhead made their peace. In asking the King for a dissolution Baldwin
had obtained permission to bring them into his government. Because
there were no resignations they could not in the end be given places;
a post might have been found for Chamberlain if he would have
deserted Birkenhead, then at the nadir of his fortunes in the Conservative party on account of a flamboyant rectorial address at
Glasgow in which he proclaimed that "the world continues to
offer glittering prizes to those who have stout hearts and sharp
swords".[37] The speech offended the rising pacifist sentiment in the
country and the faith in the League of Nations fostered by the
League of Nations Union and officially professed by all parties; but
Austen Chamberlain would not desert his comrade. Baldwin's
plunge had so far succeeded, and the Conservatives went to the
country united in a policy of complete freedom in fiscal matters,
save for an undertaking that no further taxes would be placed on
essential foods; protection for particular industries; help for agriculture; and a foreign policy based on the principles of the League
of Nations.

Though the election reunited the Tories, it lost one potential
recruit of great importance. Obsessed by the socialist menace,
Churchill was feeling his way back to the party of his youth; but he
could hardly rejoin at the moment when the Conservatives were
embracing protection, for that was the issue on which he had left

them twenty years earlier. He fought—and lost—Leicester West as a Liberal free trader.

Not only did Baldwin's policy unite the Tories; it even united the Liberals, temporarily. Hearing the word "protection", the old war-horses pawed the ground and felt the joy of battle. For Asquith and his friends there were no reservations. Free trade was the pure milk of Liberalism, and they welcomed the unexpected opportunity of fighting on this issue. Many years had passed since Lloyd George had seen free trade in this light. At heart he loved the land, and was fully prepared to protect the products of the British soil from competition. He also sympathized with his friend Beaverbrook's desire for some form of economic union among the countries of the British Empire. While Baldwin was meditating, Lloyd George was making a triumphant tour of the United States. There is evidence in a letter to him from Charles McCurdy[38] that he was thinking of returning to lead a great campaign in favour of imperial federation based on imperial preference. Later in life Baldwin told Tom Jones, if Amery's account is to be trusted, that he got wind of Lloyd George's intentions and called the election to "dish the goat";[39] but Tom Jones does not himself give this story anywhere in print, and it is inherently improbable. Lloyd George set sail from New York on 3rd November. At sea he was still toying with empire union and protection, but when his ship berthed at Southampton he found a message from Winston Churchill, borne by the hand of Archibald Sinclair, begging him not to desert the free trade camp; and a Liberal deputation led by Alfred Mond also strove to rescue his soul from traffic with the enemy. Their importunity swayed Lloyd George's mind. When he met a host of journalists in the ship's ballroom a few moments later, speaking as an "unrepentant and convinced free trader", he denounced Baldwin's decision as "unutterable folly" and "an insult to an intelligent but starving people". As that moment, as Frank Owen observes,[40] he made his choice, "not so much between protection and free trade, as between Toryism and Liberalism". He slammed the door, not only upon any further association with the Tories, but upon the creation of a centre party. A dinner-party at Beaverbrook's country house, in which Lloyd George and Churchill were balanced by Chamberlain and Birkenhead, came to nothing. Once again the importance of personal relationships in the history of party is demonstrated. "Baldwin knifed me," Lloyd George told Hamar Greenwood, "and I shall knife Baldwin." There was only one Liberal election manifesto, signed jointly by Asquith and Lloyd George in that order, which happened conveniently to be the alphabetical order.

The Labour party had no strongly formed views on the question of free trade. It was caught unprepared by the early dissolution, with only 239 endorsed candidates, but another 188 were hastily adopted within the next fortnight. Leaving the Liberals and Tories to fight out the issue of protection, Labour under MacDonald's leadership sought public backing for a capital levy and nationalization.

These were at least the nominal issues, but the Labour movement was really a rising of masses hitherto barely represented in Parliament in protest against the apparent indifference or late conversion of both the historic parties to their newly felt aspirations. "We are the people of England," wrote Chesterton, "that never have spoken yet,"[41] but in 1923 the voice was becoming more articulate. The great mass of Labour supporters who demanded a capital levy and nationalization had not the least idea of the economic consequences of these policies. It was merely a polite way of saying "To hell with the bosses". The character of Labour leadership in those years is well illustrated by a speech of MacDonald's at Bristol.[42] It throws a flood of light on the emotional basis of the Labour movement in those days and the difficulties into which Labour subsequently ran when it had to take decisions on serious economic problems.

"[This is] 1923, and I stand here with this wonderful, moving crowd in front of me. In 1885, I stood in a public place in Bristol, and three people came to listen. Ah! who will say that there is not something like the finger of Providence in all this. And how little the other side understand us: how little! How small is the vision that they direct upon us! We, the expression of a great uprising of the human spirit, never old, never satisfied, never finding a permanent habitation in any of the stable habitations that men build, but always like the Bedouin, sleeping in tents that he folds up in the morning in order to go on his pilgrimage. But, my friends, I see no end of the journey. We have come, we shall journey, and we shall go, and our children coming after us will go on with their journey, and their children will go on with theirs. And, my friends, what you and I have to take care of is that the journey is both onward and upward."

"On and on and on, up and up and up"—we shall hear those accents again when the Labour movement had begun to ask angrily where the journey was going to end. For the time being it was content to be charmed by a vibrant voice leading to the promised land.

Nearly three-quarters of those on the register recorded their votes, and the result provided a pretty problem for the party leaders. The Conservatives with 5,359,690 votes obtained 258 members; Labour, with 4,347,379 votes, came second with 191 (including four standing as Cooperative candidates); the Liberals with 4,251,573 votes, had 157 members; and there were two Nationalists, one Sinn Feiner and six Independents who between them polled 226,796 votes. The single Communist of the previous Parliament lost his seat.

NOTES

Chapter 1 ORIGIN OF PARTY 1640–1689

1. Benjamin Disraeli, Speech at Meeting of Society for Increasing Endowments of Small Livings in the Diocese of Oxford, 25th Nov. 1864: "Parties in the Church have always existed . . . What, my Lord, is party? Party is organized opinion, and as long as the nature of man is of that various and varying character which we all know it is, so long will there be various and varying parties by which it will express itself, or by which it may consult on religious matters" (*The Times*, 26th Nov. 1864); Edmund Burke, *Thoughts on the Cause of the Present Discontents* (*Select Works*, edited by E. J. Payne, vol. 1, p. 86); R. M. MacIver, *The Modern State*, p. 396.

2. "We begin to see conservatism as a distinct force when we approach the Reformation" (Hugh Cecil, *Conservatism*, p. 25).

"The first germs of Whig and Tory in England may be dated (like Florentine Guelfs and Ghibellines) from a wedding—the sacrament which united Henry VIII to Anne Boleyn and signalized our definite disunion from Catholic Europe. Having then the same nativity with Queen Elizabeth, the embryo parties grew in accord with the actions and reactions of the Elizabethan age, at the close of which two twin schools of thought may be discerned, decisively opposed to each other on the causes which most divide mankind—on religious truth and political power" (Keith Feiling, *A History of the Tory Party 1640–1714*, p. 13).

3. Samuel R. Gardiner, *History of England*, vol. 9, p. 281.

4. *Oxford English Dictionary*, s.v.; Narcissus Luttrell, *A Brief Historical Relation of State Affairs*, vol. 1, p. 124; Nigel Birch, *The Conservative Party*, p. 7. (Mr. David Ogg also notes the analogy of the Old Contemptibles, *England in the Reign of Charles II*, vol. 2, p. 608.)

5. The term "undertaker" had come into use in this sense with the first Stuart king, and is defined in the *Oxford English Dictionary* as meaning "One of those who in the reigns of James I, Charles I and Charles II undertook to influence the action of Parliament, especially with regard to the voting of supplies."

6. "Why, after we have played the fool with throwing Whig and Tory at one another, as boys do snowballs, do we grow angry at a new name, which by its true signification might do as much to put us into our wits, as the other hath done to put us out of them? This innocent word Trimmer signifieth no more than this, That if men are together in a boat, and one part of the company would weigh it down on one side, another would make it lean as much to the contrary; it happeneth there is a third opinion of those, who

conceive it would do as well, if the boat went even, without endangering the passengers" (Preface to *The Character of a Trimmer, Works,* ed. 1912, p. 48).

7. George Macaulay Trevelyan, *History of England,* pp. 464–5.

8. Keith Feiling, *A History of England,* p. 557; David Ogg, *England in the Reign of Charles II,* pp. 608–9.

9. "Nothing could have saved the country in 1679 but a union of Whig and Tory statesmen, laying aside their mutual animosities and compromising their rival claims, as they did ten years later after a cruel schooling in adversity. The Whigs, with whom the game first lay, behaved disgracefully . . . Whig violence was soon countered by Tory violence no less pernicious" (G. M. Trevelyan, *History of England,* pp. 462–3).

10. Danby, Bishop Compton and Lord Lumley were Tories; Devonshire, Russell, Shrewsbury and Henry Sidney were Whigs.

11. John Locke, *Second Treatise,* ch. 19. Mr. Peter Laslett in his critical edition writes: "We owe *Two Treatises* to the wonderful knowledge of state affairs which Locke acquired from the first Earl of Shaftesbury; indeed the evidence suggests, as we shall see, that he actually wrote the book for Shaftesbury's purposes" (p. 27). He argues convincingly that Locke really was attacking Filmer and not Hobbes by proxy (pp. 67–78). "A controversy between Locke and Hobbes would have been within one party only, and could never have given rise to the characteristic political attitude of the modern world. A clash between two such men as Locke and Filmer was a symbolic, a necessary occurrence: it changed men's minds" (p. 70). This strengthens his argument that Locke had begun writing in 1679, and was moved to the particular form of his work by the publication of *Patriarchia* in 1680. The fact that *Two Treatises* was published in 1689 has led to the erroneous view that it was a posthumous justification of the revolution. Locke was particularly concerned to refute Filmer's belief in a primitive common ownership of property. His solution in the *Second Treatise,* ch. 5, is: "Though the earth, and all inferior creatures be common to all men, yet every man has a property in his own person. This no body has any right to but himself. The labour of his body, and the work of his hands, we may say, are properly his. Whatsoever then he removes out of the state that nature hath provided, and left it in, he hath mixed his labour with, and joined to it something that is his own, and thereby makes it his property." Few more pregnant political sayings have ever found expression, and it foreshadows not only the capitalist doctrine of private property but the labour theory of value approved by Marx.

Chapter 2   PARTY MINISTRIES 1689–1714

1. "The best party is but a kind of conspiracy against the rest of the nation . . . Ignorance maketh most men go into a party, and the same keepeth them from getting out of it" (Halifax, *Political Thoughts and Reflections, Of Parties, Works,* ed. 1912, pp. 225–7).

2. *A Dissertation upon Parties; in Several Letters to Caleb D'Anvers, Esq.* (N. Amhurst), is a collection of letters that first appeared in the *Craftsman* 1733–4. Bolingbroke's *Letter on the Spirit of Patriotism* was written in 1736, his *Letter on the Idea of a Patriot King* in 1738, and his *Letter on the State*

of *Parties at the accession of King George I* also in 1738. The three were published in one volume in 1744, but Pope, contrary to a promise, had allowed the *Patriot King* to be printed in 1741. See below, Chapter 3.

3. Edmund Burke, *Thoughts on the Cause of the Present Discontents, Select Works*, edited by E. J. Payne, vol. 1, p. 82.

4. *Ibid.*, pp. 82–3.

5. *Ibid.*, p. 89.

6. Mr. Carswell has written: "Wharton's was one of the first, and probably one of the greatest personal borough interests, and from the Revolution onwards he was acknowledged on all sides to be the most expert political manager, whether in the house or out of it, that England had yet produced. The discipline of the Whig party, which created and conserved the Revolution settlement, owed more to him than to any other single man" (*The Old Cause*, p. 76).

7. John Carswell, *The Old Cause*, p. 84. This was the first Junto. In the second Junto, which led the government from 1708 to 1710 and the opposition from 1710 to 1714, the place of Shrewsbury, who had repeatedly begged to be relieved of office, was taken by the younger Sunderland.

8. We get a glimpse of the Whig machinery for evolving a common policy during the long proceedings against Sir John Fenwick that were terminated by his execution in 1697. "Meetings of the leadership at Russell's house in Covent Garden," says Mr. Carswell, "hammered out the policy which was discussed at larger meetings of the parliamentary party either at Somers's chambers in Lincoln's Inn or in the famous taproom of the Rose Tavern" (*The Old Cause*, p. 85).

9. *Bishop Burnet's History of His Own Times*, ed. 1823, vol. 5, p. 10.

10. Keith Feiling, *A History of England*, p. 629.

11. William Coxe, *Memoirs of John, Duke of Marlborough*, ed. 1818, vol. 2, ch. 51, p. 137.

Chapter 3 THE WHIG OLIGARCHY 1714–1761

1. G. M. Trevelyan, *History of England*, p. 513. Squire Western, in Fielding's *Tom Jones* (1748), is a typical Tory squire whose appointment as a justice of the peace by the Whigs did not prevent him from constantly railing at them and the "Hanoverian rats".

2. Macaulay's observations on the Leicester House opposition in his essay on the Earl of Chatham are very much to the point: "Nothing is more natural than that, in a monarchy where a constitutional opposition exists, the heir-apparent of the throne should put himself at the head of that opposition. He is impelled to such a course by every feeling of ambition and of vanity. He cannot be more than second in the estimation of the party which is in. He is sure to be the first member of the party which is out." After noting that "since the accession of George the First, there have been four Princes of Wales, and they have all been almost constantly in opposition", Macaulay judiciously adds that the disagreement between Frederick and his father, though creditable to neither, served a very useful constitutional purpose: "A

large class of politicians, who had considered themselves as placed under sentence of perpetual exclusion from office, and who, in their despair, had been almost ready to join in a counter-revolution as the only mode of removing the proscription under which they lay, now saw with pleasure an easier and safer road to power opening before them, and thought it better to wait till, in the natural course of things, the Crown should descend to the heir of the house of Brunswick, than to risk their lands and their necks in a rising for the house of Stuart" (*Essays*, ed. 1914, pp. 294–5).

3. Sir Ivor Jennings analyses the extent of "Old Corruption" in two chapters of *Party Politics*, vol. 1, *Appeal to the People*, pp. 80–111.

4. British Museum, Add. MS. 33044; L. B. Namier, *The Structure of Politics at the Accession of George III*, ed. 1957, pp. 173–234, 427–82. "The vast fund of parliamentary corruption called 'secret service money' has proved surprisingly small, a mere supplement to places and other open favours; and on further inquiry it is found that there was more jobbery, stupidity, and human charity about it than bribery" (*op. cit.*, p. 234).

5. Horace Walpole, *Memoirs of the Last Ten Years of the Reign of George II*, ed. 1847, vol. 2, p. 58.

6. *Ibid.*, vol. 3, p. 84.

7. Sir Keith Feiling is reluctant to accord him the title. See below, Chapter 4, n. 12.

8. Professor Archibald S. Foord's recent work, *His Majesty's Opposition*, includes many valuable remarks upon the nature of parties in this period, for example: "The principles supposedly dividing Whig and Tory were, in reality, little more than general tendencies or traditional prejudices. Where a politician took his stand upon an issue depended much more upon whether he was in or out of office than upon what label was attached to him. For Whigs and Tories did not constitute political parties as they came to be in the late nineteenth and twentieth centuries. Those labels were often adopted by, or foisted upon, men who had little in common and few or no real ties. In 1714 and for many years thereafter, the basic political unit was the group or connexion, often called a party, formed under the leadership of a successful politician" (p. 20). Reflecting in private correspondence on the number of "years thereafter" in the light of the three volumes of *The History of Parliament* subsequently published, Professor Foord agrees with Mr. John Brooke that the 1770s was the time when political parties began to be formed. See below, Chapter 4, n. 14.

The same point with a different terminal date had been made earlier, almost at the same time as Namier's first edition, in that stimulating work by F. S. Oliver, *The Endless Adventure*, ed. 1930–35. Oliver writes: "From a few years after the accession of the House of Hanover until the eighteenth century was drawing to a close, the names of Whig and Tory are of little value for discriminating the currents of political opinion. During the greater part of that period, the contest was for office, not for doctrines; and even in those few cases where a principle was involved, the cleavage, as a rule, cut across the nominal party divisions. It is not easy to discover that, between 1720 and 1790 any influence or motive, stronger than family tradition or a supposed personal interest, led people to describe themselves by the one title rather than by the other. But, as Bolingbroke has told us, 'the names and, with the names, the animosity of parties may be kept up when the causes that formed them subsist no longer'." (*The Endless Adventure*, vol. 1, pp. 204–5.)

Chapter 4 YEARS OF CONFUSION 1761–1782

1. L. B. Namier, *The Structure of Politics at the Accession of George III*, ed. 1957, p. x.

2. L. B. Namier, *Monarchy and the Party System*, pp. 4, 10, 12.

3. L. B. Namier, *The Structure of Politics at the Accession of George III*, ed. 1957, p. xi.

4. *Ibid.*, p. 150.

5. *Ibid.*, pp. 25, 29–31.

6. *Ibid.*, p. 39.

7. Lord John Russell, *Bedford Correspondence*, vol. 1, pp. 4–8, as corrected by L. B. Namier, *Monarchy and the Party System*, p. 14, from the originals at Woburn Abbey.

8. Sir Nathaniel Wraxall, *Historical and Posthumous Memoirs*, ed. 1884, vol. 3, p. 236.

9. Donald Southgate, *The Passing of the Whigs*, p. xiv.

10. *Ibid.*, p. xiv.

11. Sir Keith Feiling, *The Second Tory Party 1714–1832*, p. v. We may reflect that although we speak of the *Quatrième République* and the *Dritte Reich* no one denies the historical continuity of France and Germany.

12. Sir Keith Feiling, *A History of England*, p. 701. He makes the same point about Bute in *The Second Tory Party*, pp. 67, 72 ("Bute was no Tory", "To call the Bute system 'Tory' is half legend, half retrospective confusion of thought"), and about North, *ibid.*, pp. 100, 101 ("Actually, North was not a party man at all", "If North must be labelled, which he would have disliked, he can only be called a Conservative").

13. Royal Archives, Windsor, Geo. 484, cited by Sir John Fortescue, *The Correspondence of King George the Third from 1760 to December 1783*, vol. 1, p. 385, and W. S. Taylor and J. H. Pringle, *Correspondence of William Pitt, Earl of Chatham*, vol. 3, p. 21.

14. I can only regret that the three volumes of *The House of Commons 1754–1790* in *The History of Parliament* edited by Sir Lewis Namier and John Brooke were not published until this book was already in type. Mr. Brooke's introductory survey and the biographies of members of the House of Commons constitute a rich quarry to which I must refer readers who wish to study these years in greater depth. Among the main features of the development of the House of Commons in the years 1754 to 1790 Mr. Brooke distinguishes the growth of party as "the most significant feature of all" (vol. 1, p. 1). One of the contentions in the text is confirmed by what Mr. Brooke has to say about the analysis of the new Parliament of 1754 made by Lord Dupplin, Pelham's election manager. "According to Lord Dupplin's classification of the Parliament elected in 1754, almost every member of the House of Commons was either a Whig or a Tory. This happy anticipation of nineteenth-century

conditions, when every person in the land was said to be either a Liberal or a Conservative, presents the appearance of a two-party system which, if viewed superficially, can be deceptive. It is true that on closer examination the 410 members classed as Whigs in 1754 resolve themselves into followers of the Duke of Newcastle, the Duke of Bedford, the Prince of Wales, and of half a dozen smaller party leaders; and that their political behaviour could never be depended upon even by their own leaders. As for the 106 Tories, they did not profess to acknowledge any leader, but were independent members, voting according to their own lights whether of principle or prejudice. Still, the words Whig and Tory must have meant something or Dupplin would not have used them" (ibid., p. 184).

Mr. Brooke adds a warning. "When the names Whig and Tory were first used as party labels in English politics in the late seventeenth century they denoted two different attitudes towards a particular set of political circumstances. It by no means follows that in 1754, when political circumstances had changed, that those attitudes remained the same or that the words Whig and Tory meant what they had done in 1679 . . . It was universally recognized around 1754 that the old party denominations of Whig and Tory no longer corresponded to political realities and that the issues which formerly distinguished them were dead . . . The durability of parties depends less on the ideas they represent than on the strength and coherence of party organizations. There were no party organizations in 1754, apart from the Treasury, which acted as a kind of party organization for the Whigs, though its influence was limited to those members whom it provided with seats or who looked to it for favours. The Tories had not even a leader who could command the confidence of the whole . . . Party struggles in the last years of George II and the early years of George III were essentially struggles for office, with political principles used as shibboleths, a means of distinguishing friend from foe" (ibid., pp. 184, 186, 190).

"The period of short-lived ministries, from 1762 to 1770," Mr. Brooke continues, "was pre-eminently a period of personal politics. Each successive minister—Bute, Grenville, Rockingham, Chatham—was able in office to build up his own party and to lead it into opposition after he had left office, but the longer he remained in opposition the smaller his following grew" (ibid., p. 197). The system, however, was not static. "The era of personal parties came to an end about 1770 . . . One party only survived the era of personal parties: that led by Lord Rockingham . . . The era of political parties, as contrasted with personal parties, dates from about 1775, though the two types overlap: personal parties had political questions thrust upon them and had to adapt themselves accordingly. Parties were shaped by the great issues of the American war and of reform, and from 1775 to 1782 five groups can be distinguished in the House of Commons, each differentiated on a political basis" (ibid., pp. 198, 199).

"After the general election of 1784," Mr. Brooke concludes, "when Pitt had consolidated his power, the house settled down on something like a two-party basis, superficially resembling the house of to-day. On the one side was Pitt, holding a position like that of a modern Prime Minister; on the other was Fox, holding the position of a modern leader of the opposition. Between 1780 and 1784 there had been a consolidation of parties; the smaller groups had disappeared; and every member of the house appeared to have taken sides, either for Pitt or for Fox. The names of Whig and Tory had long since ceased to have any meaning, or rather were in the process of acquiring entirely different meanings from those they had held in 1754; and the speculative historian can see in Pitt the founder of the modern Conservative party, and in Fox the inspirer of the Liberal party of the nineteenth century" (*ibid.*, p. 203).

Chapter 5 RE-FORMATION OF PARTIES 1761–1807

1. Mr. John Brooke, for example.

2. George Otto Trevelyan, *The Early History of Charles James Fox*, p. 333.

3. *Ibid.*, p. 524.

4. Ian R. Christie, *Wilkes, Wyvill and Reform*, p. 76.

5. S. Maccoby, *The English Radical Tradition 1763–1914*, p. 1. The origins may be studied in greater detail in the same author's *English Radicalism 1762–1785*, one of six volumes in which he covers the whole history of the movement.

6. *Junius*, ed. 1812, vol. 2, pp. 267–8. The author of the series of letters attacking the Grafton and North administrations which appeared in the *Public Advertiser* from 1769 to 1772 under the pseudonym "Junius" is now identified beyond doubt as Sir Philip Francis. Beckford's *Political Creed* may be read in the *Gentleman's Magazine*, March 1770, p. 109. Lucy S. Sutherland's Creichton lecture, 1958, *The City and the Opposition to Government 1768–1774*, may be studied with advantage.

7. S. Maccoby, *English Radicalism 1762–1785*, p. 106.

8. *Annual Register*, 1769, pp. 78–9.

9. George Rudé, *Wilkes and Liberty*, p. 195.

10. S. Maccoby, *English Radicalism 1762–1785*, p. 170.

11. *Gentleman's Magazine*, 1773, p. 579. Alderman Bull was Lord Mayor that year.

12. *Ibid.*, 1774, p. 444. Serjeant J. Glynn ran with Wilkes and gave the same undertakings.

13. See p. 80.

14. *Oxford English Dictionary*, s.v., citing J. Jebb in Disney, *Life* (*Works*, ed. 1787). The first example of radical as a substantive cited by the same authority comes from 1806, and then as though it was a naughty word—"The sagacious only could have foreseen that he should have become a r-c-l."

15. G. M. Trevelyan, *History of England*, p. 556.

16. Stanhope, *Life of William Pitt*, vol. 1, p. 58.

17. George Tomline, *Life of William Pitt*, vol. 1, p. 89. The bishop adds: "This was, I believe, the last time Mr. Pitt was in a private room with Mr. Fox; and from this period may be dated that political hostility, which continued through the remainder of their lives."

18. Stanhope, *op. cit.*, vol. 1, p. 100.

19. *Ibid.*, vol. 1, p. 116. On the resignation of Shelburne George III gave a pressing invitation to Pitt to form a government, but with rare self-control—

he was not then twenty-four—he declined, and accepted only when the coalition fell. It was Henry Dundas who urged the King to send for Pitt.

20. But N. C. Phillips in his monograph *Yorkshire and English National Politics, 1784*, p. 9, *n.* 3, says: "The figure of 160 is almost certainly an over-estimate." He cites a contemporary pamphlet which identifies only ninety-seven "martyrs"

21. Wordsworth, *French Revolution* (1804), *Works*, ed. 1904, p. 208; Lord John Russell, *Memorials and Correspondence of C. J. Fox*, vol. 2, p. 361; Burke, *Reflections on the Revolution in France, Works*, ed. 1815, vol. 5, p. 149.

22. The Constitutional Society, or in full the Society for Promoting Constitutional Information, had been founded in 1780 on the initiative of John Cartwright. It undertook to print and distribute free of charge both original works and reprints of pamphlets supporting the reform of Parliament. From 1789 onwards it sought to manifest its sympathy with the revolution in France. The Revolution Society was a club with a yearly festival in commemoration of the events of 1688. It was remodelled and enlarged at the time of the French revolution, but retained its old name to proclaim an affinity between the principles of 1688 in England and those of 1789 in France.

23. Sir Philip Magnus, *Edmund Burke*, pp. 218–19.

24. Fox to Lord Holland, 9th March 1794: "You will perceive from the newspapers to what numbers we are reduced, though, small as they are, they are better than I expected. I mean the fifty-nine upon the first day" (Lord John Russell, *Memorials and Correspondence of Charles James Fox*, vol. 3, p. 64).

25. *Memoirs of the Lady Hester Stanhope*, vol. 2, p. 22.

26. The Corresponding Society and the Society for Constitutional Information combined their efforts in 1794 and sought to call in London a convention which would be more representative of the people than Parliament. Eight members of the societies were brought to trial for high treason. After listening to Scott for the prosecution and Erskine for the defence in three separate trials, juries acquitted Hardy, Horne Tooke and John Thelwall; the case against the others was abandoned.

27. G. M. Trevelyan, *History of England*, pp. 579–80.

28. In a letter to Addington written on 22nd March 1803 Lord Melville (as Henry Dundas had become) communicated Pitt's unwillingness to enter the government under a Prime Minister acceptable to them both. Melville added: "Besides this consideration, he stated, not less pointedly and decidedly, his sentiments with regard to the absolute necessity there is in the conduct of the affairs of this country, that there should be an avowed and real minister, possessing the chief weight in the council, and the principal place in the confidence of the King. In that respect there can be no rivality or division of power. That power must rest in the person generally called the First Minister, and that minister ought, he thinks, to be the person at the head of the finances . . ." (Stanhope, *Life of Pitt*, vol. 4, p. 24).

29. Yet as Secretary of State in 1807 Fox, seizing the opportunity afforded by a French lunatic's revelation to the Foreign Office of his plan to murder Napoleon, opened negotiations with Talleyrand for peace (Christopher Hobhouse, *Fox*, ed. 1948, pp. 264–5).

Chapter 6 THE TORIES ENTRENCHED 1807–1830

1. The first impulse of the assassin, John Bellingham, had been to kill Granville Leveson Gower, British ambassador to Russia, against whom he had a grievance, and at his trial he said he wished he had done so (Denis Gray, *Spencer Perceval*, pp. 461, 470).

2. Liverpool offered him the Foreign Office in 1812, but on condition that Castlereagh led the Commons, and he declined. In 1822 he received both posts.

3. "Both the old parties seemed to be dissolved" (Keith Feiling, *A History of England*, p. 819).

4. Memorandum by King George IV, 8th Aug. 1827, Royal Archives, Windsor, 24110–1, cited by W. C. Costin and J. Steven Watson, *The Law and Working of the Constitution*, vol. 2, p. 372.

5. Bolingbroke, *A Dissertation upon Parties*, ed. 1735, p. 5; Memorandum by the Duke of Newcastle, 2nd Aug. 1762, "An account of the Duke of Devonshire's conversation on Saturday, July 31st," British Museum, Add. MS. 33,000, f. 96; Edward Gibbon, letter to Lord Sheffield, 7th Aug. 1790, J. E. Norton, *The Letters of Edward Gibbon*, vol. 3, p. 195.

6. Keith Feiling, *The Second Tory Party*, p. 13.

7. G. M. Trevelyan, *An Autobiography and other Essays*, p. 197.

8. Reproduced by C. K. Webster, *Cambridge History of British Foreign Policy*, vol. 2, pp. 623–33; and by Harold Temperley and Lilian M. Penson, *Foundations of British Foreign Policy*, pp. 48–63. Canning is usually credited with having a hand in the composition of this paper, and in 1823 he claimed it as the basis of his policy. It is in the final paragraph that there may be found the words: "We shall be found in our place when actual danger menaces the system of Europe, but this country cannot, and will not, act upon abstract and speculative principles of precaution."

9. Stanhope, *Life of Pitt*, vol. 2, p. 141; vol. 3, p. 220.

Chapter 7 REFORM, CONSERVATIVES AND LIBERALS 1830–1841

1. Until his founding in 1830 of the Birmingham Political Union for Public Rights, most of Attwood's connexions had been with the Tory party.

2. [J. W. Croker], *Quarterly Review*, Jan. 1830, vol. 42, no. 83, p. 276; Louis B. Jennings, *The Croker Papers*, ed. 1885, vol. 2, ch. 16, pp. 116–17; Daniel O'Connell, *Spectator*, 25th May 1832; *Blackwood's Magazine*, Jan. 1832, p. 115. Geoffrey D. M. Block, *A Source Book of Conservatism*, p. 65, notes incidentally in the course of a well-documented essay on "The name of the party" that the word "Conservative" had been used by Canning at a city dinner in 1824, and by J. C. Herries (as reported by Greville) in 1829, but they did not suggest it as a new name for the Tory party. Élie Halévy, *A History of the English People*, vol. 3, p. 68 *n.*, gives examples of the use of "conservative" and "conservator" as alternatives, and he regards this usage as showing the French derivation of the term. He and Sir Ivor Jennings, *The Growth of Parties*, p. 59, *n.*, give other early examples of the use of the term "Conservative" for the revived Tory party, as Geoffrey D. M. Block also does in the work cited.

3. Lytton Strachey and Roger Fulford, *The Greville Memoirs 1814–1860*, 14th June 1835, vol. 3, p. 206.

4. Southey, *Quarterly Review*, 1816, vol. 15, p. 69; *The Journal of Sir Walter Scott*, 19th Nov. 1826, ed. 1939, vol. 1, p. 279. By "them" Scott was referring to the high Tories, and especially the Duke of York and the Duke of Wellington.

5. Donald Southgate, *The Passing of the Whigs*, p. 39.

6. J. C. Hobhouse, House of Commons, 10th April 1826, *Hansard*, New (Second) Series, vol. 15, col. 132.

7. Monypenny and Buckle, *The Life of Benjamin Disraeli*, vol. 1, pp. 254–5.

8. Macaulay, *Gladstone on Church and State* (*Essays*, ed. 1914, p. 468).

Chapter 8   BEGINNINGS OF PARTY ORGANIZATION 1832–1841

1. G. O. Trevelyan, *The Early History of Charles James Fox*, p. 145.

2. C. S. Parker, *Sir Robert Peel*, vol. 2, p. 368.

3. Sir Ivor Jennings, *Party Politics*, vol. 2, *The Growth of Parties*, p. 100.

4. Mrs. Fawcett, *The Rt. Hon. Sir William Molesworth*, p. 76.

5. Edmund Burke, *Works*, ed. 1826, vol. 3, pp. 18–19. Burke, as noted in Chapter 5, was replying to the claim of some Radicals that members should be bound by instructions from their constituents.

6. Stanhope and Cardwell, *Memoirs by the Right Honourable Sir Robert Peel*, vol. 2, p. 58.

7. *Ibid.*, p. 59.

8. Public Record Office, CAB 41/6/2, 23rd Jan. 1874; John Morley, *The Life of William Ewart Gladstone*, Bk. 6, ch. 14, ed. 1903, vol. 2, p. 486.

9. For Disraeli's offer, British Museum, Add. MS. 40425, f. 413, cited by G. Kitson Clark, *Peel and the Conservative Party*, p. 397. The Tamworth manifesto is reproduced by Stanhope and Cardwell, *Memoirs by the Right Honourable Sir Robert Peel*, vol. 2, pp. 58–67. There is an excellent essay "Printed party manifestos" by Geoffrey D. M. Block in *A Source Book of Conservatism*, pp. 69–73.

10. Norman Gash, *Politics in the Age of Peel*, pp. 193–201, 438–9.

11. Winston Churchill made the point with his usual felicity in asking the House of Commons to appoint a select committee to consider plans for the rebuilding of the chamber after it had again been destroyed. "The party system is much favoured by the oblong form of chamber. It is easy for an individual to move through these insensible gradations from left to right but the act of crossing the floor is one which requires serious consideration" (House of Commons, 28th Oct. 1943, *Hansard*, Fifth Series, vol. 393, cols. 403–4).

Chapter 9   CONSERVATIVE REVIVAL AND SPLIT 1841–1846

1. British Museum, Add. MS. 40428, f. 15, cited by N. Gash, "F. R. Bonham: Conservative 'Political Secretary', 1832–47", *English Historical*

Review, 1948, vol. 63, p. 512. "Thanks to you," Graham wrote to Bonham, "and to your indefatigable industry, no party out of office ever before possessed such sources of intelligence and such means for active war" (6th Jan. 1841, Add. MS. 40616, f. 194, quoted by Gash, *loc. cit.*).

2. "I made a most capital speech on Chartism last night," he wrote on 13th July 1839 to his wife. "It was a very damaging and disagreeable speech to the government, and they didn't like it." (Monypenny and Buckle, *The Life of Benjamin Disraeli*, vol. 2, p. 64. The background to the speech is admirably analysed on pp. 75–84 of that work, the distinction made between the philanthropic and the philosophic Radicals being particularly helpful.) Disraeli makes Charles Egremont in *Sybil* make a speech on this occasion no less "capital" than his own and as puzzling to his leaders.

3. According to a story derived from Lord Houghton which is related by Monypenny and Buckle, *op. cit.*, vol. 2, p. 122. In an anonymous article written in 1854 George Smythe attributed Disraeli's exclusion to "the political parasites by whom it was the weakness of the great minister to be surrounded, and we owe to this circumstance those immortal sketches of the Rigbys, the Tadpoles, and the Tapers, which Beaumarchais never surpassed" (*ibid.*).

4. Benjamin Disraeli, *Sybil*, Bk. 2, ch. 5, ed. 1868, p. 59.

5. Benjamin Disraeli, *Coningsby*, Bk. 2, ch. 5, ed. 1962, pp. 118–19.

6. *Ibid.*, Bk. 2, ch. 6, p. 122.

7. Monypenny and Buckle, *The Life of Benjamin Disraeli*, vol. 2, pp. 175–8; Robert Blake, *Disraeli*, 177.

8. Monypenny and Buckle, *op cit.*, vol. 2 pp. 179, 181–2, 185–6, 187–8.

9. "The Duke says, 'Rotten potatoes have done it all; they put Peel in his d—d fright'" (Greville *Memoirs*, 13th Jan. 1846, ed. Strachey and Fulford, vol. 5, pp. 282–3).

10. Peel's own record of these events is contained in Stanhope and Cardwell, *Memoirs by Sir Robert Peel*, vol. 2, pp. 97–325. See also C. S. Parker, *Sir Robert Peel*, vol. 3, pp. 220–55, 283–94; Monypenny and Buckle, *The Life of Benjamin Disraeli*, vol. 2, pp. 334–7, 343–57; Cecil Woodham-Smith, *The Great Hunger*, pp. 39–53. The similarity in Peel's relation to the Conservative Cabinet in 1845 and MacDonald's to the Labour Cabinet in 1931 has often received comment, but Peel had more immediate success with his colleagues than MacDonald. See below, vol. 2, ch. 25.

11. Benjamin Disraeli, *Lord George Bentinck*, pp. 38, 93, 95.

12. John Morley, *The Life of William Ewart Gladstone*, Bk. 2, ch. 10, ed. 1903, pp. 289–90.

Chapter 10   WHIGS AND PEELITES 1846–1867

1. Disraeli was provoked to make this remark when a Liberal member of Parliament, James Clay, gave him a protectionist pamphlet with the comment that in the author's mind protection was in the plight of Lazarus, not dead but sleeping (Monypenny and Buckle, *The Life of Benjamin Disraeli*, vol. 3, p. 241). Later in the same year (16th Oct. 1850) he wrote to Manners:

"As for protection in its old form, I look upon that as dead" (*ibid.*, vol. 3, p. 264). Once Disraeli saw that the peasantry was no less averse than the manufacturing classes to a revival of protection he was quick to abandon it; Stanley's mind moved more slowly.

2. Morley, *Gladstone*, Bk. 3, ch. 1, ed. 1903, vol. 1, pp. 327–36.

3. Morley, *Gladstone*, Bk. 3, ch. 3, ed. 1903, p. 353.

4. In a letter to his father, Morley, *Gladstone*, Bk. 3, ch. 3, ed. 1903, vol. 1, p. 351.

5. Monypenny and Buckle, *Disraeli*, vol. 3, pp. 138–9. Stanley had first tried in vain to get Granby and then Herries to accept the sole leadership in the Commons.

6. Evelyn Ashley, *Life of Palmerston*, vol. 1, p. 334.

7. Morley, *op. cit.*, Bk. 3, ch. 7, ed. 1903, pp. 419–23.

8. The amendment moved by Palmerston (then independent of party) and supported by the government, the Whigs and Liberals, and the Peelites was carried by 468 votes to fifty-three. Its first paragraph reads: "That it is the opinion of this house that the improved condition of the country, and especially of the industrious classes, is mainly the result of recent legislation, which has established the principle of unrestricted competition, has abolished taxes imposed for the purposes of protection, and has thereby diminished the cost and increased the abundance of the principal articles of the food of the people." It marked the formal acceptance by the Conservatives of free trade as a national policy.

9. So Morley records Disraeli's words (*op. cit.*, Bk. 4, ch. 1). In Monypenny and Buckle, *op. cit.*, p. 474, there is a letter from Disraeli to Londonderry: "I apprehend that the difficulties of the *personnel*—sixteen Secretaries of State—are minor obstacles compared with the daily, or rather hourly, increasing *émeute* of Brooks's and the Reform; especially the latter, the mainstay of a Liberal government, and now finding the cake is to be cut up without their having a slice."

10. Morley, *Gladstone*, Bk. 4, ch. 9, ed. 1903, vol. 1, pp. 587–8.

11. *Ibid.*, vol. 1, p. 621.

12. In a speech at Blairgowrie, Sept. 1863: "With regard to domestic policy, I think we are all very much agreed, because the feeling of the country, and of those who have conducted great reforms, is very much like that of the man who, having made a road in your own highlands, put a stone on the top of the mountain with an inscription, 'Rest and be thankful'" (Spencer Walpole, *The Life of Lord John Russell*, vol. 2, p. 402).

13. "The right honourable gentleman [E. Horsman] is the first of the new party who has expressed his great grief by his actions—who has retired into what may be called his political cave of Adullam—and he has called about him everyone that was in distress and everyone that was discontented. The right honourable gentleman has been long anxious to form a party in this house. There is scarcely at this side of the house any one who is able to address the house with effect or to take much part in our debates that he has not tried to bring over to his party or cabal—and lastly the right honourable gentleman has succeeded in hooking the right honourable gentleman the

member for Calne [Robert Lowe]" (John Bright in the House of Commons, 13th March 1866, *Hansard*, Third Series, vol. 182, col. 219, referring to David's refuge in the cave of Adullam as described in I Samuel 22, 1–2).

14. Morley, *Gladstone*, Bk. 5, ch. 13, ed. 1903, vol. 2, p. 204.

Chapter 11 REFORM ACT OF 1867—BEFORE AND AFTER

1. "These wretched colonies will all be independent, too, in a few years, and are a millstone round our necks" (Disraeli to Lord Malmesbury, 13th August 1852, *Memoirs of an ex-Minister* by the Earl of Malmesbury, vol. 1, p. 344).

2. In so describing the Public Worship Regulation Bill, 1874, Disraeli was adopting a phrase from Gladstone's speech, but as Buckle complains, it has always been fathered on him (Monypenny and Buckle, *Disraeli*, vol. 5, pp. 324–5); and Disraeli was under strong pressure from the Queen.

3. Morley, *Gladstone*, Bk. 5, ch. 8, ed. 1903, vol. 2, p. 135.

4. "The right hon. gentleman caught the Whigs bathing, and walked away with their clothes. He has left them in the full enjoyment of their liberal position, and he is himself a strict conservative of their garments" (Disraeli, House of Commons, 28th Feb. 1845, Monypenny and Buckle, *Disraeli*, vol. 2, p. 314). "Don't you see how we have dished the Whigs?" (Derby to a friend as related by Granville, Monypenny and Buckle, *Disraeli*, vol. 4, p. 551). Though Derby presumably meant no more than that the Liberals had been out-manoeuvred, Dr. Southgate sees a true word spoken in jest, for after 1867 there was no future for Whiggery (*The Passing of the Whigs*, p. 321).

5. Morley, *Gladstone*, Bk. 4, ch. 4, ed. 1903, vol. 1, p. 509.

6. "Whig and something more" Morley, *Gladstone*, Bk. 3, ch. 7, ed. 1903, vol. 1, p. 420; Élie Halévy, *History of the English People in the 19th Century*, vol. 3, p. 180; Sir Ivor Jennings, *Party Politics*, vol. 2, *The Growth of Parties*, p. 75, n. 2 (as continued on p. 76); Bell, *Palmerston*, vol. 2, p. 214; Donald Southgate, *The Passing of the Whigs*, p. 291; *Letters of Queen Victoria*, vol. 3, p. 138 n. ("The last Whig administration was that which left office in 1852. Had Lord John Russell succeeded in his attempt on the present occasion, the Whig party might have endured *eo nomine*; but Palmerston had, notwithstanding Cobden's distrust, been popular with the Radicals, and henceforward his supporters must be known as the Liberal party.") Dr. Southgate, *op. cit.*, pp. 292–3, adds some powerful considerations for making the meeting at Willis's rooms in 1859 the decisive point: "The meeting at Willis's Rooms was necessary to constitute a party by registering agreement between leaders *and* mutual obligation between leaders and followers. It was a conscious effort to restore the two-party system of 1835–45, because of the inconvenience experienced since it collapsed. That this was so was shown by some of the speeches in the debate on the Hartington amendment. Milner Gibson said that the issue before the house was simply 'the rival claims of two great parties in the country to political power'. . . . With few dissentients (but they included Gladstone) all who were not Tories voted with Hartington; after Willis's Rooms to vote against him was to opt for Toryism."

U

7. Report of the Bridgwater Bribery Commission, 1869, cited by M. J. Hanham, *Elections and Party Management*, p. 352.

8. Speech at the Crystal Palace, 24th June 1872 (*Report of Proceedings at the [6th Conservative] Annual Conference*, 1872, p. 16. Also published separately as Publication No. 16 of the National Union.)

9. Morley, *Life of Gladstone*, Bk. 5, ch. 14, ed. 1903, vol. 2, p. 227.

10. *Ibid.*, vol. 2, p. 225. The quotation is from a record written thirty years later.

11. Disraeli's account of this surprising development is contained in a letter to his principal lieutenant, Gathorne Hardy (Monypenny and Buckle, *Disraeli*, vol. 4, pp. 540–1).

12. Derby and the dishing of the Whigs, v. supra, n. 4; " 'I met Gladstone at breakfast,' says Lord Houghton (May), 'he seems quite awed by the diabolical cleverness of Dizzy' " (Morley, *Gladstone*, Bk. 5, ch. 14, ed. 1903, vol. 2, p. 230); Lowe and Cranborne, *ibid.*, p. 235; Derby, "No doubt we are making a great experiment and taking a leap in the dark," speech on third reading in the Lords, 1867; [Thomas Carlyle], *Macmillan's Magazine*, vol. 16, no. 94, Aug. 1867, "Shooting Niagara : and After?", pp. 319–36.

13. Thanks to the courtesy of Mr. H. V. Armstrong, secretary of the National Union of Conservative and Unionist Associations until 1952, this extract from the manuscript minutes was published in *The Party System in Great Britain*, p. 22.

14. *Report of Proceedings at the [7th Conservative] Annual Conference*, 1873, pp. 9–10.

15. *Report of Proceedings at the [6th Conservative] Annual Conference*, 1872, p. 16.

16. *The Times*, 18th April 1883.

17. Monypenny and Buckle. *Disraeli*, vol. 4, p. 600; Gladstone to Granville (Morley, *Gladstone*, Bk. 5, ch. 15, ed. 1903, vol. 2, p. 240; *ibid.*, pp. 245–8); Disraeli, House of Commons, 16th Feb. 1844, *Hansard*, Third Series, vol. 72, col. 1016 (Monypenny and Buckle, *op. cit.*, vol. 2, pp. 188–94).

18. H. J. Hanham, *Elections and Party Management*, p. 359 n.

19. *Ibid.*, p. 358.

Chapter 12   LIBERAL *versus* CONSERVATIVE 1868–1885

1. Morley, *Gladstone*, Bk. 5, ch. 16, ed. 1903, vol. 2, p. 252.

2. *Ibid.*, Bk. 6, ch. 14, ed. 1903, vol. 2, p. 495.

3. Sir Charles Mallett, *Herbert Gladstone*, pp. 107–8. R. C. K. Ensor in *England 1870–1914*, pp. 21–2, exaggerates in saying that "from midsummer 1871 till the dissolution of 1874 nearly every public-house in the United Kingdom was an active committee-room for the Conservative party" and that from this time the brewers and distillers became the main source of Conservative funds. H. J. Hanham, *Elections and Party Management*, pp. 222–5, after a careful examination reaches the conclusion that "the issues before the electors were so clear and the swing against the government was so strong that no amount of free beer was likely to have a decisive effect on the result".

4. Monypenny and Buckle, *Disraeli*, vol. 5, p. 195.

5. Tennyson, *Locksley Hall*; *Poems of Tennyson*, ed. 1918, p. 172.

6. G. W. Hunt, *We Don't Want to Fight*.

7. Monypenny and Buckle, *Disraeli*, vol. 5, p. 186.

8. "Mr. Gladstone on Electoral Facts", *Nineteenth Century*, vol. 4, no. 21, Nov. 1878, p. 956.

9. The quotation is from an autobiographical fragment written twenty-three years later, Morley, *Gladstone*, Bk. 7, ch. 1, ed. 1903, vol. 2, p. 498 *Gladstone, op. cit.*, p. 554).

10. Monypenny and Buckle, *Disraeli*, vol. 5, p. 325.

11. An official account is given in *Proceedings attending the Formation of the National Federation of Liberal Associations*, Birmingham, 1877, and other contemporary accounts were provided by H. W. Crosskey, "The Liberal Association—The '600'—of Birmingham", *Macmillan's Magazine*, vol. 35 (1876-7), pp. 299-307; and Joseph Chamberlain, "A New Political Organization", *Fortnightly Review*, vol. 22 (1877), pp. 126-34. Moisei Ostrogorski, *Democracy and the Organization of Political Parties* may still be read with advantage on the Birmingham caucus, and there is a good modern account in H. J. Hanham, *Elections and Party Management*, pp. 125-154.

12. *Proceedings attending the Formation of the National Federation of Liberal Associations*, p. 7.

13. T. Wemyss Reid, *Life of the Right Honourable William Edward Forster*, vol. 2, pp. 209-10. We get the flavour of the 1874 election from his diary entry for 4th Feb.: "The enemy had covered the walls with 'Plump for Ripley', but we had posted over it; and we also covered the walls with 'Split for Forster' " (*ibid.*, vol. 2, p. 55). When Gladstone offered his services to end the dispute, Forster, in replying to him under date 2nd Sept. 1878, gives an interesting glimpse of the old constituency arrangements: "I, therefore, rather prefer the old system in our towns; namely, a permanent committee to look after the registration, but a choice of candidates by the whole party just before the election. It seems to me that one of the best safeguards against the wire-pullers—that is, against the real danger besetting large constituencies—is so to frame the machinery as to keep members as much as possible in communication and contact with the whole constituency, and candidates as much as possible with the whole party" (*ibid.*, vol. 2, p. 213).

14. Winston Spencer Churchill, *Lord Randolph Churchill*, vol. 1, p. 108. Lord Randolph's attack was so effective that the bill, which would have transferred county government from quarter sessions to boards elected partly by the county magistrates and partly by the guardians of the poor, was dropped.

15. Speech at Bridgwater House, 19th May 1880, as described by Lord Rowton to Queen Victoria (Monypenny and Buckle, *Disraeli*, vol. 6, p. 576).

16. Morley, *Gladstone*, Bk. 7, ch. 4, ed. 1903, vol. 2, p. 548; W. E. Gladstone, *The Bulgarian Horrors and the Question of the East*, pp. 61-2 (Morley, *Gladstone, op. cit.*, p. 554).

17. Speech at banquet in the Riding School, Knightsbridge, 27th July 1878 (Monypenny and Buckle, *Disraeli*, vol. 6, p. 356).

18. "Lord Salisbury and myself have brought you back peace—but a peace, I hope, with honour." Beaconsfield's words from a window of No. 10 Downing Street on 16th July 1878 have connected the phrase "peace with honour" inseparably with this occasion, but he had already used it in 1855 about Russell's mission to Vienna (Monypenny and Buckle, *Disraeli*, vol. 4, p. 3). Neville Chamberlain was to use it, less happily, on his return from Munich in 1938.

19. Morley, *Gladstone*, Bk. 7, ch. 8, ed. 1903, vol. 2, p. 615.

20. *Ibid.*, p. 619.

21. The story of the group has been told by Gorst's son, H. E. Gorst, *The Fourth Party*, and it gets a chapter in W. S. Churchill, *Lord Randolph Churchill*, vol. 1, pp. 119-71. See also A. J. Balfour, *Chapters of Autobiography*.

22. A jest based on the famous hotel that then existed in the Strand. Enrico Serra in *I Partiti Politici in Gran Bretagna*, pp. 83-5, carries it too far in discerning also a Hotel Churchill, a Hotel Eden and a Hotel Macmillan.

23. The choice of Northcote to unveil the statue of Beaconsfield, and of Salisbury merely to propose a vote of thanks to Northcote led Churchill to address two letters to *The Times* attacking Northcote's leadership and, after the event, to publish his reflections in an article "Elijah's Mantle" in *The Fortnightly*. The Tory party, he prophesied, would fail "unless the secret of Lord Beaconsfield's theory of government is appropriated, understood, believed in, sown broadcast among the people; unless the mantle of Elijah should fall upon some one who is capable enough and fortunate enough, carrying with him a united party, to bring to perfection those schemes of imperial rule, of social reform which Lord Beaconsfield had only time to dream of, to hint at, and to sketch" (*The Fortnightly Review*, vol. 33 (New Series), Jan.–June 1883, pp. 615-16).

24. Churchill derived "Tory democracy" from a famous speech by Disraeli: "Speaking at Manchester in 1871, by the alteration of a letter in a quotation from the Vulgate he revealed the policy which ought to guide Tory leaders at the present time: 'Sanitas sanitatum, omnia sanitas.' Such was the quotation in which a careful mind will discover a scheme of social progress and reform of dimensions so large and wide-spreading that many volumes would not suffice to explain its details . . . The expression 'Tory democracy' has excited the wonder of some, the alarm of others and great and bitter ridicule from the Radical party. But the 'Tory democracy' may yet exist; the elements for its composition only require to be collected, and the labour may some day possibly be effected by the man, whoever he may be, upon whom the mantle of Elijah has descended" (*The Fortnightly Review*, vol. 33 (New Series), Jan.–June 1883, p. 621). Disraeli's speech was in point of fact delivered in 1872—on 3rd April. He had used the same punning slogan, *Sanitas sanitatum* at Aylesbury on 21st Sept. 1864, but then it fell almost unnoticed.

25. Speech at Blackpool, 24th Jan. 1884.

26. Monypenny and Buckle, *Disraeli*, vol. 6, pp. 621-2, 628-31; W. S. Churchill, *Lord Randolph Churchill*, vol. 1, pp. 256-60. Janet H. Robb, *The Primrose League 1886-1903*, may be consulted for further details.

27. This was the committee set up after the defeat of 1880 to make recommendations, and kept in being as described in the previous chapter.

28. W. S. Churchill, *Lord Randolph Churchill*, vol. 1, pp. 308-9.

29. *Ibid.*, pp. 313-14.

30. *Ibid.*, p. 322, and for the letter in full, pp. 539-48.

31. Churchill's son and biographer says: "Lord Salisbury did not select a lieutenant. He formed an alliance on terms of comradeship for the general advantage of the party. The two men met as chiefs of almost equal powers." But he agrees that "Lord Salisbury's primacy was never disputed by Lord Randolph Churchill" and that the settlement sealed the fate of Northcote so far as the leadership of the House of Commons was concerned (W. S. Churchill, *Lord Randolph Churchill*, vol. 1, p. 357).

Chapter 13 THE LIBERAL SPLIT 1886

1. Speech at the Corn Exchange, Edinburgh, 30th Aug. 1884.

2. Queen Victoria to Gladstone, Royal Archives, Windsor, C 50/50; Morley, *Gladstone*, Bk. 8, ch. 8, ed. 1903, vol. 3, pp. 135-8.

3. Speech at St. Stephen's Club, 20th May 1885 (W. S. Churchill, *Lord Randolph Churchill*, vol. 1, p. 395).

4. Speech at Rotunda, Dublin, 11th Dec. 1883 (Morley, *Gladstone*, Bk. 8, ch. 8, vol. 3, p. 143).

5. Morley, *Gladstone*, Bk. 8, ch. 11, vol. 3, p. 200.

6. *Ibid.*, pp. 200-1.

7. *Ibid.*, Bk. 8, ch. 12, vol. 3, pp. 214-15.

8. *Ibid.*, Bk. 9, ch. 1, vol. 3, pp. 237-8.

9. J. L. Hammond, *Gladstone and the Irish Nation*, ed. 1938, pp. 455-6. See also Morley, *Gladstone*, Bk. 9, ch. 1, ed. 1903, vol. 3, p. 238.

10. Morley, *Gladstone*, Bk. 9, ch. 1, ed. 1903, vol. 3, pp. 233-4.

11. J. L. Hammond, *Gladstone and the Irish Nation*, ed. 1938, p. 414.

12. Herbert Gladstone, *After Thirty Years*, pp. 306-14; J. L. Hammond, *Gladstone and the Irish Nation*, ed. 1938, pp. 438-50.

13. J. L. Hammond, *Gladstone and the Irish Nation*, ed. 1938, p. 490.

14. Speech at St. James's Hall, 15th May 1886. "He was disputing the contention that we ought to show confidence in the Irish people by giving them independent representative government. The claim of any population to this precise expression of confidence depended upon their characteristics. 'You would not confide free representative institutions to the Hottentots, for instance'" (Lady Gwendolen Cecil, *Life of Robert, Marquis of Salisbury*, vol. 3, p. 302).

15. W. S. Churchill, *Lord Randolph Churchill*, vol. 1, p. 59.

16. *Ibid.*, pp. 61-3.

17. *Ibid.*, p. 65.

18. *Letters of Queen Victoria*, Third Series, vol. 1, p. 135.

Chapter 14 CONSERVATIVES AND UNIONISTS 1886–1895

1. Viscount Chilston, *Chief Whip*, p. 77; *ibid.*, p. 80.

2. An illuminating memorandum by Chamberlain on the relations of the Liberal Unionists with the Conservatives in the years 1888 to 1892 is reproduced in J. L. Garvin, *The Life of Joseph Chamberlain*, vol. 3, pp. 413–16.

3. Lady St. Helier (Mary Jeune), *Memories of Fifty Years*, pp. 274–5; Robert Rhodes James, *Lord Randolph Churchill*, pp. 303, 309.

4. Monypenny and Buckle, *Disraeli*, vol. 4, p. 335; André Maurois, *Disraeli*, p. 262.

5. Kipling's *Recessional* was first published in *The Times* of 17th July 1897 to mark the diamond jubilee of Queen Victoria. *Land of Hope and Glory* was the sixth song in A. C. Benson's *Coronation ode* for which Elgar composed the music in 1901. It was first produced at Sheffield in 1902, but he had used the melody as the trio in the first of his *Pomp and Circumstance* marches played at Liverpool in 1901.

6. The "unauthorized programme" was put forward in three meetings held in Jan. 1885 at Birmingham, Ipswich and again Birmingham. It was at Birmingham on 5th Jan. that he asked, "What ransom will property pay?" The Queen was horrified and Gladstone disturbed.

7. "Oh, a Secretary of State" said Gladstone. Mr. Roy Jenkins cites this remark as "a classical example of his ineptitude in dealing with Chamberlain, and records Dilke's significant comment, "Chamberlain is furious and will never forgive the slight" (Roy Jenkins, *Sir Charles Dilke*, p. 232).

8. In a speech to his constituents in 1879 (Monypenny and Buckle, *Disraeli*, vol. 5, p. 369).

9. Speech at Free Trade Hall, Manchester, 3rd April 1872 (Monypenny and Buckle, *Disraeli*, vol. 5, p. 186).

10. Morley, *Gladstone*, Bk. 10, ch. 11, ed. 1903, vol. 3, pp. 364–8; *Baptist*, 25th Feb. 1887.

11. *Ibid.*, Bk. 10, ch. 5, ed. 1903, vol. 3, p. 437.

12. Viscount Simon, *Retrospect*, p. 65.

13. Morley, *Gladstone*, Bk. 10, ch. 8, ed. 1903, vol. 3, p. 512.

14. *Gladstone Papers*, British Museum, Add. MS. 44791, f. 30, cited by Robert Rhodes James, *Rosebery*, p. 284.

15. Robert Rhodes James, *Rosebery*, p. 198.

16. *Ibid.*, p. 199.

17. *Gladstone Papers*, British Museum, Add. MS. 44790, ff. 145–6; John Viscount Morley, *Recollections*, ed. 1917, vol. 2, p. 11.

18. Robert Rhodes James, *Rosebery*, p. 337.

19. A. L. Lowell, *The Government of England*, vol. 1, p. 523.

Chapter 15 UNIONIST DOMINANCE AND DISSENSION 1895–1905

1. Viscount Chilston, *Chief Whip*, p. 269. The contest of 1835 arose through doubts about the impartiality of Sir Charles Manners-Sutton, who had been

Speaker from 1817. He had been nominated in 1831 by the Whigs, and he had been specially asked to continue in 1833 so that the reformed house, with its large number of new members, might have the benefit of his experience. The Radicals, however, had never liked this arrangement, and it was widely believed that in the ministerial crisis of 1831 he had agreed to accept high office with the leadership of the Commons. In the crisis of 1834 he certainly attended meetings of the Privy Council. The Liberals therefore felt justified in the new Parliament in putting up a candidate of their own. They compelled James Abercromby against his own wishes to be their candidate, and on 19th Feb. 1835, after a persuasive speech by Russell, they carried the day by ten votes.

2. Lady Gwendolen Cecil, *Life of Robert, Marquis of Salisbury*, vol. 3, p. 197.

3. R. T. McKenzie, *British Political Parties*, ed. 1963, p. 180.

4. Frank Owen, *Tempestuous Journey*, p. 103.

5. The author of the biting phrase was Sir Henry Lucy.

6. Sir Henry Campbell-Bannerman, Speech at dinner of the National Reform Union, 14th June 1901 (Marquess of Crewe, *Lord Rosebery*, vol. 2, p. 569; R. R. James, *Rosebery*, p. 423); Lord Rosebery, Speech to the City Liberal Club, 19th July 1901 (Crewe, *op. cit.*, p. 570; James, *op. cit.*, p. 426); Lord Rosebery, Speech at Chesterfield, 15th Dec. 1901 (Crewe, *op. cit.*, pp. 571–2; James, *op. cit.*, pp. 429–31).

6a. "The Welsh revolt" may be studied in more detail in Kenneth O. Morgan, *Wales in British Politics 1868–1922*, pp. 181–98.

7. Joseph Chamberlain, Speech at Birmingham, 15th May 1903 (*The Times*, 16th May); House of Commons, 28th May 1903, *Hansard*, Fourth Series, vol. 123, col. 185.

8. Balfour, Speech to the National Union of Conservative and Unionist Associations, Sheffield, 1st Oct. 1903 (*The Times*, 2nd Oct.).

9. Joseph Chamberlain, Speech at Guildhall, City of London, 19th Jan. 1904 (*The Times*, 20th Jan.).

10. Bernard Holland, *The Life of Spencer Compton, Eighth Duke of Devonshire*, vol. 2, p. 378.

11. Frank Owen, *Tempestuous Journey*, p. 143.

12. Asquith, Grey and Haldane, taking counsel together at the Scottish fishing village of Relugas, had agreed that Campbell-Bannerman, if invited to form an administration, should be urged to take a peerage, that Asquith should be Chancellor of the Exchequer and lead the House of Commons, that Grey should be Foreign Secretary, and that Haldane should be Lord Chancellor. In the end the "Relugas compact" collapsed because Campell-Bannerman refused to go to the Lords and Asquith was unwilling to coerce him by staying out of the government unless he did (Richard Burdon Haldane, *An Autobiography*, pp. 155–62, 168–82; Roy Jenkins, *Asquith*, pp. 145–52).

Chapter 16   ENTRY OF THE LABOUR PARTY 1900–1906

1. Prospectus of the Labour Representation League, reprinted in A. W. Humphrey, *A History of Labour Representation*, p. 189.

2. Sir Ivor Jennings, *The Growth of Parties*, pp. 239–40.

3. Henry Pelling, *The Origins of The Labour Party 1880–1900*, p. 73.

4. *Ibid.*, p. 122.

5. *Ibid.*, pp. 216–17.

6. *Ibid.*, p. 221.

7. Henry Pelling, *A Short History of the Labour Party*, p. 3.

8. Charles Mallet, *Herbert Gladstone*, pp. 192–3; *Echo*, Oct. 1901, cited by Lord Elton, *The Life of James Ramsay MacDonald* (1866–1919), pp. 109–10.

9. Morgan Phillips.

Chapter 17   THE NEW LIBERALISM 1906–1910

1. Blanche E. C. Dugdale, *Arthur James Balfour 1906–1930*, pp. 28–9; Kenneth Young, *Arthur James Balfour*, pp. 261–2.

2. Lord Elton, *The Life of James Ramsay MacDonald* (1866–1919), p. 133.

3. *Ibid.*, p. 147.

4. Balfour to the Marchioness of Salisbury, cited by Kenneth Young, *Arthur James Balfour*, p. 255: "What has occurred has nothing whatever to do with any of the things we have been squabbling over the last few years. Campbell-Bannerman is a mere cork, dancing on a torrent which he cannot control, and what is going on here is a faint echo of the same movement which has produced massacres in St. Petersburg, riots in Vienna and socialist processions in Berlin."

5. Balfour to Lord Knollys, 17th Jan. 1906, cited by Blanche E. C. Dugdale, *Arthur James Balfour 1906–1930*, p. 20.

6. Senator Lodge to Balfour, 28th Jan. 1906, cited by Dugdale, *op. cit.*, p. 21.

7. Hilaire Belloc and Cecil Chesterton, *The Party System*, published in 1911.

8. Winston S. Churchill, *The World Crisis 1911–1918*, ed. 1939, vol. 1, p. 24; George Wyndham speaking at Wigan appears to have been the first to coin, or at any rate use, the rhyming slogan. The story as seen from the angle of the First Lord of the Admiralty can be studied in Stephen McKenna, *Reginald McKenna*, pp. 51–69.

9. The words "in furtherance of a trade dispute" became significant in 1963 when the House of Lords, in the case of *Rookes* v. *Barnard*, ruled that a dispute between rival unions was not a trade dispute.

10. House of Commons, 24th June 1907, *Hansard*, Fourth Series, vol. 176, col. 909. The resolution was passed by 432 votes to 147 on 26th June after three days of debate.

11. Roy Jenkins, *Mr. Balfour's Poodle*, p. 37.

12. Blanche E. C. Dugdale, *Arthur James Balfour 1906–1930*, pp. 40–1.

13. House of Lords, 27th Nov. 1908, *Hansard*, Fourth Series, vol. 197, col. 896.

14. Roy Jenkins, *Mr. Balfour's Poodle*, p. 38.

15. *Ibid.*, pp. 40–5. The theory that Lloyd George deliberately framed the budget to provoke a quarrel with the peers is put forward by Malcolm Thomson, *David Lloyd George*, especially on p. 182, but it is not supported by evidence.

16. Lloyd George, House of Commons, 20th April 1909, *Hansard*, Fifth Series, vol. 4, col. 548; Balfour, *ibid.*, 3rd May, col. 773; Carson and Lansdowne, Jenkins, *op. cit.*, p. 48; Rosebery, Speech at Glasgow, 10th Sept. 1909; Lloyd George, Speech at the Edinburgh Castle, Limehouse, 30th July 1909 (*Slings and Arrows*, pp. 93–109); Duke of Beaufort, Jenkins, *op. cit.*, p. 56.

17. Sir Almeric Fitzroy, *Memoirs*, vol. 1, p. 389.

18. The Marquess of Crewe, in winding up the debate on second reading in the House of Lords on 30th Nov. 1909, assured the peers that they were not the victims of a ministerial plot as "the great majority of my colleagues, including—unless I am mistaken—the Chancellor of the Exchequer himself— have been infinitely more sanguine than I have been all through that your lordships would pass the Finance Bill", *Hansard*, Fifth Series, vol. 4, col. 1338; Lloyd George, Speech at the National Liberal Club, 3rd Dec. 1909.

19. Balfour to Lansdowne, 13th April 1906, cited by Lord Newton, *Lord Lansdowne*, p. 355.

20. Henry Chaplin had claimed that the House of Lords was the "watchdog" of the constitution, to which Lloyd George retorted: "You mean it is Mr. Balfour's poodle! It fetches and carries for him. It barks for him. It bites anybody that he sets it on to" (Frank Owen, *Tempestuous Journey*, p. 169).

21. Rosebery to Queen Victoria, 7th April 1894, Royal Archives, Windsor, A 70/22, cited by the Marquess of Crewe, *Lord Rosebery*, vol. 2, pp. 451–4.

Chapter 18 PARTIES AND THE CONSTITUTION 1910–1914

1. Asquith, Speech at Albert Hall, London, 10th Dec. 1909, J. A. Spender and Cyril Asquith, *Life of Lord Oxford and Asquith*, vol. 1, p. 268; *ibid.*, pp. 261–2, memorandum by Asquith's private secretary recording an interview with Lord Knollys: "The King regards the policy of the government as tantamount to the destruction of the House of Lords and he thinks that before a large creation of peers is embarked upon or threatened the country should be acquainted with the particular project for accomplishing such destruction as well as with the general line of action as to which the country will be consulted at the forthcoming elections."

2. Asquith, House of Commons, 3rd March 1910, *Hansard*, Fifth Series, vol. 14, col. 972. "Wait and see—a phrase first used as a threat by my husband in the House of Commons", *The Autobiography of Margot Asquith*, ed. 1962, p. 306. In 1916 it was used against him to support charges of dilatoriness in the prosecution of the war.

3. Asquith, House of Commons, 14th April 1910, *Hansard*, Fifth Series, vol. 16, col. 1548.

4. Royal Archives, Windsor, King George V's Diary, 18th May 1910; cited by Harold Nicolson, *King George the Fifth*, p. 131.

5. Roy Jenkins, *Mr. Balfour's Poodle*, pp. 101–9. The story has since been retold by Mr. Jenkins in *Asquith*, pp. 194–232.

6. David Lloyd George, *War Memoirs*, ed. 1938, vol. 1, pp. 20–3.

7. Viscount Chilston, *Chief Whip*, p. 345; Roy Jenkins, *Mr. Balfour's Poodle*, pp. 115, 116.

8. Harold Nicolson, *King George the Fifth*, p. 133.

9. Blanche E. C. Dugdale, *Arthur James Balfour 1906-1930*, pp. 62–3.

10. Royal Archives, Windsor, K 2552(1)/60; cited by Harold Nicolson, *King George the Fifth*, p. 136.

11. Sir Harold Nicolson, *King George the Fifth*, p. 137.

12. *Ibid.*, p. 135.

13. Royal Archives, Windsor, K.2552(2)93; Nicolson, *op. cit., p.* 129n.

14. Royal Archives, Windsor, King George V's Diary, 16th Nov. 1910; Nicolson, *op. cit.*, p. 138.

15. Lloyd George, Speech at Mile End, 21st Nov. 1910; Balfour, Speech at Albert Hall, London, 29th Nov. 1910; Sir Charles Petrie, *The Life and Letters of the Right Hon. Sir Austen Chamberlain*, vol. 1, pp. 269, 272.

16. *Journals and Letters of Reginald, Viscount Esher*, vol. 3, p. 41; Spender and Asquith, *Life of Lord Oxford and Asquith*, vol. 1, p. 306.

17. A. Wilson Fox, *The Earl of Halsbury*, p. 232; Lansdowne, House of Lords, 20th July 1911, *Hansard*, Fifth Series, vol. 9, col. 585.

18. But on another occasion Wyndham said: "He is a fool, for he might have been the next Prime Minister" (John Biggs-Davidson, *George Wyndham: A Study in Toryism*, p. 208).

19. Lord Newton, *Lord Lansdowne*, p. 423; Blanche E. C. Dugdale, *Arthur James Balfour 1906-1930*, pp. 69–70.

20. A. Wilson Fox, *The Earl of Halsbury*, p. 258.

21. Morley, House of Lords, 10th Aug. 1911, *Hansard*, Fifth Series, vol. 9, col. 999.

22. Blanche E. C. Dugdale, *Arthur James Balfour 1906-1930*, pp. 83–92.

23. Sir Charles Petrie, *The Life and Letters of the Right Hon. Sir Austen Chamberlain*, vol. 1, p. 295.

24. The best accounts of the events by which the Unionist party obtained a new leader may be found in Sir Charles Petrie, *The Life and Letters of the Right Hon. Sir Austen Chamberlain*, vol. 1, pp. 290–311; the same author's *Walter Long and his Times*, pp. 165–73; and Robert Blake, *The Unknown Prime Minister*, pp. 71–86.

25. Robert Blake, *op. cit.*, p. 86.

26. Lansdowne, Speech at Albert Hall, London, 14th Nov. 1912; Bonar Law, Speech at Ashton-under-Lyne, 16th Dec. 1912.

27. *The Times*, 16th, 23rd, 30th Jan. 1911.

28. Sir Alexander Acland-Hood, Speech at Taunton, 26th Jan. 1911 (*The Times*, 27th Jan.).

29. Bonar Law Papers 41. I. 2, cited in Robert Blake, *The Unknown Prime Minister*, pp. 99–100.

30. Bonar Law, Speech at Belfast, 9th April 1912; Asquith and Law, House of Commons, 11th April 1912, *Hansard*, Fifth Series, vol. 36, col. 1425.

31. Austen Chamberlain, Speech at West Bromwich, Sir Charles Petrie, *The Life and Letters of the Right Hon. Sir Austen Chamberlain*, vol. 1, p. 319.

32. It was this declaration that provoked G. K. Chesterton to write his satirical poem beginning, "Are they clinging to their crosses, F. E. Smith."

33. Robert Blake, *The Unknown Prime Minister*, p. 130.

34. Austen Chamberlain, *Politics from the Inside*, pp. 486–7.

35. The rough draft of this memorandum has survived among the Bonar Law Papers (39.E.6) and is reproduced by Robert Blake, *The Unknown Prime Minister*, p. 151.

36. Bonar Law to Carson, 18th Sept., 1913, Bonar Law Papers 33.5.57, cited by Robert Blake, *The Unknown Prime Minister*, p. 156.

37. Bonar Law To Stamfordham, 26th Jan. 1914, Bonar Law Papers 34.1.16, cited by Robert Blake, *The Unknown Prime Minister*, p. 169.

38. Robert Blake, *The Unknown Prime Minister*, p. 174.

39. There is a good recent study by Sir James Ferguson, *The Curragh Incident*.

Chapter 19   WAR AND COALITION 1914–1918

1. Robert Blake, *The Unknown Prime Minister*, p. 222.

2. Earl of Oxford and Asquith, *Memories and Reflections*, vol. 2, p. 33.

3. Robert Blake, *The Unknown Prime Minister*, p. 243.

4. That the exclusion was deliberate is shown by a paper of Asquith's in the Bodleian Library with the statement "This was intended to prevent B. Law taking either the office of Munitions or the Exchequer". (MS. Asquith 27 f. 216.) These words were omitted when the paper was reproduced by Spender and Asquith, *Life of Lord Oxford and Asquith*, vol. 2, p. 171, but are given by Robert Blake, *The Unknown Prime Minister*, p. 251, with "either" transposed.

5. The party system has the defects of its virtues, and in all its long history there is perhaps no more deplorable example of party spirit triumphing over national interests than the campaign against Haldane. His incomparable achievements in seeing that the British army was ready for war on the continent, and his dignified acceptance of the vendetta against him, can be studied in his *Autobiography*, pp. 183–209, 275–88.

6. Robert Blake's statement, *The Unknown Prime Minister*, p. 289, on the authority of the late Lord Beaverbrook, that Bonar Law was told to wait while Asquith finished a hand of bridge was challenged by Lady Violet Bonham Carter in *The Times*, and her objections are stated by Mr. Blake in the later impressions of his book. See Lady Violet Bonham Carter, *The Times*, 9th Jan. 1956, Mr. Robert Blake, *ibid.*, 13th Jan. 1956, and subsequent correspondence.

7. Lord Beaverbrook, *Politicians and the War*, is an important source for the events leading to the formation of the coalition in which, as Max Aitken, he played no small part. Asquith gave his own account in *Memories and Reflections* and Lloyd George in his *War Memoirs*, while Bonar Law's part can be studied in Mr. Blake's biography, which also gives an excellent conspectus of the whole evidence. Mr. Roy Jenkins's fine new biography, *Asquith*, is also now available, but was not published in time for me to consult it. In making Lloyd George the villain of "a palace revolution", I do not think he does justice to the necessity of getting a more vigorous grip on the prosecution of the war if it was to be won. The solution proposed, that Asquith should remain Prime Minister while leaving the effective control of war operations to Lloyd George, was an honourable one which Asquith was ill-advised not to accept.

8. David Lloyd George, *War Memoirs*, ed. 1938, vol. 1, p. 588.

9. Lord Beaverbrook, *Politicians and the War*, ed. 1960, p. 413.

10. *The History of The Times*, vol. 4, pt. 1, p. 297.

11. Bonar Law to Asquith, 5th Dec. 1916, MS. Asquith 31 f. 43, cited in Spender and Asquith, *Life of Lord Oxford and Asquith*, vol. 2, p. 271.

12. Robert Blake, *The Unknown Prime Minister*, p. 338.

13. Spender and Asquith, *Life of Lord Oxford and Asquith*, vol. 2, p. 278.

14. Frank Owen, *Tempestuous Journey*, p. 353.

15. *Ibid.*, p. 413.

16. *Ibid.*, p. 377.

17. Robert Blake, *The Unknown Prime Minister*, p. 385.

18. *Ibid.*, pp. 387–8.

19. *Ibid.*, p. 388.

20. Frank Owen, *Tempestuous Journey*, p. 501.

Chapter 20   COALITION CONTINUED 1918–1922

1. Lord Beaverbrook, *The Decline and Fall of Lloyd George*, p. 20. This work is as important a source for the history of the post-war coalition as *Politicians and the War* is for its formation.

2. It was disputed until recently whether Baldwin or Keynes was the author of this cutting description, but an article by Kingsley Martin in *Encounter*, Feb. 1965, p. 83, quoting from a letter sent to him by Keynes in 1941, establishes Baldwin's title. See note *a* to this chapter.

3. G. D. H. Cole, *A History of the Labour Party from 1914*, p. 71.

4. *Ibid.*, p. 62.

5. House of Commons, 16th April 1919, *Hansard*, Fifth Series, vol. 114 col. 2953; Frank Owen, *Tempestuous Journey*, p. 542.

6. Lord Beaverbrook, *The Decline and Fall of Lloyd George*, p. 9, n.

7. *Ibid.*, p. 10.

8. G. D. H. Cole, *A History of the Labour Party from 1914*, pp. 102–3.

9. *Ibid.*, pp. 112–13.

10. Sir Charles Petrie, *The Life and Letters of the Right Hon. Sir Austen Chamberlain*, vol. 2, p. 157.

11. *Ibid.*, vol. 2, p. 159.

12. The title he gave to Chapter 4 of *The Decline and Fall of Lloyd George*.

13. *Ibid.*

14. Sir Charles Petrie, *The Life and Letters of the Right Hon. Sir Austen Chamberlain*, vol. 2, p. 153.

15. Lord Beaverbrook, *The Decline and Fall of Lloyd George*, p. 89; M. J. Macmanus, *Eamon De Valera*, pp. 129–30. The full story of the negotiations is well told by Frank Pakenham, *Peace by Ordeal*.

16. Lord Beaverbrook, *The Decline and Fall of Lloyd George*, p. 101. The 2nd Earl of Birkenhead in *The Life of F. E. Smith*, ed. 1959, p. 371, has finely portrayed the courage and statesmanship shown by his father at this time: "With his eyes open he had imperilled his position in the Unionist party, and laid himself wide open to the odious charge of treachery to a trust . . . He more than any other minister, stood to gain from stultifying a settlement, and more to lose by advocating it. So many bitter and unjust words were lavished at the time upon his 'apostasy' that it is necessary to say now that at this great moment he took a decision which he believed to be right, knowing that it was directly at variance with his own interests and destructive to many old and valued friendships. It is necessary also to say that he never swerved from this decision, and that once he had cast himself as the advocate of negotiations he remained throughout them the most resolute Unionist delegate, no mere sorcerer's apprentice to Lloyd George, but the man who most won the liking and confidence of Griffith and Collins and entered most deeply into their hearts and minds."

17. Stanley Salvidge, *Salvidge of Liverpool*, pp. 205–13; 2nd Earl of Birkenhead, *The Life of F. E. Smith*, ed. 1959, pp. 379–81.

18. Collins replied "I may have signed my actual death-warrant" (2nd Earl of Birkenhead, *op. cit.*, p. 388); eight months later he was shot dead.

19. Robert Blake, *The Unknown Prime Minister*, p. 436.

20. Lloyd George to Austen Chamberlain, 10th Jan. 1922, cited by Lord Beaverbrook, *The Decline and Fall of Lloyd George*, pp. 290–1.

21. Lord Beaverbrook, *The Decline and Fall of Lloyd George*, pp. 134–5. "He was practising deceit," says Lord Beaverbrook, "the election project was his own brain-child."

22. According to H. J. Hanham, *Elections and Party Management*, p. 375: "The sale of honours was begun by the Liberals when in 1891 the Liberal chief whip prevailed upon Mr. Gladstone to exchange a promise of peerages to two insignificant but wealthy men for substantial contributions to the Liberal party funds."

23. The subject may be studied in Gerald Macmillan, *Honours for Sale: The Strange Story of Maundy Gregory*.

24. L. S. Amery, *My Political Life*, vol. 2, p. 233.

25. *The Times*, 7th Oct. 1922.

26. Robert Blake, *The Unknown Prime Minister*, p. 451.

27. Lord Beaverbrook, *The Decline and Fall of Lloyd George*, pp. 197–9.

28. *Gleanings and Memoranda*, Nov. 1922.

Chapter 21 UNIONIST INTERLUDE 1922–1923

1. R. T. McKenzie, *British Political Parties*, ed. 1963, p. 36.

2. Robert Blake, *The Unknown Prime Minister*, p. 460.

3. Maynard Keynes, *Essays in Biography*, pp. 42–7.

4. Sir Charles Petrie, *The Life and Letters of the Right Hon. Sir Austen Chamberlain*, vol. 2, p. 206.

5. David Lloyd George, *War Memoirs*, ed. 1938, vol. 1, pp. 811, 642.

6. Sir Charles Petrie, *The Life and Letters of the Right Hon. Sir Austen Chamberlain*, vol. 2, p. 207.

7. Robert Blake, *The Unknown Prime Minister*, p. 462; 2nd Earl of Birkenhead, *The Life of F. E. Smith*, ed. 1959, p. 452 (Lord Birkenhead points out that the "second-class brains" did include three fellows of All Souls), p. 454.

8. The manifesto issued by Bonar Law on 4th Nov. declared: "The crying need of the nation at this moment—a need which in my judgement far exceeds any other—is that we should have tranquillity and stability both at home and abroad so that free scope should be given to the initiative and enterprise of our citizens, for it is in that way far more than by any action of the government that we can hope to recover from the economic and social results of the war." Lady Violet Bonham Carter commented in a speech in her father's constituency, Paisley, that whereas Lloyd George's government had suffered from St. Vitus's dance, Bonar Law's was suffering from sleeping sickness.

9. Lord Beaverbrook, *The Decline and Fall of Lloyd George*, pp. 211–12; L. S. Amery, *My Political Life*, vol. 2, pp. 241–2; Robert Blake, *The Unknown Prime Minister*, p. 468.

10. Lord Beaverbrook, *The Decline and Fall of Lloyd George*, p. 215.

11. Margot Asquith to Bonar Law, Bonar Law Papers, 108.1.23, cited by Robert Blake, *The Unknown Prime Minister*, p. 465.

12. G. D. H. Cole, *A History of the Labour Party from 1914*, p. 126.

13. Winston S. Churchill, "Election Memories", *Thoughts and Adventures*, p. 213; Colin R. Coote, *Sir Winston Churchill: A Self-Portrait*, p. 44.

14. H. H. A(squith), *Letters of the Earl of Oxford and Asquith to a Friend*, vol. 2, p. 37.

15. But he was not prepared to confine the Liberals to four or five seats on the opposition front bench as desired by the Labour party, see below. Even so, Asquith—who had been Prime Minister for so many years—had a daily hard battle to preserve his few inches of space when the Labour leader took his seat (L. MacNeill Weir, *The Tragedy of Ramsay MacDonald*, pp. 110–11).

16. Sir George Younger to Bonar Law, 15th Jan. 1923, cited by Lord Beaverbrook, *The Decline and Fall of Lloyd George*, p. 298.

17. Bonar Law to Lord Fitzalan of Derwent, cited by Lord Beaverbrook, *The Decline and Fall of Lloyd George*, pp. 298–9.

18. L. MacNeill Weir, *The Tragedy of Ramsay MacDonald*, pp. 104-11.

19. Writing in 1963, Shinwell was still of opinion that "the only possible choice was MacDonald" and that if Clynes had been elected—as he well might have been if a score of members, mostly of the old guard, had not been absent—"the party would have had a totally unsuitable leader of the opposition who would in a little more than a year become Prime Minister" (*The Labour Story*, pp. 112-13).

20. L. MacNeill Weir, *The Tragedy of Ramsay MacDonald*, p. 109; Emmanuel Shinwell, *The Labour Story*, p. 113; Hugh Dalton, *Call Back Yesterday*, p. 191; Viscount Snowden, *An Autobiography*, vol. 2, p. 574. Clynes himself gives no figure.

21. An account of the meeting is given by one of them, David Kirkwood, *My Life of Revolt*, pp. 194-8, and he says of the Clydesiders: "We had no doubt. We were Ramsay MacDonald's men . . . When the votes were counted, MacDonald was elected by a narrow majority. The Clyde men had supported him solidly. His majority was less than the number of their votes." They had their first disappointment in MacDonald that evening when he did not turn up to what was intended to be a great demonstration of welcome to their new leader. "Clynes gallantly took his place, and made a magnificent speech, ringing with loyalty and unity. That night he rose very high in our estimation."

22. He gave a brief and objective account of the election in his *Memoirs 1869-1924*, pp. 330-3, and merely commented: "Since that time Ramsay MacDonald has struck such a blow at British Labour as will never be forgotten, though it will be survived. It is possible that, had I been able to see into the future, I might have taken another line of action in 1922 which would have deprived him of the power to strike that blow. I was not in the least troubled by my defeat at the time, but when, later, I learned of the complicated plans and schemes made for my defeat, I confess feeling that some of my colleagues had been ungrateful as well as disloyal, in face of the two previous years of work which had been so successful in securing Labour's return as the official opposition."

23. *The Times*, 14th Dec. 1923.

24. Mr. R. T. McKenzie, *British Political Parties*, ed. 1963, p. 307, regards the motion of confidence passed by the joint body, endorsed later in the day by the executive committee of the parliamentary party, as the seizing of an "opportunity to demonstrate that he had every right to claim to be the leader of the Labour movement as a whole". This is going rather beyond the words of the resolution, but Mr. McKenzie's whole section on the evolution from chairman to leader may be read with advantage.

25. "A truly remarkable case of collective amnesia", the Earl of Ronaldshay, *The Life of Lord Curzon*, vol. 3, p. 330.

26. Winston S. Churchill, *Great Contemporaries*, p. 287, There seems no reason to doubt this charming story though it is not given by either of Balfour's biographers.

27. Robert Blake, *The Unknown Prime Minister*, pp. 520-5. The memorandum by Waterhouse which he reproduces on pp. 520-1 is catalogued in the Royal Archives, Windsor, as K.1853.5.

28. Harold Nicolson, *Curzon, The Last Phase*, p. 355.

29. Winston S. Churchill, *The Second World War*, vol. 1, p. 26.

30. G. M. Young, *Stanley Baldwin*, p. 71.

31. *Ibid.*, p. 65.

32. *Ibid.*, p. 66; "The Plymouth Policy", Supplement to *Gleanings and Memoranda*, Dec. 1923.

33. Robert Blake, *The Unknown Prime Minister*, p. 531.

34. A memorandum which he wrote on 22nd Oct. 1923 for Baldwin is reproduced by Randolph S. Churchill, *Lord Derby*, pp. 523–4. Mr. Churchill says: "All this was most painful for Derby. He was no doctrinaire in these matters. But his knowledge of Lancashire and Lancashire interests was even more profound and intimate now than it had been in 1912 when he had prevented Bonar Law and Max Aitken from re-saddling the Tory party with the incubus of food taxes. He was convinced that protection, and, above all, food taxes would be disastrous for the party."

35. Stanley Salvidge, *Salvidge of Liverpool*, p. 254.

36. Edward Wood to Baldwin, 8th Nov. 1923, cited by G. M. Young, *Stanley Baldwin*, p. 66.

37. Rectorial address, Glasgow University, 7th Nov. 1923.

38. Charles McCurdy to Lloyd George, 12th Oct. 1923, cited by Frank Owen, *Tempestuous Journey*, p. 672.

39. L. S. Amery, *My Political Life*, vol. 2, p. 280.

40. Frank Owen, *Tempestuous Journey*, p. 674.

41. Gilbert Keith Chesterton, *Poems*, ed. 1926, p. 120, "The Secret People".

42. Ramsay MacDonald, Speech at Colston Hall, Bristol, 20th Nov. 1923, *Western Daily Press*, 21st Nov.; L. MacNeill Weir, *The Tragedy of Ramsay MacDonald*, pp. 127–8.

ADDITIONAL NOTES TO THE SECOND EDITION

Chapter 1   ORIGIN OF PARTY 1640–1689

a. One side of the story can be studied in detail in J. R. Jones, *The First Whigs: The Politics of the Exclusion Crisis 1678–1683*. Mr. Jones notes that "the defeat of the first Whigs, who were essentially a parliamentary party, was due primarily to the superior power of the royal prerogative. Their domination of successive parliaments proved to be inadequate because Parliament was still not an essential part of the government of the country. . . . By making it obligatory for the King to rule with the assistance of Parliament, the Revolution changed the structure of politics and the circumstances under which they were to be conducted in future" (*op. cit.*, p. 211).

Mr Jones rightly maintains against Mr Carswell that the first Whigs are entitled to be called a party. "In rejecting the right of the first Whigs to the title of 'party', John Carswell, *The Old Cause*, [p.] 2, stipulates as a test: 'there will be a directing committee, membership cards, a programme, a platform, a leader'. With the exception of the cards, hardly an essential, the first Whigs had all these qualifications" (*ibid.*, p. 212 n.)

As Mr Jones notes (*ibid.*, p. 216 n. 1), none of the biographies of Shaftesbury is really satisfactory, certainly not from the point of view of the history of party. The standard life is still perhaps that of W. D. Christie, *A Life of Anthony Ashley Cooper, First Earl of Shaftesbury 1621–1683*, ed. 1871, the most recent that of L. F. Brown, *The First Earl of Shaftesbury*, ed. 1933.

b. Falkland's speech was delivered on the "root and branch bill" for the total abolition of episcopacy, either on 27th May 1641 on second reading or on some subsequent day when the bill was in committee. (So Samuel R. Gardiner in the *Dictionary of National Biography*, and this is reasonable, though J. A. R. Marriott, *The Life and Times of Lucius Cary Viscount Falkland*, p. 197 n. 2, says he "can find no positive evidence of this".) It was not included in the first edition of Falkland's *A Discourse of Infallibility* edited in 1651 by his chaplain, Thomas Triplett, later Prebendary of Westminster, but was printed in the second edition, 1660, as "a draught of a Speech concerning Episcopacy by the lord Viscount Falkland found since his death amongst his papers, written with his own hand". As we have here an early statement of the Conservative position which has never failed to attract, and which marks the real Conservative temperament better perhaps than anything else, it may be as well to set out the actual words in their context as given by Triplett: "I now proceed. And my first inconvenience of this change, is the inconvenience of change it self, which is so great an inconvenience, when the Change is great and suddain, that in such cases, when it is not necessary to change, it is necessary not to change" (Lucius

X

Cary, Viscount Falkland, *A Discourse of Infallibility*, ed. *1660*, p. 3; see also
J. A. R. Marriott, *op. cit.*, pp. 199–200).

Chapter 2   PARTY MINISTRIES 1689–1714

a. By applying to the reign of Queen Anne the Namierian methods of
analysis developed for the early years of George III Robert Walcott, *English
Politics in the Early Eighteenth Century*, ed. *1956*, came to the conclusion that
there were then no parties in the true sense but only factions. "If a careful
analysis reveals not two parties but numerous party groups, if it shows that
the ministries of this period were inevitably coalitions of several party groups
and that there are no examples of a single party in office faced by a single
opposition party, then surely the traditional interpretation of how the
constitution worked in this period needs revising" (p. 4). "If neither the
Whigs nor the Tories were effectively organized as national parties, there
could hardly have been a 'two-party system' in the usual sense" (p. 5).
"The process by which the Godolphin ministry changed from a Court-
Churchill-Harley-Rochester-Nottingham coalition into a Court-Churchill-
Newcastle-Junto combination is a logical one, if one recognizes that the
architects of governments and of parliamentary majorities worked within
a multi-party framework. This assumption often fits the facts far better than
the two-party interpretation; but the party history of the period 1688–1714
has been explained so universally in terms of 'Whig' and 'Tory' exclusively,
that the many similarities between it and the later eighteenth century
political structure have been commonly overlooked. The more one studies
the party structure under William and Anne, the less it resembles the two-
party system described by Trevelyan in his Romanes Lecture and the more it
seems to have in common with the structure of politics in the age of Newcastle as explained to us by Namier" (p. 160).

Professor Walcott's view has recently received an effective answer—and
Sir Keith Feiling, *A History of the Tory Party 1640–1714* has to that extent
been vindicated—in J. H. Plumb, *The Growth of Political Stability in England
1675–1725*. Among many relevant passages may be specially cited: "The
confusion, the complexity of politics in this period does not derive, as
Walcott would have us believe, from the absence of a two-party system,
but from the failure of either party to secure effective domination over the
other, a situation that was further complicated by the needs of two great
wars. Coalitions were forced on both parties by circumstances; principles at
times were moderated by events; and, of course, there were desertions and
conversions, loss of nerve and beady-eyed compromise—all of which factors
help to create a sense of confusion at the centre. At least for historians;
contemporaries were less distracted and they rarely had difficulty, at least
after the middle 1690s, in distinguishing Whig from Tory. When lists of members of the 1713 and 1715 Parliaments were drawn up, probably for the en-
lightenment of George I's Hanoverian ministers, the compiler had no hesitation in dividing the majority of the House of Commons quite simply into
Whigs and Tories. And to politicians of these two reigns, Whigs and Tories
were as discernible as day or night" (pp. 130–1).

Professor Plumb's reference in the penultimate sentence quoted is to the
Worsley MS. in the Lincoln Record Office, *Liste Exact du Dernier Parlement*

et du Celuyci avec de Remarques. This fascinating paper, partly cited by Plumb, *op. cit.*, pp. 190–4, and to be published in full by Mr. Romney Sedgwick in the *History of Parliament*, lists every member as Whig or Tory, distinguishing those Whigs who occasionally voted Tory and the larger number of Tories ("Whimsicals") who occasionally voted Whig.

One of the interesting points made by Professor Plumb in this important work is that more general elections, and more contests at these elections, took place between 1689 and 1715 than for the rest of the eighteenth century, and they always left the "committed Junto Whigs" in a minority in the House of Commons (pp. 136–7). This forced the Whigs into unity. The Tories were more riven by faction, but were nevertheless clearly recognizable as a party.

Chapter 3 THE WHIG OLIGARCHY 1714–1761

a. It is now usual to regard the ascription of the growth of the Cabinet system to George I's ignorance of the English language and consequent withdrawal from the Cabinet as a myth. It was accepted by Basil Williams, *The Whig Supremacy 1714–60*, ed. 1939, pp. 35–40, but C. N. Stuart in his notes for the second edition, 1961, published after that author's death, describes it as "traditional" (*The Whig Supremacy 1714–60*, ed. 1961, p. 38 *n.* 1) and "old-fashioned" (*ibid.*, p. 40 *n.* 1). The contemporary view derives from an essay by L. B. Namier in the *Manchester Guardian* 11th Jan. 1937, reprinted as "The End of the Nominal Cabinet" in his collection *In the Margin of History*, ed. 1939, pp. 105–14. Namier says "the story which ascribes the King's withdrawal from the Cabinet to an accident—George I's ignorance and George II's imperfect knowledge of English—is a crude and, by now, exploded legend" (*op. cit.*, p. 106). Prof. J. H. Plumb, *Sir Robert Walpole*, vol. i. p. 71, claims that "George I possessed more than a smattering of English, and all his ministers, including Walpole, had a fair or fluent knowledge of French, the language used naturally by the King" (see also, pp. 202–3). Namier does not make so strong a linguistic claim, but says that "the thirteen years of George I's reign would not have wrought such a change if deeper forces had not been at work, one of them being the gradual transference of the real business of the Cabinet to a new body" (*op. cit.*, p. 106). He proceeds to distinguish between the "nominal Cabinet", composed largely of the great officers of state, and the "efficient Cabinet" consisting of those ministers who had the discharge of current business in their hands. From the "nominal Cabinet" the King never completely withdrew, but "that Cabinet itself gradually faded away, till it sank into an anonymous grave", while the "efficient Cabinet", which the King never attended, grew in importance and is the real ancestor of the modern Cabinet.

This phenomenon—the rise of an inner Cabinet which eventually became the only Cabinet—deserves all the emphasis that Namier places upon it, but the question with which we are concerned is only pushed one stage farther back. Why did George I never attend the "efficient Cabinet"? One reason must surely have been the barrier of language. Let it be granted that he had more English—and his ministers more French—than has hitherto been allowed, but he would nevertheless have found a meeting of the "efficient Cabinet" irksome, while it must certainly have been easier and speedier for his ministers to transact business without the necessity of explaining every detail to him, whether in English or in French. The defects of his English, along with his "ignorance and stupidity", must be reckoned a factor in the development of an inner Cabinet which he did not attend, with all the consequences noted in the text.

The distinction between the "nominal Cabinet" and the "efficient Cabinet" is not the same as that between the "Cabinet" and the "lords of the committee" which existed in the reign of Anne and survived until 1717. For this, see J. H. Plumb, "The Cabinet in the Reign of Queen Anne", *Transactions of the Royal Historical Society*, Fifth Series, vol. 7, 1957, pp. 137–57.

To the above references must now be added as these notes are in proof J. H. Plumb, *The Growth of Political Stability in England 1675–1725*, ed. 1967, especially p. 107. While conceding that "Here was no withdrawal by the monarchy from politics, no sudden growth of political stability at the centre through the King's inability to speak the language of his country or understand its customs," I cannot agree that "the character of the King and his alleged withdrawal from business may be dismissed as irrelevant as a factor in constitutional and political development after 1714" or that "language was no barrier". This is against common sense. Professor Plumb seems to me to take too seriously Horace Walpole's good story that George I and Walpole could converse only in dog-Latin. To demolish this story is not to establish that the King and his minister found conversation easy.

b. Basil Williams's brilliant study, *Carteret and Newcastle: A Contrast in Contemporaries*, based on his Ford lectures at Oxford in 1921 but not published until 1943, is now again available in a new impression (1966). He makes a point very relevant to the theme of this book. "Carteret never lacked a policy, but could never command a party to carry it through: Newcastle, until the Patriot King found out the secret of his power and turned it against him, had always a party bound to him by self-interest, but never a policy on which to exercise the formidable instrument he had forged. For twenty years and more the two men, one with the grandiose ideas and the touch of genius, the other with the pedestrian talent, were rivals: and the victory at last rested, not with the brilliant statesman, but with the industrious politician, who, to make his triumph quite complete, swept his rival within his net". (pp. 2–3). The same author's lives of Stanhope and Chatham complete a trilogy that is invaluable for the study of the period. (Basil Williams, *Stanhope: A Study in Eighteenth Century War and Diplomacy*, ed. 1932, and *The Life of William Pitt, Earl of Chatham*, ed. 1913, reissued 1966.)

Chapter 4   YEARS OF CONFUSION 1761–1782

a. Professor Archibald S. Foord dates the formal beginning of the Rockinghamite party to the establishment of a regular dining club on 23rd Dec. 1762. "The party chiefs began meetings on 2 Dec. 1762 to plan their opposition to the preliminaries of peace (Add. MSS. 33000, f. 200). Not until Fox's 'thorough rout' was well under way could the 'young Whigs' persuade the old to consent to an organization which had the appearance of formed general opposition" (*His Majesty's Opposition 1714–1830*, p. 31 and *n.* 4).

Chapter 5   RE-FORMATION OF PARTIES 1761–1807

a. It is the view of Professor Archibald S. Foord that the two-party system of the nineteenth century had its origins in the reorganization of Court parties cast into opposition, in particular that of the Rockinghamites in 1762 and that of the Pittites in 1806. "The ouster of Newcastle and his most loyal colleagues [*i.e.* King George III] turned the opposition in a new direction. More deeply injured even than the haughty dispossessed of 1733, they assumed the tactical heritage of the oppositions they had so long decried and the ideological heritage of the Whig myth which for so long had sustained their morale in office. Their failure to recapture their predominant position at Court drove the Rockinghamites to lay the foundation of an enduring party, whose undisguised intent was to storm the closet *malgré le roi*. George III frustrated them after their brief triumphs in 1782–3, but the party survived, as earlier parties had not, because it was supported by institutions which outlived both failure and success.

"The Pittites, who professed to despise party and a formed systematic opposition, came ultimately to adopt the constitutional views of the Foxites. The summer of 1806, when Pitt's followers reached a common agreement to resist the allurements of Grenville, marks the commencement of the two-party system in its nineteenth-century form. The second party came into existence in the same fashion as the first: the dispossessed leaders of a Court party, regarding themselves as the true friends of the monarchy, formed a union for the purpose of restoring themselves to office" (*His Majesty's Opposition 1714–1830*, p. 469).

Though the view taken in this book is that there is no point later than the reign of Charles II at which the party system can truly be said to have begun, it may readily be conceded that the movement into opposition of the Rockinghamites in 1762 and the Pittites in 1806 marked decisive stages in the continuous evolution of the system.

Chapter 6   THE TORIES ENTRENCHED 1807–1830

a. These qualities can now again be readily studied in W. R. Brock, *Lord Liverpool and Tory Liberalism 1820 to 1827*, ed. 1967, at least for the later and more liberal phase of his career. In this Thirlwall Prize essay, first published in a small edition in 1939, Mr. Brock takes the view that "Liverpool as much as Canning was responsible for the experiment of Liberal Toryism. Within the Cabinet Liverpool was the mainstay of 'liberal' opinion, he was perhaps the only man who could persuade the Tory party as a whole to sanction such opinions, and he was certainly the only man who could hold together the Cabinet between 1822 and 1827" (p. 3).

b. Since the first edition of this book was prepared there have been new lives of Addington, Castlereagh and Canning, which, even if they do not draw upon new material, are valuable for the portraits they paint—Philip Ziegler, *Addington: A Life of Henry Addington, First Viscount Sidmouth* (1965), C. J. Bartlett, *Castlereagh* (1966), and P. J. V. Rolo, *George Canning* (1965). Mr. Ziegler's fair summing up of his subject's repressive administration after Waterloo is: "Sidmouth, as Home Secretary, did little to alleviate the lot of the poor and distressed. His measures to repress the discontent which followed were harsh, viewed in retrospect unnecessarily harsh. He may be accused of short-sightedness and lack of imagination. But with all this it cannot be denied that he, personally, was kind, tolerant and scrupulously fair. Though there was much to criticize in his laws, his execution of them was admirable in its temperance and humanity" (op. cit., p. 355).

Mr. Bartlett is unable to deny that Castlereagh was an obstacle to necessary domestic reforms, and that his ideas of foreign policy made him the supporter of tyranny abroad, but he questions "the old description of Castlereagh as the driving force of Ultra-Toryism" (op. cit., p. 269). (The extreme Tories, opposed to parliamentary reform and other forms of change, in the first third of the nineteenth century were designated the Ultra-Tories, commonly abbreviated to Ultras.) He was, in Mr. Bartlett's view, too pragmatic and flexible to be reckoned an Ultra. "Castlereagh thus falls far short of the arch-villain, the arch-tyrant, conjured up in the overheated minds of radical young poets" (p. 272).

What is undeniable is that both men left with the Tory party a reputation for reaction, whether fully deserved or not, which it took a long time to eliminate..

In the three studies which make up his George Canning Mr. Rolo accepts the modern toning down of the contrast between Castlereagh and Canning and sees in him the first statesman to appreciate that public opinion was not confined to Westminster. This makes him one of the architects of the party system, even though he did much to confuse the lines of party division.

Mr Rolo perhaps goes too far in saying: "In spite of party loyalties there were no real political parties in the late eighteenth and early nineteenth centuries. There were political groups held together more or less closely and for long or short terms by identity of interest, by personalities, by common enmity as by principle. All governments were coalition governments" (p. 59). It is hard to deny that in the strictest sense, apart from the absence of extra-parliamentary organization, there were parties from 1807; and even today the Conservative and Labour parties are in a real sense coalitions.

Chapter 7   REFORM, CONSERVATIVES AND LIBERALS 1830–1841

a. Mr. George Kitson Clark's brilliant study Peel and the Conservative Party: A Study in Party Politics 1832–1841, which was published in 1929, and is indispensable for the study of the period, is now again available in a second edition, 1964, with a new introduction by its author. In it he emphasizes the decisive character of the Duke of Wellington's resignation as Prime Minister in 1830. The Duke resigned because the King's government, though it was still in full enjoyment of the King's favour, was defeated in the House of Commons. This had happened before, in 1782 when North had to go, and in 1783 when Shelburne was driven out of office. But in 1783 the King's position was recovered. After November 1830 there was to be no recovery, as was shown when William IV tried in the Reform crisis and in 1834. The Whig government survived, "partly by virtue of the support for the principles for which they had come to stand and partly through the agency of their own party organization, but not at all because they enjoyed the King's favour" (op. cit., ed. 1964, p. xviii). But the two-party system as we have known it in modern times might not have developed "if it had not been for the fact that the Reform Bill crisis also produced an opposition party more permanently and extensively organized than the family groups, casual alliances and ephemeral agitations which had been the instruments of the opposition to the Crown before 1830" (ibid., pp. xviii–xix). In this development Peel played a fundamental but paradoxical rôle. Though he and his colleagues were party leaders, they had not been educated in the business of faction but in the business of government. This paradox, which Mr. Kitson Clark so perceptively analyses, explains much that is otherwise puzzling in the actions of Peel—"the strong conscientious ex-minister, for whom other men organized a party which he reluctantly led"—notably his carrying of measures which he had been put in power to oppose. Though the first of the modern party leaders, he always conceived himself, whether in office or in opposition, as carrying on his Sovereign's government.

b. The best account of the Chartists until 1842 is still Mark Hovell, The Chartist Movement, first published in 1918, but re-issued in a third edition in 1966 with a bibliographical note giving reference to recent literature. This includes Asa Briggs, "Chartism reconsidered", Historical Studies: Papers read before the Third Conference of Irish Historians, 1959, pp. 42–59; Asa Briggs, "National Bearings", Chartist Studies, 1959, pp. 42–59; and F. S. Mather, Chartism: the present position of historical studies", Britain and the Netherlands, ed. J. S. Bromley and E. H. Kossman, 1964, vol. 2, pp. 181–204. After 1842 Hovell's work becomes more sketchy. J. L. Hammond and Barbara Hammond, The Age of the Chartists, though now censured by many historians as over-drawn, gives a vivid picture of the movement.

There had been previous alarms before the Chartist Movement. In 1833 Robert Owen, industrialist and philanthropist, started the Grand National Consolidated Trades Union. The membership was soon said to have reached a quarter of a million. Its policy was defined as "to establish for the productive classes a complete dominion over the fruits of their own industry", and its aim was a general strike which would enable the manual workers to take over every type of agricultural and industrial enterprise. At Tolpuddle in Dorset the wages of agricultural workers were cut to eight, then seven shillings, a week, with a threat of a further reduction to six. One of them, George Loveless, made soundings about the desirability of founding a local branch of the Grand National Consolidated Trades Union. In the end two delegates from a trade society helped them to found a "friendly society" of their own. The rules stated "that the object of this society can never be promoted by any acts of violence", but they adopted a secret ceremony of initiation, which exposed them to the rigours of the courts against unlawful combination and conspiracy. On 24th February 1834 all six founder members (George Loveless and his brother James, Thomas Stanfield and his son John, James Hammett and James Brine, all of them Methodists save one) were sentenced by the Dorchester magistrates to be transported for seven years. The Grand National Consolidated Trade Union and other bodies organized a huge meeting of protest in Copenhagen Fields, near where King's Cross station now stands. Between twenty and thirty thousand people were said to have marched in an orderly and picturesque procession, and between one and two hundred thousand to have attended the meeting. The demonstration had no immediate effect. The Grand National ceased to administer secret oaths and collapsed for lack of financial support in the autumn of 1834. But the London Dorchester Committee, which had been formed to help the "Tolpuddle martyrs" and their families, continued to bring pressure to bear on the government, and in 1836 the sentence was remitted by Lord John Russell. Unhappily no one thought of telling the unfortunate victims in Australia, and it was 1838 before they again set foot on their native soil.

Chapter 9   CONSERVATIVE REVIVAL AND SPLIT 1841–1846

a. Robert Blake in his scholarly and perceptive *Disraeli* published in 1966 develops the parallel between Young England and the later quartet known as the Fourth Party (pp. 168, 176).

Chapter 10   WHIGS AND PEELITES 1846–1867

a. For the significance of this meeting in the development of the Liberal party, *v. infra*, p. 107 and notes. During the election campaign Austria had issued an ultimatum to Piedmont, and this was a major factor in bringing together Palmerston, Russell and Gladstone, all strong supporters of the Italian *Risorgimento*. When Derby resigned the Queen, embarrassed by having to choose between the two Whig charmers, first sent for Granville, but he was soon obliged to throw in his hand.

Chapter 11   REFORM ACT OF 1867—BEFORE AND AFTER

a. Since the words in the text were written the point has been made in evidence before the Fulton committee on the Civil Service both by the Labour party (*The Times*, 2nd Jan. 1967) and by the Trades Union Congress (*The Times*, 28th Jan. 1967). The stock answer, that this is a sign of a weak minister, is not entirely convincing, for what is one against so many? Especially when he can be dismissed at a moment's notice if he is thought to be at loggerheads with his department?

b. In his recently published study of Palmerston, *The Most English Minister*, ed. 1966, Dr. Southgate states even more emphatically his view of the critical importance of the meeting held in Willis's Rooms. "The two rivals Palmerston and Russell thus set in train a development which has received far less attention and emphasis than it deserves—the deliberate re-creation in 1859 of the two-party system which had broken down in 1846. . . . The meeting of 280 M.P.s at Willis's Rooms on 6th June 1859 may legitimately be regarded as the formal foundation of the Liberal party." (*op. cit.*, pp. 455–6).

c. Much new evidence is now available in John Vincent *The Formation of the Liberal Party 1857–1868*, ed. 1966. This important work is both narrower and broader than the title suggests—narrower, because it consists of four studies of the Parliamentary Liberal party, the rank and file, leadership and policy, broader because Mr Vincent often ranges outside his dates. For Mr. Vincent, "the chief historical problem lay in the evolution from the parliamentary party system to the national party system. The sudden adoption by provincial society of the official parties as the expressions of their political feelings, by no means a natural development, occurred with such speed in the 1860s that it has been largely lost sight of. This mutual convergence of provincial feeling and parliamentary politics was not accompanied by, still less brought about by, changes in central or local party organization. A chapter on the subject attempts to bring out the insignificance of official party machinery in creating that largely unorganized community of sentiment called a party. The creation of a (predominantly Liberal) cheap daily press outside London, the action of organized Labour and militant Nonconformity, the Reform agitation of the 1860s and the representative significance of Gladstone, were the chief influences in changing the context of the Parliamentary Liberal party. Up to 1865, that party had been the expression of personal rivalries and political differences within the aristocracy, broadly defined. After 1865 the Liberals, without important changes in their parliamentary personnel, came to represent great and dynamic social forces in the country, by reason of their vitalizing connexion with their rank and file. The representative of that connexion was Gladstone" (op. cit., p. xxxiii).

This is well put, and on this basis Mr. Vincent naturally does not make a great deal of the meeting in Willis's Rooms. "The educated mind has always dwelt on parliamentary history, the parliamentary party, and its politics. It is its natural limitation. In this view, the Liberal party came into being in 1859 through the agreement at Willis's Rooms brought about by the Italian question: and so on in that vein. Whereas, what was really new was not the slow adaptation of the parliamentary party: but the adoption of that parliamentary party by a rank and file. The great frontier is not the division between Whig and Tory in Parliament, but that separating the parliamentary parties from the national party" (ibid., pp. xix–xx). This is true, but the situation did not change completely in the second half of the nineteenth century. Hilaire Belloc and Cecil Chesterton felt exactly the same about the identity of the Liberal and Conservative front benches in the House of Commons, and their divorce from the mass of the people, in the first decade of the twentieth century (The Party System, ed. 1911); and even today the front benches in the House of Commons are often accused of having more in common with each other than either has with its mass following.

d. The circumstances leading up to the extension of the franchise in 1867, and the measure itself, have recently received careful study at the hands of Mr. F. B. Smith, The Making of the Second Reform Bill, ed. 1966. He observes: "The Reform Bill of 1867 survived because a majority of both Houses of Parliament dared not throw it out. They did not want it, they did not like it, they feared what it might do, but they passed it."

Chapter 12   LIBERAL versus CONSERVATIVE 1868–1885

a. Butt's part in the formation of Irish nationalism has now received a close study in David Thornley, Isaac Butt and Home Rule, ed. 1964. He makes the point that "the extent to which the Irish people were immutably committed to separatism throughout the nineteenth century can be grossly exaggerated" (*op. cit.*, p. 10). A study of the election of 1868, which he makes his point of departure, "reveals, perhaps, how close Ireland came in at least one period to the acceptance of Liberal unionism". Gladstone's dis-establishment of the Irish Church made Roman Catholics feel more kindly disposed towards the Liberal party and the union, but by the same token the attachment of Protestant Conservatives (such as Butt himself) to the union began to weaken. (This was a major theme of a work, *New Ireland*, by one of the nationalist leaders, A. M. Sullivan, that ran into fourteen editions by 1882.) The home rule movement is usually regarded as having been launched at a meeting in Bilton's Hotel, Dublin in May 1870 when, on the motion of Butt, the Home Government Association was founded. It was Butt's achievement in the first phase of the movement to have destroyed the attractions of Liberal unionism; but the by-election victories which were won by the home rule candidates in 1871 (including Butt him-self for Limerick) and 1872, demonstrated "the separation of the Home Government Association in Dublin from the spontaneous enthusiasm of the constituencies". A great conference of the home rule movement held in the Rotunda, Dublin, from 18th to 21st Nov. 1873 refused to require the Irish members to act in accordance with the decision of the majority, but set up a new association to be known as the Home Rule League. Though the league had only a few weeks in which to find candidates for the eighty seats, it is commonly reckoned that fifty-nine home rulers were returned; but Mr. Thornley has no difficulty in showing that they were far from constituting a homogeneous party (*op. cit.*, pp. 195–203).

b. For Parnell and the Irish Nationalist party under his leadership and subsequently Conor Cruise O'Brien, *Parnell and his Party, 1880–90* (1957), F. S. L. Lyons, *The Irish Parliamentary Party, 1890–1910* (1951) and *The Fall of Parnell* (1960), and Jules Abels, *The Parnell Tragedy* (1966) may be con-sulted.

c. The first home rulers did not sit together. "Members of the party sat wherever they chose in the house; Bowyer, Montagu and later King Har-man sat on the government benches, the ex-liberals upon the opposite side. Butt himself and his closest allies appear to have sat below the gangway on the opposition side, which became traditionally Irish in later years, but their colleagues were not bound to join them" (David Thornley, *Isaac Butt and Home Rule*, ed. 1964, p. 216).

d. Three volumes of *The Life of Joseph Chamberlain* were written by James L. Garvin before his death and a fourth, bringing the story to 1903, has been written by Julian Amery. There were at least twelve other studies of this enigmatic character before Peter Fraser, in 1966, published *Joseph Chamberlain: Radicalism and Empire, 1868–1914*. Mr. Fraser tries to find more consistency between the early and later phases of Chamberlain's career as a "socialist" Radical and an "imperialist" Conservative than is usually allowed, or is indeed possible. He is on sure ground in seeing in Chamberlain "the first 'professional' politician" (*op. cit.*, p. xii).

e. The six months, July to Dec. 1876, in which the Bulgarian atrocities occupied the centre of the British political stage have received a minute study from R. T. Shannon, *Gladstone and the Bulgarian Agitation 1876*, ed. 1963. Mr. Shannon emphasizes "the greatness of Gladstone's debt to the agitation and, conversely, the smallness of his contribution to it, despite the myth to the contrary" (p. vi). *Bulgarian Horrors* is for him a "rehash" with "no particular literary merit" (p. 109), and its significance "lies in its character as a unique response to a particular series of stimuli which coloured its form and content and made it the supremely representative expression of a passionate moment of history" (p. 110). But Mr. Shannon does not underestimate the political and party significance of "the fact that Gladstone was called out of his retirement".

f. Sir Sidney Lee brings out the Prince's "lifelong reverence for Mr. Gladstone", but adds, "There was small ground for the current gossip that Queen Victoria's private regard for Disraeli, and her steadily maturing impatience with Gladstone, caused in the Prince an inverse attitude to the two men" (Sir Sidney Lee, *King Edward VII: A Biography*, ed. 1925, vol. 1, p. 208).

Chapter 14 CONSERVATIVES AND UNIONISTS 1886–1895

a. To them and Cross should perhaps be added William Henry Smith (1825–91), son of a London newsagent, who turned his father's modest business into the great distributing enterprise of W. H. Smith and Son Limited. Having left the Wesleyans in his youth, he became deeply attached to the Church of England, won the Westminster seat as a Conservative in 1868 against the tide, and through the prestige this gained brought himself to the notice of Disraeli, who made him Financial Secretary to the Treasury in 1874 and put him in the Cabinet as First Lord of the Admiralty in 1877. Randolph Churchill's resignation in 1886 opened the way for him to become First Lord of the Treasury and leader of the House of Commons. In recognition of his public services his widow was made a peeress in her own right as Viscountess Hambleden. Smith played a notable part in giving a more middle-class appearance to the Tory party. Sir Herbert Maxwell's two-decker *Life and Times of the Right Honourable William Henry Smith* (1893) has now been succeeded by Viscount Chilston, *W. H. Smith* (1965).

b. This "celebrated saying" was attributed to Harcourt by John Morley, *Recollections*, ed. 1917, vol. 2, p. 97, and by George Bernard Shaw in "Sixty Years of Socialism", a postscript (1947) to *Fabian Essays*, ed. 1962, p. 313. Though A. G. Gardiner does not mention the phrase in his biography, *The Life of Sir William Harcourt*, ed. 1923, it is more credible that the statesman was the author rather than the Prince of Wales, the future King Edward VII, as has sometimes been stated.

Chapter 15 UNIONIST DOMINANCE AND DISSENSION 1895–1905

a. For Morley's account of these events see his *Recollections*, ed. 1917, vol. 2, pp. 81–4. He does not explain why Harcourt should have sent his letter of resignation to him, except that it was "after much discussion between us".

b. Balfour's handling of the Cabinet crisis caused by Chamberlain has recently been acutely analysed in Alfred Gollin, *Balfour's Burden: Arthur Balfour and Imperial Preference* (1965).

Chapter 16   ENTRY OF THE LABOUR PARTY 1900–1906

a. The origins of the Fabian Society were described by G. Bernard Shaw, Fabian Tract No. 41, 1892, *The Fabian Society: What it has Done and how it has Done It* (reprinted as *The Early History of the Fabian Society* and also reprinted in *Essays in Fabian Socialism*, 1932). In 1916 another of the pioneers, Edward R. Pease, wrote *The History of the Fabian Society*, 3rd ed. 1963. More recent accounts have been given by Anne Fremantle, *This Little Band of Prophets*, 1959, Margaret Cole, *The Story of Fabian Socialism*, 1961, and more exhaustively, by A. M. McBriar, *Fabian Socialism and English Politics 1884–1918*, published in 1962 (2nd ed. 1966). *Fabian Essays* was re-issued in a sixth edition in 1962 with a new introduction by Asa Briggs.

b. The *Workman's Times* was published weekly on Saturdays at first in Huddersfield, then in London, and finally in Manchester. Joseph Burgess's leading article inviting applications to join an independent Labour party appeared on 30th April 1892 and the first list of adherents on 14th May in the same year. The conference at which the Independent Labour party was formerly constituted was held at the Labour Institute, Peckover Street, Bradford, on Friday and Saturday, 13th and 14th Jan. 1893; the report of the proceedings and the comments on them occupy nearly two pages of the *Workman's Times* for 21st Jan. On the Friday there were 115 delegates present, and an additional eight arrived on the Saturday. Keir Hardie was invited to take the chair. Bernard Shaw and his two fellow-delegates from the Fabian Society caused some bewilderment by explaining that the Fabian Society could not affiliate to the new party because it wished to be able to keep it up to the socialist mark. Ben Tillett struck a discordant note by denouncing "the hare-brained chatterers and magpies of continental socialism", especially as Eduard Bernstein was there to represent the German Social Democratic party. Otherwise the unity of purpose and particularly the determination to have a Labour party that really should be independent were complete.

A history of the Independent Labour party which is reasonably complete, even though its author disclaims the description of "exhaustive", is now available—Robert E. Dowse, *Left in the Centre: The Independent Labour Party 1893–1940*, ed. 1966. In it he "seeks to explain the reasons underlying the decline of the 'left wing' of the Labour party after the Great War", and he adds, "My basic proposition is that the decline was a consequence of structural factors which left little room for manoeuvre" (p. ix).

c. It is curious that in discussing with fellow-undergraduates the possible dates at which the Liberal party began to fall Dr. Trevor Wilson did not realize the climacteric importance of this decision; nor, apparently, does he today. "One considered the Liberal party doomed from the time of the home rule split in the 1880s; another from the foundation of the Independent Labour party in the 1890s, or anyway the Labour Representation Committee in 1900; another from the election of Labour M.P.s in 1906; another from the political upheavals of the period 1910–1914 ('The Strange Death of Liberal England'). Thus to satisfy every view about when and why the Liberal party met its doom, one might as well go back to the time when there was a party bearing the name Liberal at all" (*The Downfall of the Liberal Party 1914–1935*, pp. 15–16).

The view that the Liberal party received its mortal wound in the political upheavals before the First World War may be studied in George Dangerfield, *The Strange Death of Liberal England 1910–1914*, first published in 1935 and issued in a new edition in 1966.

Dr. Wilson gives his own view of pre-war relations of Liberals and Labour in these words: "By and large, the Labour parliamentary party still existed in 1914 by Liberal indulgence—that is, because the Liberals deemed it advantageous to give Labour a free run against the Conservatives in certain seats. There is no way of knowing what would have happened before the war if Labour had set itself up in rivalry to the Liberals. On the basis of electoral evidence up to 1914, both would have suffered, but Labour would have fared much worse than the Liberals" (*ibid.*, p. 17). Though this may well be true, it does not invalidate the argument of this chapter that in concluding an electoral pact the Liberals admitted a Trojan horse. Dr. Wilson goes on: "Whether, in that event, Labour would have persisted in hopeless battles, or would have made a new (and probably more favourable) agreement with the Liberals, is a matter for speculation. It did not appear inevitable that Labour would persist in the former course" (*ibid.*, p. 17). It is the argument of this book that after the decision to "go it alone" in 1903 Labour would never at any time have been prepared to enter into a permanent alliance with the Liberals, and that this decision ultimately spelt the downfall of the Liberal party.

In Dr. Wilson's view it was the First World War that destroyed the Liberal party; according to the argument of this book, the First World War (and particularly the quarrel between Asquith and Lloyd George) accelerated a downfall that was in any case inevitable after the Labour decision to "go it alone".

Professor Samuel H. Beer in *Modern British Politics*, ed. 1965, pp. 137–45, regards the "door mat" incident as a turning-point in the history of the Labour party and the acceptance of socialism in 1918 as the real explanation of the final break with Liberalism. "In its effect on the future relations of the Labour party with the Liberals, the commitment to socialism was crucial. It ruled out the old cooperative relation as well as any closer union of the two parties. Or to put the matter a little differently: the adoption of socialism set the seal on the decision of 1900 to form a separate and independent political party. In spite of the words of 1900, Labour's independence in actual practice had been far from resolute" (*op. cit.*, p. 140). This is true, but I would suggest to Professor Beer that the decision of 1903 went beyond the decision of 1900, and this was really the crucial point.

d. There is a large (but uneven) literature on the origins and later history of the Labour party. Among general works which may be recommended are Herbert Tracey (editor), *The Book of the Labour Party* (1925), G. D. H. Cole, *A Short History of the British Working Class Movement* (1927) and *A History of the Labour Party from 1914* (1948), Henry Pelling, *The Origins of the*

Labour Party, 1880–1900 (1954) and *A Short History of the Labour Party* (1961), and Carl F. Brand, *The British Labour Party: A Short History* (1964).

Chapter 19   WAR AND COALITION 1914–1918

a. The test could be only a rough and ready one, but it was nevertheless a real one. Dr. Colin Wilson (*The Downfall of the Liberal Party 1914–1935,* p. 145) challenges the view that the Maurice debate has "a crucial place in the demise of the Liberal party" on the ground that 229 Liberal candidates were denied the coupon and one of their opponents given it, while "the Maurice division could only have caused the proscription of seventy-one Liberals". (Of the 108 members of Parliament, including the tellers, who voted against the government in the Maurice division, twenty-five did not stand for re-election and twelve more did not stand as Liberals.) Furthermore, six of the seventy-one stood in constituencies where no coupons were issued, and the remaining eleven received the coupon, so that only fifty-four were actually proscribed. Four Liberals who voted with the government in the Maurice debate found that the coupon was given to an opponent. Of the 159 Liberals who did receive the coupon, only fifty-four had actually voted with the government in the Maurice debate, the others not having been members of the House, or absent, or in some cases voters in the Asquithian lobby. Though Dr. Wilson makes some telling points, the Maurice debate remains fairly decisive for those who took part in it. Of seventy-one Liberal candidates who had voted for Maurice, fifty-four had the coupon given to an opponent; and of fifty-eight who had voted against Maurice, only four were denied the coupon. Something must be allowed for the confused circumstances in which the election arrangements had to be made.

b. It is not quite true to say, as J. M. Keynes did in a letter to Kingsley Martin in 1941 (*Encounter,* Feb. 1965, p. 83) that the speech was reported only in the local paper. *The Times,* 10th Dec. 1918, attributes the following words to Sir Eric Geddes at the Drill Hall (*sic,* but presumably a mistake for Guildhall), Cambridge at his adoption meeting the night before: "If I am returned Germany is going to pay restitution, reparation and indemnity, and I have personally no doubt we will get everything out of her that you can squeeze out of a lemon and a bit more." But the speech would certainly not have had so wide a circulation but for the circumstances mentioned in the *Encounter* article by Keynes: "He invented this perfect expression in an election speech at the Guildhall in Cambridge, during the coupon election, which was only reported in the local paper. It would have been entirely lost to fame if my mother had not cut it out and sent it to me, and it was impressed on my memory when I came to write the *Economic Consequences.*" In the *Economic Consequences of the Peace,* published in 1919, Keynes reported the speech as follows: "The grossest spectacle was provided by Sir Eric Geddes in the Guildhall at Cambridge. An earlier speech in which, in a moment of injudicious candour, he had cast doubts on the possibility of extracting from Germany the whole cost of the war had been the object of serious suspicion, and he had therefore a reputation to regain. 'We will get out of her all you can squeeze out of a lemon and a bit more,' the penitent shouted, 'I will squeeze her until you can hear the pips squeak' " (*op. cit.*, ed. 1942, p. 131).

Chapter 20   COALITION CONTINUED 1918–1922

a. "The phrase about the hard-faced men, which you quote, I stole from Stanley Baldwin, who invented it. I was sitting in Chalmers' room in the Treasury having tea on the first day of the new Parliament after the Coupon Election. Baldwin, who was then Financial Secretary and had the adjoining room, poked his nose through the door, as I can see him now, to us at tea. I asked him—'What do they look like?' And he replied in the famous phrase—'A lot of hard-faced men who look as if they had done well out of the war' " (J. M. Keynes to Kingsley Martin, 13th Nov. 1941, cited by Kingsley Martin, "Arguing with Keynes: A Memoir", *Encounter*, Feb. 1965, p. 83).

b. Dr. Colin Wilson in *The Downfall of the Liberal Party 1914–1935*, pp. 23–48, takes the view that it was not the rise of the Labour party, nor the rivalry between Lloyd George and Asquith, but the First World War which destroyed the Liberal party. His argument is that for a Liberal government to lead Britain into war, and to direct a war-time administration, seemed almost a contradiction in terms; while some Liberal principles were suspended for the duration, others seemed unlikely ever to become important again; and Nonconformity, on which the Liberal party relied so heavily, was itself disintegrated by the war. While the strength of Dr. Wilson's arguments must be recognized, and the Liberals could hardly have emerged from the war as the ruling party, if there had been no other alternative to the Conservatives they would in due course have recovered their position, albeit with many changes in their outlook and doctrines. It was the existence of another radical alternative to which erstwhile Liberals transferred their votes in large numbers that made a Liberal recovery impossible.

A former Conservative chief whip, James Stuart (Viscount Stuart of Findhorn), in an autobiography that is as diverting as it is informative, expresses the following opinion: "My own belief is that Lloyd George's 'coupon election' of 1918 and Asquith's support of the Socialists in 1923 combined to lose for the Liberal party the popularity which they had enjoyed for so long" (*Within the Fringe*, ed. 1967, p. 70). Lord Stuart foreshortens the time scale; Liberal popularity on the mass scale had already gone.

INDEX TO VOLUME I

The principal entry for persons known by different names at different stages of their careers will be found under the title by which they were known when politically most active, but with cross-references when desirable. Thus, Charles II's Tory minister may be found under Danby, Earl of, with cross-references from Osborne, Thomas, and Leeds, 1st Duke of. In order to increase the utility of the index, a few references in square brackets to events not recorded in the text are given.

Y

Y2